PRESCRIPTIONS
FOR
PROSPERITY

OTHER BOOKS BY ELIOT JANEWAY

The Struggle for Survival
The Economics of Crisis
What Shall I Do With My Money?
You and Your Money
Musings on Money

PRESCRIPTIONS FOR PROSPERITY

· ELIOT JANEWAY ·

Times
BOOKS

Published by TIMES BOOKS, a division of The New York Times Book Co., Inc.
Three Park Avenue, New York, N.Y. 10016

Published simultaneously in Canada by Fitzhenry & Whiteside, Ltd., Toronto

Library of Congress Cataloging in Publication Data

Janeway, Eliot.
   Prescriptions for prosperity.

   Includes index.
   1. United States—Economic policy—1981-
I. Title.
HC106.8.J35   1983   338.973   82-40364
ISBN: 0-8129-1036-2

MANUFACTURED IN THE UNITED STATES OF AMERICA

83 84 85 86 87 5 4 3 2 1

For Elizabeth Hall Janeway,

my wife and co-worker of half a century,
whose wisdom has taught me to
respect the laborious processes that ripen
events and challenge us to change
their direction, and whose pioneering probes
into relations between the sexes
have broadened my perceptions and raised
my sights on what all of us together
can do for each other

Acknowledgments

The author and publisher would like to thank the following for permission to quote material from their publications:

Jacques Gansler and the MIT Press for excerpts from *The Defense Industry*, 1980

Chaim Herzog and Random House for excerpts from *The Arab-Israeli Wars*, 1982

J. B. Kelly and Basic Books for excerpts from *Arabia, the Gulf and the West*, 1980

Henry Kissinger and Little, Brown and Company for excerpts from *Years of Upheaval*, 1982

Gerald Krefetz and Ticknor & Fields for excerpts from *Jews and Money*, 1982

George Lichtheim and Columbia University Press for excerpts from *Marxism: An Historical and Critical Study*, 1982

Michael Parrish and The Free Press/Macmillan for excerpts from *Felix Frankfurter and His Times: The Reform Years*, 1982

George Reedy and Andrews and McMeel, Inc. for excerpts from *Lyndon B. Johnson: A Memoir*, 1982

Marvin N. Strauss, CLU, and the Strauss Agency, Inc. for their tabulations of whole life insurance benefits

Preface

THE OLDEST PROPOSITION in formal logic, contrary to contemporary practice, is neither a philosophical abstraction nor a mathematical equation. It simply puts us on notice that either the moon is made of green cheese or it is not. The application of this basic proposition to the problem posed by the depression of the early 1980s is just as simple: Either, as President Reagan promised, the economy will prove to be "on the mend" by itself (with a little bit of help from a friendly Federal Reserve Board) or it will not. If it does, this book might better have been entitled, with apologies to Shakespeare, *Love's Labor Lost.*

If it does not, then who will mend the economy? The only alternative to self-mending for an economy in the throes of a depression is government-mending. Mere economic recessions suffered without complications of a financial, social, or military nature again and again correct excesses and trigger recoveries. The question about a recession, however, is always diagnostic: When is a case of cramps a diversion from a heart attack? The economy cannot place itself in an intensive-care unit, nor can it perform open-heart surgery on itself.

By constitutional injunction, moreover, the self-policing reach of the domestic economy stops at the water's edge. The Founding Fathers knew their business. They barred businessmen from meddling in the foreign affairs and military security of the United States. The rules they laid down followed the lines of force dictated by the continuous struggle for power and advantage between governments. They charged the government with the responsibility of protecting America's interests, beginning with her economic interests, against foreign governments threatening her security.

America's failure to do so brought on the depression of 1980, which was too well-engineered a product to bear an American brand; it was imported with every barrel of oil on which America paid tribute—and with the blessing of the government. Predictably, the spectacle of

OPEC collapsing after a decade of extortion legitimized by Washington's appeasement stirred up hopes and even symptoms of market-induced recovery. Just as predictably, Washington's failure to have put the cartel out of business left the economy crippled and unable to prime the pumps of recovery on cheaper fuel. Just as extortionate money costs had hurt the economy enough to stop it and cheaper money costs had not helped it enough to start it, so extortionate oil costs had contributed to the overkill and cheaper oil costs had not contributed to its revival.

If prescriptions for prosperity emerge as the order of the day, America's political parties, their 1984 primary contests, their 1984 national conventions, and their candidates will assume a fearsome responsibility. In a bygone world ridden with superstition and abused by tyranny, Descartes came up with a practical compromise for the war between science and religion. His calculation was aimed at buying peace for scientists without selling their souls. If the universe runs like a clock, he reasoned, the fine-tuning of its mechanism presupposes a blueprint designed by a clockmaker—God! But word-weaving will not put America on the mend again. Mending, as Descartes's logic tells us, calls for a mender. If the mending to be done is in the foreign relations of the United States, only the president can do the mending, Congress willing. If the power vacuum opened by OPEC's collapse is to be filled and Russia's readiness to exploit it is to be checked, a policy lead from Washington will be needed. As this book goes to press, none has been offered, except for the simplistic slogans of Reaganomics that have failed at great cost.

Consequently, the tremors shaking America's economic society and financial structure have been forcing a switch in national focus from the plausible to the workable. Either America, with her "domestic tranquility" jeopardized beyond the limits contemplated in the Constitution, is enjoying tranquil relations with the rest of the world, or she is not. If not, either the government will "provide for the common defense," as the Constitution charges it to do, or it will not. No matter what the brand of governmental advertising or management may be, the government has long since extended its responsibility to "promote the general welfare" to include the effective direction of the economy —with particular emphasis on its financial and economic relations with other economies. Success in the mission, if moon gazing will not work, calls for prescriptions for prosperity. Accordingly, this book is offered as a work kit for all of us to use in guiding the Mender in Chief who will be charged in 1985 with managing the switch from show business to serious business. More than incidentally, it is also offered as a guidebook for those of us who want to know what to do to help themselves if, providentially, the government turns out not to be made of branded green cheese, and how to protect themselves if, tragically, it does.

This book was sent off to press the week after the stock market made its all-time highs, just as the gold market was hit by the selling panic that accompanied the discovery that OPEC had lost control of the price of oil. Given the gravity and the urgency of the situation, the book was conceived and written under pressure. I am indebted to John Shutt, the managing editor of Janeway Publishing & Research Corp., for support beyond the call of occupational duty, for the sacrifice of more leisure time than can be counted, and, above all, for guidance in threading the continuity of the manuscript. Ms. Melinda Rothel, the executive vice president and editor-in-chief of Janeway Publishing & Research Corp., has watchdogged the project with characteristic zeal and severity, firm in the faith that writing a book combines an act of desperation with a commitment to contemplation. Readers can thank her for managing the transition between prescriptions for national prosperity and prescriptions for personal prosperity until that happier day arrives. Her wise and shrewd counsel guided the identification of the market barometers that measure the difference. Michael C. Janeway of the Boston *Globe* and Dr. William H. Janeway of F. Eberstadt & Company have given me the benefit of their expertise and their perspective. My friend and fellow student Charles Brophy, the virtuoso former editor of *Bond Buyer,* has done the same. The editor-in-chief of The New York Times Book Company, Jonathan Segal, has been the severest taskmaster of all and the most helpful in his relentless insistence on fitting the diagnosis of America's flawed past to prescriptions for her curative future. Elizabeth Janeway has imposed her incomparable deftness and sternness of literary discipline on fine-tuning my various sensibilities. All of us can thank our company's two veteran manuscript typists, Elizabeth Parr and Manuel X. Rad-Cliff, for their indefatigable patience, accuracy, and speed in turning jungles of scrawl into models of clarity.

ELIOT JANEWAY
New York City
February 1983

Contents

PART III
Political Strategies, the Economy, and the Markets 255

PART IV
Prescriptions for Personal Prosperity:
A Financial Strategy for All Seasons 271

· PART I ·

DIAGNOSIS OF THE AMERICAN DISEASE

CHAPTER ONE

America's Enemy
in the 1980s: Time

ON THAT DAY in March 1933 when Franklin Roosevelt was inaugurated for his first term, he paid a symbolic call on Mr. Justice Holmes, America's revered elder statesman, after taking the presidential oath. The country was in the midst of the banking crisis of 1933. That very same month, Adolf Hitler was in the process of taking over in Berlin. Holmes greeted the new and untried president with characteristic pragmatism: "Young man, you have a chance. But hurry."

Voltaire's throwaway line about God—that if He hadn't existed, we would have had to invent Him—applies to elder statesmen as well. Countries that have made their way as powers rely on elder statesmen to lay down simple and practical guidelines for their up-and-coming politicians, who temperamentally travel too fast to know where they are going. FDR had run fast and hard making his way to the White House. Once perched "at the top of the greasy pole"—Disraeli's term for the pinnacle of power—he needed a policy and he needed a target. The old man's warning to the young man to hurry went to the heart of the problem of crisis management. FDR, always ready to rise to a competitive challenge or to best a rival, followed Holmes's advice to the letter and hurried in playing his domestic political hand; the prevailing political pressures called for action against the Depression. He deferred it, however, in playing his foreign political hand for the simple and sufficient reason that the prevailing political pressures were also isolationist.

Both Holmes's warning and FDR's responses to it proved prophetic. Half a century later, Ronald Reagan's America was still faced with the decision whether to hurry or wait, as was every president in between, notwithstanding the country's success in accomplishing more than any power ever had before and in less time. By the time the 1980s arrived, America had landed in the well-known position of Alice in Looking-Glass Land: Running fast barely kept her in the same place; the more she accomplished, the more unfinished business she found confronting

3

her; the more her leaders talked, the less they accomplished; the clearer she thought she became about her domestic economic priorities, the more muddled her foreign political priorities grew.

A country at bay can offer only two responses to a challenge to hurry: It can wait, or it can act. This book makes the case for today's America to stop waiting and to start acting. It is written on three assumptions: (1) that Russia has caught this country in the worst of both worlds, a nonstop political war America has not known how to fight and a financial exposure she has not known how to ensure; (2) that America can counter by plunging Russia into a new style of economic war that Russia cannot win and that America cannot lose; and (3) that the alternative is to invite the entire world into a nuclear arms race that no country can win but in which America, by virtue of having the most, will have the most to lose. America's enemy is not Russia; it is time. America's immediate vulnerability is not to missiles. It is to her loss of time in changing her priorities. When time is of the essence in any test of strength between rival powers, even the best-tested weapons of war are risky because they take so long to activate. That's precisely when the weapons for waging peace are most effective; their delivery schedules are quicker and more reliable.

America has been conditioned in the twentieth century to expect to be brought into long wars in time to bail out beleaguered allies and mercenary clients. The changed terms of military combat, however, now stack the strategic cards against belligerents who wait for wars to start before preparing for them. By the same token, they offer an incentive to any superpower that can improvise economic and financial alternatives to the trigger-pulling route. As the arms race accelerates and draws in more participants, it is going to put America at a disadvantage, first against Russia and then against Third World dictatorships, particularly its oil dictatorships flexing their new nuclear muscles. The reason is simple: Militaristic competition is not the race in which America has been trained to excel; economic competition is. The more effective her economic weaponry proves to be, the less destructive her military weaponry will need to be.

I regard the prompt mobilization of the American economy as the one timely and practical alternative to an arms race that is accelerating and to the holocaust it is threatening. America's economy is her proprietary asset. Her best hope of keeping the peace militarily is to make war economically, using her economy as a mercy weapon. America lacks the combination of military muscle and political persuasiveness to talk Russia into disarmament. But she has the economic muscle to trade Russia into buying the economic stability the USSR has never enjoyed. Moreover, her economic resources can be stretched to lead the rest of the world into a return to the political stability the USSR, with a deadly assist from its oil satellites, has upset all the way from the Baltic to the Persian Gulf and back around the world to the Caribbean.

The prescriptions for prosperity put forward in Part II of this book are formulated for adoption by the government as the economic equivalent of war. The idea may seem alarming at first blush, but FDR made it seem reassuring in his first inaugural when he declared war on the Depression. A declaration of economic war calls for methods different from those familiar in a shooting match. It begins by subordinating random dollar incentives to competitive national purposes, and by fighting with commodities and technology—what the old-time Chinese warlords called silver bullets—rather than with manpower sucked into mudholes and missiles tucked away in silos. The economy is a battlefield too, and each new chapter of history establishes it as a more decisive battlefield than before. The economic interpretation of history assumes a continual clash of hostile economic forces, where strategic ends are pursued through economic means.

America's fallback arsenal is her agripower—her distinctive agricultural productivity. Today the United States has a unique opportunity to use this food power—by no means her only advanced technological economic weapon—to neutralize Russia's nuclear firepower. Russia cannot do without America's distinctive product mix of crops, nor can she duplicate it. For Russia, a first-strike nuclear attack risking the sterilization of America's croplands would be an exercise in slow-motion suicide. She would sentence herself to starvation, if not necessarily for wheat in the short term, then certainly over the long term for the feed grains she cannot get anywhere else. Agriculture is America's shield and sword, exactly the designation the Kremlin has given the KGB. *Vive la différence!*

Clarification is in order on the strategy and tactics of waging economic warfare against Russia. The way to begin is to get clear about how *not* to wage economic warfare. It is not to rely on embargo, as popularly supposed and recurrently practiced. Washington, blissful in its belief that business is business and politics is politics and never the twain shall meet, had originally been content to permit the market to "do its thing" between embargoes. Then the false start Reagan made at waging economic war compounded the problem. European charges of hypocrisy were justified when Reagan called for embargoing the Russian gas-line project into West Germany—which was good business for Europe—while continuing to sell grain to Russia—which was good business for America. Unfortunately, embargo has crystallized into a code word for "economic warfare," consistent with the hair-shirt philosophy of salvation through suffering.

The self-defeating assumption that the way to soften up Russia is to keep our food weapon in the storage bin has predictably turned the farm bloc in the Senate—its strongest single bloc—against the thoroughly bipartisan idea of declaring economic war against Russia. The farmers would be all for it if they could see themselves moving more tonnage to Russia instead of none at all. In fact, once America pits her decisive source of strength, her agripower, against Russia's most glaring deficiency, her agriweakness, America would have every incentive to step up her food dealings with Russia, not to stop them. The red herring of the embargo has distracted us from the real issue: not whether to sell to Russia, but in what coin and on what terms to get paid. We can make her population an offer the Kremlin could not refuse. America has never put Russia on the spot to pay what the political traffic will bear. Reciprocal trade, to revive the slogan of Roosevelt's first secretary of state, Cordell Hull, is the way to resolve the muddled debate between the hawks and doves on Russia. It is the way to reassure the responsible and literate constituency of George Kennan, and other eloquent and constructive advocates of a halt to the Soviet-American nuclear arms race, that economic initiatives offer the most practical hope of avoiding nuclear confrontations and, in the process, satisfying economic incentives.

I would regard my efforts as incomplete if I simply catalogued a pharmacopoeia of policy prescriptions for managing the crisis (Part II) whose evolution from the 1950s to the 1980s is analyzed in Part I. Accordingly, I have supplemented my diagnosis with a second kitful of prescriptions in Part IV aimed at helping all Americans who participate in our economic society by voting their hopes and fears about money —their earnings and their capital, as well as their lack of either or both —along with their opinions and preferences. Here I offer them a three-phase personal financial strategy: how to play the defensive game for the duration of the high-risk period in which the crisis incubates and the prevailing insecurity intensifies; when to switch to an offensive stance as the American government shows it has met the danger by adopting the variants of the prescriptions detailed in Part II; and what to select as the investment vehicles for maximizing the rewards when the momentum of prosperity is regained. On that happy day, our government, with no blood on its hands, will repeat with confidence Commodore Perry's laconic message to a tranquilized world: "We have met the enemy, and they are ours." On that same day our people will have reason to stop repeating the refrain of defeatism popularized by the cartoon Pogo, "We has met the enemy, and it is us."

A word on the method I have adopted. The writings of economists too often recall the old bromide about the weather: "Everybody talks about it, but no one does anything about it." Contrary to the preoccupation of model builders, computer tenders, and statistical scorers, I believe that the performance of the economy, interacting as it does with the conduct of our foreign relations, offers a standing challenge not only to the diagnosis of complaints but to prescriptions for cures. This dedication to cures has led me, during the forty-five years of my involvement in what Justice Holmes termed the "marketplace of ideas," to describe myself neither as an economic analyst nor a political activist, but rather as a political economist, a policy engineer.

For those who, in the past, have sought a definition of that calling (before brokerage firms began sprouting them), I offer the simplest, if the most arcane, explanation: A political economist is what Sir William Petty called himself in the middle of the seventeenth century when, as Karl Marx noted (and he knew the business!) Petty emerged as "the father of economics." A more contemporary definition is provided by Professor Michael E. Parrish in his judicious and scholarly study of Mr. Justice Frankfurter, where he recalls an abortive encounter that Frankfurter, ever the power broker, had arranged between FDR and John Maynard Keynes in 1934. Roosevelt complained to "Madame Perkins," his very idealistic but not very effective secretary of labor, about Keynes: "He left a whole rigamarole of figures. He must be a mathematician rather than a political economist." This was a case of intuition rediscovering history for FDR, who had never heard of Petty or Schumpeter, or read Marx or, for that matter, very much of anything. But FDR knew that he was a politician in need of an economist. Keynes, in one of his most memorable dicta, had warned economists, including himself, that the acid test of their work is in the quality of the political clients it wins for them.

This casual put-down of Keynes by Roosevelt points to a badly overdue definition of the mission of a political economist: to show politicians, who know how people behave, how the economy can be made to behave when it is given a substantive lead from Washington. America has spent her entire history as an organized society confronted by the challenge to reconcile the political ends proclaimed by Thomas Jefferson with the financial means engineered by Alexander Hamilton. Since their day, a new complication has been added to the circuitry of political communication. FDR was a past master of the fine art of political packaging; he bought new political programs crafted for him by his advisers and sold them to his constituents around the country. His freewheeling style has been institutionalized. Today, not just the president, but every officeholder and candidate deals through open intermediaries, specifically, through economists, pollsters, and pundits, just as money users—individuals, corporations, and governments—deal through financial intermediaries. The economists float the slogans, the pollsters measure the waves made by them, and the pundits look back on the ride they give the country. Reagan taught America the hard lessons that slogans without substance behind them will not work. America wasted valuable time she did not have flirting with this detour. With time the enemy and Russia the adversary, the war may not be lost, but the margin for error is—certainly in the choice of weapons.

The peace and prosperity America secured for herself after World War II are now suddenly in danger. The challenge to economists in the 1980s is to fit slogans that sell to programs that work in time to manage a near miss, avoiding the twin blight of depression and war. The country is in urgent need of precisely the "quick fix" that the prevailing defeatism in the Reagan White House has told us is not to be found and has warned us not to be tempted to seek. Yes, we do have a chance, but we need to hurry.

CHAPTER TWO

The Calculus
of Security

AMERICANS SPENT the 1970s growing complacent about living with a chronic inflationary crisis and even doing well out of it, while shrugging off the hard evidence of their country's deteriorating international political position. They had forgotten their ordeal of survival in the 1940s, when they learned firsthand that domestic economic failures colliding with foreign political disturbances flung them into military confrontations. Consequently, they were dismayed to find themselves catapulted into the 1980s on notice of a ghastly new war danger and, nevertheless, living with two pocketbook crises disrupting their daily lives, each pushing them in a different direction: debt inflating out of hand and income deflating below levels needed to pay interest. As they felt the twin pinch of this complicated new phenomenon of "flation," they also watched it paralyze the annual budgeting process, which had been trusted too long to keep the country's mind off its longer-range needs and the money flowing between credit crunches, debt-limit crises, and worries about the arrival of monthly Social Security checks. But this budgetary paralysis is the symptom of a deeper disorder, political in nature and foreign in origin.

The defense budget is at the heart of our chronic budgetary disorder. We will not bring the budget, and the money flows it unleashes, under control until we bring the defense budget under manageable control—a budget projected not one year at a time, or even two or three, but decade by decade. Neither wishful nor angry denunciations of the defense budget as the unbalancing factor it is in the budgetary equation will simplify the perplexing calculation. We are conditioned to weigh the budget quandary in terms of dollars, but the requirements of defense programming, realistic or otherwise, are figured in units of firepower, the cost of deployment where needed, and the burden of overhead when not. As fast as defense claims are totted up in physical terms, however, they collide with fiscal pressures and dollar limitations.

9

The availability of financial rations for the defense budget rises and falls with the level of earnings in the domestic economy, that is, with the flow of funds in and out of the Treasury, supplemented by borrowings. Annual fluctuations in the level of Detroit auto sales influence our ability to finance new reconnaissance planes on the naval base at Guantánamo in Cuba. The harsh realities that determine such defense needs are apt to escalate them in direct response to any and every deterioration in our domestic economy, whose performance we are convinced is insulated from such strategic vulnerabilities, while at the same time we rely on it to finance our strategic commitments.

I remember, as a young man of twenty-seven, at the outset of the first faltering, furtive defense effort in 1940, talking with Carl Vinson, then chairman—or "Admiral," as he liked to be called—of the old House Naval Affairs Committee and still treating Roosevelt as a promising protégé. Vinson (for whom one of the House Office Buildings is named) was a power and, therefore, felt no need to be a voice. He used the ascendancy he enjoyed over the president and over his colleagues to build the navy that won World War II for America in the Pacific (when the Atlantic theater claimed her top priority) and provided the support at sea needed to win the land war in Europe. Vinson's new navy went off the drawing boards and into the shipyards while Pearl Harbor was still a gleam in the eyes of Japan's high command.

Vinson was a potent mentor for developing a sense of defense programming as the complicating factor it has since proven to be in every crisis, confusing the management of America's foreign relations and the management of her domestic economy. He was not himself oriented toward the world of finance, but he possessed an astonishing (and instructive) grasp of the intricacies, the cost, and, above all, the length of time involved in fitting defense programs into their indispensable support role behind foreign policy and, simultaneously, in fitting the resources of the economy into their indispensable support role behind defense programs. From that time on, my thinking has been dominated by the underlying calculation that peace and prosperity together will remain elusive goals for any administration not in command of its defense programming and defense budget.

Vinson's philosophizing, in fact, added an extra dimension to the built-in problem defense finance poses for finance and politics. He used to say that the basic problem of a democracy is to reconcile the requirements of national security with "heppin' seff," as he put it in his inimitable south Georgia drawl. Strength for America and "heppin' seff" are once more the two horses Americans are being challenged to ride at a full gallop and with a firm hand through the 1980s. The challenge to mobilize America's resources puts any administration presiding over an impending emergency on trial to tap the teeming reservoir of American talent and wealth that is visibly dammed up. That same challenge also puts Americans on notice to help themselves and not be distracted by rhetoric about "the magic of markets" while waiting for the government to blueprint ways and means to protect the citizenry as only the government can do in confrontations involving other governments.

America entered the 1980s as she had entered the 1930s—thrown onto the defensive preparatory to being plunged into crisis, facing another threat of demoralizing political paralysis, devastating economic disintegration, and apocalyptic military activism. Yet the most rudimentary scrutiny of the situation that existed in the American economy at the time of the 1929 crash reveals a startling contrast with the state of affairs in 1982: 1929 was a better year than 1982. Not only was 1929 a banner year of balanced growth for the American economy, but even 1930 chalked up a remarkable performance, conjuring up visions to hindsight of a chicken first pacing, then walking, and finally limping all the way to the butcher's block on the other side of town. Outside of the fireworks in Wall Street, the economy where representative people of all incomes lived was marked by the conspicuous absence of the three blights of 1982: no inflation, no unemployment, and no taxes. Interest rates were not a source of complaint outside the call money market where, however, the high demand for brokers' loans to finance the buying of stocks on margin punctuated Calvin Coolidge's solemn dictum: "The business of America is business." Mortgage rates were not burdensome, though the ten-year limit on mortgage loans was escalating risks that were not recognized. As the stock market enjoyed its blowoff, not only 1929 fashion but also 1982–1983 fashion, it radiated the assurance that America, and every business in it, was a going, dividend-paying concern.

The 1929 crisis of foreign bank failure and government debt repudiation hit the stock market when the U.S. economy was still going strong. But until Hitler ended the charade of reparations payments to England and France in March 1933, thus choking off their war-debt payments to America, we threw good money after bad in repeated efforts to lend our debtors the money they owed us and to keep our banks out of trouble. In 1982, we dedicated ourselves to the same strategy of shoring up the unshorable, namely oil prices, for the same reason—to keep our banks out of trouble. The oil cash flows collateralizing so much of the 1982–1983 international bank debt load were dwindling and drying up. The foreign debt repudiation threatening to hit the U.S. banking system this time around would have broken the economy even if it had been strong. In fact, the world economy was already devastated and the banking system was already suspect as a direct result of OPEC's extortionate pricing. By the time the foreign lending caper was over in the summer of 1982, the unmanageable, uncollectible float of loans had grown to $750 billion. A highly fragmentary and gross underguesstimation of the damage by *The Wall Street Journal*, identifying less than

$500 billion, included three OPEC members—Nigeria, Venezuela, and Indonesia—among the dominoes being toppled by defaults. Canada failed to win even an honorable mention in this superficial evaluation of the debt derby. So did the busted borrowers in the Mediterranean/ Gulf oil patch. The default illustrated the classic definition of bankruptcy: It happens "when you can't borrow the interest." Any bank willing to join in throwing an extra couple of billion dollars for interest payments to Mexico or Argentina by 1982 could be confident of extending the daisy chain of distress from the busted borrower to the busted government behind it. Spokesmen for wounded banks had a canned answer to the anxious questions plaguing them about the exposure of major banks to foreign loans gone bad: "Only a small portion of our outstanding loans are foreign." They neglected to add that the write-offs ate up from two-thirds to double their capital. They also overlooked one straw blowing in the wind: The Saudis had cut back their depositories to two New York City banks. Of these, one, Morgan Guaranty, went public in *The Wall Street Journal* with an offer to provide a haven for customers of the busted Canadian banks left homeless.

While bank loan portfolios mushroomed, so did the major debtor nations' arms burdens, as did not happen between 1929 and 1933. In 1982, every government in distress owed more than it could have managed had its national income been rising. In fact, national incomes were falling, unadjusted for the twin bite of inflation and taxation. Nevertheless, nations without exception were finding it easier to take on new obligations for armaments than to meet old obligations for interest.

Militaristic competition, indeed, took over as the only growth market in sight. Time and again war challenged politics as its principal competitor for front-page headlines. In the bloody month of June 1982, with the Falklands, Lebanon, and the Iran-Iraq border all in flames, Sweden launched a mammoth (for Sweden) $4.5 billion military aircraft program, in spite of her reputation for stubborn neutrality. She had no bona fide domestic defense need of her own for this program; she certainly had no security need to protect herself from encroachments by Russia, her bad neighbor, though not her imminent invader. But in her desperation, Sweden identified arms as the only sure growth market that could support her entirely export-dependent economy. In the average good year, at least two-thirds of Swedish production needs to find overseas buyers, but in 1982, the markets for wood, steel, and glass, her commercial mainstays, were dead. Then, adding insult to injury, even this strategy of despair was cut off before 1982 turned into 1983, when Sweden found herself forced to cut back production schedules at her Bofors munitions operation for lack of export orders. She could not compete with Israel's merchants and America's subsidies.

In this strange new economic environment in which wars, far from

alleviating depressions as of yore, were deepening them, another example was provided by Alejandro Orfila, the head of the Organization of
American States, who saw the British invasion of the Falklands as
guaranteeing a wide-open, uncontrollable drive for nuclear armaments
by every dictatorship in Latin America. A simple political calculation
underlined the allure of nuclear armaments for Latin America's militarily inexperienced but politically battle-scarred generals and admirals; it
offered them a formula for retaining their own formidability without
putting them in need of troops to train for combat or of young people
to trust with weapons.

Reagan's astonishing run of popularity, months after the depression
of 1982 deepened precipitously, demonstrated how slow Americans are
to draw political conclusions from economic mishaps. It was not until
the winter of 1983 that his poll rating dropped below 50 percent, even
lower than Carter's midterm rating. True, the stock market explosion,
which started in August and ran through the 1982 election campaign
(and into the summer of 1983), bought time for Reagan and lent plausibility to the White House's bumper-sticker campaign slogans: "Give the
guy a chance" and "Stay the course." People free to wonder and worry
about the stock market generally take its recovery moves during hard
times as a reassuring promise that the economy will follow.

The dislocation in the economy riveted the attention of IRS victims
on their private pocketbook problems. Those who were still swayed by
the Great Communicator were invited to wait for the domestic economy to cure itself with a beneficial assist from his program and its
inspirational effect on the stock market. Never mind the merits of
Reaganomics (dealt with in detail in Chapter Six), its purely domestic
approach to the collapse of the domestic economy obscured the foreign
political sources of economic disaster. By its domestic focus, the administration defaulted on the responsibility for its stance in the world,
a responsibility even larger and more urgent than that which it had
necessarily assumed in managing the economy. Every administration
inherits the obligation to ask itself: How can the United States, acting
through its government, earn its way and defend its position in the
outside world, helping itself without hurting its friends and clients
abroad? No administration in Washington can lead, or look credible
even trying, while it encourages the country to look inward and concentrate on coping with its close-to-home pocketbook problems.

The father of modern political thought, Thomas Hobbes, in making
the case for a strong, centralized government in the England of the
1600s, warned in his colorful prose that, lacking a powerful sovereign,
"every man's hand is against every man's." This description of domestic
anarchy in the absence of a delegation of police power to a sovereign
government applies perfectly to the state of international affairs in the

1980s: Every government's hand is against every government's. Every government's hand is also to be seen reaching for money, which for two generations has been the Yankee dollar. In good times and bad, every foreign government deals across its borders with its foreign competition as the uninhibited and unapologetic bargaining agent for the national economy it represents. Traditionally, the backlash from a slump starts a push for economic improvement at the expense of trading partners. Every country but America knows enough to handle its foreign relations with a sensitive eye on its need to make a living in a world of governments looking out for their own economies. America handles her foreign political relations on the twin assumption that (1) the money problem raised for her is how much of it she will hand out rather than take in, and (2) her domestic affluence does not depend on her foreign practicality. Americans are not conditioned to seek reprisals abroad when their own economy collapses or to look abroad for signs that the Horsemen of the Apocalypse are mounting their murderous chargers. No poll will show more than the barest fraction of older Americans recalling that, while Hoover's depression was getting ahead of him, the Japanese army happened to be riding roughshod over Manchuria. At the time, no one worried, because the Japanese military were charging in the opposite direction, a long way from Pearl Harbor.

True, America is subject to a special hostility because she is bigger, stronger, and richer than other countries. But, notwithstanding the universal foreign suspicion of the "ugly American" and the universal foreign experience that it pays to take the hard line against America, the United States persists in traveling as the perpetual innocent abroad. Consistent with this national habit, Reagan proclaimed his confrontation with the Kremlin, and America's with Russia, in moral terms. But any confrontation between governments is either a sham or, more dangerous, a provocation, unless it is a power confrontation. The sinister embrace of Hitler and Stalin, which opened the way for World War II, stands as a reminder that all governments are potential adversaries, even when they take turns at experimenting with alliances. It's axiomatic that all economic and financial dealings between countries are basically political and, therefore, potentially military. This holds true even for traditional allies, as Britain and Argentina proved when they had their falling-out in the spring of 1982. Morality may shape politics, but it is no substitute.

Under three successive administrations—Kissinger's, Carter's, and Reagan's—the American government engineered a disaster by ignoring the adversarial element always present in foreign relations, even among allies, and particularly with any combination of governments that extends into the Americas, and by defaulting on its responsibilities in coping with OPEC. Kissinger set the pattern when he greeted OPEC as a friend, an ally, and a ward. He compounded the miscalculation by inviting the international oil companies to become the cartel's messenger boys and, more naïve still, by endowing them with ex officio expertise on OPEC's politics. The costly lesson it taught has jolted everyone ready to learn from experience that any effort to deal with OPEC by relying on purely economic, or political, or financial, or military responses is foredoomed to failure. America's unpreparedness was revealed and her innocence bared in the reaction that led her to focus on all four challenges posed by OPEC as separate and distinct from one another, instead of grappling with them as interwoven.

The United States, for lack of a coordinated, double-pronged attack on her interrelated domestic economic and foreign political malfunctions, developed a new export: depression. In one year it spread around the world, developing an epidemiology of its own, so that country after country came to think of it as the American disease. Its impact was painfully simple, but its symptoms were complicated. It surfaced as economic in its symptoms but political at its roots; financial in its distress but military in its responses—recalling the bloody scenario that began to unravel in 1929. Its fever rash was a domestic infection reaching epidemic proportions in Detroit in 1981, before spreading across the country in the summer of 1982, when the stock market broke loose from its moorings and ran wild, only to fall apart in the summer of 1983, after the economy showed some faint sign of recovery. The virus was as mobile as it was deadly. It originated beyond America's borders in the world's oil-producing areas, and during the 1970s it spread to every foreign testing ground destabilized by America's loss of strategic purpose and supporting economic initiative or military capability. As the depression epidemic developed momentum, every foreign country, developed or undeveloped, complained that it was importing the American disease and packaged it promptly for reexport. By mid-1982 the European economy was leading the American economy downhill; even the Japanese economy was following; the economies of the Third World were grounded; and the sick list was suffering additions by the month. Horror stories from Poland of domestic shortages suffered and export prices slashed were no surprise, but they were unexpected in Yugoslavia, where the regime proclaimed its determination to mete out punishment to violators of "economic laws"—as if it had spent the previous generation under the yoke of Adam Smith and not Tito. Even South Korea, the dynamic new entry in the world's industrial growth derby, was reduced to undercutting Sweden's idled shipyards by two-thirds (and in bids to build bottoms for Sweden) and Japan's by one-half.

A superpower that exports a depression is on notice to prepare for the wars that depressions beget. But while the depression at hand was visibly eroding large blocks of the capital embodied in America's productive plant, she was hardly getting her money's worth from the trillions she was sinking into her preparations for the various wars in prospect. The failures of her marketplace efforts reflected the impracticality of her economic thinking, and the flabbiness of her military muscles reflected the impracticality of her strategic thinking. A sad dichotomy exists inside America, where professional economic thinking is not conditioned to calculate politically, nor are realistic political observers accustomed to maneuver in markets, and where military programming has been left to the initiative of foreign enemies to set in motion, even though, ironically, Russia has been successful in branding America the scheming nuclear aggressor. Because Americans have been prone to blame their domestic dollar discomforts on impersonal economic developments, and to attribute their foreign political frustrations to miscalculations in Washington, they have been conditioned to go along with the pressure to cope with each set of problems separately. They have accepted the reckless compulsion to jump to conclusions about their own economy, about politics in foreign countries, and about the worldwide arms race without making the connection between one hook baited for their economists, another baited for their strategists, and another for their generals, all strung on the same line.

Complaining comes as naturally to Americans as smugness. They ended the 1970s complaining about the performance of their own economy, complaining about the behavior of their supposed allies and admitted enemies, complaining about the fecklessness of their politicians and "deep thinkers," complaining about the irresponsibility of their young people, and complaining about the high cost of maintaining their military establishment. The list of complaints was long, and every entry on it was justified. By the time the depression hit in 1981, American opinion was angrier than it had been for years, but its thinking remained as smug as ever. No vision had yet taken shape that would trace the deepening of the country's domestic economic distress to Washington's foreign political miscalculations during the 1970s, much less back to its foreign military misadventures of the previous two decades. Nor did the prevailing despair identify the domestic economic collapse in 1981 as the direct cause of U.S. foreign political floundering in 1982.

When America bloodied her nose in Korea and Vietnam, she found she had lost each war and came close to suspecting that she had not known what winning would have meant. Both excursions against Soviet satellites in the mudholes of Asia turned out to be entrapments. Each unfolded as an expression of America's simplistic assumption that Communist "conspiracies" are her political danger and that Soviet expansionism on the other side of the world is a military threat to America's military security on her side of the world. At the time America rushed into both wars, she was blinded to the inconsistency of dividing up the world into Soviet and American spheres of interest and then presuming to play policeman inside the sphere of interest America had yielded to the Kremlin. She also failed to recognize that time was her enemy, that space, represented by Asian mudholes turned into battlefields, is a decoy, and that her economy is her distinctive and decisive asset.

Soon after America found herself knee-deep in Korea, she realized it was a decoy and put it behind her, taking comfort from the tremendous long-term economic expansion that the war had provoked her into launching. But no comparable economic gain offset her military defeat in Vietnam. When her indignation over discovering that Vietnam was a decoy too finally forced her disentanglement from it, she proceeded on the innocent assumption that she was out of it too. A full decade after the disaster was admitted and the pullout completed, she had not yet put it behind her. On the contrary, every time she turned around, the nemesis she spawned in Vietnam tripped her up again. Job's lot was a joyride to seventh heaven compared to America's ongoing retreat from Vietnam. She can thank the war for the alienation of her youth; for the slippage of her economy from boom into stagflation; for her progressive isolation from her former allies; for the aimless disintegration of her high-cost defense establishment; for the glazed daze with which she contemplates Russia outsmarting her in the Cold War; for the outbreak of the oil inflation and the eruption of the Middle East into a tinderbox; and, as a tax on it all, for the runaway in governmental debt and the resumption of the tax spiral, despite the depression. Consciously or otherwise, she was driven by the trauma of defeat in Vietnam into a new conditioned reflex of defeatism—her compulsion to play the appeasement game in the oil war—and into her confusion of thought and purpose in the 1980s.

For Vietnam she can thank the demented political genius whose image, at once charismatic and chilling, has come increasingly to dominate the vacuum between Roosevelt and Reagan: Lyndon B. Johnson. With each passing year, Johnson's successors have discovered to their dismay that their agenda is dominated by the demonic role he played in activating the American tragedy in Vietnam. Henry Kissinger and Richard Nixon charged into the same trap that the self-styled Texan country bumpkin had. In fact, they wasted four full years, plus more lives and resources than anyone would subsequently care to count, and belied their self-admitted claims to sophistication at the strategic chessboard. The obsession of the Nixon White House with chasing Communist guerillas around every tree in the jungle distracted them from the fatal blunder committed by our British allies in vacating their entrenched power base commanding the then still ignored sea lanes of the Middle East. This same obsession lulled them into acquiescence in the coup that the Kremlin map readers scored on the heels of the departing British innocents. Not only did the Soviet power players show themselves to be every bit as shrewd as Kissinger and Nixon claimed to be, but they set the stage for OPEC to declare the oil war on when America was ready to call the Vietnam War off.

During the following four years, Jimmy Carter offered a moral response to the challenge to American power in the Middle East. To recall the sinister taunt in vogue in post-Pearl Harbor America, he did not know there was a war on, nor did he show any sensitivity to the sophisticated assist that Soviet forces, political as well as military, were giving to the strident anti-American belligerents. Instead, he attested to the provincialism of his world view by greeting the inflation of oil costs as an opportunity for America to strengthen her moral fiber through sacrifice.

Governor Reagan's incumbency in the Oval Office confirmed the danger of naïveté in office acted out by his predecessor. Reagan took over innocent of the ghosts that haunted the Situation Room and certainly of our bloody entanglements overseas. With the same perilous innocence he proclaimed his proprietary possession of a magic formula to restore America's strength and security. To his credit, he also warned that the time had come for America to realize her jeopardy. His focus, however, was blurred. While he turned one of America's eyes to the road that beckoned ahead toward the dead end of nuclear confrontation, he turned the other back down the memory lane dominated by the statue of Herbert Hoover. This eye-crossing vision identified Hoover as his economic mentor and FDR as his political mentor. He ignored the opportunity at hand to declare economic war against Russia before Russia could involve America in the real thing against one or more Soviet satellites in one or another colonial outpost for the third time since 1950. Because Reagan failed to make the connection between the country's domestic economic travail and its foreign political frustrations, the Kremlin made the connection for him between the fiery rhetoric he unleashed against it and the mudholes into which he began to dispatch American fire fighters. The traps it baited for Reagan in the Caribbean were more dangerous than the ones it had baited for Truman, Eisenhower, Kennedy, Johnson, and Nixon, because they were located inside America's defense perimeter and not inside its own.

American presidents have hardly been running for elevation to the exalted role Plato reserved in ancient Greece for the philosopher-kings. But if presidents were expected to be thinkers, and not doers in need of counsel and advice from thinkers, they would have a ready alibi to justify their fruitless and frustrating pursuit of divergent foreign political and domestic economic aims. In that case, they would simply point to the great tradition of philosophical speculation the modern world has inherited from the Greeks, which taught us to think in an orderly way by separating specific categories of thought, like space and time or physics and biology. The simple, practical way for America to pacify the jungle of international relationships is to outgrow the formalism and structure of ancient philosophy, and to adapt her thinking to the realistic integrations of modern science. She can stabilize society if only she will revolutionize her thinking about it—by overcoming the traditional separation of two categories of thought, one domestic and economic, the other foreign and political. Smaller and weaker countries habitually integrate the foreign political and domestic economic strands of their national policy. Only America tolerates their divergence. The separation between the two categories threatens to detonate a military explosion America is committed to avoid. Where we have been plagued (and still are) by the separation, we are now challenged at long last to improvise a foreign economic policy, to put it to work not only in the marketplace but at all the political pressure points within our reach abroad, and to get down to brass tacks in doing so.

CHAPTER THREE

The Cunning of History: How Vietnam Invited Johnson's Rise and Engineered His Fall

THE QUESTION about history is always where to begin: How far back in the genealogy of a crisis must we go to reach its roots? The history of countries is the history of their crises, even when historians set out to celebrate eras of goodwill. The crisis of depression and endemic war in the 1980s erupted after germinating for three troubled decades. Its immediate cause surfaced in the aftermath of the oil war of the 1970s —the oil war went military as the oil boom went bad, and the Middle East ignited as the American economy collapsed. But the grandparent of the crisis of the 1980s and the parent of the oil war of the 1970s was the Vietnam War of the 1960s, which had been smoldering for over a decade before it erupted. All roads to an understanding of America's confrontation with Russia lead through Vietnam. Any realistic perspective on Vietnam, in turn, requires tracing the career of Lyndon Johnson, whose rise to and fall from the pinnacle of power parallels the history of that disaster.

The tragedy of Johnson dramatized the most abstract and intricate philosophy that has influenced the modern world: Hegelianism, which nevertheless is pending business for America because it inspired Marxism. Johnson undoubtedly never heard of Hegel, yet Johnson's role in Vietnam acted out Hegel's concept of the cunning of history. It enmeshed Johnson in its web and turned him from its unsung hero into its target. His meteoric rise to national prominence had been accelerated by his initiative in 1954, advising Dwight Eisenhower to avoid taking the Communist bait in Vietnam. His fall from power came with the blame for taking the same bait himself ten years later.

Any realistic audit of the cost, still pyramiding in the 1980s, of Johnson's decision to go all-out in Vietnam during the mid-1960s calls for striking a balance between his strengths and his weaknesses. Other figures exuded the charm he lacked. The pretentiousness of others sharpened his paranoia. Still others earned a reputation for character, which he certainly lacked. Statesmanship eluded him. But he was the most creative political animal who ever roamed the American political jungle—and he was an animal, the least philosophical and least literate of politicians. When Wendell Willkie's campaign pamphlet, *One World,* became a brief best seller in 1943, Johnson told me that the effort of trying to read it put him to sleep before he finished the first page. Two decades later, his associate counsel, Hobart Taylor, Jr., to whom Johnson looked as a resident intellectual, told me of receiving one of the Boss's frantic post-midnight calls asking who "Malrax" was the night before the distinguished French author André Malraux, then De Gaulle's minister of culture, was scheduled to attend a White House dinner.

During his first year as Jack Kennedy's trustee, when he performed on every one of Kennedy's unfulfilled promises, Johnson was the most effective president that America has had. He went on to become the most destructive president America had had until Nixon's performance granted him a reprieve. I was one of the first "Easterners" he met when, as a young congressman with a lean and hungry look, he took over as Washington's new monument. I helped him raise the first money he ever found outside Texas for his first Senate race, which, canards to the contrary notwithstanding, he won at the polls but lost in the voting machines.

This is neither the time nor the place to recount the ups and downs of my relationship with Johnson. I do remember, however, Lady Bird, always the patient, understanding, never self-pitying foster mother and head wife (as they say in Southeast Asian palace circles), telling me, in her husband's presence, that she and Lyndon were anxious for me to meet George Reedy, whom they had just hired from the United Press (as it was then called), to mediate the then majority leader's savage, nonstop guerilla war with reporters and pundits. I also remember heaving a sigh of relief and remarking what a mercy that would be for everyone in between Lyndon and friends in the media—for everyone but the unsuspecting George in his new martyr's role as Lyndon's press secretary. Just as I was sending this book off to press, my travail was relieved by the exhilaration of proper rib-busting laughter and was distracted by genuine agony of spirit when I discovered George's magnificent memoir, *Lyndon B. Johnson,* in my mail. As a biography, it is larger than its subject, and its subject was larger than life. To avoid any possibility of misunderstanding, George makes one thing perfectly clear about Lyndon: "As a human being, he was a miserable person— a bully, sadist, lout, egotist." Reedy's rapier is deadly when he laughs at Johnson as the comic figure Johnson was. But the tears Reedy weeps come from the agony of despair when he writes: "I, myself, am glad to get him out of my life at last. . . . What I would like, of course, would be a Lyndon B. Johnson who was *not* a bastard. . . . He was a tormented man. And while we will never know why he was tormented . . . I only hope we really accept him that way—not a saint and not a demon but still a towering figure on the landscape of American history." No gift for prophecy from the perspective of the crisis brewing in the 1980s is needed to see that, as it comes to a head, win, lose, or draw for our effort or for our default, he is destined to become and we are fated to see him become a more towering figure still. "Torment" is the word Reedy uses for the ecstasy and the fear Johnson found in the mechanics of power. Before the advance copy of Reedy's memoir reached me, I had written in this very space that this is the time and the place to explain how he transmitted his torment to all of us and to all of ours behind us when he charged—he was not lured!—into the decoy that had been prepared for him in Vietnam.

The drama of Johnson's involvement in Vietnam began in 1954. America had pulled out of Korea; France had been knocked out of Indochina. President Eisenhower knew enough not to let anyone talk him into starting up Truman's war again. After all, he had won his election by satisfying the country that he would stop the fighting there. No sooner had America's war ended at the 38th parallel, however, than the pressure came on Washington to renew France's war at the 17th parallel. Eisenhower had permitted his fire-eating, fiercely anti-Communist secretary of state, John Foster Dulles, to go up to the Senate on an informal mission and request permission from Senator Richard Russell of Georgia, chairman of the Senate Armed Services Committee, and Majority Leader Johnson, then chairman of the key subcommittee on defense of the Senate Appropriations Committee, for authority to send military technicians to Vietnam. Russell and Johnson refused it and promptly adjourned Congress.

A few weeks later, Dulles instructed one of his assistant secretaries, Thruston Morton, later senator from Kentucky, to call Senator Russell to inform him that the President had, nevertheless, exercised his prerogative as Commander in Chief to dispatch the operatives to Vietnam. Russell was subsequently rueful in recalling his shocked reaction at the time: "Before you know it, we're likely to have 20,000 men there," he warned, not realizing how right he was in identifying America's miscalculation or how wrong in underestimating its scope.

Dulles had not acted alone in urging Eisenhower to send the first corps of "technicians" to Vietnam in preparation for intervention in force. His ally in this hawkish exercise was Admiral Arthur Radford, the formidable new chairman of the Joint Chiefs of Staff whom Eisenhower had appointed. In August 1982, the publication of Volume XIII of *Foreign Relations of the United States* provided official confirmation of the scheme Dulles and Radford had hatched to persuade Eisenhower to send American troops to hold the line the French had scuttled. In a perceptive review in *The Washington Post* of the grim narrative in this volume's 2,497 pages of documents, Murray Marder noted that eight years after Hiroshima, Ike was being pushed to approve the use of three tactical A-bombs on the treetops and gullies of Vietnam. Marder's remarkable digest of the passages at arms, recorded during Eisenhower's privy council, quotes the President as responding to the proposal with the not at all unwise judgment that a leader "would want to ask himself and all his wisest advisers whether the right decision was not rather to launch a world war."

"If our allies were going to fall away in any case," the President continued, "it might be better for the United States to leap over the smaller obstacles and hit the biggest one with all the power we have. Otherwise we seemed to be merely playing the enemy's game—getting ourselves involved in brushfire wars in Burma, Afghanistan, and God knows where."

Eisenhower was by no means alone, however, in parrying the gung-ho onslaught from his senior advisers in the National Security Council. The official documents recording the deliberations among the President, the secretary, the admiral, and all the other participants to the discussion within the executive branch are necessarily limited to their formal interchanges. A Commander in Chief like Eisenhower, with his head screwed on straight and with two spare eyes in the back of his head, will always take the precaution of conducting necessarily informal interchanges with the leaders of the legislative branch when a military crisis is brewing. These were Eisenhower's fallback in America's near-brush with a brushfire war of nuclear dimensions, and they proved to be America's salvation at the time.

My subsequent involvement in the drama resulted from the initiative of H. Struve Hensel, whom Eisenhower originally appointed counsel of the Defense Department, but who by that time had been promoted to the new assistant secretaryship of defense for international affairs. Knowing of my relationship with Johnson and of my interest in the relationship between the defense apparatus and the economic mechanism, Hensel agonized with me over his twin concern that the administration was on the verge of a major policy involvement in Vietnam without congressional approval, and that the military merits of the venture seemed more dubious to him than the hawks in the administration were willing to grant. Before he had come to Washington with Eisenhower, Hensel and I had often discussed the Truman administration's rashness in plunging into the Korean War and particularly in doing so without the benefit of congressional approval. The contrast was even more glaring because Harry Truman and Dean Acheson had made their move in the full light of day, whereas Eisenhower was on the verge of being rushed into his by the cloak-and-dagger crowd. As an Eisenhower loyalist with large advisory and administrative responsibilities to the Pentagon high command, Hensel was concerned that the Eisenhower administration was poised to repeat the Truman administration's error—doing the wrong thing without the right approval —to no better purpose.

I had learned early in my relationship with Johnson that he was too cautious and too political to consider any recommendation on its merits. Instead, he could be counted upon to hold back and wait to see how allies with political muscle might be encouraged to support any initiative of his. Accordingly, I decided to share Hensel's policy concerns with Supreme Court Justice William O. Douglas—for three reasons I thought sufficient. The first was that Douglas knew more, from firsthand observation, about the mainland of Asia than anyone else in the Washington power structure—certainly more than Dulles. The second was that Douglas had transferred his own frustrated presidential ambitions in the 1940s to support the option Johnson was staking out in the 1950s to the Democratic succession in the 1960s. Douglas had been entirely passive when his own availability as the heir of the New Deal was under scrutiny during the 1940s, yet he exerted himself continuously and effectively in behalf of Johnson's future availability during the 1950s. My third consideration was that the dominant political pressures in Texas, as well as in the Senate, were driving Johnson to positions right of center. Therefore, he was in increasingly anxious need of a senior sponsor with impeccable liberal credentials who would be willing and happy to vouch for him no matter how far to the right he might be driven by any local pressures. Douglas knew the problem, he knew Johnson, and he had the liberal credentials.

Separately and together, Douglas and I persuaded Johnson that Dulles and Radford did not have the cards to play with Eisenhower but that Johnson did and that Eisenhower would respect him if he played them. With characteristic prudence, Johnson took the precaution of persuading not only Senator Russell but also House Speaker Sam Rayburn to move with him. Rayburn's support was decisive because he was not only Johnson's link with the realistic oil money that ran Texas politics but Eisenhower's too.

Texas was bulging with oil multimillionaires, but only one of them had the sense to keep his mouth shut, his wallet open, and his eyes focused on the real world. Sid Richardson was his name. He was reputed to have begun his fabulous career as a faro dealer; he ended it by naming Governor John Connally as one of the five trustees of his vast estate. Of all the big-time Texas money moguls, Richardson was the one with the Rayburn connection. And both of them had the Eisenhower connection dating back to when Ike, like Herbert Hoover before him, had gone after the Democratic presidential nomination before the Republican presidential nomination came to him. The common tie that bound Eisenhower to his Texas sponsors, and his Texas sponsors to Rayburn and Johnson, was the reliance of the Richardson Establishment on Rayburn and Johnson to protect the tax shelters that made oil profitable for Texas at seventy-five cents to one dollar and thirty-five cents a barrel and, therefore, that made Texas attractive to Northern money, with which it then still financed itself.

Under cover of his genial smile, warm personality, and "aw shucks" aloofness from ideological commitments, Eisenhower was as cold and calculating a master of the fine art of personal politics as anyone who ever went to West Point before vaulting the army ladder. Lines are drawn, and line-ups are drawn up, at the card table inside the West Point club before they can be on the battlefield. A memoir of Ike in action, in of all places, the "Bridge" column of *The New York Times*, recalled his gut reaction after having accepted an offer from President Truman to take over as commander in chief of NATO in 1950 and being asked whom he proposed to take as deputy. "I'd like to take Bedell Smith, but I think I'll take Al Gruenther. He's the best bridge player." Ike knew that the hard core of Texas oil operators, who had won the Republican presidential nomination for him against Senator Robert A. Taft by swinging the make-or-break Texas primary to him, was not infatuated with his *beaux yeux*. Richardson and his cohorts could not count on "Mr. Republican," Senator Taft's nom de guerre, to deal in their behalf with Johnson and Rayburn, but they could count on Eisenhower to fit into a cozy threesome without stirring up a backlash against themselves. Turnabout being fair play, the drift to the right in Texas politics had put Rayburn and Johnson in need of a nonpartisan Republican president with a liberal appeal and the charisma that a war hero commands in the Alamo State. When Ike reached for the brass ring in the Texas primary, he was on clear notice that the Texas players with political clout had held their noses and hung onto their long-standing options on Democratic decision making in their own backyard, while buying brand-new rights to participate in Republican decision making nationally. But Ike also knew that the oil money that preferred his personality to Taft's cantankerousness was insistent on a clear understanding in return; Ike was to cut their old Democratic allies in Congress in on their new deal with him in the White House. Everybody was happy, particularly Rayburn and Johnson, who picked up a free option on the best of both worlds.

For Ike, the choice between the pressure from Dulles and Radford to go into Vietnam and the respectful admonition from Rayburn, Russell, and Johnson about the prudence of staying out was an easy one, all the more so because Dulles and Radford were his appointees, to be eyed warily, while the Democratic triumvirs were his friends, entitled to be handled with care. Moreover, they controlled the check-writing pen, which in American politics is more powerful than the sword. Ike had no incentive to rock the boat that Rayburn and Johnson were trying to keep on an even keel for him across congressional party lines. Eisenhower recognized that wars are made in the same way as laws: with congressional approval. Besides, the personal relationships Eisenhower enjoyed with members of both parties in both houses were too cordial to tempt him into the provocative course of action that Secretary of State Acheson, who looked down on Congress with disdain, had led Truman into taking when he pulled the trigger in Korea. So the leaders of Congress took advantage of their warm personal relations with Eisenhower to warn him that the war his strategists were starting was not likely to make sense to Congress, especially if Eisenhower put his seal of approval on it barely two years after he had stared Douglas MacArthur down and extricated a hurt and humiliated America from Korea. Also, Ike had already won a big war and needed little persuasion to see that he would have everything to lose and nothing to gain by risking a small guerilla war in Asia, even one authorized by Congress. Johnson had told him that Douglas regarded such a war as unwinnable, adding that Douglas knew what he was talking about. More to the point, Johnson warned him that the liberal political activists, who regarded Douglas as their mentor, would have the political artillery to shoot at Eisenhower on the home front if he sent American manpower and firepower to Vietnam.

The initiative worked. Eisenhower's "secret" decision remained his secret. Dulles's public pronouncements gave off a great deal of heat but started no fire. Radford grumbled but did not resist Eisenhower's orders to keep the lid on defense spending and avoid overseas adventures. Ike remained a popular war hero in hawkish Texas and emerged as a political hero in dovish Washington. Johnson and Rayburn bought time for the tightrope-walking act that enabled them to make common cause with Eisenhower in representing the conservative sponsors they shared in Texas, while still leading the liberal opposition in Washington. Vietnam was left to simmer for another decade.

Johnson, for his part, was careful to claim no public credit for his role in this constructive bipartisan episode of legislative and executive interaction. LBJ was content to win acceptance inside the Republican White House as a welcome and appreciated courtier, while he relished the recognition he was winning for the dictatorial power he asserted over the Democratic congressional establishment. At the peak of his congressional power, Johnson established himself as the first Senate majority leader in American political history to assert direct control over the House, through his personal ascendency over Rayburn, as well as the Senate.

Johnson was also the playmaking figure entitled to the credit for defusing the Sputnik crisis of 1957. Its onset coincided with one of the recurrent stoppages that marred the performance of the American economy in the 1950s. Its impact broke the stock market, sending Eisenhower into a panic. Its upshot started the space race and thrust America into the new era of decade-spanning governmental procurements, previewing the fiscal challenge of the 1980s: how to fund trillion-dollar program obligations with mere billion-dollar annual spending authorizations.

In my account of the Sputnik crisis in *The Economics of Crisis*, I did not feel free to mention the entirely accidental spur that prompted me to take a stab at activating Johnson, with the happy effect of calming Eisenhower and ending the freeze he had ordered on the government's backed-up bills to defense contractors. The death of Edwin L. Weisl, the crafty political lawyer who was the gray eminence behind Lehman Brothers, removes this restriction. The Federal Reserve Board had precipitated the failure of the economy by tightening credit just when the economy was moving into a healthy, expansive phase and needed more of it. Just then, the Soviets had induced a national failure of nerve in America when they scored their memorable first in space. A few months before the market broke, Weisl and I had had a falling-out over a trivial interchange, mischievously prompted by Johnson after his fashion, over who had or had not said what to whom about an item Johnson wanted planted in the Hearst papers. Weisl was the Hearst counsel. At the worst of the Sputnik market break, his lifelong confidant, Daniel Arnstein, who had played tackle alongside Knute Rockne on Chicago's first pro football team, had supervised the construction of the Burma Road in World War II, and, finally, had controlled distribution for Esso in New York harbor, told me that Weisl was aggravating himself to death because he was getting hit with margin calls and that "Eddie says we can get Lyndon to do something about the market if only you'll just figure out what to tell him to do." I told Arnstein to tell Weisl I loved him and to have him call me.

Within minutes Weisl was on the phone, smooth as syrup, as if we had never had a spat, bragging about the favorable mention of Lyndon that he had persuaded the Hearst San Antonio paper to run. I played dumb and told him that we needed to get the market up for the country's sake, adding that the way to do it was to show Lyndon how he could help himself without, of course, taking any risk or doing any work: just by getting old reliable Dick Russell to go to Ike with him on the standard mission of freeing the president from the custody of the palace guard. The purpose of the mission I proposed was for Russell and Johnson to threaten Eisenhower with the long-term gravity of the Soviet's space challenge and at the same time to promise him immediate relief from the panic by holding hearings to demonstrate the urgency of an American scientific effort to catch up. At this point, Weisl would have bought the idea of decorating the Washington Monument with a circus tent. He extracted from me a promise not to let on to Johnson that he was caught in the market break.

I called Johnson and told him that Weisl was alarmed for the country. "You and Weisl scheming together again?" he asked, always meticulously informed about the ups and downs of feuds and friend-ships. I could hardly tell him that our reconciliation was barely five minutes old.

"You know Eddie," I said. "He's always thinking about the country, but he's scared to ask you to stick your neck out. He has an idea, however, that he thinks Dick Russell might do something with, and he asked me to try it out on you for size." Over the long-distance line, I could practically see one of Johnson's nostrils dilating with suspicion, and the other with jealousy.

"Why doesn't he call Russell himself?" Johnson asked.

"Because I talked him into letting me try it out on you to see if you wanted to talk it over and get Russell to help you put it across yourself."

Johnson's defense investigating subcommittee was one of his many obscure mechanisms tucked away in cubbyholes under the Capitol dome. When I suggested that he take it out of mothballs and crank it up into the vehicle for moving on "Weisl's idea" of investigating what the Soviets were doing to us in space, I added that he could talk Russell into serving with him. He agreed to ask Russell to go to Eisenhower with him, not to ask for any action from the administration but to tell Ike everything they were going to do to get him off the spot. He said that Russell would not mind so long as he did not have to do anything about it himself. "Dick's no worker," he cautioned, a classic case of articulate expertise. I bet him that, if Russell went along, Eisenhower would too. He did.

Only one snag remained. Who would do the work? It was a legiti-mate question. No congressional hearings are any better than the staff preparing and running them. "It's Weisl's idea," I told Johnson. "Why not draft him?"

"He wouldn't get off the phone long enough to do any work," John-son grunted. "Besides, he's too busy rolling in the dough."

"You should know, Lyndon," I needled him. "Doesn't Eddie keep you up to date on all the money he's been making in the market?"

The complaint that came back was predictable. "How can the son of a bitch let me get stuck with all of Lehman's lemons?"

In fact, Weisl had been a great lawyer before he evolved into a political and financial mover and shaker. When I came back to him with the sale and its terms, his complaints shifted from his market losses into laments over his bad luck in getting caught with the responsibility for getting his friends out of the jams they were always getting into.

Weisl found support beyond the call of duty in Cyrus Vance, to whom he turned over the arduous job of preparing the hearings. He himself did a penetrating and painstaking job of laying out the strategy of the hearings, which stand as a neglected mine of invaluable informa-tion. On the low road at the time, I recall Weisl sneering about the fiasco of Edward Teller's appearance. Teller, the prize-winning physicist, had made an important contribution to the breakthrough at Los Alamos. He was also as fierce a nuclear hawk as any right-wing Republican in Texas. Weisl had spent grueling hours preparing Teller. He had also bragged to Teller of what he could do to get Johnson to act on his ideas. At the hearing, Teller outdid himself, while Johnson slept (as he always did when he was not the center of attention), but with one ear open. This habit served him well because it woke him up at precisely the point in Teller's testimony where he was explaining how space technology could be harnessed to control precipitation and to irrigate the desert. "Can you grow more wheat from space on our dry land in West Texas?" Johnson asked.

The hearings, nevertheless, served their purpose at the time. Eisenhower recovered his composure. The government resumed payment of its backed-up bills. Its contractors paid down their emergency bank loans. Interest rates fell. Inflationary pressures were no problem. America proclaimed her entrance into the space race. The Pentagon expanded the military-industrial complex into the military-industrial-educational complex, typified by the rise of Silicon Valley in Stanford University's backyard and the parallel development of Route 128 in the backyard shared by Harvard University and the Massachusetts Institute of Technology. The stock market was on its way, and so was Johnson as he eyed the campaign trail and resolved to elect a new crop of Democratic senators on the twin claim that the Republicans were responsible for the recession and that his leadership was responsible for working with Eisenhower to get the country out of it. The pattern was set for the unintelligible yet unmistakable fiscal quandary of the 1980s: $500 million first-year cash down payments as icebreakers to launch programs entailing obligations of $10 billion to $20 billion (before adjustment for inflation) further out into the future than anyone could calculate. Johnson took care to make himself chairman of the new Senate Aeronautics and Space Science Committee, and Houston emerged as the new space center.

Throughout the Eisenhower years, Johnson vacillated between being tempted by the encouragement Douglas and I, along with others, were giving him to "go national" in quest of the presidency and being sobered by the caution from Lady Bird that "the only thing Lyndon would ever be president of was the bank in Johnson City, Texas." Even Eisenhower, while disparaging Johnson as "a small man . . . superficial and opportunistic," felt no inhibitions in telling visitors he would feel "comfortable" with LBJ succeeding him. At the height of his power in Congress, when Eisenhower's term was running out, Johnson continued to turn a deaf ear to friendly warnings that he was missing his chance to head Kennedy off in the race for the presidential nomination in 1960. "I'm too busy minding the store to run," he used to say. But when this line fell on deaf ears, he switched stance and exploited his belated challenge to Jack Kennedy by making a secret deal with Joe Kennedy—unbeknown to the candidate or to the candidate's formidable campaign manager, his brother Bobby—to balance the ticket and assure victory in the South by running for vice-president.

The controversy, stirred up by publication of the first volume of Robert Caro's encyclopedic biography of Johnson, over the always racy subject of campaign contributions calls for a footnote to the secret deal. Johnson's political campaigns had never lacked for money. (After his first race for the Senate, his patron George Brown of Brown and Root, the giant international construction firm, told me, "Eliot, we was never in danger of running out of money, but we damn near run out of names.") He financed the lost-cause start he made toward his shrewd deal at the 1960 convention in Los Angeles more successfully than he mounted it. Joe Kennedy never went beyond alternatively complaining that Jack's nomination had cost him $11 million and that "he had laid it all off by October" with bandwagon chasers and favor seekers. But the informed belief at the time, fortified by hallowed custom, assumed that Johnson had done as well with Kennedy "in getting back his campaign expenses" as frustrated presidential candidates who settle for the second spot are expected to do. In Johnson's case this meant double-dipping on his expenses—which in fact he had already covered in his habitual way from his various sources. Joe Kennedy, who had extensive dealings of his own in "the oil patch" with Johnson's backers, knew it but was in no hurry to tip the IRS off to the fact.

After the convention, I told Douglas that Lady Bird had been against the deal and had remarked to my son, Michael Janeway, then a Harvard undergraduate working on Johnson's staff, and me of her feeling that she and LBJ had lost their freedom of action. "We are prisoners," she had said sadly. "Nixon will blow it," Douglas replied to me, "and someone will take a shot at that kid."

The Kennedy administration took office with notice that Eisenhower had left it two trouble spots, Cuba and Vietnam. The setback it quickly suffered at the Bay of Pigs and the embarrassment it made for itself when the Berlin Wall was dropped on it left it with a special incentive to redeem itself in Vietnam; the remoteness of Southeast Asia made it more inviting. Perhaps the administration's most compelling incentive for stepping up the pace of operations there, however, fell in the realm of personal politics behind the headlines, where the Kennedys revealed a naïveté in sharp contrast to their well-advertised Ivy League sophistication. They had inherited a problem in Francis Cardinal Spellman of New York, the vicar general of the U.S. Armed Forces. In his early days as bishop of Boston, he had been an intimate of the colorful founding father of the Kennedy clan, before the two began to feud. The brothers knew that Spellman was an outspoken hawk on Vietnam; they were also sensitive to the comfort the cardinal took pleasure in giving to conservative Catholics who looked askance at the brothers' escapades in tomcatting, invariably shadowed by gossip columnists. With an eye to placating Spellman as well as diverting attention from their two reversals closer to home, the Kennedys resolved to push forward in Vietnam, while Johnson watched and muttered.

When Johnson's turn came to make the decisions on America's involvement in Vietnam, he had good reason to feel that his mind had been made up for him during his three years of captivity under the Kennedy brothers. Johnson had no doubt that it was good for him to make a public commitment to finish the secret commitment they had made. This was consistent with his solemn pledge to complete every other project the Kennedys started. But this tactic reckoned without the contrast between Johnson's reputation at that stage of his career and the aura surrounding the brothers. LBJ was viewed as an oily and unprincipled backroom wheeler-dealer. Everyone expected him to compound ignorance with venality, stumbling into foreign policy decisions beyond his grasp. His interplay of self-pity and resentment was punctuated by his complaint that the Kennedys were credited with being statesmen who knew what they were doing and for what high policy purpose.

Adding bitterness to frustration, Jack Kennedy was no longer there to share the blame with LBJ over Vietnam and Bobby Kennedy was seizing the chance to fix it on him. Adding frustration to bitterness, Johnson always believed that Bobby had engineered the assassination of General Diem, America's swaggering, reactionary ally in Saigon, just three weeks before JFK was shot in Dallas. (Diem's widow had publicly greeted the Dallas shooting as retribution for the Saigon execution.) Still smarting from the wound suffered when JFK had bested him in the dramatics of national politics, Johnson decided to outdo his fallen "leader," as he called JFK during his vice-presidential phase. The Kennedys had thought it safe to order a small-scale escalation of "Eisenhower's war" in Vietnam, as they called it, and were smart enough to order a not-so-small escalation of "Spellman's war," as Johnson said they should have called it. Johnson, who could have given both Kennedys cards and spades in the manipulation of Washington politics, decided that it would be smarter still to escalate "Bobby's war," as he called it, on a large scale. The chain reaction of personal blamesmanship was carried on in the name of grand strategy, on the pretense of fighting Communism wherever it sought America out.

Johnson relied on the complexities of the military appropriations process to cover his tracks. His studied technique for mounting his secret plan of war escalation in Vietnam was to understate the need for new appropriations to prosecute the war and to cover the cash he wanted for it with unauthorized diversions of equipment and supplies from American forces already activated in other potential theaters of war under legally budgeted authorizations. When a plane took off from a carrier of the Seventh Fleet off the coast of Vietnam and failed to come back, a replacement was commandeered from the Sixth Fleet patrolling the Mediterranean; no appropriation was requested to replace it or to pay for the stepped-up cost of supporting it in combat. When ammunition rations in the jungle were exhausted by the escalation in the fighting, reserves stored elsewhere were flown in; no appropriation to replace them was requested either.

This technique of "cannibalization," as the military call it, was systematic, but its results were erratic and disruptive. When spare tires clocked in past-year appropriation bills were stripped from other commands and smuggled into Vietnam, the damage was hidden from congressional scrutiny, but the other commands wound up long on planes they could not use because they were short of tires with which to support them. The inflationary damage was compounding by the day, thanks to the consumption of mountainous reserves of military inventory, which had been put in place back when costs were substantially lower. Consequently, the cannibalization disrupted the inventory profit the Pentagon had collected on timely purchases made before the onset of the cost push due to the war.

My first sense of alarm over the trouble brewing in Southeast Asia had been touched off simultaneously with Johnson's in 1954, when I helped him talk Eisenhower out of walking into the ambush awaiting him in Vietnam. Between then and 1963, I confess, I had allowed the problem festering in Saigon, with a still unadvertised assist from Washington, to slip into the periphery of my own thinking. Elizabeth Janeway and I were shocked into thinking about it again one autumn Saturday in 1962 when Ben Cohen came to lunch at our home. Ben had been the brain truster's brain truster in the New Deal, instrumental in drafting much of its pioneering legislation. He had since taken the high road to elder statesmanship in the Truman administration as counselor to the State Department during the stormy tenure of Jimmy (formerly Mr. Justice) Byrnes and had increasingly concentrated his interests on foreign affairs. So when he remarked in his quiet, whiny drawl, "I am very much worried about what is happening in Southeast Asia," the two of us took notice. This was before the Washington rumor mill began to buzz with suspicions of responsibility for the assassination of Diem.

Moral opposition to war has never persuaded presidents to turn to pacifism. Final decisions are made on other grounds. Three years later, when Johnson started to escalate the war that, by that time, was America's war, there were two excellent pragmatic arguments for pulling back, one strategic and one procedural, but neither could be made to weigh with Johnson. Strategically, it was clearly the height of folly to commit America, whose proprietary strength is economic, to a military escalation beyond the fringe of the world economy, where even victory was likely to mean defeat but where defeat was more likely. The Mediterranean, unlike the South China Sea, connects the main arteries of the world economy. America's commitment to protect Europe (which Europe took more seriously in the 1960s than it did subsequently) hinged not only on America's ability to police the North Atlantic but also on the supporting ability of the U.S. Sixth Fleet to keep the Mediterranean open and safe for European commerce. Escalation in Vietnam was obviously a commitment to fight the wrong war at the wrong time in the wrong place—and all the more so because its hidden cost had to be borne by America's Mediterranean fleet, whose mission it was to ensure America against having to fight another war in another place at some future time. The United States had three client governments on its hands there—Turkey, Greece, and Italy. None of them had enough muscle in Washington, as West Germany and the other Western European host governments did, to resist LBJ's cannibalizing raids on America's floating strength in the region. Another nearby client, Israel, if inspired by the wisdom of the Prophets, might have been up to it and, if she had tried, would have enjoyed more leverage over Johnson than the others, but she did not.

Procedurally, Johnson's shrewdness and skill in wangling, wheedling, and bullying the congressional elders whom he had served on his way up the ladder could only be seen as a danger. He knew that Senator Robert Taft had committed political suicide by challenging Truman's unpopular "police action" in Korea. Taft, a stickler for the rules, had declared that he would have supported an official declaration of war, a constitutionally correct position but hardly one to be taken by a serious presidential contender. "Not even the Republicans would be dumb enough to take him in 1952," Johnson told me at the time of the Taft-Truman confrontation in 1950, when he wrote Taft off as a pompous loser. By 1964, the impression of Taft's blunder was still indelible on Johnson. Carrying pragmatism to the point of prophecy, LBJ reckoned the world was not outgrowing wars; it was outgrowing declarations of war. This calculation emboldened him to lure the Senate Foreign Relations Committee into accepting the time bomb known to history as the Tonkin Gulf Resolution of August 1964. It could not have been more cynically timed or more artfully unveiled.

Earlier that summer the Senate's Democrats had been tasting political blood. Their eyes were focused on the landslide victory that Johnson was building against Barry Goldwater and on the rich patronage commanded by the new subcommittee chairmanships sprouting within their reach. Johnson was filling senators' ears with fire and brimstone, branding Goldwater a warmonger and baiting him into his fatal attack on Social Security payments (although the system's solvency had not yet been threatened).

Just then two clouds, too small to seem worrisome, were spotted across the American political horizon. They blew in from the Gulf of Tonkin where two U.S. destroyers happened to be on patrol and were hit by an air attack. Few Americans indeed knew where the Gulf of Tonkin was or what our destroyers were doing there. Still, patriotism declared that the two ships had every right to show the flag on any open sea. So, to avoid a possible misunderstanding abroad or at home and to assure the Senate of the President's dedication to the spirit as well as the letter of their partnership, Johnson asked for senatorial approval of the Tonkin Gulf Resolution. Drafted in the classic Emily Post tradition, the resolution offered a nice balance of firmness and restraint. It did not ask for war appropriations, nor did it bristle with any war threats. It merely called upon the Senate to affirm its awareness of the American naval presence in the Gulf of Tonkin. The old wolf disguised as Little Red Riding Hood's grandmother, tucked up in bed and licking his chops, was the soul of candor by comparison with Johnson at his craftiest.

Johnson was too clever to ask the Senate for a grant of authority to start shooting inside Vietnam. On the contrary, he asked it only to bear witness that he was not using his authority as Commander in Chief to do so on his own when, in fact, he already had. Not until a year after the trap had been sprung on them and the escalation had surfaced did Johnson's dupes in the Senate discover that the noncombatant naval presence they had approved had turned into a belligerent military operation they had neither approved nor even been invited to consider. By then, however, the land forces could be seen disembarking from the sea forces and their weaponry could be seen following. Not only had Johnson put senators who supported his promise of the Great Society on the spot; more provocative still, he had taken protective cover behind them. They, after all, had approved the resolution. He was simply carrying out their mandate in his capacity, as he was given to explaining, as "just one little person."

LBJ set out to demonstrate America's ability not only to afford guns and butter but to do well going all-out for both. He outdid Truman, who had fought the Korean War by raising taxes and mothballing the civilian economy. Johnson insisted on pushing forward with his Texas hawkishness, promoting his Great Society programs, and sticking with his tax cuts. He added a fourth ingredient to this witch's brew—the mudholes of Vietnam. Johnson's start-up success left no doubt that America, contrary to the conclusion drawn from the war, can afford guns and butter. His climactic failure removed any doubt that America cannot afford guns, butter, tax cuts, and mudholes. The muddling of priorities that would turn up to haunt America in the 1980s originated with this inflation of priorities during the 1960s. If Ronald Reagan but knew it, Lyndon Johnson left behind the blueprint for his failure.

Johnson's string of successes had sent him flying. He could claim credit for orchestrating prosperity without inflation, and he was pointing to the stock market at its new high above 1,000 on the Dow Jones industrial average to prove it. He had rebuffed Bobby Kennedy's demand for the vice-presidential nomination and, instead, had maneuvered Bobby out of the troublesome power base at the Justice Department and into the powerless position of just another freshman senator. Like others before him, Johnson came to nurse delusions of grandeur, wrapping himself in the mantles worn by Roosevelt and Churchill and claiming to have compressed into three short years the historic achievement Roosevelt had needed twelve full years to accomplish: first, establishing himself as the New Deal president at home and, then, as the war president who institutionalized a new era of peace for the entire world. Johnson never tired of recalling that the day Roosevelt died he had crashed into media headlines declaring, "FDR was like a daddy to me." Sons are driven to emulate and outdo their fathers—especially their adopted fathers.

Despite his image as a bully, Johnson was always running scared, never more so than when he seemed to be running strong. As 1965 churned violently into 1966, his "Alamo complex" was driving him into the same trap he had advised Eisenhower to avoid. Normally so calculating and so intelligent in applying the experiences of others to his own situation, LBJ completely forgot the outcome of the siege of the Alamo. As his nemesis, Senator Eugene McCarthy of Minnesota, remarked when he broke with the President, not one Texan walked out of the Alamo alive.

The political tide crested for Johnson in 1966. Consequently, the stock market crested then too. The fears stirred up by the war eroded the confidence that Johnson's miraculous first year had inspired. So did the confusion he stirred up over whether the military were winning the war, whether he was going to call on the country to do so, or whether the war was indeed winnable. Through angry demonstrations, students voted their disapproval with their feet. As the campuses erupted, the stock market voiced its dissent too, stalling at the magic barrier of 1,000 confronting the Dow. I drew more than my normal quota of catcalls when I pronounced the great postwar bull market dead. Tom Murphy, the bookkeeper who presided over the fall of General Motors, christened me "Mr. Gloom Boy" when we appeared together before the Los Angeles Chamber of Commerce. Yet the arrival of 1983 found the stock market not only perched uneasily aloft the biggest, top-heaviest "triple top" in market history but still unable to transform its 1965–1966 ceiling into a floor stabilizing it against new declines and serving it as a base from which to mount the long-promised takeoff into the promised land. My judgment was confirmed throughout the two intervening decades by the comparison, increasingly unfavorable, between the amount of market buying power needed to get the Dow average into four-digit territory the first time, in January 1966, before the markets sensed the onset of the Johnson crisis, and the immeasurably greater volume needed to get it there the last time, when the Reagan crisis receded in the autumn of 1982. On the first go-round, fewer than 20 million shares were enough to do the trick; on the last, a 150 million–share day, climaxing a series of days above 100 million shares, was needed to give the market its reckless thrust above this same top.

The raw price performance of stocks in dollar terms unadjusted to allow for the erosive impact of the Vietnam inflation on capital values, let alone on the dividend returns they paid, was sorry enough. It was positively dismaying once the adjustment was calculated. Stocks that had failed to advance between 1966 and 1983, or at least to double the dividend-paying potential behind their prices, were seen to have eroded to half their former values.

Meanwhile, back in the Senate, another index harder to quantify but easier to track—the index of political discomfort—was confirming the refusal of the stock market to improve. Senators, bristling with resentment, began to search for a formula calculated to nullify the record LBJ had made in clearing his undisclosed war with them when they were still rallying behind his campaign rhetoric. At the same time, their resentment was tempered by a healthy respect for Johnson's knowledge of their weaknesses and a prickly fear of his ingenious methods of exploiting what he knew—diverting patronage to their enemies, feeding choice tidbits to the media, harassing and prosecuting their allies, infiltrating their staffs, and even investigating them. They were caught in a dilemma between the future consequences of going along with the war and the immediate hazards of coming out against it before it turned unpopular, as even popular, seemingly winnable wars eventually do. Serious senators recalled how unpopular the Korean War had become as its escalation diluted prosperity with inflation and turned average people from puzzled observers into frightened participants.

Politics being the art of improvising third alternatives to dilemmas, those senators moving from scrutiny of the Vietnam escalation, to mistrust of its risks, to outright opposition to its costs, found themselves groping for a formula designed to have the same political effect as shouting "Stop, thief!" at a fleeing pickpocket. But they were at their wits' end to improvise a way to whisper to the President or even to gesture at him, let alone to oppose him openly. Of all the rebels whom Johnson subsequently sneered at as "Nervous Nellies" as they took their stand against him, the only one who had seen through the Tonkin Gulf ruse and voted against it was Gaylord Nelson of Wisconsin. The Senate's ranking doves, Eugene McCarthy of Minnesota, George McGovern of South Dakota, and J. William Fulbright of Arkansas, then the chairman of the Senate Foreign Relations Committee, had all gone along with it. No doubt Bobby Kennedy would have done so, too, if he had won his Senate seat in time, if only because he had had the decisive voice in stationing the destroyers in the Gulf of Tonkin in the first place.

The ringleader of the rebel group was Vance Hartke of Indiana, a Johnson protégé in 1958, a Johnson stalwart against Kennedy in 1960, and subsequently a Humphrey intimate. LBJ had introduced Hartke to me over the telephone from Indianapolis in 1958. I had seen Hartke more or less casually during his first term, generally with Gene McCarthy, with whom he had served on the Senate Finance Committee, but we had never really squared away on any project together. Now, however, Hartke called me in deadly earnest as the resentment among senators over Johnson's trickery in sneaking the Tonkin Gulf Resolution through the Senate was coming to a boil. I asked him how he thought I might be of help. "Johnson used to tell me that you were so effective when you were with him," Hartke replied. "So, when I found that you were against the way he was playing his hand, I figured you would be just as effective."

In subsequent conversations, Hartke reeled off a long and impressive list of colleagues whose uneasiness on grounds that ranged from moral to military was prompting them to build defenses against the secret escalation techniques Johnson was devising and the public war fever he was fanning. I was quick to tell Hartke that I thought Johnson had dealt himself a winning hand with the Tonkin Gulf Resolution by acting out the story told in Texas about his card game with his partner in a real estate deal. The punch line reported LBJ remonstrating, "Now, Reuben, I expect you to play fair and square. Besides, I know what I dealt you." Moreover, I cautioned Hartke that after Taft's legalistic fiasco during the Korean conflict any senator would be foolhardy to oppose the constitutional right of any president to make any war he pleased by unconstitutional means.

The scale of the fighting in Vietnam, and the violence of its backlash throughout the entire country, led Johnson to expect violent frontal counterattacks on constitutional, political, military, and moral grounds, and he was ready to resist each and all of them. But he was not braced to cope with a new political application of the tactic of encirclement that the guerilla insurgents of Asia had perfected against establishment military formations. Above all, he did not want public disclosure of the secret of his fiscal embezzlement. The effective way to stand up to Johnson, it seemed evident, was to flush out Johnson's secret with a secret maneuver, counterattacking with the one weapon he least expected to be unleashed against him by his former protégés in the Senate Democratic caucus: the fiscal weapon. Moreover, the front to open up against him, I reasoned, was the one on which he felt most ill at ease and on which he least expected a hostile flare-up: Europe, about whose support for the war Johnson was bragging most aggressively in Washington.

Europe's initial reaction to the Vietnam escalation had been to welcome it, but from the sanctuary of the cheering stand. There was, of course, relief when the Communist encroachment was opposed. Nor could Europe fail to be pleased by a counteroffensive launched as far from its own frontiers as it was possible to get. It was likely, however, that this applause was guaranteed to turn into a chorus of complaints the moment Europe's financial interests discovered that Johnson's plunge into Vietnam would expose their substantial dollar investments to risk without offering any prospect of tangible advantages in return.

The purpose of political maneuvering for position is always to stick one's adversary with a dilemma. Johnson was adept at the art, and he confronted his targets in the Senate with the uncomfortable choice of either cutting themselves off from his patronage or acquiescing in his escalation by stealth. The trick was to find a tactic aimed at sticking LBJ with a dilemma of his own: either to stand pat on his fraudulently understated war budget or to abandon it as just that, so that he would be forced to come clean on the full extent of his undercover war spending and to admit his need for a war tax. If Johnson dug himself into his bunker and tried to stare his critics down, the inflation being unleashed by the war was bound to whip up a pocketbook backlash against him. Alternatively, if he compromised his always precarious reputation for integrity by admitting that he had lied, and then atoned for it by hitting the country with an unpopular tax—reneging on his commitment to administer Kennedy's tax cut—he was bound to provoke not only a pocketbook backlash but a moral one as well. During a war boom, resentment against inflation always runs neck and neck with resentment against taxes; the two together fuel resentment against casualties.

No doubt, once the magnitude of Vietnam's hidden cost was flushed out, Johnson would come up with a third alternative as a fallback. Hartke and I expected him to air his grievances against the fate he had suffered when he was vaulted into the vacancy left by Kennedy's assassination. In this vein, he was likely to complain that he had to go on fighting in Vietnam because it was "Bobby's war," because JFK had fought it too, and because he was bound by his sacred commitment to finish every fight Jack had started. The moment he took the "total war" approach, however, he would run into a political buzz saw. His posturing as the son of Roosevelt, avenging Pearl Harbor and cornering Hitler, while invoking the echo of Churchill's rhetoric to prove it, was likely to grate on the nerves of older people, who remembered World War II as a defensive war of mass participation against active aggression spiked with barbaric inhumanity, and to infuriate young people, who were already up in arms against draft calls. His chance of justifying the escalation as a commitment to Kennedy was flimsy, but his exposure to a backlash from reversing the Kennedy tax cut was ominous.

The probability upon which Hartke and I calculated was the tax-increase alternative. We expected the discovery of Johnson's deception to put him under irresistible pressure from Europe by way of the dollar markets to acknowledge the escalation by admitting the need for tax increases. When he did, we concluded, he would undo all that he had accomplished by his celebrated 1965 trade-off with Congress: enacting the spending cut Kennedy had not proposed in exchange for the tax cut Kennedy could not pass. Instead, LBJ would awaken memories of the "petty cash" $100 billion spending limit he had promised Chairman Harry F. Byrd, Sr. of the Senate Finance Committee to impose in 1965. Johnson consequently stirred up a fuss over his spending $135 billion just one year later and $157 billion the year after that. And, with an assist from the tax cut, he engineered deficits that then seemed horrendous—$3.8 billion in the first year and $8.7 billion in the second. More abrasive still, he managed to put a sober and representative mass constituency of outraged taxpayers behind the draft protests and, therefore, to turn the war unpopular sooner rather than later. Either way, the calculation assumed that an effective attack on LBJ's fiscal embezzlement would throw him onto the political defensive—especially if the upshot was a tax increase. Hartke had no doubt that, as a senator who was a thorn in Johnson's side, he had more influence on Johnson's ultimate policy decisions than any courtier could have.

It was Hartke, at any rate, who ferreted out the hard, inside evidence of fiscal embezzlement and who figured out how to win unimpeachable confirmation for his suspicions. He was convinced that the emotional fallout from Vietnam would whip him, and every other Democrat running in Johnson's shadow, out of office. And his political brokering became all the more persuasive with his colleagues on both sides of the aisle because he scared them, not one by one, but by twos and threes, into moving to save their political skins too. In his self-appointed role as the gadfly of the Senate rebels, Hartke was shuttling back and forth between outspoken critics of the war—mainly liberals who Johnson hoped would attack him with the same legalistic weapons Taft had blunted against Truman—and uneasy ones, apt to be more conservative, afraid to surrender their cover. Johnson, always shrewdly informed, if not always wisely directed, was well aware of these "closet critics" of both political colors, and he was deathly afraid of the political consequences from public outcry against him on the war. The "Confederates," as they were called because so many of them were Southerners with seniority, controlled the key committees Johnson needed in his pocket, four in particular: Foreign Relations, Appropriations, Armed Services, and Finance. The record LBJ had made with the Senate Foreign Relations Committee had neutralized it as the Senate's instrument for discharging its constitutional duty to advise the president in his conduct of foreign relations and to consent to his actions. Johnson was confident that he could also handle Senator Carl Hayden of Arizona, the chairman of the Senate Appropriations Committee, under whom he had served. Hayden was less important to him than the two other Senate chairmen in his sights, not only because they were concerned with future spending rather than past appropriations but because of the power they wielded as "Confederates" inside the Senate club.

Specifically, Johnson's nightmare was that his old friend and mentor Dick Russell, the dean of the Senate and also its unspoken but acknowledged statesman, whose sponsorship had helped give him his big push into power, might stifle his personal loyalties and his austere sense of his responsibilities, and jump the fence into the rebel camp. Russell's chairmanship of the Armed Services Committee, his knowledge of the Pentagon, his integrity, his prestige among the military, and his firm political leadership over the "Confederates"—demonstrated by the solid bloc of delegates he had delivered to Johnson at the Kennedy convention in 1960—put Johnson in need of winning the war for Russell's soul in order to continue fighting the war in Vietnam. The first whisper that Russell had become a doubter—and Hartke had the biggest mouth in the Senate—was guaranteed to raise the first question about Johnson's ability to keep control over his old stamping ground and to solidify the new bloc of anti-Vietnam senators. It did.

The fourth committee holding the key to the control of the Senate power structure was the Finance Committee. Once the chairman of the Armed Services Committee put his confidential auditor's seal on the extent of the embezzlement, Chairman Russell Long of Finance would be flushed out too. He could be expected to put his seal of disapproval on escalating the war without raising taxes. Long had no stomach for sponsoring a tax-increase bill on the heels of the tax cut the Finance Committee had passed during Johnson's first year.

Hartke had been in close touch all along with both Russell and Long, sharing his misgivings with each that stakes bigger than Democratic chairmanships were in danger. Both chairmen preferred to bide their time and to wait to use their power rather than to flaunt it. Russell, the only civilian other than Johnson himself who had the honest inside count on the unauthorized funding that Johnson had directed Secretary of Defense Robert McNamara and the Chiefs of Staff to divert piecemeal for combat use in Vietnam, became so alarmed that he confided it to Hartke. It came to a cost of $2 billion a month—not a king's ransom but, on the dollar scale of the mid-1960s, at least a sheik's.

Once Russell passed Hartke the ammunition, finding the gun from which to shoot was easy. The mechanism Hartke and I worked out called for using the vulnerability of the steel mills to import dumping, already surfacing in the shadow of the guns-and-butter boom, as cover;

Indiana is a major steel state, and no concern could have been more natural for Hartke. Trade relations fall under the jurisdiction of the Senate Finance Committee. Hartke had seniority on it, and he had already enlisted its chairman as an ally and a covert sponsor. Other senators from steel states who were in on the scheme readily agreed that White House pressure on the steel mills to stay out of the import-dumping fight proved how important lip service from Europe for Vietnam was to Johnson. Johnson was determined not to permit any petty local commercial or financial frictions to disturb the public relations solidarity on the Vietnam issue that he had orchestrated with the Europeans. Besides, he had spent the previous year trying to buy support all over the Free World by dangling offers of trade plums to countries willing to cooperate.

I had been clear with Hartke from the outset of our cabal that the purpose of our audit would be to share it with Johnson's gallant allies and militant supporters in Europe. The flimsiest of official-sounding passports would do, and Hartke undertook to latch onto the most impressive one imaginable: authorization from the chairman of the Senate Finance Committee to make an informal investigation of European steel-export-subsidy practices on his behalf. Long's approval of Hartke's expenses, confirming his entitlement to draw local funds for his own expenses from the U.S. Embassy in each country we visited, would assure him all the status he would need with title-happy European officials. Elizabeth Janeway and I agreed to accompany Hartke to Europe at our own expense but with Long's knowledge. The informal nature of his investigation and the entirely private nature of my role as his unofficial adviser would avoid the nuisance of a report on steel imports upon our return, when the illicit financing of the war in Vietnam was the issue. Once in Europe, in September 1966, we would be free to launch our counteroffensive by alerting the relevant ministers and bankers to the alarming $2-billion-a-month fiscal gap between Johnson's tame Vietnam War budget and his wild war spending.

From our first day in Germany, we were relieved of any concern over the impact our investigation was having. We never had a chance even to discuss a visit to a steel mill in any capital. Each U.S. Embassy was under stern orders to keep us busy on the cookie-pushing circuit and not to let us out of sight. But a week of stumping from Frankfurt through Bonn to Zurich, Paris, and London sent shock waves back to the White House, which had the calculated effect of hitting its hypersensitive incumbent on his exposed fiscal and foreign financial fronts. We found that every European financial figure of consequence had the publicized Vietnam budget at his fingertips and was shrugging it off as inconsequential fiscally and, therefore, marginal for the markets. But every one of them needed tranquilizers in response to our revelation that the actual amount was three times higher. The evidence that the systematic fiscal cover-up had thrown the European financial establishment and the financial markets they managed off the scent proved even more unsettling than the raw numbers. We were at pains to explain that senators had pieced the story together; not even the Treasury, the Budget Bureau (as the Office of Management and Budget was then called), or the Council of Economic Advisers was privy to true figures. The European establishment had been mumbling clichés in praise of America's "leadership" in Vietnam, but its spokesmen quickly became concerned for their own financial stake in the stability of the dollar markets.

To the surprise of the European financiers, the dollar markets had already begun to slip, despite the apparent strength of the American situation and the small-scale outlays claimed for the pursuit of high principle in Vietnam. When they were shown the actual cost of the war inflation Johnson had unleashed, they expressed bewilderment over why the dollar markets were not slipping more. When we explained the high risk to which Johnson was exposing Europe as he cannibalized the Mediterranean fleet, their concern over the dollar markets turned into uneasiness for their own future. I still recall my worry that the conscientious head of the German Bundesbank, Karl Blessing, may have suffered his subsequent heart attack as the result of our revelations.

We wound up the Continental phase of our investigation of steel-dumping practices in Zurich, although Switzerland has no steel industry. It is, however, the financial capital of Europe. At that point, we flew to Athens, where we were introduced to Andreas Papandreou, the controversial and flamboyant son of the recently deposed (July 1965) Republican prime minister, who became prime minister himself in 1981. To our surprise, our visit coincided with the preliminaries for the Greek military putsch, sponsored by the CIA and the DIA (the undercover Defense Intelligence Agency, an arm of the Department of Defense).

When we had decided to make the detour to Athens, we had no idea of what was being planned. The excursion filled a gap in our otherwise tight schedule; it was entirely unrelated to the purpose of our trip. Upon our arrival at the Greek capital, Elias P. Demetracopoulos, a well-known journalist, arranged the meeting with the younger Papandreou and the Greek Establishment, gave us an incisive and documented briefing on the impending putsch, and appealed for our help in Washington to forestall it. When his early warnings appeared in *The Janeway Letter* of September 28, 1966, Johnson hit the ceiling. In September 1967, after the military had taken over and Demetracopoulos had escaped from Greece with UN help, the Johnson administration blocked his entry into America. Fortunately, it was possible to enlist the formidable help of Dean Acheson, and, with the assistance of allies in Congress, Johnson was finally persuaded to let Demetracopoulos settle in

Washington, where he became a dedicated and effective opponent of the Johnson-supported Greek dictatorship and, subsequently, ambassador-without-portfolio to Washington.

Johnson's move to install the junta in Athens on April 21, 1967, came as an admission of America's deteriorating combat capability in the area. In mounting the coup, LBJ revealed his awareness of the trap he had set for himself when he diverted strength from the Mediterranean to put behind his gamble in Vietnam. When we left for Europe, Johnson knew what he was doing and he wanted to be sure he knew what we were doing. Our appearance in Athens so soon before the takeover caused him to jump to the conclusion that we really were spooking him instead of simply encircling him—especially because he knew that we were scheduled to meet in London with Prime Minister Harold Wilson the day after we left Athens. So the waves stirred up by this coincidence aggravated the tensions created by our trip and explained the confrontation awaiting us on our return.

In London, we were greeted with instant evidence of the success of our strategy. I recall with a chuckle the pompous disorientation of *The Times* of London in reporting our arrival as an invasion from the sinister "steel lobby." When Hartke and I returned from meeting with Wilson at 10 Downing Street, the hall porter at Claridge's greeted Hartke with the momentous intelligence that Senator Mike Mansfield, the Democratic majority leader, had called to summon him home to Washington for a roll call and had an Air Force plane standing by.

Johnson turned our exercise in encirclement into a confrontation with me soon after our return, but, always wary of leaving his own tracks in the sand, he tapped Vice-President Hubert Humphrey to patch up our feud, as he saw it. Humphrey, always warm and increasingly reliant on Hartke to do his battling for him, lived in admitted terror of Johnson's whiplashing. He could never decide whether he was more anxious to run Johnson's errands or more afraid of failing to complete them. Humphrey arranged for me to see him with Hartke in his Senate hideout. He began by reminding me that I had been his friend, independently of Johnson, ever since we met at the 1948 Democratic Convention in Philadelphia. Hubert then came right to the point and told me that the President had asked him to remind me of all the help I had given him in the past and of how fond he still was of me.

"The President would like to patch things up," Humphrey volunteered, "if only you would stop publishing those dreadful attacks on him."

"You can tell Lyndon, with my compliments, that he can kiss my ass," I replied. "If he will stop doing those dreadful things in Vietnam and stop lying about how he'll pay for them, he won't have to invite me to any dinners for two-bit potentates from outfits he can't find on the map, and I'll go back to bragging about what a great president he could be. But if he goes on with this secret escalation, I'll go on lambasting him for lying." From that point until the end of the tragedy, Johnson counted me among his declared enemies.

The markets demonstrated a voice of their own and voted their disapproval of the impracticality of the war in lockstep with the disapproval voiced by Europe. One good reason why this expression of discontent from the markets proved decisive is that it removed any lingering doubt over the motive behind the escalation. Public opinion could find no moral justification for it. The word was out that Johnson's own secretary of defense, Clark Clifford, who was still a believer when he replaced McNamara, had satisfied himself that the war made no sense militarily. And Clifford's disillusionment carried special weight because he had run the Truman White House during the Korean disaster. The easy alternative that public opinion had fallen back upon between 1966 and 1968 was the hypothesis that the war, though wrong, was profitable. As the markets undermined this unhappy justification, Johnson's political base splintered under him.

Hindsight leaves no doubt that Johnson's defeat had been sealed in January 1968, when Eugene McCarthy declared war on him and found the sinews of war that any challenger of an incumbent president ruthless and sophisticated in the uses of patronage would need. From that day on, the only question about LBJ's fate was whether a Democrat who declared independence from him, or Nixon, would emerge as the beneficiary of the political suicide he had already committed in Vietnam. Sometime that January, McCarthy first sounded me out about the New Hampshire primary. I told him that Manchester was close enough to Boston for a relatively small war chest to finance a big political win for him in that bellwether state; and for the momentum from that victory to produce a still bigger one in Wisconsin immediately following. I gave him my judgment that two successive primary defeats would have the effect of frightening Johnson and his closest personal adviser, Justice Abe Fortas, into throwing in the sponge. McCarthy's wise and gifted wife, Abigail, who presented a baffling and lovable study in paradox—at once unworldly in her idealism and yet deadly effective in her ability to organize the campaigns that had established McCarthy's early magic—registered her concern that her husband's conscience, as well as his destructiveness, would cost him his career. Though their marriage was clearly wearing thin, she was still entirely dedicated to his presidential potential.

I warned McCarthy that I agreed with Abigail, at whose judgments he always felt impelled to scoff, that the price he would pay for challenging Johnson would be the forfeiture of his own presidential aspirations. The convention was not likely to nominate a "spite" candidate; it would blame him for depriving the party of the advantages of incumbency. Moreover, if any effort of his showed up Johnson's vulnerability,

Bobby Kennedy could be counted on to elbow McCarthy out of the way and to rush in for the kill at the convention. Consequently, any McCarthy campaign would be foredoomed by its very effectiveness as a no-win effort. I told McCarthy that I would do whatever he wanted: either forget his probe or raise the money for him. He told me that his mind was made up, and he asked me if I could help finance his martyr's crusade from the Wall Street Establishment.

At the time, no project could have seemed more unlikely, more impractical, or more hopeless to finance. I happened to know, however, that the most influential opinion maker of consequence in the Wall Street power structure, Howard Stein, the securities marketing genius who managed the Dreyfus Funds, was ready and anxious to try. When I arranged for Stein and his wife, Janet, to take McCarthy and me to lunch in February 1968, Stein expressed gratitude for the opportunity. He had already paid for a succession of sorties by one of his aides with McGovern in Vietnam. This had satisfied him that the war was unwinnable and that, therefore, the markets were unsupportable.

Stein put only one question to McCarthy: "How much would you need to stop Johnson in New Hampshire?" I believe that McCarthy still bears a welt on his right knee where I kicked him when he replied that only "about $50,000" would be necessary. What followed illustrates the old Wall Street rule that when a sale can be made, only one customer need be called. The indignation came from the students, and the money came from Wall Street. Stein had enough clout with the other heavy hitters in Wall Street to raise what was needed; the bearishness in the atmosphere directly attributable to the escalation turned the chore of raising campaign money into a romp. No doubt some of those sensing Democratic defeat in disunity were Republicans.

The McCarthy victory in New Hampshire, however, was merely moral because Johnson actually won the primary. To Johnson's indignation, the media had treated McCarthy as the winner because he had come so close to tying the President. Just before the votes were counted in Wisconsin the following week, Elizabeth Janeway and I found disturbing confirmation of our worst fears for the stability of arrangements inside the Oval Office. Abe Fortas, philosophical about our having drifted apart after my break with Johnson, had invited us to enjoy a reunion dinner at his home. He asked justices Douglas, Marshall, and Brennan and their wives to attend, along with Herbert Salzman, the assistant secretary of state for GATT (General Agreement on Tariffs and Trade) matters, and his wife, Elizabeth. Babs and I joked together afterward that Abe would not trust us with a majority of the Court. During cocktails, Abe went on about how he had spent the afternoon with "the Boss" and in what terrific form he was. Justice Douglas and I sat across the den from one another, and as we listened, he winked at me, flashing his magnetic grin.

When Carol Fortas led us into dinner, I fell into step with Douglas and asked about LBJ, "Can you still talk to the son of a bitch?"

"He's gone crazy," he replied. "I've tried by the hour. It's no use. Even Abe admits it." Fortas was also Douglas's favorite protégé.

By that time, the late winter of 1968, Johnson had gutted America's strength in the Mediterranean. Reedy in his Johnson biography confirms that "no one will ever know the exact cost of that military effort because no rule exists for sorting out the money spent in Southeast Asia from the money spent for general defense." A full fourteen years after Johnson finished depleting the Mediterranean fleet, further official confirmation that his reckless scheme had not been corrected came from Admiral William J. Crowe, Jr., NATO's commander of allied forces on the alliance's southern flank. In an interview in *The Wall Street Journal*, "painfully underequipped, with most of its weaponry of Korean War vintage" was his description of Turkey's military capability to play its part in carrying out NATO's strategy, either in Western Europe, in the Mediterranean, or in the Gulf. Yet Turkey had the only army that the NATO plan relied on in the area.

Johnson was also unaware of the power vacuum that, as we shall see, the British were leaving behind in the region. The British, who are not normally bashful in pressing Washington for help, even when they have no advantage to offer, suffered from the same myopia. In a tragic default of responsibility on both sides of the alliance, although the simple geography of the situation gave them a great deal to offer, the British left their base in Aden (subsequently rechristened South Yemen in 1967) without so much as canvassing the penny-ante cost of being invited to remain on sentry duty. They had been responsible enough to alert Truman to the problem created by their retreat from the eastern Mediterranean in 1948. Twenty years later, only Russia grasped the opportunity to move into the gap left by Britain's withdrawal from the Middle East and America's advance in Southeast Asia. Once Russia transformed the rundown British facility at Aden into an ultramodern base, the stage was set for the oil war to wind up as the Vietnam War wound down, and for the nuclear arms race to speed up.

CHAPTER FOUR

The Oil War:
Henry Kissinger in an
Economic Wonderland

ILLUSTRATING THE OLD adage that "many a truth is spoken in jest," Senator George Aiken of Vermont gave Lyndon Johnson a bit of sage advice at the height of the Vietnam escalation: "Declare victory and pull out." When Richard Nixon's turn came to take the same sane and shrewd advice, he did the exact opposite. He accepted defeat in the Vietnam theater of war but kept America's forces engaged in it for another four years. In fact, belying his vaunted reputation for expertise in foreign affairs, Nixon actually extended the scope of the war into Cambodia. He followed where Johnson, who had no reputation even for familiarity with foreign relations, let alone expertise, had led.

The political consequences of Nixon's wrongheadedness were momentous. In the first place, it revealed the CIA's involvement in terrorist tactics overseas, making the agency suspect to Congress and making Congress resentful of the White House for covering up for the agency. Beyond this, Nixon missed a golden opportunity to clear the air of the strains left over from his unwelcome and uneasy tenure in the Senate as the vice-president Eisenhower barely tolerated.

Nixon had not been accepted as a member of "The Club" while he was a senator. Eisenhower's calculated snubs had hardened the suspicions against Nixon that were shared by all factions; mistrust is a more worrisome political liability than straightforward opposition. Predictably, therefore, by the time Nixon was installed in the White House, winning the confidence of Congress was his most serious problem. He insisted on ignoring it, and he, of all political loners, acted as if he enjoyed special immunity from the congressional scrutiny that seals the fate of all presidencies. Yet Nixon owed his presidency to the Senate and to the triple stroke of luck that first embarrassed the presumed Republican nominee, Governor Nelson Rockefeller of New York, for permitting romantic ardor to interfere with political ambition; that then unhorsed Johnson on his own turf; and that finally caught Humphrey in the crossfire over Vietnam.

Worse still, when Nixon and and his trusted expert on foreign affairs, Henry Kissinger, were enjoying their joint honeymoon in 1969, Kissinger too ignored Congress. Contrary to his reputation for shrewdness, Kissinger came to Washington so remote from the realities of the political game, and so intoxicated with the chichi of the publicity game, that he relied on Nixon to handle the special problems with Congress that he began to accumulate. In spite of Kissinger's admitted mastery of the international checkerboard, on taking office with Nixon he showed no awareness that the Vietnam theater was not where the action was. The access Kissinger's position gave him to the cables, the archives, and the dealings did not alert him to the time bomb that had been ticking for four full years in the Persian Gulf.

The round robin of conflict among the oil-producing countries and between them and their customers, which fueled the oil-price inflation, proved as deceptive as the bloody conflict fought in the swamps of Vietnam. There was no shooting in the oil markets to fire up anyone's suspicions, but the hostilities set in motion an international economic power struggle over the cost of oil, the control over capital, the access to weaponry, and the command of sea lanes and air bases. The oil war carried with it a potential for bloodshed immeasurably greater than the carnage winding down in Vietnam, and, as the years passed, that potential was realized. The loot from the oil-price war was rich enough to fight over. The looters without exception were too weak to defend themselves, yet, like their money lust, their appetite for high-powered armament was insatiable. As they continued to demand more money in anticipation of selling more oil and as, instead, thanks to the glut, they began to collect less for more, they came under pressure to collect more for less. Accordingly, they fell back on the standard cartel expedient of agreeing to cut back production in the hope of holding prices up. When cutthroat pricing nevertheless intensified, the cartel members took to cutting each other's throats. Hence the Iran-Iraq War and the effort it represented to knock out two producers (or at least one) altogether as the statistical equivalent of cutting back all the producers a little.

The origin of the oil war can be traced to the flawed marriage between America and Britain. By 1968, though the marriage still seemed very much on, at least west of Vietnam, the partners were going their separate ways. America was bogged down in Vietnam, for which Britain had no patience and to which her eyes were shut. Britain, for her part, had been complaining about the high cost of maintaining a naval base at Aden on the Arabian Sea, from which she commanded the mouths of the Persian Gulf and Red Sea and, therefore, the potential to defend or to cut off the oil traffic originating there. Britain solved her penny-ante problem by creating a monumental one for America and the world.

J. B. Kelly, in his masterful work *Arabia, the Gulf and the West,* has laid out the details of this historic disaster. Britain's Labor government guaranteed itself annual savings of £12 million—a mere $28.7 million at the rate of exchange in force then—by its panicky pullout. America would have found a real bargain and insured herself against costs and risks measured in trillions if she had simply done what has come naturally in so many other crises: offer to put up the money to keep the British presence in the Persian Gulf, even without being asked. But America did not know, or want to know, about the consequences of Britain's blunder. This failure of her high-powered, high-cost, and intellectually pretentious intelligence operation revealed a fatal flaw destined to become routine: ignorance of history and, indeed, a laxity in probing its precedents. The British had set a prophetic pattern for dismantling the crumbling Middle Eastern segment of their empire during their evacuation of Palestine in 1948. As General Chaim Herzog (who was named Israeli president in 1983) notes in his definitive history, *The Arab-Israeli Wars,* they "withdrew from successive areas of the country without being able to transfer administrative authority to anybody, leaving a vacuum." The KGB, however, had drawn the practical conclusion from the British method of retreat. As Kelly shows, the Russians were prompt to pour into the vacuum left by the British naval withdrawal from Aden and to build a formidable naval air base that went on to dominate the Arabian Sea and interdict American sea and air power from protecting it.

Soon after they did, the Iranian shah and the Arabian sheiks decided that the time had come to take advantage of Britain's pullout, America's distraction, and Russia's incursion to turn the commercial distress caused by chronic oil surpluses into a profitable price push. Nixon's reelection in 1972 coincided with the decision to spring the great oil-shortage hoax on an innocent world conditioned to panic in response to pricing ploys and disoriented by sloganized theories about free-market forces. The campaign of commercial piracy against the energy have-nots on the part of the Organization of Petroleum Exporting Countries (OPEC) was a governmental operation. Only governmental countermoves could neutralize it.

Washington offered the only hope of an effective initiative in this direction. Before Nixon's disgrace shelved any solution, he had been posturing as a world strategist. To prove his expertise, he bragged about the argument he had had with Nikita Khrushchev over iceboxes. He bragged about being spat upon in the streets of Caracas by an anti-American mob. He bragged about his feat in arranging foreign franchises for Pepsi-Cola. When the promotion of Gerald Ford in 1974 made the vacancy in the Oval Office official, Kissinger, who had been content to bide his time in Nixon's shadow, took over. Public recognition that first Nixon, and then Ford, had not known what they were doing reinforced the hope that Kissinger did. Kissinger, for his part, was diligent in harnessing his formidable powers of persuasion to show that he was the one who knew what needed to be done. The strategy he selected was to appease OPEC as a matter of philosophy, policy, and practicality.

To be sure, the mere fact of Kissinger's de facto regency did not accelerate the oil war. The coincidence, however, did invite its subsequent speedup if only because the OPEC powers in the saddle—principally the Saudis—realized that they could deal with Kissinger from strength. Their partners in OPEC had waited five years since the British departure from Aden before making their first predatory price move in 1973, demonstrating the healthy respect they had for America's retaliatory capabilities. Kissinger's declared indifference to the cost consequences—"Economics is for bookkeepers," he allowed himself to be quoted as saying—sent them in hot pursuit, first of prices they had never before dreamed of cashing in, then of armaments and other indulgences financed by the spoils of war. So, while Kissinger does not bear the responsibility for inviting OPEC to unveil the full extent of its economic war aims, his condescending attitude toward what the Victorian upper crust used to call "trade" had the effect of emboldening the cartel and cementing the shaky solidarity of its members.

The impression Kissinger created was that he believed that capitalism, democracy, and, therefore, America were on the defensive, fighting a rearguard and increasingly isolated action against the Communists and the sheiks. Clare Boothe Luce, who certainly was sympathetic to his premises and who had come to share them after the failure of her efforts to persuade her husband, Henry R. Luce, to mobilize his publications to lead America and capitalism onto the counteroffensive, once remarked to me, "Henry [Kissinger] thinks time is running against the West." Given this premise, Kissinger's translation of his own philosophy into American policy could not have been more logical or more sincere. Estimating America's adversaries as vigorous and knowing them to be greedy, Kissinger believed the only serviceable stratagem for buying time was to execute rearguard maneuvers.

Though not an imaginative strategist, Kissinger was an ingenious tactician: a craftsman rather than an architect. His prototypical hero, whom he never tired of citing, was the Austrian architect of the coalition against Napoleon, Prince Metternich, and his maneuvering recalls Metternich's determination to buy one last gasp for the Old Order, before the forces of modernism picked up where the French Revolution left off. Basically, of course, the Metternichian premise is defeatist. As applied by Kissinger, it suggests that the more a power on the wane pays to buy time from an enemy on the make, the better the bargain it will be able to strike. His aim was defensive: to buy time, not to secure the advantage. It didn't work. The consequence of the foreign policy he designed for America (and, therefore, for the world) was to lose time and to be left with the disadvantage.

Kissinger seems not to have discriminated between Russia and OPEC. At any rate, he challenged neither; his posture cast him as the Neville Chamberlain of the oil war. His defeatism justified the demands each antagonist put forward, while what can only be seen as intellectual arrogance led him to shrug off the exorbitant cost of catering to each. Awed by Russia's military capability as a superpower and by her aggressive political drives into exposed Western frontiers, Kissinger overestimated her bargaining power and failed to factor her economic weakness into his calculations. In similar fashion, he exaggerated OPEC's economic power without allowing for its political disarray, military primitiveness, and precapitalist genius for the dissipation of financial resources.

America's grand strategist was too complacent, it seemed, to learn two rudimentary lessons. The first, in dealing with Russia, was that arms buildups cannot buy America parity with any belligerent rival without mustering our supportive economic strength. On the military battlefield, Russia was the power able and anxious to husband her head start; on the economic battlefield, America has unwittingly been ready to relinquish her head start and has certainly hesitated to exploit it. The second lesson Kissinger ignored, at America's peril, is that OPEC oil power cannot be converted into real power. In fact, oil power was fated to deteriorate of its own weight into fissioning weakness within a decade.

In any balancing exercise between Kissinger's personal vision of world politics and the realistic substance of policy making, the outcome was a foregone conclusion: Substance finished second. Thus, Kissinger gave an overriding priority to the claims of the incumbent oligarchs of the oil industry on the presumption that they must surely know best, when in fact what the oil men know best is simply the oil business. They certainly did not know how to bring political power to bear on the oil-producing sheikdoms, and they were babes in the woods at the ancient art of selling them military protection. Instead, they urged Washington to pledge free protection, when the sheiks were anxious to buy it.

At the time of the unexpected oil crunch, an innovative secretary of state was granted a rare opportunity to seize the initiative from the tradition-bound sages of the State Department. Growing public impatience with received wisdom that produced mile-long, around-the-clock gas lines would have supported dramatic and novel action. Indeed, the media claimed that the secretary was ignoring the department as a political resource. In economic matters, however, the same secretary let the bureaucrats shape his policy and did little but lift the ceiling on their habitual requests for funds with which to buy "friendship." As the rich oil-producing countries demonstrated their nuisance power, Kissinger lavished more arms on them; the poorer ones got cash. His concurrent avoidance of any policy calculated to bring American economic or financial pressure to bear on Russia was perfectly consistent with his attitude toward the sheiks. The result: a lost opportunity to develop a bargaining stance that might have solved the world's oil problem while time was still America's ally.

Instead, Kissinger's acquiescence in dealing with OPEC on its chosen terms tempted him into further miscalculations. He discounted the importance of Latin America (which, ironically, was his 1983 comeback issue); he gave credence to the political clout of the Saudis; and he accepted the shah of Iran's valuation of his own status.

First, Kissinger turned a blind eye to the affiliation of oil-rich Venezuela and Ecuador with OPEC. In accepting the presence of a hostile Old World energy-power bloc inside American waters, he put himself in the awkward position of ignoring, if not denouncing, the time-honored Monroe Doctrine. Though liberals may define the doctrine as little more than a convenient justification for ventures into imperialism, it commands adherence from many Americans across party lines and, most unquestionably, from the constituents of Kissinger's own presidents, good patriotic Republicans. For them, a lapse on the foreign-policy front in the Caribbean could be taken as a domestic political affront: witness Jimmy Carter's later troubles over the Panama Canal Treaty. True, Kissinger could have claimed that Castro's seizure of Cuba had set the precedent for such a violation. But no one could deny that the Kennedys had risen to the challenge and had gained great kudos when the unpleasant memory of the Bay of Pigs was wiped out by their success in negotiating the publicized Russian retreat from the Caribbean during the missile crisis.

Kissinger's second exercise in appeasement set the Saudis up as the future repositories of financial power, committing America to play the oil-and-dollar game and the political-and-military game their way. This calculation attributed a capability for political finance to them that they failed to combine with their natural oil wealth. It stipulated America's direct dependence on Saudi oil in an oil-short world—palpable nonsense *exactly* reversing the increasingly apparent reality of OPEC dependence on American protection in an oil-glutted world. The myth of American dependence distracted public attention from the sources of oil supply that matter more than Saudi Arabia: Nigeria, Venezuela, Ecuador, and Indonesia inside OPEC, and Mexico and Canada outside it. None of them could command any bargaining power against the United States; all of them were dependent on the United States for welfare. Moreover, by assuming that America would need to pay whatever price OPEC set, Kissinger invited the Saudis and their partners in the cartel to insist that America manage the dollar to suit them. He put America in the absurd position of paying the Saudis for the privilege of protecting them.

Kissinger's third analytic blunder centered on the shah of Iran, Mohammed Reza Pahlevi. It was a recipe for catastrophe. The shah imagined himself a new Darius, the reincarnation of the warlord of Persia's Golden Age. Kissinger, buying that image and accepting at face value the shah's claim to be America's buttress against Russia along the "caviar curtain" and a formidable ally on whom America could rely to keep the area's oil flowing, agreed to feed the shah's insatiable appetite for arms. Ballooning oil prices in turn permitted the Iranian ruler to buy F-15s by the dozen. Kissinger's deference to the shah's demand for special consideration as America's ally-on-the-spot against Soviet aggression was oddly perverse. It ignored the shah's blatant role as OPEC's most rapacious instigator of price increases.

This political premise and its economic conclusion added up to a rationale for appeasement more destructive than Munich had been on the eve of World War II, because it was completely deceptive. At Munich, it had been too clear for comfort for the British and French that they were in the presence of a powerful, determined, and absolutely crazy enemy. They capitulated because his offensive had caught them unprepared. After they did, they at least recognized the need to make up for lost time; they saw it as a challenge. Kissinger's road-show revival of the original tragedy ran for a full decade. It mistook foe for friend, gouger for ally. It saluted the shah for unleashing the cost inflation that unhinged the American economy and trusted him to man a new Maginot Line on the frontier he shared with Russia. It imagined that weakness for the American economy, paid for without buying military strength from the shah in return, worked out as a fair trade. Kissinger's claims and stratagems ended by blasting any lingering hope that America might defend herself on the economic front without being driven into the vicious circle of going for broke buying weapons and threatening to use them. Any second-year law school student should have been able to see that the shah, as the price hawk incarnate, had turned himself from an ally into a player of what the lawyers call an adversary role. Yet Kissinger, despite his sophistication and his well-developed instinct for the jugular in hand-to-hand combat, never appeared to discern a contradiction between the two conflicting roles the shah played as America's presumed military ally and as the actual aggressor on her economic lifeline.

Meanwhile, at home, Kissinger was coming under the widespread suspicion of being puppet rather than puppeteer. Its source was a plot theory peddled during his years in power in the large market for right-wing pamphlets. This global whodunit claimed that David Rockefeller, when still head of the Chase Manhattan Bank, had woven a web known as the Trilateral Commission for the purpose of entangling the American government in a scheme calculated to hand it over to an undisclosed foreign power, presumably Russia. The Wall Street Establishment, of course, can function as a target for left-wing critics, too, and this scenario had sex appeal for them as well, particularly on campuses. The left-wing version dispensed with the agency theory and projected David Rockefeller as the new Machiavelli plotting through Kissinger et al to take over in his own right rather than to act as Moscow's quisling. Like most exploitable myths, this one rested on a shred of evidence, namely, that the Trilateral Commission did and does exist. It is a private debating society, but it has no power base, nor is it even a disciplined lobbying operation. Opinions of David Rockefeller's performance at Chase Manhattan may vary—which after all is what markets in money or opinions are all about—but the picture of him at the heart of a worldwide web of power is outrageous as well as funny. The wonder and the warning was that the idea took, but take it did, and on a scale commensurate with the cult of personality that Kissinger has enjoyed. In practice, the myth of the Trilateral Commission as a world conspiracy did little more than contribute an unpleasant aura of nut-case credibility to the public picture of the shah, but that it did do too.

The Pentagon, normally critical of Kissinger and resistant to him, was all for his buildup of the shah. It had acquired a financial stake in the Iranian ruler's share of the loot from the oil war. Sophistication could not be expected from the military in anticipating that turning the Persian Gulf into an arsenal might turn the oil war into a shooting war. Defense-project commanders, like operating managements in industry, develop tunnel vision when concentrating on their own costs and schedules. The military were shocked to discover how fast and how far the runaway in oil costs escalated procurement costs not directly related to fuel. But they were also relieved when the shah's apologists explained that he had paid hard cash for all the firepower on his Washington shopping list. And, indeed, he was happy to do so. Why not, when Washington was inviting him to take oil-price increases as fast and as often as he needed them to gather in the dollars to pay for his arms purchases from the Pentagon? And when the U.S. military, which does not share the responsibility of its civilian superiors for setting a grand world strategy, was in desperate need of a cash-rich export customer to keep assembly lines going for unfunded weapons and to supplement its own allowances from appropriations with export earnings? Clearly, Kissinger was not alone in his enthusiasm for underwriting the shah.

The exaggerated lip service the shah paid to the West as he promised to contain the Red Army on its own side of the Caucasus, away from Persian Gulf oil, concealed a reckless and incendiary purpose. His strategy called for him to take over the oil fields for himself, beginning with an air strike against the Saudis with his brand-new American-built air force, in flagrant disregard of Kissinger's reliance on collaboration between the two Gulf powers—Iran on the firing line against Russia and Saudi Arabia in the marketplace. The shah was shrewd enough to supplement his exaggerated promises to protect American interests with blandishments that were convenient to America and profitable to him. Being ethnically and religiously a bona fide Moslem, but not an Arab, created an unusual opportunity for him, which he exploited to the hilt. He undertook to protect Israel's inflation-ridden economy against the ravages of the oil gouge as an additional trade-off for his entitlement to American weaponry.

While Kissinger did not see through the sham of the shah, his principal rival in the Ford administration, Secretary of the Treasury William Simon, did. Simon never carried his feud with Kissinger over America's strategic alliance with the Iranian ruler to the point of going public, but he did go public against the shah. Simon used the occasion of the shah's state visit to Washington in 1975 to stir up the most colorful social flap in Washington since President Warren G. Harding was caught hiding naked girls in closets. Simon called the shah "a nut" and refused to attend the White House gala in his honor. At the time, the laughter provoked by this seemingly trivial episode was directed against Simon. But in the short space of a few years, the joke was seen to be on the country. Simon had the last laugh. Late in 1982, when cuts in the price of oil were threatening to force write-downs in bank-loan portfolios, Kissinger, who never had Republican credentials, was maneuvering his way into the administration's confidence, while Simon, who had impeccable Republican credentials, was articulate in putting distance between himself and the Reagan White House. Simon typified the conservative breach with Reagan that widened through 1983. Simon saw, as he had from the outset of the oil war, that without a bargaining policy toward OPEC, America was fated to navigate without a manageable foreign policy, a manageable defense policy, or, therefore, a manageable fiscal policy. Without the last, she was out of business.

Back in the 1970s, Simon and Kissinger were at loggerheads over methods of keeping the shah in line. Simon was looking for bipartisan allies, and I was able to play a role in shaping a coalition with various influential members of Congress, particularly Democrats with seniority on the Senate Armed Services and Finance committees and the House Ways and Means Committee. Some of them were concerned over the extent to which the Ford administration was taking on the air of a "Kissinger administration" in foreign relations; others were more immediately alarmed over the inflationary impact of the escalating oil costs Kissinger was inviting and subsidizing; still others were troubled by the extent to which the ominous erosion of weapons budgets due to inflation was bending America's strategic planning to accommodate the shah. The reasoned voices of congressional resistance to Kissinger agreed that higher oil prices would invite aggression inside the oil world by funding purchases of the arms that the OPEC powers could not produce themselves.

Simon perceived that the shah was using America's immediate political anxieties to further his own longer-range purposes as systematically as he was using his ascendancy inside OPEC to wield the oil club against the American economy. Though a financial man by background and not an industrialist, Simon had a highly developed sense of practicality, which showed him where America could assert leverage over the shah: by accelerating schedules calling for the shipment of advanced weapons to his technologically backward bases and by decelerating the backup shipments of spare parts and improved accessories needed to keep them serviceable. He saw that tanks without treads could turn unreliable allies into hostages. His perception fit the facts: Oil is a consumable common item, while weapons and parts are durable and standardized but in need of continuous and meticulous repair if they are to remain usable. Japan had applied this technique with apparent innocence and remarkable effectiveness when Mitsui started making deliveries on its mammoth petrochemical construction project in Iran. Japan managed to improve the terms of her oil "take" with predictable regularity as she expedited deliveries of previously delayed shiploads of missing components.

Simon saw that any society that, like Iran's, included widely disparate levels of development would devour spare parts. Not only would an inexperienced work force run up catastrophic breakage rates, but in addition the shah's rapacious courtiers and hangers-on could be expected to keep parts coming in order to keep their own commissions coming (and their payoffs to the palace following). Simon deserves credit for being the first to see that Washington had the leverage to bend the shah to its purposes, and in the process to hinder those of his confederates in OPEC, by the simple expedient of dangling the weapons bait and pulling in the parts hook.

Simon observed how Kissinger's all-out support for the shah's contradictory demands was undermining his own hope of fashioning a bipartisan oil policy. In my talks with Simon, I was able to assure him that congressional Democrats with political clout were ready to go public in support of his efforts to neutralize Kissinger's influence with the President and to stiffen America's stance toward the shah, and he urged me to talk to members with this in mind. But the support he sought would have required a public lead from him; none was likely to be volunteered without it. This understandable Democratic hesitation left Simon on the horns of a dilemma: outgunned inside the White House if he voiced his dissent only in private and targeted as disloyal if he took on Kissinger in public with support from the political opposition.

Late in 1982, I found myself reprimanded by Kissinger for failing to understand that he had been "the principal advocate of mobilizing the oil-consuming countries to form a united front against OPEC and the principal advocate of a strategy to restore the balance of market conditions in favor of the consumers." My provocation had been innocent enough: a review in the *Los Angeles Times* of a book entitled *Jews and Money* by Gerald Krefetz, in which I had cited the author's reference to a bitter confrontation between the two most powerful Jews in America, Kissinger and Arthur Burns, over the issue on how to deal with OPEC. Kissinger wrote me, referring to his own *Years of Upheaval* as evidence of his claim to be leader of the charge against the embargo. He goes so far as to claim: "I was advocating a common front of consumer nations, including plans for emergency sharing in case of an embargo." (He goes on to pin the responsibility for the failure of this noble resolve on his French counterpart, Michel Jobert; French exports were well known to have had the inside track on the Iranian market.) But token resistance to the embargo was by no means the pragmatic equivalent of effective resistance to the price gouge. The Arab partners in OPEC instigated the embargo. The shah led the fight inside OPEC to jump the price; Sheik Ahmad Zaki Yamani of Saudi Arabia was in fact a moderating influence in the ongoing argument about OPEC's prices. Kissinger's explanation does not explain away his own unwavering support of the shah.

My reaction to Kissinger's complaint was simply to send his letter to Simon and Burns. Simon, though no student of Marxist exegesis, snorted, "Revisionism." Burns wrote me, agreeing with Simon's characterization. In fact, a passage in Kissinger's book documents in painful detail the embarrassing extent of his disorientation from the realities of the marketplace. He summarizes the stance he took at the outset of the price hike by citing the speech he made in London in December 1973 in which he gave OPEC the keys to the safe: "We must bear in mind the deeper causes of the energy crisis. . . . It is the inevitable consequence of the explosive growth of worldwide demand outrunning the incentives for supply." It is a basic rule of politics that when caught with your records showing you either issue a flat denial or change the subject; you never repeat the gaffe. By the time Kissinger sent his book to press, every sophisticated international consultant in the financial world was aware that the price pyramid OPEC had jerry-built was collapsing. By the time he wrote me, every television viewer of programs sponsored by the clients of those consultants was being filled in on the excruciating details of the boomerang that OPEC had thrown when it claimed a shortage, gulled its dupes, and whipped up the biggest flood of unwelcome liquid since the Deluge. Apparently, only Kissinger himself failed to realize as late as 1982 that in 1973 he could have relied on an ally more formidable than even the shah in his one-man fight to hold the line against OPEC. It was the market.

Instead of respecting the market's warnings while he was still in power, Kissinger compounded his original error. He started out by trusting OPEC to remain rich, and he ended up assuming that it would remain solvent. At any rate, when the miscalculations of the oil powers began to catch up with them, Kissinger encouraged the multinational banks to advance cash to the poorer ones, like Mexico, which they continued to do after he had lost his power and they were losing their deposits from the richer ones, like Kuwait. Consequently, the liquid glut the oil producers built up while he was in office was matched by the unpayable paper glut they built up after he left office.

The damage that Kissinger's policy set in motion was institutionalized when first Jimmy Carter and then Ronald Reagan took over. Strategies, once in place, tend to take on a life of their own and become hand-me-downs from one administration to the next, just as the appeasement of OPEC did. From daily inconvenience and expense to ordinary citizens, it grew to threaten America's security, financial and even physical. If Kissinger's intellectual arrogance kept his policy in place, Carter's commitment to hair-shirt economics turned it into a crusade. It was launched with the same zeal that his successor was to display in escalating his war of words against the Soviet military machine. Like Reagan, Carter relied on dramatics to do double duty for him in his campaign against domestic oil consumption. The stage setting for his first television show as president told the story: His pollster and his television impresario dressed him up in a sweater, sat him in front of a roaring fireplace, and, lo and behold, America had an energy policy. That same afternoon I was given a preview of how the Carter administration was going to work, and it chilled my lukewarm hopes for a change for the better. Bert Lance, the President's confidant and director of the Office of Management and Budget (OMB), called me with the gist of the fireside chat.

I was aghast and pleaded, "Can't you even get him to take a paragraph with language referring to the creativity and practicality of American technology to raise the supply side"—two code words not used at the time in their later sense—"instead of preaching hellfire against our insatiable appetite for oil?"

"I can talk sense with the President on most other things, but I can't do anything with him on oil," Lance replied. For the first time since I had known Lance, I sensed a note of discouragement in his normally optimistic tone. His defeatism was particularly dismaying to me because of what Carter himself had told me in 1974 about his dependence on Lance. I had told Carter over the phone that I was scheduled to make a speech to a convention in Atlanta, and he asked me to come down to the Governor's Mansion the Sunday before.

I had not heard of Bert Lance at the time. He and a small group were leaving as I arrived, and Carter introduced him as his highway commissioner, adding, "Anytime you want to make sense with me, Eliot, just talk to Bert." Between then and Carter's first year as president, I found this to be the literal truth, extending to the energy problem as well as to just about everything else. Two aspects of Lance's admission that Carter was limiting his energy decisions to his Bible, his pollster, and himself struck me as positively alarming. The first was that Carter was aware of Lance's extensive network of intelligence sources across the Arab world and, therefore, that Lance's realism about the oil bubble was well founded. But Carter, notwithstanding all his claims of exper- tise as an engineer, did not let any facts distort his judgment.

My second source of alarm was even more pointed: In December 1976, when Carter was assembling his Cabinet, he had reached an impasse in his negotiations with James Schlesinger, who had served as director of the CIA and later as secretary of defense in the Nixon and Ford administrations. Richard Whalen, the well-known writer, had asked me if I could be helpful. After Schlesinger had been told that he was wanted, but not in the post of his choosing, secretary of defense, we agreed that a meeting was in order, and that duly took place in December 1976.

Previously, I had told Whalen that a chat with Carter's designated conduit was indicated, suggesting that Schlesinger could help both him- self and Carter by taking on the energy spot. Lance, however, was not convinced that Schlesinger would accept the job. Under the circum- stances, I said, I thought he might be persuaded to sign on. A post that offered a real opportunity for successful and effective intervention would surely be attractive to an energetic administrator whose aims had been sadly frustrated in two previous administrations. In the end, Lance told me that Carter would agree to appoint Schlesinger if Schles- inger would agree to join up. The argument that OPEC was ripe for splitting carried weight, and Schlesinger came aboard. But within the five-week span between Carter's agreement to take Schlesinger for the energy job and his inaugural, Carter had reversed course and had taken over as the thinker-in-residence on energy policy for his administration. The results were predictable: OPEC's racket was safe for another four years with official American blessing. As for Schlesinger, he was stuck with an oil-shortage story to sell.

Carter found a new rationale for continuity with Kissinger's policy. The shah would help America lower its oil consumption by helping himself to higher prices. At the same time, Carter assured the Saudis that they could count on America to recognize their need to tag along behind the shah in the oil-price push. He signaled the Saudi royal family, which for all intents and purposes owns Saudi Arabia, that it enjoyed equal rights as America's ally and protégé with the shah and that the shah's respect for the three-way relationship would make any attack by Iran on the Saudis unthinkable. It did not occur to Carter to add an explanation of how America's special relationship with the kingdom might protect it against an attack by Iran after Ayatollah Khomeini drove the shah from his throne and used the remnants of his army to drive into Iraq.

Neither Carter nor Kissinger ever recognized the self-defeating thrust of their open-ended commitment to the shah. The more domineering a figure the shah became outside Iran, the weaker he became inside Iran and the more suspect inside the Moslem world. The shah's troubles deepened as fast as he drove oil prices up. The ambitious projects he launched to reinvest his country's inflated income in "westernization" aggravated the cleavages in Iranian society. They activated a basic rule of inflation applicable at any stage of national development, particularly in an early stage of industrialization when inflation invites conspicuous consumption by resident upper-caste foreigners: Either the benefits accompanying the inflation—beginning with domestic debt relief and increased importing capability—are democratized, or the deprived revolt. The shah did nothing to spread the precarious benefits of Iran's inflation. His refusal to share the booty of his piracy in the time-honored way, by allotting a part to the hierarchy of Moslem mullahs, won him a powerful group of enemies. It provoked the violence of their takeover, and it invited them to extend their violence against Iran's Arab neighbors, particularly Saudi Arabia. Like so many revolutionary movements, the mullahs' revolt against the shah was reactionary in origin, populist in support, clerical in leadership, and militarist in purpose.

After the Shiite fundamentalists took to the streets of Iran and sent the shah on his quest for a place to die, first to Mexico City, then to New York, Panama, and finally to Cairo, spot oil prices and gold prices were driven sky-high on cocksure calculations that anarchy in Iran would cause a fuel drought around the world. When, to cap the climax, Iran's theocratic dictatorship took the U.S. Embassy staff hostage in Teheran in 1979, it put the fear of God into Carter that Khomeini would be his real opponent in his reelection campaign—and would beat him. For once Carter was right. The unity of OPEC never seemed more invincible; in fact, it was never more vulnerable.

Khomeini's first act on taking over, after denouncing America as Satan, was to disrupt the cozy family-circle arrangement among America, Iran, and Israel that had been so convenient under the shah. The ayatollah cut off oil shipments to Israel (although he permitted the flows to continue to India, which had been cut in on the shah's oil-subsidy deal with Washington as America's way of buying New Delhi back from Moscow). But not even this angry effort at an oil embargo proved effective. The concern of Americans in and out of government for the security of Israel was understandably anxious; they had fallen for the hoax of the original OPEC embargo in 1973. The response from Israeli officialdom, however, was at once revealing and prophetic: "Khomeini is America's problem," inquiring Americans were told. "Oil is Israel's problem, and Israel will handle it in her own way."

Israel was close enough to the front-line trenches in the oil war to feel as secure as Americans felt insecure about where her oil was coming from; she was also conditioned to shrug off any add-on to inflation. When at last the farce was played out, the Khomeini regime was pressing more oil on Israel than it was prudent for her to store within range of PLO artillery. But nothing so commercial as cash on the barrelhead or money in any form was a consideration for the normally cash-conscious mullah hierarchy. Instead, the theocracy in Teheran chose to make payment in oil for Israel's superior military technology.

Meanwhile, the sheiks—all of them members of the conservative Sunni sect, which is structured to serve family hierarchies—put up a $24 billion start-up purse for their mercenary hit man, President Saddam Hussein of Iraq, to take out Iran. One of their aims was to stave off the nightmare of a mullah-led Shiite revolutionary assault on their privileges by the downtrodden Moslem masses, that is, to keep the mullahs' rockets aimed away from Riyadh. The sheiks had been uneasy enough about the shah's ultimate intentions toward them, but the mullahs positively petrified them. They were revolutionary incendiaries and much, much harder to deal with than a fellow magnate, however hostile. The sheiks were also motivated by a more immediate commercial need: to soak up the oil glut by using the militaristic OPEC member they could control to stop the flow of the oil from the theocratic OPEC member they could not control, slashing overall cartel production without any need to cut back their own in the process. The sheiks calculated that the cost of the war would be a bargain compared to the cost of letting the oil companies and Washington in on the secret that the glut was increasingly out of control. The trouble was that after three years and $36 billion of wasted payoffs Iraq had failed to deliver value received by knocking out Irani production. The mullahs remained in a position during OPEC's convulsive winter of 1983 to point a gun at Sheik Yamani's head. In public, they demanded that OPEC stand pat not only on its unenforceable posted price but also on the admitted rate of overproduction that was responsible for the price cutting in the first place. In private, the mullahs were the ringleaders in the price-cutting scheme and, more provocative still, were relying on prominent Jewish firms to move distressed Iranian barrelage on a barter basis for well under $30 a barrel.

Israel was quick to diagnose this Arabian power play and to begin supplying the sinews of war to Iran. It was a fair trade. As Iran joined the extensive roster of Israel's arms customers, Khomeini found it expedient for the time being to shuffle Israel from the top of his list of Satans to a place nearer the bottom. All hands involved in the Iran-Iraq War subsequently agreed that Israeli armor helped Iran even more than Israel's preemptive strike at Iraq's nuclear facility had hurt Iraq. It was Israel's way of reminding both the moneyed Arabs and the radicalized Arab masses that her expertise was more than a match for their guerillas.

Meanwhile, the prophets of an endless oil shortage were systematically misreading the meaning of the Iran-Iraq War. They ignored hard evidence that had been building up since the summer of 1979, cited in my article on ways and means of stretching gasoline supplies (*Atlantic*, November 1979). The glut had been growing. World production had been running almost 6 percent above 1978 levels despite the Iranian situation, and tankerloads were being offered at slashed prices, subject to slow pay. Nonetheless, an oil shortage was still all too credible to many worried Americans who were suffering from the promised consequences and finding their pocketbooks tapped by overseas marauders from unknown backgrounds with unfamiliar motivations. Scare interpretations were easy, since they seemed to be supported by common experience, and many "experts" pointed to Iraq's invasion of Iran as confirmation of their belief that the sheiks were out to buy control of OPEC and that OPEC would then be able to control oil sales at prices it could dictate in a persistently shortage-ridden market. In fact, this exaggeration of OPEC's power had the ironic effect of bolstering hopes of Saudi moderation to keep further price increases gradual—if appeasement could only be guaranteed. I offered counterarguments at the time, suggesting that "The Oil Shortage Is a Malthusian Myth" (*The New York Times*, February 24, 1980), and went on to predict that even the Iran-Iraq War would fail to contain the overflow of glut, which indeed it quickly failed to do.

Another disorder loaded another dislocation onto the oil inflation. In 1981, Europe was bulling the dollar like a hot new stock. Foreign buyers of dollar goods, trying to cope with inflation, routinely speculated in dollars for future delivery and earned speculative windfalls of up to 25 percent, which amounted to rebates on their import costs. One tangible consolation for the oil-exporting countries was that the dollars they collected on their invoices were marked up more than the oil they shipped was marked down. Consequently, though the weaker oil-exporting countries had been hurting for some time, the stronger ones did not begin to worry until they started to fear that the dollars they were collecting might lose market value as fast as the cargoes they were shipping. Spot prices began to plunge and oil companies, which had "protected" themselves against a shortage that wasn't there by signing jumbo supply contracts at peak prices, lost their appetite to take deliveries. For the first time since the birth of the OPEC conspiracy, an abrupt paralysis of activity sent oil producers running after customers.

The oil glut turned the atmosphere in the Persian Gulf turbulent as the oil war went military. If there was anything good that could be said about the shooting in Vietnam, it was that it did not produce any military or financial fallout around the world. America was its only victim outside the battle area. Unfortunately, this has not been true of the oil inflation. It spread as the first phase of commercial piracy escalated into shooting matches and as brushfire conflicts leapt from one combat zone to another. In fact, the first gun fired in the shooting war preceded the commercial campaigns: The sheiks financed Anwar Sadat's Israeli adventure on Yom Kippur, 1973. When Israeli tanks brought it to a halt by crossing the Suez Canal and carving the Golan Heights out of Syria, the sheiks announced their first breathtaking price increase—from $3 to $5 a barrel! The very next day they went on to impose an embargo against Israel's suppliers in the West. Their willingness to pay for Israel's destruction in 1973 is part and parcel of their anxiety to pay for Iraq's confrontation of Iran, which under the mullahs presented much more of a threat than it had under the shah. The expedient of using Iraqis as mercenaries to keep the mullahs busy sending their troops against a buffer state instead of Saudi Arabia itself was a bargain. Just as surely as too much money chasing too few goods fuels inflation, too much money running too many guns crosses oil and fire with predictably explosive results. America hit Libya's planes in 1981, and in the same year Libya threatened to retaliate against Egypt, which by that time had been labeled an outcast for being a party to the "Camp David peace process" and had become fair game for Moslem hawks. Israel wiped out Iraq's nuclear capability in 1981 and the military emplacements the sheiks had given the PLO in 1982, taking a sideswipe at Syria and, finally, devastating Beirut.

In the wake of this multinational salvo, Argentina provoked Britain into sending an armada to the South Atlantic, diverting it from NATO. Britain then proceeded to give the prevailing chaos a new impetus— and, inadvertently, added a new dimension to America's confusion of purpose—by justifying her intervention in the South Atlantic on the grounds that the Atlantic alliance needed her naval presence in the Falklands to police the oil traffic coming around the Cape of Good Hope. This claim revealed a disconcerting inconsistency at worst, or amnesia at best, on the part of Britain's civil service mandarins who make the decisions for her cabinet members. As recently as 1970, they had rejected an offer, after pulling out of Aden, of a South Atlantic naval base at Simonstown, South Africa. In the end, America wound up on both sides of both wars: tied to Israel, but trying to deal with the rich Arab states; supplying Britain, though tied to Argentina.

The linked events that led to this unpleasant situation started in Vietnam. Distracted by her involvement in Southeast Asia, she failed to take the precaution of anchoring her British ally in the Middle East, when the cost of persuading Britain to sit tight in Aden would have been nominal. Thus, when America's ill-conceived military initiative in Asia invited the outbreak of the oil war, she had no European partner with a power base in the Persian Gulf area. Then, tragically, America proceeded to repeat the lapse that has marred her historical performance as a world power. She has never failed to meet a crisis after it has exploded, but she has never succeeded in planning how to get ahead of one that is painfully sizzling at home and abroad simultaneously. In the case of the oil war, America saw no need to use the leverage at her disposal to end it at its source. Consequently, the oil war ended up undermining the political and military power behind America's economic and financial muscle.

Under pressure from OPEC, Kissinger gradually turned America's focus back from Vietnam and Cambodia to the Middle East, but he marred his performance by putting America in pawn to the oligarchs of OPEC. By the time the shooting started in 1980, however, OPEC was not only beginning to break up; it was beginning to go broke clinging to the extortionate price structure its customers could not afford to live with, while lavishing sheiks' ransoms on arms, the indiscriminate purchase of luxury, and industrial white elephants. Increasingly, these transactions were settled by bartering parasitic imports, like missiles, rather than cash. Even the Saudis woke up to find themselves paying for their imported follies by living on capital. What with the compounding inflation they had unleashed in the United Kingdom, Switzerland, and the other countries they favored for the exile they anticipated, this discovery left them feeling as insecure as if they had already lost their capital along with their net operating income. This spectacle of the oil-producing powers losing their oil income, the oil-consuming powers writing off oil-financed loans and losing oil-financed deposits, and the Third World losing its sources of credit challenged America to mobilize her economy to launch a desperate peace offensive on pain of being thrown onto the defensive in a shooting war.

CHAPTER FIVE

The Oil War:
Milton Friedman in a
Political Wasteland

AMERICA'S ISOLATION in the world started with the Vietnam War and hardened when the onset of the oil war spread the realization around the world that America did not know what had hit her, much less how to strike back. The countries—large and small, rich and poor, powerful and weak—that had watched with sharpened skepticism as America bogged herself down, walking loudly and carrying no stick in Vietnam, had shrugged the exercise off as America's private affair.

America's political isolation resulted from her economic naïveté. This, in turn, was the direct result of the mass conversion of America's business and financial elite, especially her bustling army of confident young MBAs on the make, to the old religion of laissez-faire whose new prophet was Professor Milton Friedman, still ensconced during the Nixon years in his authoritative pulpit at the University of Chicago. Friedman preached faith in a simple trinity: supply, demand, and price. Of the three, he saw supply and demand as the contestants and price as the arbiter. Price change was seen as the only force that matters in markets. This simplistic definition of markets leaves room for cartels, which prevent independent workings of free markets by rigging prices and choking supply.

In his theory, popularly known as monetarism, Friedman speculates that buyers and sellers grappling one another for competitive advantage move prices, and explains market events by the tracking and control of money flows. This is easier said than done, however, thanks to the literally immeasurable capacity of the credit system to obey the biblical injunction to multiply and to do so even faster than the monetary authorities can regulate it. A self-defeating paradox built into monetarism is its insistence that the Federal Reserve Board maintain a strict system of control over credit in order to ensure liberty for all money users. The monetarists have led the Fed into an extension of this same paradox as they horsewhipped it into its predictably unsuccessful efforts to control a money supply that by its own admission it cannot even count. As I told the Joint Economic Committee of Congress on June 2, 1982, "The money supply calculation is irrelevant. Over $200 billion is sitting in the money market funds. Over $170 billion is in the commercial paper market. That's a lot of money. You have Lord knows how many more billions floating through the foreign branches of U.S. banks" into the Eurodollar and Asiadollar markets. Dollar loans by these branches and dollar deposits in them are not included in the money-supply calculation. Neither are dollars created by U.S. Treasury advances to its client governments abroad or to the International Monetary Fund (IMF) for transmission to those clients. Altogether, the exclusions from the money-supply calculation bulk larger than the inclusions in it.

Friedmanism came into vogue in the midst of a violent inflationary surge; it denied the existence of inflation and downgraded it into a mere matter of price adjustment. Thanks to the authority monetarism commanded, its very denial of inflation invited a wild expansion of prices on the faulty premise that higher prices function as confirmation of higher demand and justification of expectations for still higher demand.

This is not as abstract as it may sound. The flesh-and-blood experiences behind the theory are very simple: Suppose the supply side of the romantic equation in a Klondike mining town is represented by one ambitious blonde, a participant in the oldest market of all, and five miners show up on Saturday night loaded with overtime pay to tilt the equilibrium of the flesh market violently onto the demand side. Friedmanism assumes that the market price of love will jump. It will, indeed, until or unless the blonde figures out that investing pays better than wholesaling and uncorks a supporting cast of younger, or at least newer, girls. The arrival on the scene of the reserve army of labor will bestow an extra dividend on the customers: faster action at a collapsed price. The wild card in the market deck, never taken into account by the Friedmanites, is inventorying. It is the balancing item between supply and demand, a composite of old supply stuck in the pipelines and new demand pumped into them.

To listen to the Friedmanites go on about the workings of the free market, one would think that price levels, to paraphrase Keats on truth and beauty, tell you all that you know—and all that you need to know —about demand levels in any market at any time or, indeed, throughout the economy as a whole. It is more realistic to recognize that price levels alternately stimulate and kill the incentive to inventory. Everybody rushes to buy anything they think will cost more tomorrow or, what comes to the same thing, will be harder to get; nobody wants to be stuck with anything needing to be peddled off at bargain-basement prices because it is a drug on the market. Consequently, inventorying changes follow price changes and determine when buyers are taking sellers off the hook and when they are leaving sellers in the lurch. The analytical problem for forecasters and policy makers alike is to figure out when buyers' eyes are bigger than their stomachs and vice versa and, in either case, by how much and for how long. Despite all its preaching for the liberation of the profit motive, monetarism ignores the governing practicality of market life. Markets develop more momentum on the upside from greed and lose more on the downside from fear than from actual supply and demand for immediate use. The interplay of greed and fear shows up in the endless guessing game about inventories, best summed up in the familiar question "Who will wind up holding the baby?"

Monetarism ignores the inventorying problem, much less its fundamental importance. Inventorying is invariably and almost entirely financed by bank borrowings. Two English economists, R. H. Hawtrey and D. H. Robertson, who exerted great influence on Keynes's formative thinking, argued that the cost of borrowing and the ability to borrow had the decisive effect on the impulse to buy during upswings in the business cycle. This susceptibility of buying to borrowing fortifies the bull's-eye scored by Dr. Henry Kaufman of Salomon Brothers in his definitive criticism of the relevance of monetarism in a credit-fueled economy. "The dilemma of monetarism," Kaufman declares, "is that its concept of money keeps changing. The awareness of that change occurs with a considerable lag. The monetarists follow the classical economists in making a sharp distinction between money and credit." Monetarists insist on measuring money as cash but propose to regulate it as credit. "But," Kaufman says, "the private sector has a blurred view of what is money and what is credit and hardly ever distinguishes between the two." Of course, the more illiquid businesses become during the prepanic phase of a depression, the less sensitive they will be to this basic distinction. Therefore, the more irrelevant to the facts of market life rigid monetarist dogma becomes, the more destructive it is certain to become as businesses struggle to survive on credit and as monetarists crusade to clamp down on credit as original sin.

More fundamental still, however, is the stubborn philosophical insistence of the monetarists on the separation of market and state. All monetarist calculations follow from the premise that the basic decision-making entity in the marketplace is the individual decision maker, personal or corporate, and therefore that all governmental decisions, actions, and participations in markets set chain reactions of distortion in motion. My own observation is that, accept the consequences or not, the basic decision maker—the market's market maker—is the government. It follows, then, that private decision makers merely react to governmental actions already taken or anticipate the results of governmental actions they expect to be taken. Objections to the soundness of governmental actions merely accentuate the market power the government wields, even—or especially—when the objectors prevail. When they do, the case they make invariably stirs up memories of New York's colorful Mayor Fiorello La Guardia's rueful admission: "When I make a mistake, it's a beaut." The shark cannot take a small bite, and the government cannot make a small mistake. It certainly cannot make a mistake in a market vacuum, if only because every mistake it makes or corrects has a backlash on tax rates, interest rates, and the government's dealings with other governments. The mistakes made by Johnson first and by Reagan afterward in cutting taxes while raising arms outlays are classic examples, and the markets made no bones about casting votes of no confidence in both.

All modern political theory goes back to Thomas Hobbes and his concept of the Leviathan, or the state, as an entity more powerful and more stable than the floating majority of the citizens, or any combination of minorities in need of protection. In the early seventeenth century, Hobbes's England was busy cutting off the head of her king and looking for a successor strong enough to protect her but scared enough not to threaten her himself. The economy, as the modern world has learned to think of it, was not yet a gleam in the eye of the government. How the government, contrary to the myth perpetrated by Adam Smith a century and a half later, fathered the modern economy in the reign of England's next king, who died in bed, is another story. I plan to probe the mystery of its birth in my next book. For the scope of this book, suffice it to say that Hobbes's concept of the state has come to apply to the modern economic mechanism as well as to the modern political structure. Hobbes thought of the state as a political power center, separate and distinct from all the people subject to its sovereignty and in need of its protection from generation to generation.

The exact same definition applies to the state as the activating force it is in the marketplace to which all its participants respond—all the way from the scramble for food stamps to the auction market for securities, not forgetting the competition for defense dollars and tax advantages. When Hobbes spelled out the power of the state to protect the people subject to its sovereignty, he was talking politics; in his day, politics was the only language of power, even in time of war. Three hundred years later, when John Maynard Keynes added up the obligations of the state to provide for the feeding, the housing, the schooling, the employment, the arming, the healing, and the retirement of the people protected by the state, he was talking economics. By his day the grammar of politics had evolved into the arithmetic of economics, especially in time of war and certainly under the stresses brought on by preparations to fight wars or to avoid them. This evolution from the thinking of Hobbes to the thinking of Keynes was direct, compelling, and obvious, as was the evolution it reflected of economics into the vehicle of politics and the simultaneous expansion of politics—that is, government—into acting as the pilot of the economy.

The subsequent transition from the thinking of Hobbes through the thinking of Keynes to the thinking of Friedman, however, has turned the clock back; Keynesians and Friedmanites agree on this point if no other. Friedman took his stand firmly in support of the police powers Hobbes claimed for the sovereign state but in opposition to the economic obligations Keynes charged up to the welfare state. (Despite the impression spread by the Friedmanites and the Reaganites that he was Marx reborn without a beard, Keynes was in fact the target of fierce and justified attacks by Marxists for his determination to save capitalism.) Given Friedman's major premise—that the welfare state is a modern dinosaur—his inescapable conclusion became subject to only two ifs: if we lived in a domestic political vacuum, and if the sole purpose of all governments, pushing one another for advantage, was the innocent exchange of money for goods and services in free world markets.

The complicating factor for the Friedmanites is implicit in their battle cry, which calls for stripping the government down to its police powers, namely, law and order at home and national defense across its borders. Whether the Friedmanites know it or not, their stance leaves them with no alternative but to vest the government with the exact same arsenal of economic powers that Keynes armed it with. In fact, when he did, with Hitler breathing fire against both England and America, he taunted the laissez-faire economists of his generation with the reminder that the government could implement his program through its military departments no less effectively, if less compassionately, than through its welfare departments. The welfare state can function without being called upon to do double duty as a garrison state, but the garrison state cannot function under the conditions of modern warfare —or preparation for it—without forcing the government to finance it on at least the scale called for by the welfare state.

The constitutional power to provide for the national defense carries with it the political obligation to finance the requirements arising from the ongoing revolution automating military technology, and this obligation is incompatible with the monetarist demand to straitjacket the creation of bank credit. To claim that the national defense can be financed within the monetary confines of a 3 percent or even a 5 percent annual increase in the money supply, granting that it could be counted for purposes of control, is to invite the vulgarization of serious debate over national economic and defense policies to the innocent intellectual level of Reagan's ad-libbed claim on television that defense spending is not inflationary, only nondefense spending is. It is to ignore the fundamental difference, by Friedman's own definition of inflation, between the two. The Treasury can disburse cash for direct subsidies to claimants for entitlements of one kind or another by recirculating tax collections, but the Pentagon routinely relies on its contractors to finance its procurement awards at their banks. And the extension of bank credit for any purpose—defense or nondefense—fuels the explosion of the money supply.

The lawyers have a term, *stare decisis,* which translates as "frozen decisions" or "precedent makes policy and tradition molds theory." The economists have not yet adopted it. But the plight of the monetarists, caught between the rock on which they had built their dogma and the hard place where the reality refutes the dogma, makes them ripe targets for the strictures of *stare decisis.* The Union Bank of Switzerland (UBS) operates on a more disciplined analytical level than the Great Communicator in Washington did when improvising his lines; it speaks with the voice of financial authority. In its *Foreign Exchange News Bulletin* of November 1982, it invoked the principle of *stare decisis* to read the monetarists out of court. The UBS report detailed a technical analysis of the growing disparity between the money supply and industrial production in the United States with this verdict:

> An upward trend in the real money supply, for example, has always been followed by a gain in industrial production after a time lag of several months. But it appears that this parallel movement has ceased to exist in just under 18 months. Rather, the real money supply has exhibited an upward trend since the late summer of 1981 whereas industrial production has moved lower. This means that industrial production no longer reacts to a rise in the real money stock.

During this same period, however, the Federal Reserve Board, knuckling under to intense pressure from the monetarist zealots in the Reagan administration, was slavishly implementing the doctrines of monetarism. The Fed's experiment was a failure, setting in motion the forces that discredited the dogma that was on trial. By the time the inflation in the money supply did spur production, it inflated interest rates.

Monetarism overlooks another harsh fact of economic life in most of the world. The theory assumes the free and continuous interchangeability of income-account and balance-sheet uses for money, that is, of income into capital and back again from capital into income. This is a reasonably valid assumption in free societies having optimal conditions of liquidity, stability, and prosperity. It bears no relationship whatever to financial decision making, however, in such Third World dictatorships as Chile and Argentina, the very ones that have sought Friedman's counsel in changing their ways but have ended up in abrupt reversals of course instead. In any of these countries or, for that matter, in countries as disparate as Greece and Mexico, money is almost never moved from an income-statement purpose, like paying wages in local currency, to a balance-sheet purpose, like building domestic factories with the profit earned on the same working-capital expense. On the contrary, all investable cash earned or borrowed is routed across the border as fast as it is received, and once out of the country, it stays out. The early 1980s saw the world's money havens swimming in excess cash, while the world economy was choking for lack of productive investment. When Italy, for example, enjoyed her round of dynamism during the late 1970s, Milan emerged as "the largest city in Switzerland." True, the lurid atmosphere of mystery surrounding the collapse of the Banco Ambrosiano of Milan in 1982 revealed a studied strategy that called for siphoning cash out of Italy into Caribbean lockboxes in order to finance raids on other Italian institutions. But the shady genius behind it wound up hanging from a London bridge in vivid recollection of Talleyrand's grim gag: "It is more than a crime, it is a blunder." More typically, in Argentina, hides to be made into two-toned suitcases, brown on the outside, green on the inside, enjoyed a brisk and steady demand. Pesos, once converted into dollars for traveling, never came home.

No country that invites money out through a one-way valve can function for very long or with much plausibility, notwithstanding the precepts of Friedmanism. *The Wall Street Journal,* which is dedicated to the gospel of monetarism and routinely pays homage to Friedman as its apostle, published a revealing audit of the impact of Friedmanism on Chile in the midst of the 1982 depression there. The resident Friedmanites in the saddle—the "Chicago Boys," as they were called in Santiago because the diplomas they brandished came from the University of Chicago—found themselves blamed for engineering a flat-out depression and advising an obdurate military dictator, Augusto Pinochet, who to their chagrin decided "to relieve the load of bad debts crushing the bank system." At the same time, with unemployment at 20 percent and rising due to the collapse of world demand for copper, Chile's main source of income, the Chicago Boys were pressing Pinochet to decree a wage cut instead of waiting for the magic of market forces to determine how sharp it was to be. Pinochet knew better. He settled for warding off power grabs by insurgent strong men before the theories of Friedmanism collided with the practicalities of Darwinism. The government got out from under the pyramid of bad debts by following the fashion of the 1980s and ignoring them. When the banks finally did fail early in 1983, it loaded their floating liabilities onto its own and tabulated them in the "No Problem" column on the national ledger.

One of the paradoxes plaguing monetarism is that the governments anxious to sponsor it are the reactionary dictatorships, which soon discover to their discomfort, however, that societies that do not tolerate freedom of political preference cannot invite freedom of economic choice. Friedman's personal dedication to the principles of nineteenth-century liberalism is beyond dispute, but the "contradiction," as Marx would have called it, between his evangelism and his disciples puts the countries most congenial to the monetarists on display as exhibits of their failures.

Even democracies with established status structures and anxious for one reason or another to give monetarism a whirl have not been able to tolerate its rigid impracticalities. Israel tried it and rejected it. When Menachem Begin took over, he enlisted the Nobel laureate's counsel. Israel is not a dictatorship, but it is a socialist state that, however, allows elbow room for private enterprise to coexist with government operations, and even to piggyback them. Moreover, Israel has learned to live with inflation (its annual rate is far enough over 100 percent to make counting meaningless) by treating it as just a price adjustment, in accordance with monetarist doctrine. To prove it, Israel has asserted its competitiveness in the biggest growth industry in the world economy, arms export, by pole-vaulting into a strong number-two position behind the United States and gaining, despite the lift U.S. arms exports get from the Pentagon's willingness—and even anxiety—to buy sales by cutting prices and making soft-money loans. Nevertheless, one whiff of holy writ was the only one Begin could take. He and Friedman quickly and quietly arrived at a nonaggression pact. Friedman was not invited back.

In Israel, says Gerald Krefetz in his book *Jews and Money,* Friedman "felt the full weight of two conflicting traditions at war with one another." He quotes Friedman: "One of them was a very recent tradition —a tradition 100 to 150 years old . . . the tradition of socialism." The other, emphasized by Friedman, was the 2,000-year-old tradition "of how you get around government regulations. How you find chinks in controls, how you find areas in which the free market operates and make the most of it. It was that tradition which enabled Jews to survive during centuries of persecution." So where Begin found monetarist dogma to his disliking, Friedman found prudence the better part of valor and departed, admittedly confused—not a familiar stance for him —by Israel's crazy-quilt structure of socialism subsidizing capitalism and making it pay, even amid the rigors of international market competition, supposedly the acid test.

If monetarists were of any use to themselves (let alone to their clients) as pragmatists, they would limit their experiments to countries that are inclined to show skepticism in buying their wares. But the monetarists are armed with an ironclad alibi for their unbroken record of boomerang throwing in their encounters with the workaday world. No so-called free society is free enough to submit to the water torture prescribed by monetarism until all the domestic inflation and uncompetitiveness in unsubsidized foreign dealings have been squeezed out of its economy. Free societies are by definition endowed with a humane sense of social responsibility, and they are burdened with a corresponding cost structure for the funding of social obligations. No free society can submit to the martial code of Sparta; Sparta was not a free society. Monetarist dogma unleashed upon mere human beings in a money crunch treats them more harshly than they can bear but less harshly than the rules of Sparta require. Any national economy allowed to run free by the monetary authorities is bound to be reined in by the political authorities once its performance fails to observe "a decent respect to the opinions of mankind," to recall the simple and noble language Thomas Jefferson employed in the Declaration of Independence.

The fatal flaw in the monetarist logic is revealed by its devotees when they invoke the principles of Jeffersonianism to justify the double standard assumed by their credo. They reserve the right of unlimited freedom for the economy, but they deny that same right to society for its claim to put the economy on a performance basis subject to rules it retains the right to impose. Society always does impose rules; even Victorian society did in the heyday of "neo-Darwinian" economics, when it put limits on the "right" of mine owners to abuse child labor. American society always has and always will do the same when the economy and the government between them fail to stop unemployment short of collision with "a decent respect to the opinions" of the voters. As a practical matter, the signal that a new monetarist experiment has sent the social discomfort index past the point of tolerability never comes from the politicians. The first call to rush first aid from the government to the wounded comes from organized business. The strong demand help from government before the weak can get it.

This is exactly what *The Wall Street Journal* itself admitted one month into the business year that began September 1, 1982. As business opinion showed dismay at the spectacle of the economy falling through the floor after it had spent the first part of the year falling out of bed, Lindley H. Clark, the *Journal*'s economics writer, posed the question: "How much time does Ronald Reagan have?" His answer was to quote the ranking monetarist spokesman in the banking fraternity, Leif Olsen, chairman of the economic policy committee of Citibank. "If the Christmas season turns out to be a dud," Olsen conceded, "the Reagan administration will be under great pressure to do something." Added Clark: "And the pressure will be coming not from the Democratic opposition but from the Republican businessmen who voted for Reagan in 1980." Just two weeks to the day after the midterm election results put the lame-duck question mark on Reagan, the businessmen spoke up for themselves. *The Wall Street Journal*'s front-page headline summarizing the results of its nationwide survey told it all: "Business can't survive another year of Reaganomics." The very next day, the Republican congressional leaders went to the unusual length of informing the media that they had tried to break the news to the President that he did not have the votes to "stay the course" and beat off demands for the "quick fixes" the monetarists had programmed him to resist at all costs. The President may not have believed them, but the media did, and the Democrats knew that their opposite numbers had read the political omens realistically.

So the monetarists travel with a "can't-win" formula for performance and a "can't-lose" formula for debate. They shrug off the dire political consequences of any market development they welcome as just another effort on the part of an unbalanced market to find equilibrium; they target the economic consequences of any political development they deplore as political interference with the healthy efforts of a free market to do so—as if any markets ever were free (except upon the blackboards at the University of Chicago) and as if any existed without governments patrolling them when they work well and protecting them when they do not. In this vein, the monetarists scoff at the suggestion that unemployment can ever be a problem, insisting instead that their complaints about it are nothing but evidence of the need for a downward adjustment in the price of labor. They greeted the opening gun OPEC fired in the oil war as a market event whose "ripple" effect changed price quotations, not power relationships. This judgment was consistent too. The theory assumes that market forces fluctuate with continuity and, therefore, that market prices do as well. Market survivors know better, and so do victims of the oil war. When economists strain the political substance out of the markets whose performance they scrutinize, they outwear their welcome with their political clients. Their political prestige loses its luster soon after they lose their political entree.

The economic interpretation of history is subject to the domination of economics by politics. But each new generation of monetarists learns the hard way that markets pivot in response to the impact of shocks and that the shocks are invariably political, which explains why markets themselves are too. The "shocker" that disrupted the continuity of market life in 1973 was the oil embargo by the OPEC sheikdoms in the backwash from the Yom Kippur War. The sheiks had demanded that all companies doing business with them fill out an elaborate form declaring that they did no business with Israel and were free from any internal contamination by Jewish owners or executives.

Only America took the charade seriously. The fact that the sheiks aimed the embargo primarily at America in retaliation for America's role as Israel's principal arms supplier gave the ploy the ring of plausibility. More than incidentally, the proclamation of the embargo also gave the ring of authority to the widespread illusion that America herself was dependent on oil from the sheikdoms. The panic that followed was aggravated when the American companies that were free to fill out their forms hesitated for fear of punishment by the American government; the companies that were not hesitated for fear of being punished by the sheikdoms. No one in authority in Washington, from Kissinger on down, seemed to realize that what the other side wanted was simply the declaration, not the compliance. To carry Tallyrand's cynicism one step further—which is fair play in assessing Kissinger's performance—this was worse than a blunder, it was a confession of innocence. Scarcely the way to reenact the saga of Ali Baba locking the forty thieves back in their oil jars for the benefit of sheiks brought up on the *Thousand and One Nights.*

America was the principal target of the embargo but not the only one. The Netherlands landed right behind America on the embargo list ostensibly because that it is where Royal Dutch Shell is headquartered; Royal Dutch is targeted as Jewish by OPEC. It is also where Rotterdam, the world's largest and busiest oil port, is located. The impact of the embargo on the European Establishment, however, was nil. Europe yawned and promptly delivered its confirmations to the sheiks; the sheiks winked, and business went on as usual, as it does between Israel and the Arabs under cover of their rhetoric (provided, that is, no land-ownership transactions are involved).

The official provocation of the embargo had nothing whatever to do with the state of the oil market. If anything, it seemed to represent a costly act of self-denial on the part of the sheiks as a token act of solidarity with their poor, embattled blood brothers in Egypt and the Palestinian camps, with a bit of greed thrown in. And the traumatic impact of the threatened holdback sent prices skyrocketing. At the outset of the oil gouge, the Friedmanites, in their impracticality, and the oil companies, in their practicality, echoed each other's studied assurances that the market knew best how to price the products in it, proving the existence of the supply shortage. The Nixon administration readily agreed. The reality, however, was the exact opposite. The price markups triggered the inventorying chase and loaded an artificial layer of buying pressure onto the demand side of the market. The fact that the price hikes had this impact is a testament to the tendency of economists to swallow political hoaxes. The gas lines were real; the alarm that sent innocent and susceptible people out in the middle of the night to line up in them was false.

The proof of the sham at the height of the hoopla over the 1973 embargo was the other long line—of tankers and barges loaded to the waterline with full cargoes waiting for berths in Rotterdam. At the time, I wrote in the newspaper column I was then publishing that it was possible to walk the vast span of the Rotterdam harbor—without any theological implications or fear of wet feet—just by stepping from one loaded vessel to the next. In the same vein, year in and year out, I urged doubting Thomases on the television networks who believed in the myth of the oil shortage to check it out by the simple expedient of chartering planes and flying a hundred miles out to sea past America's principal ports of entry to photograph the traffic jam of tankers waiting for berths. NBC finally scored a lazy scoop by doing just this out of Galveston, while the contributors to the consensus of economic thought still droned on about the shortage that never was. But from opening salvo to closing whimper, the piece of news that sent the price spiral whirling skyward and triggered the rush to fill storage capacity on land and at sea with enough bloated inventory to strain supplies was the phony embargo.

Through the regimes of Kissinger, Carter, and Reagan, the intellectual commitment to monetarism in the marketplace, fortified by political commitment to appeasement in government (the latter being entirely bipartisan), dignified the barefaced oil-price gouge as a law of nature and a mercy to America. So, therefore, did the sons of the sheiks, whom the media lionized because they had gone to American graduate schools of business administration and "learned all about the law of supply and demand" before going home to gun oil prices. The newly educated sheiks-to-be were operating under the misimpression that they were chasing demand when, in fact, they were encouraging inventories. The cult of monetarism back in America had eyes only for the cartel's pricing; it mistook OPEC's success in imposing its prices on the market for the strength of bona fide market demand. The true believers in the gospel of free-market pricing had everything going their way. They therefore felt neither the pressure nor the incentive to sort out the price structure to see how fast pricing was prompting inventorying or how much inventorying was exaggerating actual demand.

Oil buyers wasted eight years and hundreds of billions of dollars failing to do this sorting job. They paid up for all the oil they could get and for inventorying more of it than they themselves knew. The higher they drove oil prices, the higher they drove the interest rates they were paying to store the oil their customers did not need. The biggest oil companies, all of them with more money than the best banks are supposed to have, were doing it. Everybody therefore assumed that they knew what they were doing. The parent companies lent out the cash they had to the money markets, and their operating subsidiaries borrowed back from the banks the credit they needed to carry the inventories they did not need.

No oil users discovered that they had paid too much, or had too much, in time to stop the costly charade. None of them ran out of cash or credit. On the contrary, oil-using companies led the rush to siphon billions of dollars of idle cash out of the banks to finance energy takeover bids all through 1981 until mid-1982; they were shocked into laying up tankers, shutting down refineries, overloading jobbers, and recognizing that the shortage they thought they had seen was really a glut. The booby prize for gullibility went to du Pont, the traditional symbol of market power and wisdom. In the summer of 1981, months after the glut had surfaced, du Pont borrowed $3.9 billion to win a spirited bidding contest to take over Conoco for its treasure trove of unexplored reserves of oil for the living, gas for their children, and coal for their grandchildren. The total cost was over $10 billion. The rationale for du Pont to spend on this scale was to buy these reserves as an option on a shortage-ridden future rather than to invest in anything so humdrum as operating income. One short year later, dismayed by the stubborn refusal of interest rates to fall as promised, du Pont rushed to dump these proven reserves, which it had been so insistent on paying up for, onto a market too demoralized and cash poor to inventory energy reserves for the future. The cash pinch brought on by du Pont's naïveté in taking the oil-shortage hoax at face value and borrowing to anticipate an even greater shortage was a "first" for the corporation.

Anything American corporations and banks tend to do poorly their Canadian counterparts excel at doing worse. This settled rule of financial performance found classic confirmation as a by-product of the du Pont–Conoco affair. The locale was the western Canadian oil and gas fields. Under cover of the "Canadianization" of energy resources, Ottawa offered substantial incentives to Canadian companies with unexploited reserves to buy out their U.S. partners. Dome Petroleum, *The New York Times* reported, "bit the bait." It paid Conoco over $1 billion (U.S.) for the privilege of buying Conoco's majority interest in another Canadian oil company that was big by Canadian standards. Dome wound up owing Canadian banks more than Ford and Chrysler owed American banks: $5.8 billion (Canadian) and, as *The New York Times* reported, with no cash or short-term debt whatever. Moreover, Dome did unto at least three of its neighbors in the banking business exactly what it had done unto itself: It ran them out of approximately half their net worth, one of them so conspicuously that the London money market rejected its commercial paper. One of those banks sent routine notice to U.S. holders of its certificates of deposit (CDs) to invoke the fine-print clause entitling it to claim that "due to the volatility of the money markets, the non-preincashable clause [note the authentic Québecois patois] in U.S. term deposits will be strictly adhered to. Accordingly, it will no longer be possible to obtain your funds prior to maturity of your investment." The exercise left Dome rolling in high-cost oil reserves it could neither develop nor sell. Dome had been the hottest growth stock in sight when the energy crisis was guaranteed to be endless and oil prices were guaranteed to be topless. If ever there was a case of borrowing for long-term purposes, entrapping short-term lenders—the classic recipe for financial disaster—this was it.

Dome's destructiveness and du Pont's disorientation made even U.S. Steel, never noted for its managerial achievements, look good. U.S. Steel had borrowed up to the hilt, too, to take over Marathon Oil. But its response to the interest-rate pinch was more realistic than du Pont's:

It sold its own assets, not Marathon's. Almost nobody asked why the oil companies had drifted toward dependence on oil-producing countries dominated by dictatorships and then surrendered their independence and proprietary engineering skills to every one of them. Not even the indignant participants in the nationwide tax revolt, who complained about the power exercised by the oil companies in bludgeoning and wangling tax advantages out of Washington, were provoked to the point of expressing curiosity about the glaring anomaly in the foreign political operations of the oil-company managements. The companies were impotent in asserting their own commercial interests, let alone the political interests of the United States, in dealing with the dictatorships in the producing countries. But their persuasiveness as the unofficial ambassadors of the producing countries to the foreign policy-making apparatus of the U.S. government was irresistible.

The turn in the oil market came as turns always do: when expectations collide with realities. This abrupt reversal was touched off when the obsession with inventorying, intensified by scares of still higher prices, collided with the physical reality of the glut. The oil companies simply ran out of storage space while Jimmy Carter was still mumbling his exit lines on the campaign trail, exhorting people to burn less oil in order to enjoy better lives. The discovery of the oil surplus was first made by Japan. America's delay in confirming it revealed the operational difference between the secret of Japan's success and the saga of America's failure. Japan is the world's most conspicuous, import-dependent oil have-not. Nevertheless, her costs were never inflated by any oil-price or oil-supply problem. The stability of her low interest rates during the entire decade of the oil war is proof that she was able to take in all the oil she needed or wanted on her own terms. No doubt one explanation of this apparent anomaly surfaced with the enormous fleet of supertankers the Japanese built in their bustling shipyards to swap—first and foremost with the Saudis—for oil; oil and tankers make a neat, indeed indispensable, fit. The elastic prices of tanker charters provided a leading indicator of OPEC's successive oil-price hikes; the higher OPEC jumped oil prices, the more anxious its members became to sell cargoes. Its intoxication with its own propaganda showed up in its anxiety to pay up for tankers for future delivery after it lost its ability to peddle its oil for immediate delivery. The Japanese smiled as they took in oil at OPEC's prices, and they laughed as they collected their own charter rentals. This game was so good that the Japanese continued to push overpriced tankers at the Saudis after they ran out of spare floating storage space for surplus oil.

Where the Japanese authorities reacted with pragmatic incisiveness to the discovery that oil had become a drug on the market, the American authorities shrugged off the hard evidence as a series of random events. Where Japan, in her sophistication, exploited her own accumulated surplus of imported oil to compound the long-standing advantage she had enjoyed as a buyer of cheap oil, America, in her naïveté, continued to pay hard cash for marked-up oil that had nowhere else to go. While Japan continued to get her oil from OPEC countries by building tankers for them that the market could no longer absorb, the American oil companies were content to lay up tankers on which they were paying rent.

Economic analysis is a matter of judgment, but economic geography is a matter of fact. The simple facts of economic geography explained the ominous portents of Japan's exhaustion of storage space, on land and at sea, for imported oil. These portents also found positively explosive confirmation in the first announcement that America had also exhausted her storage capacity. It came, of all places, from the northeasternmost refining point in North America. The obscure district manager of the Gulf Oil refinery in Newfoundland blurted it out in a chance interview with *The Wall Street Journal* in September 1980. He explained that he had ordered the refinery shut down because it had run out of storage facilities. All of northeastern North America is an oil have-not; its dependence on oil imports becomes more pronounced and, therefore, more costly due to transportation charges on each leg up the coast from Florida to Newfoundland. To anyone with an eye on the map, let alone on the marketplace, this announcement left no doubt that market points closer to continental points of crude production were even more overloaded.

The commercial evidence that the glut was cascading out of control corroborated the physical evidence from Newfoundland. Of all the Seven Sisters, which serve as America's links to the overseas potentates of the oil world, Gulf was the most import-dependent; its ratio of domestic reserves to total needs was the lowest of any major international oil company. Gulf's import flows came from the richest per capita member of OPEC, Kuwait, as well as from the poorest, Nigeria. The revelation surfaced not from any sleek, high-powered public relations headquarters but from a literal-minded superintendent out in the boondocks; it was therefore not only credible but irrefutable. It showed that Gulf's overseas captive sources, to which Gulf itself was held hostage, were dumping more oil on its refineries than they could digest. Gulf itself admitted its disadvantage due to a deficiency of domestic reserves when it offered to pay an above-market premium to take over Cities Service, incurring stockholder criticism and wrecking the market for its stock. Nevertheless, America did not heed the SOS from Gulf in 1980, no doubt because it was strictly factual and originated in the field.

The Japanese, true to form, figured out how to make a profit out of this glut, while their American competitors were still hell-bent on buying expensive insurance against a nonexistent shortage. Hosannas to the Japanese miracle ignore the real source of that efficiency: The Japanese, like all dumpers onto export markets, are able to sell cheap, thanks to their shrewdness in buying cheap in the export markets of their customers. Buying cheap is always the key to profits. Selling merely cashes in on them. Cheap raw-material import costs and dependent overseas suppliers make the difference for Japan. This skill applies with particular force to Japan's participation in the world oil market.

Darwin wrote the book on the survival of species. His observations on the rewards of adaptability and the penalties of rigidity also apply to competitiveness in the marketplace. Government needs business to do well because it needs to collect taxes; the fattest cows give the richest milk. Business needs government to manage well because it has finally discovered that business cannot manage the economy, and it no longer trusts the economy to manage itself. In Darwinian terms, Japan proved herself adaptable, not inflexible. After World War II, she launched a systematic offensive for the supplies and markets she needed from abroad. Ever since, when her business operatives, foraging around the world in her national interest, have discovered a change in combat conditions on the market firing line, they have signaled their government, which has responded by doing something about it. By contrast, when America went back to business-as-usual after Vietnam and on the eve of the outbreak of the oil war, her businesses were invited to range all over the world. They were expected to prosper in a political vacuum, although the economic landscape in every country outside the United States was under vigilant political control by the local powers-that-be. Consequently, American businesses up against foreign competition have all along been on the losing end of a game that the Japanese have been organized to win.

America, if she had had eyes to see her plight, would have recognized that she was importing the wrong product from Japan: a subsidized flood of hard goods, whose impact on America's markets attracted consumers but cut off the earnings from her own dismembered industries. If, instead, America had been imbued with enough of a Darwinian sense of survival to import Japan's proprietary government-to-business and business-to-government signal-and-aid mechanism, she would have recognized and acted on the twin symptom of oil-market distress: the first from the most import-dependent region of North America and the second from the most import-dependent of the major oil companies, which happened to have a refinery in that very area.

The functional separation of business and government in America explains why the United States has been on the losing end. The reason is not that Japanese business or labor is brighter and better than its American counterpart. It is that Japanese businesses operate abroad with their government behind them, while American businesses are resigned to operating alone, with their government relegated to the role of a rescuer. When American businesses stumble on a change in market conditions or practices and announce it in Washington, the government does nothing. The oil-price gouge was a classic example. Instead of resisting it as the declaration of economic warfare it was and devising a counteroffensive against it, which the Japanese government did, the American government welcomed it as a market adjustment. It was a marketing victory for Friedmanism but a policy defeat for America.

A sociological note is in order about the contrasting role of economists in Japan and in America. Though economists are prominent in America, they do not play conspicuous roles in the Japanese power structure, nor do they compete as private makers of public policy by playing the parts of lone rangers raiding the media, which in Japan are not available for such capers. The division of purpose invited by undisciplined debate is a luxury Japan cannot afford for two reasons: one nondiscretionary, the other discretionary. In the first place, her natural disadvantages dominate her thinking; she has no raw materials to support her large industrial capacity. In the second, she does not permit foreign nationals to enjoy free access to her economy. Of necessity, therefore, Japan is run by decision makers on trial to exert the nation's influence on world events and at the same time to insulate her against the impact of those events. Economists, by contrast, are trained to be observers of events, anonymous staffers, and team players, not policy makers or opinion makers with an option on charisma or power. The difference is pinpointed by George Bernard Shaw's put-down of professors: "He who can, does. He who cannot, teaches." America has been listening to the teachers instead of picking the doers. Her economists are trained to function as team players manning computers and carrying briefcases for her doers.

America's mind, meanwhile, was on a nonexistent oil shortage. Americans had become conditioned to read computer printouts of total returns from the marketplace indiscriminately and had been educated out of the habit of reading selective samplings of hard news, like the Gulf announcement. Moreover, the brainwashing to which Americans had been subjected about the oil shortage left them insensitive to the basic physical difference between the surplus of oil and the surplus of any other commodity. Food, to take the most obvious example, is readily destructible, even in the midst of hunger during depressions. Again and again, desperate producers have taken drastic steps to dispose of surpluses by plowing under crops, killing animals wholesale, and "deep-sixing" cargoes. Oil, on the other hand, is both bulkier than food and not destructible by any acceptable means. Oceans of it, once lifted from the ground, are explosive inventories waiting to be poured into boilers, engines, or storage tanks. In this day of environmental sensitivity, producers and marketers do not dare resort to oil spills, and they are as frightened of oil fires as the public is. But overspills from storage tanks whose overloads belied the clichés of shortage flared up into a perpetual fire hazard. Overspill was the admitted cause of the "inferno" created when the Texaco tank farm in the congested Newark, New Jersey, area exploded in the summer of 1982. Once oil is in the market, it is either moved or it blocks the arteries of distribution and backs up onto the points of production.

OPEC clouded the commercial atmosphere throughout the tense spring of 1982 with confident assertions that inventory reductions would soon firm up oil prices again. The oil analysts, brainwashed to accept all pronouncements from OPEC as gospel, took these assertions at face value. By July 1982, however, the oil markets were jolted into the realization that OPEC spokesmen made more sense programming American opinion—financial as well as official—than tracking the condition of the markets for their own products. Japan's all-powerful Ministry of International Trade and Industry (MITI) had been on the verge of ordering a million-barrel-a-day target in Japanese refinery runs; this directive would have slashed runs to just 17 percent of refining capacity. MITI, however, was shocked by the filings of the individual Japanese refineries calling for refinery runs of only 687,000 barrels a day, a full third below its official estimates of demand. In view of the reliance both Indonesia and Saudi Arabia place on Japan as their primary market outlet and in view of Japan's presumed disadvantage as the world's number-one have-not, the deepening of the distress in the Japanese refining industry left no doubt that Sheik Yamani and his less-exalted OPEC apologists had been taking their cues from King Canute in their efforts to talk the rising tide of unwanted inventories of petroleum products into receding. Their incantations had proven as influential as Canute's royal commands to the ocean tides.

With even the Japanese refining industry working at levels not seen during the worst of the 1929–1933 depression and with Japan's by-product petrochemical industry shutting down plants ten at a time (notwithstanding bromides from Sheik Yamani that recovery was under way around the world and, therefore, that demand levels were on the rise and inventory levels on the decline), the strains within OPEC reached the breaking point as its customers ran out of storage space. The glut left two options and two options only to the cartel members: to cut production below agreed levels or to cut prices below admitted levels. Every member of OPEC took the price option, inviting customers to get their own back through the back door. Its tougher-minded customers, none more so than the Japanese refiners, took advantage of those strains to force sharp concessions in the terms of trade, as was not yet the case in the American oil business. The fierce competition between Indonesia, which was busted, and Saudi Arabia, which was bulging with backed-up inventories for odd-lot Japanese orders, advertised the pressure for a collapse in the oil-price structure. The Reagan administration saw the distress, beginning with Mexico's hemorrhaging $84 billion debt. Insead of maneuvering to benefit from it, Washington moved to pay for it, giving Mexico a $1 billion Band-Aid for oil America did not need at the then still official price of $35 a barrel. The following month, Libya—OPEC's hawkish extremist and the member most animated by anti-American venom and with the least need for cash—cut her selling price to $32.

The following month OPEC saturated the media with declarations of its determination to hold the cash price, which, at $35 a barrel, none of its non-American customers was paying in a $25 barter market. At that stage of the gathering depression, however, the cartel was inflicting more damage on the world economy by desperately curtailing its buying than by the chaos of its selling. Nigeria, whose oil is top grade and whose selling prices are bottom of the barrel, added 150 categories of imports to its trade-prohibition list. Topping the list was all industrial equipment. Protectionism in a Third World country with no industry but only a crippled currency to protect is immeasurably more destructive than the familiar American variety bearing the McKinley-Coolidge brand, which at least stimulated investment, employment, and economic activity in an emerging industrial power. Two side effects of the Nigerian import ban were particularly destructive: The first, by effectively closing her ports to import traffic, Nigeria choked off her moonlighting income from the "skimming" of merchandise by customs personnel, a major growth business. The second dealt sterling a stunning blow just when it was falling. Nigeria was the United Kingdom's largest single export market outside Europe and the United States.

At that point oil had become more useful to busted oil producers around the world as collateral for their overextended loans than as a source of cash with which to meet their interest payments. The deeper the crack in oil prices went, the further underwater their bank loans went. In the same fundamental sense in which breathing is the function responsible for living, borrowing is the function responsible for inflation. At the outset of the oil inflation, its source seemed self-evident: the rising spiral of oil prices. From the day it started, the weak oil-producing governments, led by Iran and Mexico, projected the capital values of their oil reserves at peak price and production levels as collateral for foreign bank loans; as fast as prices were pushed up, and claims for reserves at the higher prices raised proportionally, bank borrowings were too. The loan proceeds were committed far into the future for arms programs and for uneconomic capital projects of every kind—beginning but by no means ending with cash eaters like steel mills, airlines, and, of course, petrochemical complexes. Luxuries for personal consumption claimed a preposterous share even by nouveau-riche standards. The borrowings to pay the interest on the borrowings to pay the bills compounded the insolvency that developed before the price was broken and production cut back. Billions in official borrowings were diverted to private accounts in Switzerland, Hong Kong, and the world's other competing cashboxes, and interest was borrowed to carry these government loans too.

By the time the oil bubble was pricked, however, the astronomic borrowings invited by the price gouge loomed as the undeniable residue of the oil inflation; that is to say, the oil-cash boom was over, but the debt burden it invited remained and continued to inflate as the busted oil borrowers held the banks hostage for fresh advances, not only to meet interest bills but to swell the total outstanding. Consequently, the oil inflation continued to inflict more damage on the system of international credit after the oil-cost inflation began to ease up than it had on the interrelated costs of living and doing business while its spiraling still seemed topless. Still another paradox: The easing of oil prices helped world trade, as did the switch from cash to swap transactions. The offsetting negative, however, developed with the failure of oil prices to continue going up. Their slump pulled the foundation stones out from under the top-heavy, jerry-built structure of oil credit. The banking crisis precipitated by the first easing of oil prices brought the world financial system to the brink of depression before the initial relief from OPEC-dictated oil costs could open the way for recovery.

When the evidence was building but not yet obvious that oil was backing up onto points of production, the throwaway line I publicized —that the surplus would accumulate until its custodians ran it into a shortage of storage space—was laughed off by many as an exaggeration. But President Reagan quoted me to this effect on March 16, 1979, in the syndicated newspaper column he was writing while out of office. If only Reagan the columnist had been aware of the commitment that Reagan the candidate was destined to promise but that Reagan the president would fail to implement, America might have been spared the debilitating consequences in the 1980s, of continuing the appeasement of OPEC that began under Kissinger and resumed under Carter in the 1970s. In that case, the course of history would have been happier, tricked by less cunning, guided by more wisdom. The world, dependent on America's realism for its security, would have prospered more and suffered less.

CHAPTER SIX

The Financing of Defense: The Four Frauds of Reaganomics

THE MOMENT President Reagan identified Russia as "our adversary," he set off an alarm in the Kremlin. Reagan thought he was waging a war of words, effective politically but harmless militarily. The Kremlin took it as a serious threat.

When he took over as Commander in Chief, Reagan started out on the wrong foot, outfitted with the wrong paraphernalia, heading in the wrong direction. He rushed to declare political war against Russia, unsupported by either military or economic muscle. He concentrated his rhetoric, moreover, on the weapons of war rather than on the sinews of war. Consequently, the President put America under pressure to challenge the Soviets on battlefields of their choice rather than in the marketplaces of our choice. The results speak for themselves.

America is the only country that derives her distinctive strength from her economy. She won two world wars wielding the economic weapon against her enemies more effectively than any military hardware or manpower. Therefore, to paraphrase Sherlock Holmes, it's elementary that the magic formula for reasserting America's strength in international dealings is to reinvigorate her economy at home. It's elementary, too, that the only way America can put strength on display abroad is to demonstrate it in her own economy at home. Certainly, President Reagan set out to do both, but separately. That was Reagan's trouble; the connections between the programs he launched eluded him. Instead of cranking up the economic engines to power the vehicles of American armor, he unwittingly engineered a collapse for the economy and, consequently, immobilization for his own defense program.

The question raised by any declaration of political warfare is one of weaponry, and the question raised by any choice of weapons is one of speed. Hence, the basic axiom of war, laid down by the long-since-forgotten Confederate cavalry general who attributed his victories to his knack of getting to the scene of battle "fustest with the mostest." In

Hitler's day, Roosevelt exposed America to no physical risk when he denounced Nazi war crimes in public. The ocean was America's fortress then. Though FDR confided to intimates that Hitler meant war, he nevertheless continued to allow America's antiquated army to amble along on horseback. In the era of intercontinental nuclear missilery, however, neither space nor time offers natural defenses against paranoid adversaries. Any American president intent on driving the Soviets into a line of rhetorical fire takes reckless risks unless he rushes to back up his own rhetoric by bringing America's nonnuclear defenses up to speed and, even more important, by directing an economic offensive at the weak links in Russia's armor. Political warfare unsupported by economic weaponry is more likely to trigger gunfire than not; in that case, with weapons chosen by the government walking softly and carrying a big stick, not by the government doing the talking. Economic weaponry, supported by an instinct for the political kill, is America's last hope for keeping the peace. It gives the edge to the power with the stronger economy, it reduces the risk that military weaponry may be used, and it eliminates the need for verbal bombshells.

Tragically, Reagan's diatribes against Russia heightened the risk that America might talk herself into a war that Russia was ready to shoot her way out of but that America was unready to face. Washington's break with Moscow in 1981 found America overstocked with obsolescent weapons she could use but was reluctant to activate for two reasons: first, because large quotas of manpower were needed to fight with them and, therefore, large casualties were likely to result, and, second, because America lacked the transportation backup to bring her firepower and her troops to any hot spot overseas. This twin deficiency of combat manpower and logistical capability was America's Achilles' heel. Moreover, the breach found America entirely unprepared to improvise with the unconventional mercy weapons of economic warfare—specifically, to dangle terms of trade to the Kremlin that it could not dare refuse. Russia brings no proprietary assets to any engagement on market battlefields; America does.

It was ironically the Soviet leaders who showed that Russia was able to do more with less, while America continued to do less with more. Russia read the oil war realistically, while America misread it. Russia, like Japan, saw the myth of the oil shortage drowning in the reality of the oil glut, while America looked at the weakness of the Persian Gulf states and saw strength where none existed. Russia was prepared for the oil war to go military, while America was taken by surprise when it did and positively flabbergasted by the failure of the local war between Iran and Iraq to relieve the glut. In fact, the Reagan administration remained so impressed with America's need to protect Gulf oil flows from a Soviet blockade that it offered to resume arms shipments to Iran,

America's enemy of record—forgetting Khomeini's seizure of the American hostages and how that confrontation had contributed to Reagan's defeat of Carter. Finally, while Russia put her navy in position to pick up the pieces in the Middle East when the oil war went military, America manned a new base at Oman at the mouth of the Persian Gulf, a site Anwar Sadat had sold to Carter for the quixotic purpose of protecting the sheikdoms. America thought she was doing the Arabs a favor by positioning herself to oversee their safety from Russian attack. They, however, took it as another act of treachery against the Arab cause on Sadat's part, beyond the Camp David accords, for which, to America's surprise, he was executed.

Russia, eyeing America uneasily as Washington set out to catch up with Soviet leads in conventional weaponry, was losing her appetite to risk shooting matches at the cost of scattering her forces. Her restraint in Poland spoke for itself. Her restraint in Lebanon provoked Yasir Arafat, a moderate in the PLO, to speak out against her and throw Syria, her client, into Israel's line of fire. Her restraint in the Falklands, after two years of flirting with Argentina, showed that she preferred to wait until the battle was over before moving into a high-profile presence in the South Atlantic. At the outset of the 1980s, Russia, by her own admission, still needed formidable economic resources from the industrial world. The importance she attached to her gas pipeline to Europe not only showed that she was hesitant to use the familiar military weapons she already had on hand, but confirmed the diagnosis that the confrontation between Russia and America was going economic as fast as the oil war was going military.

Postmortems on the failures of ambitious new U.S. administrations are never productive; assessments of the sources of their strengths and their weaknesses are. President Reagan asserted his distinctive strength from the moment he took over as the authentic heir of America's pioneering merchant, R. H. Macy. The secret of Macy's success had been his public insistence that "the customer is always right." Like Macy before him, Reagan was a retailer. He owed his dominant role as a political retailer to the same disciplined axiom; it helped him make skillful use of the electronic media. Reagan's media advisers had made a much more exhaustive investigation of the methods of FDR and had drawn on them more cleverly than Reagan's host of conservative followers had ever been allowed to suspect. His operation was a modernized version of Roosevelt's, updated to exploit the evolution from radio to television but still employing the same technique of direct retailing from the Oval Office to everybody within reach of the presidential personality. But the more systematically the Reagan operation copied FDR's, the more conspicuously one major contrast surfaced. It was the difference between art and artifice. Roosevelt had played his retailing by radio by feel and by flair, while the Reagan team, disciplined by professionalism rather than inspired by genius, systematically followed the preferences and the prohibitions clocked by the pollsters.

Reagan delegated the job of finding successful slogans to the functionary in his entourage with the lowest profile, his very competent pollster-in-chief, Dr. Richard Wirthlin, who held no official public office. His job was simply to feed the data to the stage directors in the junta —Mike Deaver, Bill Clark, Jim Baker, and Ed Meese—as guidelines for the Great Communicator to follow. Of the resident White House junta translating Wirthlin's numbers into policy after the purge of Alexander Haig as secretary of state, Michael Deaver was the most familiar because he had been at Reagan's side carrying the presidential briefcase when John Hinckley started shooting. The best-kept secret in the secretive Reagan White House was that Deaver was also the President's most powerful adviser because his province was the scheduling of private access and public appearances. His barony was relatively absolute because it was absolutely negative, that is, remote from policy concepts. Its power was buttressed because it was close to Nancy Reagan.

Ed Meese started out ranking second on the scale of familiarity, serving as presidential counselor. His intellectual reach made a neat fit with his background as a small-town police chief in California. Meese began his White House tenure paralleling Deaver's control over the almighty schedule, but by early 1982, Meese had clearly been targeted by a faction within the White House and was left as the only junta member standing in a game of political musical chairs.

William Clark, the junta's third Californian, became the object of international ridicule when his Senate confirmation hearings revealed that he was as familiar with a world atlas as with the Bhagavad-Gita. He owed his claim to fame to the unfortunate Richard Allen, who had committed a gaffe in embarrassing Nancy Reagan over a stray $1,000 bill left behind by a Japanese interviewer. But respect for Clark's professionalism skyrocketed when, as national security adviser, he set and sprung the trap that got Secretary of State Haig fired.

The thinking on the Reagan staff was delegated to Texan James Baker, the only non-Californian in the group. With Allen a goner and Meese a loser, the junta found itself short one policy maker with cosmopolitan credentials. From the vantage point of Reagan ranch country, Baker loomed as a junior-grade John Connally, offering a connection with the pivotal power state, though not a threat to power in the White House. All presidential juntas are on notice to protect the continuity of their status in picking vice presidents. The Californians made their deal for the succession by picking Baker; he was George Bush's manager in the primary campaign against Reagan and, therefore, had the Bush connection.

The popular perception of the government, going into the Reagan years, revealed a glaring crisis of confidence. Too many Americans for comfort, and more than enough to swing a presidential election, looked down on their government as "the pitiful, helpless giant" that Nixon in his day had vowed it would not be. Wirthlin's data projected America as a bully at home, battening on its own taxpayers, and a coward abroad, shrinking from overdue confrontations with predatory challengers and outright enemies. The President's pollster set out to count and to classify what the customers thought they wanted. His polls showed that the same customers who wanted their government to foot the bill for a stronger defense did not want to live with less in Social Security benefits. They wanted the budget balanced but didn't want to help balance it by paying more of their own money in taxes. They wanted a tax bonus for working in a world that was improving, while they wanted their government to protect them with a stronger defense in a world that was deteriorating.

Once the customers were converted into supporters, it was not Wirthlin's job to convert them to consistency. On the contrary, the White House staff used the data Wirthlin fed it from his computer to encourage the customers to indulge their inconsistencies and to thank the President for the opportunity to have their cake and eat it too. Two years after Wirthlin prepared the script that enabled Reagan to play Macy to a grateful national clientele, Wirthlin expressed his surprise to a reporter over the amount of patience the electorate had shown: "I thought we had a year from the time the President took office to see significant signs of improvement in the economy." Whenever Reagan waved his arms and aimed a harsh, open-mouthed blast against the Kremlin, Wirthlin found him winning an unprecedently high poll rating of 75 percent without coming under any practical pressure to back up his tough talk with new power plays. Whenever Reagan called for tax cuts as a social dividend on the spending cuts he promised, he won nearly as much praise. Whenever Reagan guaranteed that he would balance the budget, despite taking the hard line against Russia and the soft line on taxes, his ratings soared. Only one negative rating came into play: Whenever Reagan threatened even to slow down the rate of growth in Social Security benefit checks, much less to cut out the increases altogether, over 60 percent of the respondents turned thumbs down on the idea. The resistance came not only from those already on the receiving end but from people still in the prime of life who expected to receive their benefits when the time came for them to collect. Administrators of local governments and of health and educational institutions joined in the protest on the understandable ground that they would be called upon to raise any money that the federal government stopped spending. In 1982, the country went into hysterics over whether the American government was going bankrupt paying Social Security or whether its taxpayers would go broke either putting up the money or not collecting it. But by then America's habitual obsession with the present had long since obscured the oil war as the cause of the pressure to escalate entitlements. OPEC had lit a time bomb under the entire American structure of fixed-income benefit calculations over the decades to come when it lulled America's political strategists into welcoming oil-price gouges, which seemed a mere inconvenience, overdue as a matter of equity.

The polls registered a striking tribute to Reagan's prowess as a communicator, if not to his effectiveness as a leader at home or abroad. The high-flying, self-indulgent world of creative opinion engineering was made to order for Reagan. There it was easy to succeed in managing a merger between a balanced budget, economic recovery, a stronger defense-spending increase at a falling rate, and, to round out the tinsel on the Christmas tree, the tax cut that gave peanuts to Joe and Jane Six-Pack but took billions from the Treasury. In the real world, of course, a stronger defense does not go with a balanced budget; genius plus perseverance are needed to make a try at a stronger defense only to end up with a collapsed economy. By the same token, a weaker defense goes with a balanced budget, not with a record deficit. Through the welter of confusion and frustration punctuated by Reagan's assertion of his determination to get "leverage" on the Russians, he sold the idea that what matters about defense spending is the money paid out each year. His persuasiveness distracted attention from the need to budget for the obligations built up to make future-year outlays for each new defense program adopted. All of them that were adopted shared one characteristic: Each stretched out over years, and each cost more in each succeeding year. If spending more was all it took to guarantee the accumulation of more combat strength, the Kremlin would have thrown in its hand the day after its intelligence radar alerted it to the U.S. resolve, formalized at Reagan's first Cabinet meeting, to spend more on defense.

Basic political home truths, though easy to deride or to resent, can be educational stimulants to the voters. FDR applied them when he helped a reluctant country make up its mind about how to handle Hitler with a practical reminder that when your neighbor's house is on fire, you bring water to save your own. To take another example from the same crisis-torn era, the Japanese made America's mind up for her about how to handle them by hitting Pearl Harbor. But Reagan was not up to challenging Americans to make up their minds either to "go Quaker" and forget defense spending, or to "go Avis" and try harder not to finish second to Russia by any measure of actual muscle.

America ended up identifying defense spending with strength. This non sequitur invited two more: first, that increases were apt to go for overhead, not weapons; second, that cuts would free up increases for spending on the rival programs that every group wanted for itself. Even the most rabid Reagan supporters advocating a balanced budget felt robbed in the summer of 1982, when interest rates fell and so, therefore, did their interest income. But the crowning illustration of the fiscal illiteracy broadcast by the battle of the budget came from members of Congress in that same troubled summer. They were finding on their trips home that the customers responding to Reagan's eloquent plea for voter support on the trumped-up crisis over the budget resolution did not even know what a budget resolution meant. The voters were under the misimpression that the resolution for which the President urged their support was simply a guarantee of a balanced budget. In fact, it resolved to grant the government, with the President's blessing, the authority to spend more by borrowing more.

The Reagan administration clung to the stubborn conviction that the Great Communicator's own protection continued to lie in following the polls. Consequently, the steadiness of purpose Reagan continued to project against spending led him into a trap of his own making. His first step was to brand all spending sinful and, therefore, bad for the economy, as if the military strength he promised to assert could be conjured up on television for the world to see and the Kremlin to salute without being bought with the spending he denounced. He closed his mind to the possibility that defense spending might power the economy and buy a boom, as it had during every arms buildup in the past (although this is not the only kind of spending on which he could have relied, and the pressure to buy recovery is certainly not the reason to spend on defense). Instead, the administration continued to defer the Pentagon's access to the Treasury's cashbox and, at the same time, to create the impression that it was going forward with an urgent yet streamlined arms buildup.

The delay in actual defense outlays, however, compounded the damage done by the slump in private-sector spending. This setback for Reaganomics was aggravated by the run-up in interest rates, for which the administration had mainly itself to blame. The lost momentum in the economy was certainly not to blame for the rate explosion; the revelation that Reagan was presiding over a bigger deficit than Carter had was to blame. Any shred of an alibi the administration might have had went up in smoke when it turned its artillery loose against the wounded economy and demoralized markets. To the dismay of Republican congressmen able to peek around the corner to the post-honeymoon skirmishes looming ahead and to the relief of the entire Democratic caucus squirming under the backlash from the Carter fiasco, Reagon singled out the most unpopular of all the Carter hold-overs, Chairman Paul Volcker of the Federal Reserve Board, for his unqualified endorsement. Moreover, he turned his endorsement to co-incide with the launching of Volcker's dogged, tradition-bound campaign to beat back inflation by pushing up the cost of credit, which is the common ingredient in the cost of everything else, beginning with the cost of finding the cash to meet payrolls.

The test of effectiveness aside, the fulfillment of campaign promises also faced a race against time. The President's closest friend and lowest-profile adviser, Senator Paul Laxalt of Nevada, was realistic in recognizing that the President took office under pressure to beat the congressional calendar. In a talk in Washington at *The Janeway Seminar* of February 1981, Laxalt, with characteristic candor, declared that "if we don't get our program passed by July, we will have had it." Reagan did get his program through just a few weeks behind this rigorous schedule, giving a grateful and ebullient country what it wanted. But the upshot recalled the famous tag line about the pushy surgeon: "The operation was a success; the patient died." America did not realize that she had "had it."

Having failed on both counts, efficacy and timing, the administration wound up in a fierce, nonstop row with Congress. Perversely, the fight blossomed into Reagan's strongest political asset, providing him in the nick of time with the political "out" he desperately needed for the future of his programs. The voters gave their President credit for trying to do what they wanted, and they gave Congress the blame for the failure of his performance. By June 1982, months after the collapse of the economy had gone unchecked, but before the violent midsummer rally in the stock market, the White House's poll still found its victims blaming Congress for what had gone wrong by an overwhelming majority of three to one, while Reagan was still riding high above 50 percent.

The decisive battle for the Reagan administration was fought out not between the President and Congress, or between the bulls and bears in Wall Street, but between the President's two top movers within the Cabinet. Caspar Weinberger, the secretary of defense, knew what the President wanted for his defense budget. David Stockman, the eager-beaver wunderkind whom Reagan had installed at the Office of Management and Budget (OMB) power center, knew what the President wanted for his entire budget. Their inevitable clash put Stockman on trial to show that he could follow the President's orders without running the risk of being cut up by "Cap the Knife," the soubriquet Weinberger had won as the keeper of the purse during the Nixon administration.

Weinberger insisted on more for defense, and Stockman countered with a one-two punch: the tax cut packaged with the balanced budget. The polls showed each of them having a constituency, and, therefore, the President let both of them win. It proved to be a fixed fight, ending in one of those famous victories costing more than it was worth. Stockman temporarily emerged the victor with the media, not merely because he was brash but also because Washington always turns the spotlight on the new game in town. His meteoric vault into prominence came as an unsettling reminder that while all geniuses are expected to be eccentric, not all eccentrics are geniuses. Some are excessives who make it big as confidence men, as this dropout from evangelism did when he went from studying God in divinity school to playing God in politics. He invited the charge that he was a confidence man, not in the self-serving confidences he revealed to William Greider in *The Atlantic* but in his brash pose before the Cabinet, the media, and the Congress as the master of fiscal wizardry he quickly revealed himself not to be.

Every successful politician needs to be part actor. This fact of political life explains why Ronald Reagan (as his former assistant, Peter Hannaford, is careful to show in his definitive biography of the president as the campaigner he is) relishes any opportunity to lash back at highbrow critics who look down on him as an ex-actor, which it is clear he is not. It also explains why he took a liking to Stockman. At the outset of the campaign, the Reagan staff had been worried, with some reason, that Congressman John Anderson, the Independent candidate, might present a threat. In their careful rehearsals for the campaign debates, Stockman, who had worked for Anderson, was cast as Anderson. He played the part so brilliantly and briefed Reagan so effectively that he was awarded the role of expert-in-residence.

Stockman was an instant smash. He took as naturally to spouting fiscal expertise as John Barrymore had to declaiming Shakespeare; he brandished his heavy budget books as masterfully as Barrymore had his profile. As he dazzled his audiences with his apparent mastery of budgetary intricacies, Stockman distracted them from the four ingenious cover-ups the administration was devising. Wirthlin's findings had called for the pursuit of contradictory goals, and Stockman started by quantifying the formula for doing so. He ended by acting out Sir Walter Scott's famous warning: "O what a tangled web we weave, when first we practise to deceive!"

The first cover-up was invited by a three-way discrepancy Stockman was clever enough to spot in preliminary discussions of the budget. First, there was the traditional way of presenting the entire budget: one year at a time. Then there was the new way in which Reagan had presented the taxation side of the budget: three years at a time. Finally, beyond the tug of tradition or reform, there was the mind-boggling requirement for financing the defense budget dictated by the revolution in high-tech weapons procurement: ten years at a time. Though Stockman was counting horses, oranges, and bricks, he whipped the ingredients of a budget together as if they were all subject to the same time scale, as if they all flowed in the same direction (as, clearly, spending and taxing do not), and as if they all meant as much to Treasury calculations.

Stockman bludgeoned Congress and mystified the media by packaging a one-year defense-spending increase with a three-year tax cut and a ten-year program of weapons development. There was no way in the world that Congress could deal with this in a responsible fashion, but arguing about it at the time would have been resented as out of spirit with Reagan's honeymoon. The rationale behind the three-year tax-cut schedule was the guarantee it gave taxpayers to plan, as Senator Orrin Hatch of Utah, a Reagan loyalist if ever there was one, put it to me in response to my demurrers. The one-year defense budget that Stockman offered in order to kick off a ten-year defense program killed any hope that the tax collector would be able to plan. Therefore, it cast the Treasury in the role of an Indian giver before the bill for the first leg of the arms race fell due.

Once Stockman hit upon the first deception needed to satisfy Reagan's combined purposes, he found himself in need of improvising a second. The resultant deficits were so astronomical that they soon blacked out all memories of Stockman's—and Reagan's—earnest promise to balance the budget. Houdini the master magician once confided to me that the secret of his success was the patter, not his tricks; he played to the ears of his audience in order to divert their eyes from his hands. Stockman's evangelical instinct inspired him to discover Houdini's magic formula and to exploit it in unraveling the mysteries of finance. Stockman's studied technique for distracting attention from the imbalance he was creating on both sides of the budget was to display the apparent balance he was achieving on the spending side. He double-dipped his $36 billion cut in spending on social programs to pay for the first year of the tax cut *plus* the first-year increase in defense spending. It was as if a hot-shot stock market player had taken advantage of the 50 percent margin rule to persuade an innocent or hungry broker to let him put up $10,000 of margin in order to place the same order twice. Stockman was audacious enough to put his double dip right out on the table for everyone to see. Moreover, he got away with it. The only surprise about the runaway in the deficit was that it came as a surprise to anyone but Reagan.

Two follow-up manipulations in the government's cost figures threw the Reagan budget into chaos and guaranteed that the markets would follow, as they always do. Stockman's next two sleights of hand for putting the President's crazy-quilt budget across were built into the arithmetic of the defense budget itself. Well over half of the Pentagon pocketbook is eaten up by manpower costs before cost-of-living adjustments are factored in, before the first bullet is bought, and, needless to say, before the next missile is conceived. Consequently, the great bulk of the first-year budgeted increase in defense spending went for catch-ups in pay and benefits at the expense of the ambitious ten-year shopping list of complicated, expensive weaponry whose program costs had not even been worked out. Stockman proceeded to violate the first principle of auditing integrity, namely, the reconciliation of future cost projections with previous cost experience. The lowest responsible calculation of the compound annual rate of inflation for the procurement of defense hardware—18 percent—came from low-profile senatorial watchdogs on the Armed Services Committee, but devastating data dug up by the House Armed Services Committee claimed that it had been running above 30 percent. The alarming House figure revealed the inclination and the need of the armed services to change specifications and to order overtime, revealing the inflationary environment for the development, production, modification, maintenance, and, ultimately, combat use of all high-tech weaponry. All hands agreed that the "disinflation" reported in the popular statistical indices—the consumer price index (CPI) and the wholesale price index (WPI)—did not apply to weapons development and procurement. Nevertheless, Stockman wrote another chapter in the history of logic by assertion. He developed a calculation justifying a paltry 8 percent rate of annual compounded inflation into his defense-cost projections. This third ruse camouflaged the fact that the Pentagon, at the very time Stockman was delivering himself of this pronouncement, had found itself, on pain of losing its noncommissioned officers in droves, forced to grant 1981 pay increases of between 11 and 12 percent. Simultaneously, the gap between current payroll drains and ongoing investment in hardware for the "out years" was widening each year; the most expensive hardware programs, such as the MX missile, were subject to the longest lead times and, therefore, were compounding the most onerous annual cost increases.

Always resourceful and aggressive, Stockman was ready with a fourth razzle-dazzle move to defuse the charge that his estimate of procurement-cost inflation was too low; it targeted interest rates as too high. Fragmentary and amateurish though his grasp of the budgetary problem was, Stockman was quick to pounce upon the interconnection between the cost inflation and interest rates. He realized that the deception of an 8 percent projection for procurement-cost inflation justified the parallel deception of a 7.5 percent cost for money. This fourth smoke screen was the most clever, transforming as it did the admitted weakness in the government's inability to follow the basic rule of Hamiltonian finance—to stretch out the debt—into a source of fiscal strength. Since most of the government's debt was owed at short term, the faster and the further interest rates fell, the sooner and the lower the government's interest bill could be projected to fall too.

The full measure of the Stockman fiasco was revealed when interest rates did fall (and to the threshhold of the 7.5 percent Treasury-bill rate he projected as the future norm) but the Treasury's interest bill did not. The jump in borrowings more than cancelled the relief from the cut in rates. The Treasury's interest bill for Reagan's first full fiscal year, ended October 30, 1982, came to $112 billion, and refunds in one form or another to overoptimistic taxpayers came to $110 billion. The deficit itself amounted to $129 billion, big by any bipartisan standard of past performance, but small relative to the bloat in the making. Nevertheless, this first-year deficit of Reagan's would have been contained within manageable proportions if either significant interest costs on the spending side or revenue losses on the collection side could have been avoided. The administration's change of heart regarding interest rates did not change its luck in the first half of the fiscal year that began September 1, 1982. The Treasury's tab for interest ran at exactly the same annual rate of $112 billion, but the deficit for the first half of the 1983 fiscal year was greater than for the entire 1982 fiscal year. The backlash from the depression ripped the budget to shreds when in April, normally the cruellest month for taxpayers and the happiest for the Treasury, the Treasury still ended up with a cash deficit. This fiscal disaster was without precedent. The budget was abandoned as excess baggage in May 1983, and the emperor of the budget balancers was seen standing naked without a budget. The Pentagon then panicked and began to cancel wholesale pet projects that it had spent the last two years programming as top priorities.

The evidence available for a verdict against Stockman as the architect of this "creative financing" points to a hung jury. The case for the President being innocent of responsibility for the disaster rests on two grounds: first, that he was merely doing the job he was elected to do by giving the customers what the polls reported they wanted; and second, just as persuasive, that ignorance of finance can be a defense for a president. Reagan's defenders could, if called upon, cite the horrible examples of Hoover and Johnson to prove that the country is better off when the president is certifiably ignorant of the budgetary mechanism.

Any vote of acquittal for the President is, of course, a vote of guilt for Stockman. But he had his defenders too. Their case is simpler than the case for Reagan: the familiar one with ominous overtones, especially in the case of an aspirant preacher, that he was just following orders. Stockman's defenders claim that he knew how to do what the President wanted. Probably the truth is that Reagan erred in unleashing Stockman's demonic energies and ingenious ignorance on this mission and that Stockman erred in undertaking it, strutting about as if he knew what he was doing. Far from being a policy maker, he was just a mechanic. The suspicion lingers that his confession in *The Atlantic* was self-serving and that he used the magazine to convey publicly a coded message to the White House that he just worked there and that, though he was talking, he was not telling everything.

In any case, these four calculated deceptions were anything but fringe stratagems. On the contrary, the course of the economy, the stability of the markets, and the plausibility of the President hinged on Stockman's success in pulling off all four of them and making the sale stick. Inside the Treasury, Reagan's caper and Stockman's coup had set a time bomb ticking. The reason is as simple as the compound interest table: A program subject to cost inflation compounding at an annual rate of only 8 percent will not double until the ninth year, even on the unlikely assumption that scheduling or engineering changes will not build up the bill during the nine-year stretch. But an annual cost increase of over 30 percent will double the program's cost in two years, quicker than any engineering changes can slow deliveries or speed up costs on their own. Months before Stockman came out of the closet and displayed himself to the readers of *The Atlantic* as either a political conniver and a statistical contriver or an ambitious stooge on the make, no very sophisticated auditing was needed to support the suspicion that he had hit upon the 8 percent rate of inflation and the 7.5 percent interest rate for the budget as a whole *after* the President had accepted the decade-long time frame for both. The effect of this unobtrusive statistical ploy was to defer the doubling of Reagan's first-year defense budget until its scheduled completion a full decade later—on the cynical calculation that the next administration would pick up the tab for it.

Inside the Pentagon, the administration's battle plan created paralysis, as it reduced the overriding need for long-term defense programming and financing to provocative rhetoric. In doing so, it rusted the huge inventory of the armed services, and its defense budgeting contributed to the collapse of the economy, to the instability of the markets, and to the inability of the military to back up Reagan's threats and promises. This state of affairs was all the more demoralizing because the secretary of defense had earned his spurs in the fiscal hierarchy by his previous service in Stockman's job under Nixon. Therefore, he was presumed to know enough about the problem and the procedures needed to contain it to have kept Stockman shut up in the White House and out of the Pentagon. Weinberger's secret was that he knew as little about the defense budget as Stockman did. The mystery behind Stockman's meddling in Pentagon affairs deepened when Weinberger asserted his seniority with the President by beating back Stockman's demand for deep cuts in the defense budget. But because Reagan first backed Weinberger against Stockman and then backed Stockman against Congress, the chaos he and Stockman engineered between them was a by-product of the President's crusade to balance the budget that he was busily unbalancing. To cover up the shambles he was scheduling for the 1983 budget, as well as the enormity of the deficits he was skyrocketing into the second half of the decade, and with no thought for the deficiencies and delays he was decreeing for the country's defense posture in the early 1980s, Stockman took the position that what matters in defense budgeting in any single year are current-year outlays rather than future-year obligations.

The opposite is the case. Thanks to the time lags by which contractual commitments lead deliveries of products and disbursements of cash, the government always signs for the money first and then invites everyone entitled to raise money on its credit to do so. It pays on delivery, not in cash for the end product but in installments (technically known as progress payments based on time spent and allowable cost incurred). No Pied Piper ever led an innocent band of children into the blue with more wanton irresponsibility than Stockman did when he carried his dedication to the President and his nimbleness with the numbers to the extreme of dreaming up this cart-before-the-horse scheme. In the kingdom of the blind, the one-eyed man is king, and Stockman crowned himself inside the White House. His patter first overpowered then overwhelmed the entire administration, from the President on down. When the Reagan White House bought its impressive start-up legislative victory by packaging the $36 billion tax cut with a like amount of spending switches, it provided a preview of the technique it subsequently perfected for buying votes in Congress: offering to members spending programs, which were by no means limited to defense. Since the end sounded frugal, the profligate means employed looked sound. This technique of spending more in the name of spending less reached its high point during the midsummer 1982 fight for the budget resolution (otherwise known as the increase in the debt ceiling) when member after member of the bipartisan Reagan majority then in control of the House, took turns asking the clerk to verify their impression that a bill appropriating funds for an airport here, a post office there, and a dam or a highway somewhere else exactly conformed to the conditions present in the community that, quite coincidentally, the member having the floor happened to represent. The member, assured that the money would be there to spend in the district under discussion, dutifully cast a vote in support of Reagan's crusade against the big spenders. The record shows that their votes were bought.

One year before, in the summer of 1981, Stockman, dizzy with success, had inadvertently revealed the encyclopedic proportions of his ignorance about the budget and the defense budget in particular when he told *The Washington Post* that he had ordered Saturday morning briefing sessions to be staged for him on the workings of defense finance; this *after* he had bullied and bribed Congress to accept Reagan's topsy-turvy, deceit-ridden, politically indulgent scheme to spend less, tax less, arm more, and still bring the budget under control. Once the budgetary fiction had materialized into political fact, the White House cited the polls—specifically, the evidence that the customers were eager to see a defense catch-up, tax cuts, and a balanced budget —to prove that it knew what it was doing politically when it did not know what it was doing fiscally.

Enter Professor A. B. Laffer, the articulate and energetic high priest of the administration's new supply-side economic credo. Charles E. Walker, a senior associate of Laffer's consulting firm who had been on active duty at the Pentagon as a senior civilian adviser responsible for defense policy formulation, was responsible for translating the administration's economic program into its defense strategy. In August 1981, Walker circulated a paper entitled "Investment Strategies: The Emerging Reagan Defense Strategy." (Congressional monitors of Pentagon procedures forced Walker's removal on learning that he had been indiscreet enough to circulate his official paper on his firm's letterhead.) Walker argued:

> The dilemma that President Reagan faces, namely, the requirement to accelerate defense spending while being constrained by budget deficits and high inflation, can be overcome to a degree by opting for programs such as the Stealth bomber which have long lead times and later rather than earlier heavy funding requirements. This approach would take pressure off the need to fund many programs over the next two-three years when outlays might exceed the President's current defense spending projections. This constraint also favors the air-launched MX missile system which has a much lower initial outlay than the land-based alternative. Thus a cautious attitude should be adopted toward programs that appear to have substantial funding outlays over the next 3–5 year period. Some of these weapons systems may be substantially reduced in favor of more promising long-term weapons programs.

During the costly year of the Laffer/Walker ascendancy, its spokesman-on-the-spot was arguing for the deceleration of long-lead-time, technologically advanced, but operationally risky weapons programs on the grounds that slowdowns would buy time and save money. He promised that supply-side economics in the meantime would buy relief from inflation and produce a return to tolerable budget deficits and interest rates. The Laffer/Walker calculation ignored the national-security policy question of how, if the threat to America's physical security were sufficiently urgent to justify the priority President Reagan claimed to give it, any delay in the arms buildup could be justified on the grounds that it would be cheaper to wait. The Laffer/Walker calculation also ignored the practical question of how waiting would buy a bargain when the "swing" payroll factor in defense costs was being inflated by the very defense budget supposedly deflating them. But the larger question of whether deferral would be safe, which is the only question that matters once the president raises defense goals, was ignored. It made sense in only one respect: It provided an administrative rationale bolstering the Reagan administration's blueprint for policy chaos and security risk.

How is history likely to grade Reagan for effort, if not performance? Our judicial system is based on the ability of lawyers "to distinguish cases" relevant to the issues at hand, and our system of business education has borrowed the case system from our law schools. The approach to a judgment most likely to be both objective and practical also calls for a search for cases supporting a claim of relevance.

I have found two. We have already examined the traumatic consequences of the first: Lyndon Johnson's two-step decision, undoubtedly unpremeditated at its outset, to cut taxes preparatory to escalating a war buildup. The second case I have found carries an unmeasurably more sinister ring. It was the calculated decision on the part of Kaiser Wilhelm II's Germany to execute her meticulously engineered war plan in 1914 without preparing to finance it by imposing war taxes on German industry. Granted, Kaiser Wilhelm was a nut needing to be handled with care by his court, and granted too that his generals ran his regime. Nevertheless, the comparison between the case of the kaiser's plan of emergency finance and the case of Reagan's merely suggests a fit, like the comparison between the case of Johnson's plan and the case of Reagan's, without making a complete one. Johnson launched a limited war amid a boom he engineered. Reagan launched an expensive and disturbing arms buildup on top of a depression he triggered. This comparison is not entirely unfair to either Johnson or Reagan because both of them inherited a tax system to work with. But the comparison with the Reagan case history is unfair to the kaiser; Germany had no tax structure available for cutting.

The outcome of the German experiment of 1914 was disastrous enough to warn policy makers in every industrial country against repeating the experiment in any form and to brand any head of government who went along with such a wartime fiscal policy as ignorant. Imperial Germany's method of wartime finance between 1914 and 1918 stands as one of the most traumatic experiences of modern history, not merely because of the blood it shed but because of its still bloodier aftermath, impossible though this was to conceive of at the time. The disaster set in motion by the kaiser's insensitivity to the profits his regime showered on industry, while drowning its people in their own blood, proliferated long after he was stowed away. What he did, however, was merely wanton. The establishment thinking he adopted was as destructive as it was respectable, and it has lingered on into the 1980s, as destructive and respectable now as it was then.

Wilhelm's petulant decision to drop Bismarck raised questions about his stability and put him on trial to demonstrate the soundness of his judgment as he embarked on an expensive naval arms race with England. He therefore chose the soundest or, at any rate, the most authoritative figure in the Prussian financial establishment to be his finance minister, Karl Helfferich. Helfferich was what in football is called a triple-threat man: head of the Deutschebank, still the largest in Europe; professor of finance at the University of Berlin, then the most prestigious in Germany; and the author of the country's standard text on finance. By the time the opposition party challenged Helfferich on the tax issue in 1917, the General Staff was drafting boys of fourteen into the bloody muck of the trenches and working Belgian war prisoners as slave labor in the mines. Helfferich's rationalization stands as a classic illustration of how wrong economists can go when they insist on turning their dogma into forecasts and their forecasts into justification of their dogma: "Ours is a just war," he declared on the floor of the Reichstag with the air of a schoolmaster. "Therefore, we shall win. And when we have won, we will force the vanquished to pay the cost of the war to us."

The French have been criticized ever since for doing to the Germans exactly what he had advertised that the Germans were planning to do to the French. It raises the question of whether peace treaties may be too important to be left to the tender mercies of finance ministers. Ironically, Helfferich, and the thinking for which he stood, has been allowed to bask in posthumous respectability. His indiscretion was no mere academic abstraction, forgotten soon after. The tragic toll taken by his doctrinaire miscalculation continued to inflate long after he was gone. During his time, it set in motion the wartime inflation that monetized the mountain of debt he incurred because of his refusal to limit the liberties of German industry by taxing its war profits. The surge of wartime borrowings, in turn, led to the postwar collapse of the mark. The plight of German workmen pushing wheelbarrows loaded with worthless marks to the grocery store in the rush to convert their wages to potatoes helped to propel Hitler from the beer halls to the battlefields, where he was hailed as a noncombatant hero. It helped to unleash World War II and the nuclear nightmare in which it climaxed.

Hitler's rise from the ruins of the mark guaranteed a grisly confirmation for John Maynard Keynes's first forecast, namely, that the Versailles Treaty, which visited the punishment upon a defeated Germany, was guaranteed to end in a world depression, which, in turn, was guaranteed to start a second European war. Neither Keynes nor anyone else had heard about Hitler when he arrived at this judgment. Moreover, Keynes was still too young and too new at the financial game to have trained his sights in *The Economic Consequences of the Peace*, published in 1919, on the destructive consequences for the currency of a belligerent that monetizes its war debt in order to avoid taxing its people. By the time Keynes published his first book, the backlash from Germany's hyperinflationary method of war finance had not yet destroyed her currency, which did not go up in smoke until 1923. Nor could he have foreseen the destruction of the currency of the victorious power, France, and, six years later in 1931, the weakening of the British pound, the stability of which had symbolized the financial equivalent of the eternal verities. Keynes showed that he knew, however, that any exercise of political power that begins by destabilizing the structure of finance will end by paralyzing the economic mechanism. This is exactly what happened when the postwar reparations exacted from Germany forced the international borrowings that compounded the damage done by the original domestic borrowings that imperial Germany had relied on to pay her staggering war costs.

By the time the Reagan entourage set out to enforce the mandate it thought it had to reinstate the eternal verities of finance, as it saw them, the name of Keynes had come to symbolize fiscal irresponsibility to his conservative constituency. Reagan and his brain trusters shared the misconceptions they popularized. They had no idea that Keynes made his reputation advocating the very principles of free trade for which they stood; that he believed in a gold standard, as they do; that he was a passionate nationalist, as they are; or that it took the calamity of Dunkirk to give him his chance to put his fertile and practical imagination to work bringing British and American war finance under manageable control.

Moreover, the familiar principles Reagan extolled were all embodied in the methods of wartime finance Keynes's disciples inside Roosevelt's war administration had adopted from his thinking: pay-as-you-go taxation, war savings bonds for everyone on payrolls, automatic cash refunds on V-Day, and patriotism (backed up by an excess-profits tax). The package was inflation-proof. It extended the draft of bodies to the draft of money. It passed every test that Helfferich's irresponsible and inflationary method of war finance failed and that Reagan's conservative and nationalistic rhetoric called for. Unlike Helfferich's methods, it did not infest the future with an evil virus; unlike Reagan's, it did not stop the economy it set out to spur. The contrast between Keynes's success as a war financier and Helfferich's failure stems from the fundamental principle of fiscal politics that comes into play the moment winning peace or, as Reagan described the challenge in making the case for his MX missile plan, keeping the peace, claims top priority on the national agenda.

The principle is as simply stated as the concept of the cost-benefit ratio: Any political establishment that adopts a program of arms expenditures without the support of a balancing program of taxation runs the risk of infecting itself with the virulently inflationary German disease of 1914–1923. It carries a corollary compelling enough to defy the popular distaste for the heavy tax burdens that are the only alternative to the inflationary consequences of a major arms buildup (whether launched to fight a war or to avoid one). Any political establishment that undertakes a buildup without taking the precaution of persuading its people to pay for a meaningful portion of it as it is spent will lose its political base. Once it does, it will learn the bitter lesson the Reagan staff did, that a supportive political base is as indispensable to an industrial power in an arms race, let alone in an actual war, as a viable industrial base.

The privilege of rewriting history is a fringe benefit that goes to the brain trusters who take over as spokesmen for any new administration. But they use it at their peril, as often as not revealing more ignorance than attracting awe. The test of their realism comes with the case histories they construct from their view of the past to explain their approach to the future. The chief Reagan brain truster to compile a prospectus for Reaganomics in the 1980s was Jude Wanniski, who had been a major prophet writing editorials for *The Wall Street Journal* before he stepped down to publish *The Way the World Works* in 1978.

Wanniski's reconstitution of the crash of 1929 fixes the blame for the tragedy it set in motion on America's adoption of protectionism, that is, on the Republican party's "betrayal" of free-market principles in 1920. It was not his argument that mattered; it was his simplistic and didactic quasi-official view of how the world had evolved from the 1920s to the 1980s that did. In the first place, Wanniski revealed a monumental ignorance of the history of the Republican party, which was rooted in the protectionist appeal to industry and labor to join together to protect "the full dinner pail"; the Democrats had been stuck with the losing side of the case for free trade until FDR exploited the Hoover depression to counterattack by going protectionist, taking vigorous steps to start a recovery at home instead of waiting for it to start in Europe and spread to America. In the second place, Wanniski's thesis revealed an even more glaring ignorance of the most important cause of the tragedy of the 1930s and, with it, of the repeat performance it threatened in the 1980s: the shock of international bank and currency collapses, which confirmed worldwide market crashes and triggered a global arms race. The blockage of trade flows in 1982 was only a side effect. The fiscal politics of armament was at the root of the tragedy. Wanniski targets greedy old-guard Hoover Republicans as the villains, but they were the dupes who put up the money to subsidize the flawed peace that the hated Keynes foresaw would explode into the next war.

The Reagan administration's performance created an even more embarrassing analogy for Republicans committed to both a balanced budget and a stern military alert against Russia (not that Republicans have a monopoly on either priority). True, the fraud Reagan sold and Stockman bought in the name of strengthening America's war potential was not a carbon copy of the fraud that had begun to sap both America's financial and military strength in Vietnam sixteen years earlier, but it was similar enough. By comparison, the Reagan administration's performance made Johnson's look good—or at least professional. At least when LBJ cut taxes and inflated defense, he knew what he was doing. Where Stockman had pulled off all the stunts in Reagan's hat trick at once, LBJ, characteristically more cautious, had set the precedent by spacing his out. He cut taxes first without any big talk of preparing for war; he pumped up military spending later when he actually went to war in the big way Texans like to do things. The discrepancies in comparing the two exercises in duplicity are details, but the principle is the same: Funneling money into the Pentagon does not go with cutting taxes. Moreover, when the political crunch came, LBJ was more consistent than Reagan; he resisted the pressure for the tax increase that he subsequently accepted. The tragedy a decade and a half later was compounded by the spectacle of Reagan denouncing the Johnson legacy of "big spending," while the cunning of history trapped him into playing the part of Johnson's heir without knowing that he had become entangled in the thread of the plot.

So Reaganomics was a fable. Its strategists misread the past, misjudged the present, and misplayed the future. They failed to appreciate how Keynes, whom they pilloried, put their principles into practice; how Johnson, whom they despised, set the pattern for their deceptions; how Friedman, whom they revered, deluded them with his dogma and distracted them from their problems; how Kissinger, whom they mistrusted, taught them to trust media diplomacy instead of economic strength; or how Stockman, whom they used, outsold the support stratagems dictated by their poll results when he bought them himself as a package. The precedents were embarrassing to the Reaganites, and the results were disastrous for everyone.

For this generation the issue of war and peace has been absorbed into the terrible question of national—or worldwide—suicide by nuclear conflict. Meanwhile, however, conventional wars have come along about as often as during pre-nuclear times. If we can turn a pragmatic gaze on what has been happening and defer for the moment the terrible prospect of nuclear disaster; if we can think—that is, *not* about the unthinkable but about actual warfare during the forty years when nuclear war could have happened but did not—we may derive a few tentative guidelines from past experience for future national confrontations of the conventional kind that have taken place and have changed both the map and the political balance of power. "No taxation without representation" is the slogan that dominated the early history of America. It is a slogan that assumes confrontation between taxpayers and their heads of government in a time of peace. It is logical because our culture still assumes that peace is normal, viewing wartime emergencies as temporary interruptions of the status quo. We have learned through bitter experience that economic weapons swing the tide of battle after it starts, but we cannot bring ourselves to believe that they can be effective in avoiding the test of battle or in making the world safe as it no longer is from any power's missilery, to swing with the American economy, as—like it or not—it does.

"No taxation without representation" is a throwback to a simpler age. The slogan is a syllogism that skips the minor premise implicit in it: that elected representatives would tax their own constituents rarely and frugally. Once the welfare state mushroomed into the arsenal state, taxpayers took fright, with good reason, that their representatives would preach compassion, wrap themselves in the flag, and tax them more mercilessly than despots would even try. The triple trauma of total war, permanent preparation for it, and inflationary impoverishment from it established a corollary to the slogan: "No war—or preparation for it—without taxation," which freely translated means "No war without public participation in the national defense." If any single test stands out in modern history, it is Britain's willingness in 1940 to pay for the privilege of mass participation in the national defense at the water's edge. The presence of Hitler twenty-six miles across the English Channel silenced the familiar grumblings of Britain's Colonel Blimps against the tax burden.

When General William Tecumseh Sherman delivered himself of his memorable maxim, "War is hell," he did not have taxpayers in mind. But war is certainly hell for taxpayers, whether the government drafts their money at the outset of any arms buildup, or resorts to the inflationary subterfuge of sticking them or the banks floating on their deposits with the paper it peddles in lieu of the taxes it shrinks from collecting. The American depression of 1982 provided the clearest demonstration since the days of Kaiser Wilhelm and his impractical finance minister that arms buildups that wink at the taxpayers and exempt them from emergency tax calls end up depriving them of their options as well as their money. It confirmed the warning of Milton Friedman, the prophet the Reaganites honored but did not heed, that inflation is a hidden tax and the one that costs more than taxes that are paid.

Yet Reagan's failure was instructive, all the more so because his polls taught so well. The stern notice they served on him to take the hard line against Soviet power but the soft line with the taxpayers seemed to provide the blueprint that Stockman followed too faithfully for everyone's good, including his own. Yet it concealed a deeper purpose: to undo the bloody lessons of history as well as lethal threats of technology by making war pay. The way to do this in the age of intercontinental missilery is as old and as simple as the injunction in the Old Testament to turn swords into plowshares. Like Christianity, this has never been tried. Devastating though the American depression of 1982 was, ominous though the market boom and subsequent bust were, this biblical injunction recalled the most hopeful saying in Wall Street: Lost money is retrievable; lost options are not.

CHAPTER SEVEN

The Strategy of Defense:
Senator Nunn to the Rescue

THE NUCLEAR BOMB was conceived in sin, and America was the sinner. True, Hitler was the Satan who had tempted her into the experiment; Anglo-American intelligence detected him making the first start. But the Nazi scientists made a wrong turn in their race to perfect a nuclear device before the American scientists scored the first breakthrough. Fathoming the secret of the atom was not America's sin; exploding it over Japanese civilians was, especially after their military leaders had been beaten and America knew it. Justice William O. Douglas told me the day we dropped it that America would rue the day she was tempted to provoke the peoples of Asia to declare her guilty of genocide against them, and he was right.

A generation later, in 1982, three separate threats of nuclear holocaust, none excluding the other two, were whipping up a sense of impotent rage on a mass scale, spreading the nuclear alarm from the study to the streets—and not just in Asia. The first was the obvious danger of a desperate act, escalating a war fought with conventional weapons into a nuclear shoot-out. The second was the possibility that lieutenants pushing buttons might panic lieutenant generals who felt they were at a combat disadvantage into seizing the nuclear initiative. The revelation in the spring of 1982 that a British armada armed with nuclear warheads had steamed to a remote assault on the Falkland Islands, 8,000 miles from command communications centers at home, confirmed this fear. The third threat, stirring up even more frantic insecurity, came in the form of a postscript to George Orwell's novel *1984*, which caricatured the automation of society by its Big Brother, the government. This alert spread the fear that the ultimate guilt might fall on a couple of computers acting as impersonal brains behind the dread decision. The suburban-police-chief mentality bared by presidential counselor Edwin Meese, when he dismissed the antiwar demonstrators in Europe as "extremists," inflamed these necessarily general fears into an acute sense of alarm. So did the revelation that cruise missiles flying too low to be spotted by defensive radar nets, as the Exocet did in the battle for the Falklands, might provoke all three alternatives to materialize at once. And Reagan himself punctuated the confusion even further when he expressed the considered opinion that the U.S. nuclear-freeze movement was the handiwork of undercover Communist apparatchiks. The French have a phrase for comic responses to tragic challenges, and Reagan's simplistic response to the new challenge on the nuclear front called for it: *pas sérieux,* meaning "frivolous."

In the Kremlin, recognition of these three scary scenarios prompted a deadly serious "we told you so." For nearly forty years the Soviet Union had been troubled by the knowledge that the American government had not hesitated once before to go nuclear as a means of avoiding casualties at the hands of a savage combatant already defeated with conventional shot-and-shell. Therefore, Russia concluded, America would not hesitate to adopt the same priority, by stealth, against an enemy target like herself that, far from being defeated, was mounting an increasingly effective challenge on several fronts simultaneously, all of them impossible for American armor to check without enormous casualties. Reconsidered in light of the resentments and suspicions the Kremlin had been nurturing from Stalin's time on against the White House, the motivation behind Russia's step-up of the nuclear race could be seen as ominously sane.

Historically, Russia has been paranoid about encirclement and invasion. This atavistic fear, dating at least from Napoleon's attack early in the nineteenth century, was reinforced by the two bloodbaths she shared with Germany in the twentieth century. After Hitler's failed effort, Russia developed a reasonable sense of confidence that no one would ever launch a surprise invasion against her by land. Hiroshima left her petrified, however, that America might try a nuclear attack by air or sea. These fears, far from being allayed when Russia overcame America's nuclear head start, intensified when Washington greeted the nuclear stalemate as a provocation. From the 1950s through the 1970s, the comfort the Soviets took from the knowledge that they were prepared to fight with conventional weapons and massed manpower was balanced by discomfort over the realization that America was not, and by the sober calculation that America was the innovator of every advance in nuclear weapons technology. In the 1980s, the Kremlin greeted President Reagan's repeated promises to regain American nuclear supremacy as the preliminary to an act of war.

By that time, however, membership in the nuclear club was ready to be expanded by the various Libyas and Argentinas preparing to crash the gate. Israel had taken drastic unilateral measures to disqualify Iraq from membership by knocking out her reactor before it was completed.

Nevertheless, visions among the superpowers of "crazies" playing nuclear war games on their own, free to push buttons instead of fielding disciplined combat troops, were terrifying enough to spur worldwide demonstrations in support of a nuclear freeze. The dawn of an aggressive new movement to prevent nuclear annihilation grew out of the vested interest the two superpowers were developing.

These necessarily scattered and vague stirrings were jolted into urgent focus early in May 1982 by a remarkable initiative taken by Senator Sam Nunn of Georgia. Nunn had emerged as the acknowledged congressional authority in defense matters. Appearing before the Senate Foreign Relations Committee on May 11, Nunn pointed to the danger of a sneak nuclear strike as a common threat giving Russia and America a joint interest in policing the various Third World extremists on the horizon, along with the terrorist groups using their military bases as havens and supply depots. He noted that by 1990 as many as twenty nations would have the capability to employ nuclear weapons, either for their own use or as conduits for terrorists. Reporting on an in-depth probe he had made with the Strategic Air Command in Omaha, Nebraska, Nunn demonstrated that Russia and America are equally unprepared even to detect, let alone to defuse, "the various unconventional delivery systems that could be utilized to explode a nuclear device on U.S. or Soviet soil."

The official purpose of this unusual appearance was to inform Nunn's colleagues on the Foreign Relations Committee that he had introduced an amendment to the fiscal year 1983 Defense Authorization Bill calling for just such U.S.-USSR collaboration. The measure of the urgency Nunn attached to this proposal in his amendment was reflected in its directive to the secretary of defense to prepare a progress report to the Congress by August 1, 1982, and in its further directive to the President to report to the Congress within a month on the relevance of the secretary of defense's report to U.S. arms-control policies and proposals.

By the time of Senator Nunn's appearance before the Foreign Relations Committee, the Senate had already passed his amendment, although the media, thanks to his low-profile method of operating, had not picked up the fact. Before proposing the imaginative move to transform weapons of nuclear confrontation into instruments of nuclear control, Nunn had spoken of his fear that the Reagan arms buildup might invite administrative excesses and abuses of the kind that have plagued too many of the government's social programs adopted in the 1960s. He emphasized his concern that defense programs adopted in an atmosphere of hysteria and exempted from policing as they grew would provoke the same angry backlash and suffer the same discrediting as the social programs that had been conceived in enthusiasm, nurtured with indulgence, and dismantled with righteousness. To make a start on defense-program regulation, Nunn had taken the initiative in

1981 and organized the Military Reform caucus as a bipartisan forum drawn from presumed hawks and doves in both houses. In Nunn's careful restructuring of priorities, the need to defuse the danger of accidental nuclear catastrophe came first, the need to step up advanced conventional weapons capabilities came right behind emergency steps to cool off nuclear war threats, and the need to police all defense spending in order to limit the military's claims on the economy and demonstrate its responsiveness to the claims of public policy finished a very strong third.

The case for vigilance on the part of each superpower against nuclear trigger-happy third-party adversaries sharpened the incentive for both America and Russia to look for practical methods of safeguarding the defensive interest they shared. Nunn's suggestion that the two superpowers might identify a common interest more commanding than their obvious frictions opened up an altogether new trail for Washington to ponder and explore. The upshot of the alarm was scarcely to assure America that she could trust Russia; it was to warn both nuclear superpowers that they could trust no nuclear interlopers to respect their own security. It was also to urge the Reagan administration to free itself from its obsession with nuclear elixirs and to focus on its responsibility to reset its defense priorities.

This sober call was echoed soon thereafter, at the height of the battle of Beirut, by the commanding general of the U.S. Tactical Air Command, W. L. Creech. In an unusual complaint to Pentagon reporters against administration priorities, Creech blamed the presidential priority on the $180 billion nuclear intercontinental missile program for the shortfall in fighter planes, which he put at twenty wings on top of thirty-four in operation. *The New York Times* quoted him on August 7, 1982, as pointing with pride to the deadly use Israel had made of her U.S. fighter planes against the Soviet models flown by the Syrians, yet he admitted in dismay that the conventional forces programmed by the administration were inadequate to fulfill its military commitments.

In Reagan's Washington, talking tough to the Russians guaranteed magic results in the polls. In the Pentagon's Washington, it also guaranteed nuclear overpreparedness and military underpreparedness. Senator Nunn's challenge to Reagan called on the President to sort out the nuclear horses from the military apples in America's arsenal. Tragically, however, posturing for poll ratings blinded Reagan's staff to the basic principle that once a power identifies an enemy and then launches an arms buildup in response to the threat posed by that enemy, its one sure formula for disaster is to ignore the real enemy that then takes over: time. When Reagan strode into the White House, he had been quick to warn the country of the ominous Soviet threat and to advertise America's determination to fall back on the nuclear counterthreat. But Stockman's glibness in following administration orders to cook the books stretched the activation of the next generation of ultimate weapons too far into the future to confirm the claim of emergency in the present. Dawdling in response to an alert will maximize financial insecurity without ensuring physical security, as the Reagan team found out by its second year.

Yet the President's response to the emergency he himself had proclaimed belied its urgency. The directives he broadcast from the White House conjured up visions of gulping down sleeping pills in response to fire alarms. When the economy began its collapse in 1981, he insisted on the need for time to work a long, drawn-out cure. When Russia responded to his nuclear threats in kind, Reagan stretched out the programs, inciting the Soviets to go full speed ahead with their countermeasures on all fronts, from nuclear missiles and military concentrations to provocations by Cuba and other satellites. When the Reagan staff responded to the resistance in the polls to more spending, the White House put the pressure on the Pentagon to step up its export business in order to raise cash to fill out the deficiencies in its programs.

On that same eventful August 7 when the commander of the Tactical Air Command was airing his worries, the front page of *The Washington Post* disclosed that Deputy Defense Secretary Frank Carlucci was ordering the Navy and the Air Force "to help drum up business abroad, not leaving their marketing effort to the manufacturers." The directive Carlucci dispatched to the secretaries of the Navy and the Air Force informed them that "together with the Department of State, we have identified the following . . . as strong candidates for procurement . . . because of a strong combination of threat, abnormality and fiscal resources: Turkey, Egypt, Jordan, Malaysia, Philippines, Thailand, Bahrain [which six weeks later was promised six Northrop Corp. fighters], United Arab Emirates, Oman, and Saudi Arabia." "It is also likely then," Carlucci's memorandum added, "as our post-Falklands policy toward Latin America is clarified, we shall want to promote the FX [fighter plane] selectively in our own hemisphere." Latin America was seething with incendiary post-Falklands nuclear venom when the State and Defense departments delivered themselves of this state paper.

Carlucci revealed a new rationale for the Reagan administration's step-up of its overt tilt and covert thrust against Israel. Israel, by that time, had emerged as America's principal competitor in the arms-export business. She was getting more of it because she was more willing and able to make sales on a barter basis. Having learned to live with inflation, as America had not, the Israelis had every incentive to match every sale they made with a buy-back arrangement from their customer, who, by virtue of being an arms buyer, was busted and therefore able to pay only by shipping what it could not sell for cash. Not entirely irrelevant to Israel's breakthrough as an arms exporter, her sense of urgency had frightened her into perfecting the military technology she had started out importing; while America's trust in spending to buy strength was reflected in the chancy performance of her weapons and, even more, in her condition of unpreparedness. The most telling evidence of the technological proficiency Israel had engineered into her tiny industrial base emerged with the Pentagon's inability to fathom the proprietary improvements Israel had made in her American-made weapons.

The Israelis did not discriminate; they were as effective in besting Russia in the arms-export competition as they were in elbowing America out of her established munitions markets. Russia, smarting under the humiliation visited on her by Israel in Lebanon, was hit with a second blow; Israel sent the Russian weapons she had captured there to Argentina (also a time-honored Pentagon market presence) in exchange for bartered grain. In the process, Israel demonstrated her acquired skill in duplicating Soviet spare parts as well as her zeal in beating Russia's proficient arms peddlers in a market they had just penetrated and were trying to lock up.

Unilateral disarmament was the very last objective Reagan had in mind. The polls would have registered bitter repudiation for him if he had so much as suggested it. Nevertheless, he ended up presiding over a widened arms gap without suspecting that he had. On the contrary, Reagan's guard was down because U.S. military spending, high to begin with, was up. His instinct for misplacing America's priorities suggested that had he been a Polish commander in 1939, when the German panzer divisions started to barrel eastward, he would have starved the horses before sending the cavalry out to intercept the tank corps.

The Reagan administration failed to make the logistical connection between the protective mission it had pledged to send flying to the Middle East, its own lack of wing power to accomplish that mission, and the economy's urgent need for the work required to bring Air Force capabilities into line with its own top-priority foreign policy commitments. This was a simple case of history repeating itself, with no complications about its cunning. Consistently, under presidents of both parties, Washington has economized on defense when the economy has been throttled, only to splurge on it after the economy has moved back into high gear, with inescapable penalties in procurement costs and delivery delays.

As the result of this "stop-start" programming of conventional defense, America has fallen back upon her nuclear arsenal as the military equivalent of convenience foods. Consequently, she entered the 1980s overprepared with weapons she knew she could not use but which Russia believed her to be itching to use. The arsenal that is the most incendiary and also the largest has turned out to be the most useless: the 7,000 American tactical nuclear guns stationed in West Germany. Their potential for overkill was documented abundantly in war games conducted by the American forces in West Germany during the 1970s. In a 1977 report to the Senate Armed Services Committee on these mock passages at arms, Senator Nunn cited an anonymous German general: "During the past eighteen months, NATO has played five war games, and my country has been defended five times and destroyed five times." Not one exercise resulted in the nuclear equivalent of a glove being laid on the enemy, for the simple reason that America's tactical short-range nuclear missiles could not hit the right target; the formidable, disciplined concentration of crack Russian armored troops based in East Germany was therefore safely beyond their range. Kissinger, Carter, and Reagan, whether through ignorance or arrogance, disregarded this official record. The government in Bonn was content to go along with Washington's suppression of it until Weinberger, always the spokesman for Reagan and echoed by him, blurted out the provocation (about fighting a "limited" nuclear war) that strained the ties binding Bonn and Washington. The Reagan administration's inflammatory rhetoric, delivered in the bland tones of a come-on from a mortician, pledged America to fight a prolonged nuclear war against Russia in Europe. Weinberger's gaffe sent shivers down spines in West Germany and precipitated demonstrations by Germans of many points of view and income brackets. It put the Greens into business as an up-and-coming anti-American political force in West Germany. But even they showed no awareness of the war games. While they concentrated on the deployment of Pershing missiles, NATO strategists set to work, however belatedly, on plans to move their four nuclear units eastward, closer to their Red Army targets.

Another conspicuous source of confusion in the department of overpreparedness surrounded the controversy over the MX, the intercontinental nuclear missile projected as the ultimate weapon for the 1990s. The missile was greeted like an unwanted child, and the problem of finding a lodging for it delayed the project more effectively than any nuclear-arms protest could. The trouble started when President Reagan invoked the logic of simplistics to assert that "the U.S. needs the MX to demonstrate our commitment to the Russians," a reminder that a symbol of deterrence is *not* the reality of a stalemate. Weinberger, privy to the President's wishes, had been wrestling for over a year with alternative solutions to the housing quandary, but he belied his reputation as a careful and conservative cost controller by his decision to order the adoption of the new supermissile before finding a nest for it. Even the attempt of the President's closest friend, Senator Paul Laxalt of Nevada, to persuade the governor of the Casino State to accept responsibility for its share of the program was undone by Weinberger's susceptibility to local political pressures in a Reagan state. Lou Cannon, White House correspondent of *The Washington Post*, in his book *Reagan*, charges Weinberger with a glaring failure to follow through in treating a project so intertwined with the nation's and the world's security as if it were a "gut" campaign promise. First the secretary made headlines promising to deliver on it, and then, according to Cannon, he dumped it on a nondescript committee, which buried it. Cannon goes on to attack Weinberger for having vacillated to the point of stacking this committee with a motley crew that "encompassed so many different views it would have difficulty reaching any decision," which was in fact a problem for the secretary himself.

A secretary of defense capable of rushing into a decade-long commitment to produce an ultimate weapon without simultaneously arranging for the support commitments needed to launch and protect it winds up making the emperor with no clothes look like the best-dressed man of the year. Weinberger's ineffectual house hunting for the MX enriched the annals of defense planning with two classic lessons in how not to go about it. The first was a reminder not to arouse an enemy— especially an enemy afflicted with paranoia and armed with retaliatory weapons—with fiery threats to go nuclear against its domestic defenses from remote launching pads and then to slow down the actual start-up. The second was a warning not to begin any part of a provocative program without thinking it through from the very beginning. If funding all the financial requirements of a large-scale defense program is crucial to its success, blueprinting all its physical requirements is vital to its usability.

Meanwhile, back in the world of the Pentagon budget, the share preempted by payroll costs at one end of the budgetary spectrum combined with nuclear costs at the other was leaving less and less for the procurement of usable munitions. Even though the total defense budget continued to grow yearly, its allocations for military end products did not. The annual increases were regularly diverted from munitions to overhead. During the Korean War, LBJ had used his special subcommittee for investigating the wartime practices of the Pentagon to criticize what he branded its "chair corps," meaning its bumper crop of deskside generals. Before that, during World War II, the Russians had managed with a ratio of only four support troops behind each soldier freed for combat, while America had frozen as many as fourteen behind the lines (not counting generals). By the same token, America's allocation of human resources guaranteed excessive waste of financial resources.

By fiscal 1982, the total of manpower, much of it too unskilled to be used, and of nuclear systems, all of them too destructive to be used, was devouring 75 percent of America's defense budget. This imbalance distorted calculations of relative defense strength and future defense commitments. It confused any standard by which a realistic measurement could be made of the operative force available to the two superpowers relative to weapons or potential theaters of war. Worse, it switched the unit of comparative strength from weapons to money, counting combat readiness in dollars and rubles spent.

This method of calculation led American defense planners to muddle the requirements of security by practicing their own brand of conventional economics, offering a yardstick based on comparisons of the gross national product (GNP) that the two superpowers allocate for defense. The devotees of this monetary defense yardstick, moreover, ended up adding more heat than light to the ongoing controversy over what could be afforded for defense, what defense needs might be, and, above all, how the costs of defense could be financed without paralyzing each country's ability to pay for everything else it needed—beginning with health, education, and transportation in America's case, and with food and technology in Russia's. Matching GNPs is both simplistic and impractical, as it lures soldiers into playing at economics and economists into playing soldiers, risky business for both trades. In terms of the governing practicalities, America's GNP structure overstates money flows, while Russia's, with its emphasis on end products, understates work done to earn new entitlements, like food and shelter, paid for in kind. In America's national accounts, a pound of steel produced for tennis rackets is equated with a pound of steel fashioned into a machine tool. In Russia's national accounts, bushels of wheat routinely laid out on paved roads to dry in the sun after harvesting count for nothing positive, spoiled grain for nothing negative, and such roads as are paved show no by-product national income from crop processing, as they would in America. Americans have made a national pastime of sneering at the Soviet economy and bragging about their own without realizing that the joke may be on them, for the simple reason that the Soviet economy has so far proved adequate to support the Soviet military in the fashion to which it has become accustomed. The American economy, in sharp contrast, has found its recent growth through supplying services to support life-styles America now finds hard to afford, but has decayed as a producer of basic goods. Where the British had boasted in their day that the roots of their empire could be found on the playing fields of Eton, Americans were risking the discovery that they had dissipated their competitive drive on the ski slopes of Vail.

On her side of the "equation," Russia finances defense by preempting assets from her satellites and from less-favored sectors of her own economy. The Soviet defense planners, while subjecting their economy to harsh dislocations, are not saddled with the interest-rate burdens that plague their American counterparts. Interest charges are not a serious cost factor for Soviet accounting purposes; neither is insurance or depreciation. America's interest-rate structure, by contrast, not only distorts the comparison of defense GNP ratios but also inflates America's defense costs at a double-digit level. In any drawn-out period of double-digit interest rates, those costs bleed America but do not bother Russia.

On the American side of the calculation, the escalation in interest rates poses a qualitative policy problem, not merely a quantitative cost problem: whether America could stop wasting time programming her defense until she first rolled back her interest rates to manageable levels. Double-digit interest rates are seen as an obstacle to economic recovery, but they are not recognized as a perilous cost to defense programming.

Another endemic problem for the military has grown out of the disparities in American society, which have directed the unskilled, who face massive permanent unemployment, into the armed forces in search of training for skills and a regular pay check. Most arrive as products of inadequate schooling. The demand that any military machine also serve as a national apprenticeship program is bound to strain its efficiency severely, and this is doubly true for an army that suffered the bloody muddle of Vietnam only to survive into peacetime indifference. Wellington won Waterloo with troops that he regarded—surely unjustly—as being "the scum of the earth." He did not, however, have to teach them to handle high-tech equipment. No doubt with training they could have done it. The task—and it is equivalent to what any efficient army faces today—of training a corps of mechanics and a battle force of fighters at the same time is, to say the least, demanding. But the Pentagon's provisions for maintenance of complicated equipment have been reduced to the preparation of bilingual comic books. There's a general rule that the state of a country's military establishment reflects the maturity of its social motivation and the diligence of its work force. This maxim was tested and confirmed for America when Carter and National Security Adviser Zbigniew Brzezinski reenacted their fatal Iranian-desert version of Kennedy's Bay of Pigs caper. The spectacle of assault helicopters grounded, choking on dust, while scrambled intercontinental phones guaranteed instant coded briefing to the Situation Room in the White House, conjured up visions of American freeways jammed with stranded cars, their hoods up, awaiting rescue by tow trucks outfitted with crackling two-way radios. America was in the position of a run-down, half-paralyzed industrial dinosaur relying on advanced military automation for security and, therefore, increasingly dependent on a crack repair corps that was, unfortunately, out to lunch.

The battle for the Falklands in 1982 provided another reminder that the fighting caliber of a country's military holds the mirror up to the technical maturity of its work force. Argentina's troops, many of them teenage conscripts, were down to the standards of her technology; commanders kept them in the trenches by shooting them in the foot. Argentina fired torpedoes that hit British aircraft carriers without exploding.

The battle of Beirut, on the other hand, provides positive proof of this military maxim. Israel decisively established herself as a super-power in her 1982 invasion of West Beirut precisely because her troops showed themselves to be up to the standards of her military technology. The sophistication she revealed in Lebanon and across her Syrian border also testified to the disciplined fighting quality that her conventional ground forces retained. Israel's forces were automated, as America wanted hers to be. They were also still up to the rigors of combat, as America was no longer sure hers were.

While Israel was parading the advanced state of her military preparedness in Lebanon, the trial run there simultaneously revealed that the Red Army, far from being manned by supersoldiers fourteen feet tall, suffered from problems of underpreparedness comparable to those plaguing America's volunteer army. Of course, Russia had no immediate stake in the battle of Beirut, but she certainly took years to design, to tool up for, and to activate the high-tech surface-to-air missiles (SAMs) that she had installed on Syria's Lebanese border as cover for the Palestine Liberation Organization (PLO). Yet it took Israel only minutes to expose the high-cost underpreparedness the Kremlin had locked itself into; that was all the time Israel needed for one pilotless plane, representing an advance on American technology sold to Israel, to blind a SAM's brain. To leave no doubt that she had planned it that way, or of her methodical commitment to finish any military undertaking she launches, Israel followed through by repeating the exercise in reverse; one of her SAMs took the same few minutes to dispose of an advance Soviet MiG fighter flying over Lebanon.

Russia's position as a superpower is of course much more complicated than Israel's. She deserves the label by her dedicated commitment to achieving and maintaining the status, and she has the wherewithal to put behind her effort. But she pays for the superiority of her conventional forces by diverting skills en masse from her economy, which needs them, to the sterility of the drill ground and the barracks room. In addition, she is burdened by the same top-heavy nuclear overpreparedness as America. She brings a smaller, less-advanced economy to the arms race than does America and taxes it with heavier drains for armaments. Her determination to load her narrow industrial base with a massive military superstructure and to divert to it her scarcest skilled cadres of manpower has placed her in a state of underpreparedness despite the priority she has put on preparedness. The trial run Russia made against Afghanistan was her Bay of Pigs, her Vietnam. When she got bogged down there, all the rifts in her economic society were bared, as they always are under combat conditions. Yet Russia's frustration over the lethargy of her campaign in Afghanistan was mild compared to her shock over the destruction of her missiles in Lebanon. Under cover of PLO complaints against Moscow for not having rushed reinforcements to its rescue in Beirut, a full colonel general of the Red Army jetted to the debris in a matter of hours to inspect the shattered remnants of his prize SAMs.

Once unveiled, evidence of underpreparedness in the conventional forces of any power at war—or fear of it—is likely to unleash hysteria. An early American fighting slogan was "Millions for defense, but not one cent for tribute." The millions that were needed to ensure the infant republic's physical security were as hard to provide as trillions have since become. Moreover, whenever any power comes under attack (as America did at Pearl Harbor), it comes under pressure to reach for every weapon in sight to accomplish every purpose within reach and to chase after many purposes out of reach. But the moment every purpose and every program seem to command a priority, no purpose and no program do. When World War II, and later the Korean War, plunged America into her siege of "priorities inflation," as I called it in *The Struggle for Survival,* she suffered fever flashes of "all-at-once-itis." Everyone entitled to priorities—the military and its contractors alike— exercised claims for them strenuously enough to interfere with everyone's ability to get on with the job of fighting the war. Early in World War II, when the Army, which still had the budding Air Force under its wing, preempted claims amounting to four times the steel capacity of the United States, the redoubtable Mayor Edward J. ("Boss") Kelly of Chicago asked me to help him persuade the War Production Board to let him have ten tons of steel for rudimentary sanitation needs. General David Jones showed himself to be well aware of this problem forty years later in an interview with the media on the eve of his retirement as head of the Joint Chiefs of Staff in June 1982. He reminded them that military commanders "are in the business of priority making." With three wars blazing at once (Iran/Iraq, Israel/PLO, and Britain/Argentina), and America warding off political fallout from all three, the real news in the middle of 1982 was that this laconic and pragmatic reminder from the senior military chief with the longest tenure still made news.

After two years of turning the country upside down by the wholesale transfer of resources from bona fide social claims to military gestures, scaring clients and quarries around the world out of their wits with unfulfillable promises and threats to export the Alamo whenever the Kremlin was ready for it, Reagan had yet to demonstrate any real grasp of the business of priority making, which is the central and serious task of the Commander in Chief. Nor had the polls extended their job rating to this question, although it has again and again become the overriding issue in the reelection campaigns of presidents whose first terms had been dominated by domestic issues. No circus like it had been seen in Washington since FDR's blowhard secretary of the navy, Frank Knox, who had run for vice president on the ill-fated Landon ticket in 1936 and whom Roosevelt had appointed as a gesture of bipartisanship, made nationwide headlines with an article proclaiming that "America Can Win on Both Oceans." Knox's timing was more conspicuous than his priority making. Pearl Harbor followed in a week.

CHAPTER EIGHT

The Priorities of Strategy: What Admiral Gorshkov Learned from Admiral Mahan

"PRIORITY MAKING" was America's classic contribution to military thinking at the turn of the twentieth century, when she first turned her energies and sensitivities outward. The service rendered by the supreme strategic naval thinker of the era of boiler-powered steel vessels, Admiral Alfred Thayer Mahan, in formulating his famous standard of priority making, had been the preeminently practical strategy of avoiding "all-at-once-itis" and the excessive strains it places on national resources, which by definition are always limited at the moment the alarm sounds, when time is of the essence.

Mahan was hardly a lone ranger, as so many seminal thinkers are. His base was the Naval War College at Newport, Rhode Island, where he was sought out in 1897 by that bustling, ambitious assistant secretary of the navy on the make, the first Roosevelt to become president. Admiral Mahan—or Captain Mahan, as he preferred to be called, since he was still a captain when his writing established his reputation—put forward a very simple thesis. It stated that sea power applied around the world at key commercial "choke points" invited the nation that controlled the seas to stage a cheap and profitable triple play: to extend commercial interests, to minimize military burdens, and to consolidate international political power. The moral of "Mahanism," applied to either winning or avoiding war, is that a naval power could gain more, while risking less, than a land power. By way of analogy, the Japanese invented jujitsu as a technique for exerting leverage in hand-to-hand combat; Mahan showed countries how to use the choke-point tactic to guarantee their physical security without jeopardizing their financial security or condemning their manpower to mass slaughter. When Britannia ruled the waves, England employed the same principles to improve her financial position without weakening her defenses. He took her strategy as his model.

The Influence of Sea Power upon History was the title of Mahan's masterpiece. The power struggle in world history that he cited most effectively was the achievement of Britain (sneered at by Napoleon as "a nation of shopkeepers") in standing off the French emperor's armies and relying on her navy to tighten the noose around France's land-based empire. He credited Britain with tailoring a military priority to her national strength, which was economic, and a striking force to her military power, which was naval.

Mahan's thinking made an indelible impression upon the chapter of history dominated by America's emergence as a world power. The accident of politics that landed Theodore Roosevelt at the Navy Department under a do-nothing president and a doddering absentee secretary, rather than at the War Department under a disciplined functioning administration with a mind of its own, changed the course of history when he enlisted his energies behind Mahan's theories. The eruption of long, bloody continental land wars after Mahan's time has blurred memories of his work, as did the rise of air power. Americans have forgotten Mahan and the contribution his sea-power thesis made to strategic planning inside the United States, much less around the world. To the extent that his name still turns up in academic and journalistic use or in biographies of TR, citations are mainly in an historical context, and, as a matter of fact, his own exercises in historical application lose relevance because they hark back to the days of sailing vessels and, indeed, war galleys moved by oar.

The Soviet high command, however, which could not be more missile- or air-minded, has not forgotten the lessons taught by this pioneering American strategist. On the contrary, Russia adopted Mahanism as a strategic text. She promoted a Kremlin hierarch steeped in Mahanist as well as Marxist doctrine, Admiral Sergei Gorshkov, and charged him with the mission of factoring Mahan's concepts of sea power into the strategy of the world's largest land power. Gorshkov has followed Mahan's blueprint for leveraging power as faithfully as Mahan himself followed Britain's when she ruled the waves. Gorshkov has shown himself to be the most farsighted of the world's ranking commanders, more of a practicing Mahanist than a practicing Marxist, and apparently the most forceful at the bargaining table with his own political leaders. On the eve of Israel's invasion of Lebanon, in a wide-ranging discussion with a retired Israeli foreign service officer whom I have always regarded as one of his country's principal intelligence gatherers, I brought up Gorshkov as a figure to be reckoned with in the imminent struggle for control of the Middle East. My Israeli visitor, who had been ambassador to a major European naval power, immediately replied that during his ambassadorial duty in the 1960s, his country's chief naval officer had alerted him to Gorshkov as the coming man in the Soviet High Command and, for that matter, on the world's military horizon.

On the basis of Gorshkov's work, Russia has systematically diversified her application of Mahan's strategy. She activated it without firing a shot during the Korean War. She perfected it, again without firing a shot, during the Vietnam War. She has since put it to work by deploying her floating fortresses in the world's strategic choke points—the Persian Gulf, the Baltic, and the Caribbean. She has targeted the Caribbean as the most promising choke point on which to concentrate on the general principle that it pays to dangle military bait in the home waters of main adversaries, and, specifically, in order to exploit the insensitivity of America's policy makers to the historical and strategic importance of the southern waters into which the Caribbean leads.

War is always thought of as a test of discipline in some spartan sense but rarely as a test of intellectual discipline. Two points are relevant in considering the Soviet breakthrough into South American waters. The first reflects the depth and breadth of the intellectual discipline behind the Soviet achievement. In 1850, just two years after the discovery of gold in California magnetized the westward flow of people and production toward the southwest coast of the North American mainland, Karl Marx set down a prophetic note:

> What Tyre, Carthage and Alexandria were for the Old World, what Genoa and Venice were in the Middle Ages, what London and Liverpool were until now—the emporiums of world trade—that New York and San Francisco, San Juan de Nicaragua and Leon, Chagres and Panama are about to become. The gravitational center of world commerce . . . is now to be found in the southern half of the North American continent.

Marx anticipated Mahan by fifty years, and Gorshkov put the thinking of both of them into the operation he launched at the Caribbean choke point commanding the South Atlantic.

The second point testifies to the arrogance and the superficiality of the intellectual discipline displayed on the American side of the confrontation in the late 1960s and early 1970s, just when Admiral Gorshkov was setting the sights of his squadrons on the sea lanes of the South Atlantic. No one outside the Kremlin power structure had yet heard of Gorshkov; Henry Kissinger, however, was the toast of the cocktail circuit everywhere. The following glimpse of Kissinger explains why, with Nixon behind him and the Kremlin confronting him, he failed; he was intellectually unprepared to do battle against Marxism or to grasp Mahanism. Kissinger's interlocutor in the following dialogue was Gabriel Valdés, the foreign minister of Chile in the government whose demise the Nixon administration welcomed with much rejoicing. The source of it is Seymour Hersh, the former investigative reporter for *The New York Times* who nosed out the scent of Watergate before Woodward and Bernstein appropriated it for *The Washington Post.* Writing in the December 1982 issue of *The Atlantic,* Hersh cited Valdés's participation in a delegation of senior Latin American officials to Washington to confer with President Nixon. His call on Kissinger followed an angry interchange with Nixon. This extract isolates the serious issue from the merely shocking scandal rising out of the debacle in Santiago.

> KISSINGER: Mr. Minister, you made a very strange speech. You come here speaking of Latin America, but this is not important. Nothing important can come from the South. History has never been produced in the South. The axis of history starts in Moscow, goes to Bonn, crosses over to Washington, and then goes to Tokyo. What happens in the South is of no importance. You're wasting your time.
> VALDÉS: Mr. Kissinger, you know nothing of the South.
> KISSINGER: No, and I don't care.

Kissinger's sweeping, cavalier dismissal of the South revealed no awareness of the Mediterranean, Israel, or South Africa, all commanding access to the Cape route—a southern route!—for oil traffic from the Persian Gulf to the industrial West. Yet this strategic consideration was the presumed rationale for Kissinger's appeasement of OPEC. Even if we make charitable allowance for Kissinger's possible nervousness about being blamed by Nixon for inviting unwelcome visitors to the White House, this outburst, tainted by half-baked geopolitical quackery, suggests that Kissinger was as close to Prince Metternich on the discarded calendar of history as he himself boasted he was on the redrawn intellectual map of politics; too far back in political time and too far to the right in political space to matter. But Metternich at least held on to power. He dominated Europe the better part of half a century before Marxism was seen as a serious bid to take over, and the better part of a full century before Mahan, the strategist, applied Marx's thinking on maritime power to the global challenges confronting American power in the twentieth century. The striking parallel between Marx's world view and Mahan's is a stern reminder that the processes of power are as nonpartisan as the tables of arithmetic, and that wars are won by the warriors with the most formidable intellectual arsenals, more often than not in the quiet of the study rather than in the carnage of combat.

Bred on Marx's dynamic vision of history animating geography, and borrowing Mahan's equally forceful grasp of geography inviting naval powers to make history, Gorshkov has expanded Russia's triple pincer play by diverting America from bringing economic strength to bear against her. She has lured the United States into going military in the literal sense of overland warfare, not against the Soviet Union herself but against targets the Kremlin has dangled before her—originally Korea and Vietnam, but subsequently Cuba, Central America, and the Middle East. She spiced up her servings when she added Iran to the list. Her strategy has been tailored to the deterioration of Iran's power position and the corresponding buildup of Iran's nuisance value. First, the Kremlin put enough troops on display on its Iranian borders to invite the shah, armed by America, to pose as the militant and fearless defender of the West. Then, under cover of Khomeini's revolution, Moscow shifted its commitments of money and manpower to the factional free-for-all inside the mullah regime, staking out a base of political power among the students, beginning with those who pulled off the raid on the American embassy, and buying one among the most mercenary mullahs. With this background of feint and infiltration, the Kremlin bought itself a flexible option on the rights to any post-Khomeini bidding contest. The fact that his shortening life expectancy coincided with the oil-pricing debacle gave the option a dynamic potential.

The Khomeini regime emerged as the most aggressive oil-price cutter; the lower the price, the greater the pressure on the mullahs to mount a strike against one of the sheikdoms. Such a scenario would suit the Kremlin's crisis managers just fine. Never mind the incidental fact that the domestic American economy has no direct dependence on Persian Gulf oil. The echo of the first rocket striking the first palace in a sheikdom, with Moscow apparatchiks leading the charge, is guaranteed to blow the whistle in Washington, while Gorshkov's huge strike force runs through its training exercises outside the combat zone.

Diverse as the countries on Moscow's list of appetizers are, all of them—from Oman and Saudi Arabia to Nicaragua and around to Cambodia—share one characteristic: They are nothing but combat theaters, and dead-end ones at that. Unlike Russia herself, these areas have little to offer the U.S. economy, either as buyers or sellers. All of them desperately need access to U.S. resources, but America has no vital dependence on any of them—certainly not with the myth of the oil shortage fading. All of them are calculated to distract America's strategic planners from Mahan's concept of the choke point, which, far from being made obsolete by the advent of air power, has gained in importance. This is also true for the space race, as we shall see.

History offers many sad examples of countries exporting arms and becoming targets of their own weapons after their customers have turned into their enemies. To take the most familiar and obviously uncomfortable one, America suffered a bloody awakening at Pearl Harbor when tons of scrap iron and steel, bought in the United States and processed by American machine tools supplied to Japanese industry, rained down on the U.S. fleet and its base there. A generation later, Britain suffered the same rude awakening at the hands of Argentina, when her most modern destroyer went down under the impact of even more modern missiles that she herself had sold to the Argentines. In 1981, however, the United States took a particularly bitter blow in the realm of strategic planning when she woke up to discover that the doctrines conceived by her most formidable naval strategist had been adopted and implemented as a weapon of Russian imperialism by a Kremlin disciple of that strategist. The shock was more than a humiliating loss of face. It registered the painful difference between the overriding determination of the Russian military to do its homework and to capitalize on its insights and America's complacent dilettantism, demonstrated by her inattention to history and her self-indulgent disregard of the discipline demanded by the revolution in military technology.

After a full generation of cold war and repeated dissipation of American military power in frustrated attacks upon Soviet satellites that offered no relevant rewards, Reagan and his advisers were still failing in their third year to distinguish the country's fears of Soviet military power and her long-term antagonism toward Marxist ideology from the administration's facile dismissal of Russian economic stratagems. Given Russia's economic weaknesses and America's economic strengths, any Soviet challenge to America in the marketplace seems ludicrous. But the United States has been distracted by concentration on the politics of confrontation into a state of paranoid premonition; fear of Soviet weaponry has inhibited incentives to pursue the economics of confrontation. Americans have never been encouraged to ask rudimentary questions about comparative strength in other areas. A very relevant one indeed runs as follows: How would Russia have used the opportunity to squeeze America if she commanded an economic apparatus that matched her formidable military operation?

Indeed, Moscow has been suggesting its own answer to this question before it has been posed. Soviet strategists have already adapted their ingenious new version of Mahanism to the economic counteroffensive they mounted against Reagan's declaration of political warfare. They hit not just on the two fronts close to their home base, the individual export-dependent, oil-short economies of Western Europe and the oil-export-dependent economies of the Middle East. In addition, they landed a third blow on the American economy at its strongest point, its machinery-export-dependent sector. The Kremlin's recourse to economic weaponry certainly did not represent a moderation of its aggressive intent. The shift expressed a stepped-up resolve to probe, to press, and to penetrate Free World defenses, while conserving Russian military superiority and baiting America to divert still more of her economic superiority into increasingly dubious speculations on military force aimed at peripheral "no-win" targets.

The Soviets unveiled their new exercise in political economics mobilized for economic warfare on September 20, 1981. That was the day the USSR and Ruhrgas A.G., the major West German gas company, struck their deal to construct a pipeline to deliver natural gas from northwestern Siberia to Western Europe. The agreement represented a ten-year, $15 billion "gas-for-pipeline" barter. It was a sweetheart deal for Germany, guaranteeing her 30 percent of her total gas needs but obligating her for only 5.5 percent of her energy bill—a cheap price to pay for all the employment it promised to provide. As one European commentator explained, "Better a 5.5 percent dependence on Moscow than a 6 percent dependence on [Muammar] Qaddafi." At least Russia had an insatiable appetite for industrial products costing her no cash; Libya had none.

West Germany and the other participants in the pipeline's financing —Italy, France, the Netherlands, Belgium, Austria, and the United Kingdom—put their own economic interests above warnings about Washington's displeasure at the political embarrassment to America of any East-West rapprochement. The Germans took the lead in financing the pipeline. The French followed, undeterred by vigorous objections from then Secretary of State Alexander Haig, who hesitated to express them to the German government, while the other members of the European consortium made their own arrangements for access to Siberian gas. Meanwhile, the White House's poll readings suggested that East-West economic détente did not fit well with a Reagan declaration of cold war, and the President publicly passed on that message to America's European allies. The result was a prompt lesson from Prime Minister Margaret Thatcher on the relative value of past favors when weighed against immediate national self-interest. Her way of thanking Reagan for his decisive support in Britain's high-risk expedition in the Falklands was to lecture him about the ethics of his attempt to interfere with the sanctity of the contracts signed by British suppliers to the pipeline, especially in an atmosphere of double-digit unemployment.

If the Reagan entourage had been more inclined to books than to bridge, its members might have taken solace in falling back upon Byron's bitter denunciation of Perfidious Albion. But neither poetry nor ideological commitments to free enterprise were in a position to win debating points. England lined up with Europe against America even though the Reagan administration had abandoned the far-reaching commitments it had made to Argentina to bolster its high-priority, high-risk military aims in the Caribbean. At that point, Reagan met himself coming and going, with no easy way to explain how he proposed to reconcile his imposition of sanctions against America's NATO allies with his dedication to free enterprise. When Reagan later made amends to Argentina by granting her an export license for an electronic brain to activate her budding nuclear capability, England, like the queen who ruled over her when she still ruled the waves, was not amused.

Consummation of the deal by the West Germans came at a time when they had much to gain from such an exchange of resources and only the American connection to lose. At the end of 1981, West Germany was hungry not only for lower fuel costs but for capital-goods exports and domestic jobs as well, as the bankruptcy of AEG Telefunken demonstrated just as the project was getting started. The barter deal with Russia guaranteed all three on a massive scale, and did so quickly enough to provide insurance against dangers of a cutoff of

Middle Eastern oil. It also secured a commercial and a political advantage for Russia if she gave her blessing to disruptions in the Middle East, which would threaten those oil flows and increase European dependence on Siberian gas flows. As an immediate by-product, the deal offered West Germany's equally depressed industrial competitors in the European Economic Community (EEC) a reward in cartelized export prices and terms, which suited them better than did flying blindly into the normally competitive but then shrinking American market. Every European supplier to the expanding Russian market felt it could be sure of knowing in advance how the market would be shared, how much of it would go to whom, and what the price would be. This cozy cartel arrangement left all of them feeling more comfortable doing business with Russia than swallowing rhetoric from America, which they blamed for getting them into their depression. They looked to Russia to help them live with it.

Yet even before the West Germans entered into this agreement, they had prepared themselves for the danger of any reduction in supplies of crude oil from the OPEC cartel and had protected themselves from the threat of a total cutoff. The EEC countries, after all, could draw on domestic oil and gas reserves of their own as a fallback defense; oil from the United Kingdom and Norway, gas from the Netherlands and, marginally, from West Germany. With their sophisticated mastery of energy-conversion techniques—specifically, for changing plant facilities from refined liquid petroleum to natural gas and back again—the West Germans had routinely reserved natural gas for use in heavy industries able to switch to other forms of energy on short notice.

The managers of the energy power center based in Rotterdam and The Hague, which is an adjunct of the economic and financial center based in Frankfurt, are uniquely qualified to certify the versatility and virtuosity of West European energy engineering. Their opposite numbers in Johannesburg are in a position to serve as expert witnesses, as Melinda Rothel and I saw for ourselves in our visit to the South African coal fields (where the country's fuel-conversion refineries are based) in the summer of 1979. Thanks to Dutch technology, South Africa had equipped herself to mass-produce high-powered motor fuel directly from coal in her SASOL facility without needing to stop along the way to get crude oil as an intermediate product. American technology made a contribution, too, through Fluor Corp.—though the only benefit the American economy got out of it was an export order.

At that point, it should be noted, the technical chiefs of the American oil industry were upholding received dogmas as devotedly as any fourteenth-century theologian. The idea of getting motor fuel from natural gas or from refinery waste gases (at minimal cost relative to investment in new facilities) was, they declared, contrary to both the laws of nature and to the workings of free markets. The famous Yankee ingenuity of the past seemed to have been transformed into an American way that assured American industry's blundering through the climactic phase of the sleight-of-hand oil shortage, while proclaiming the progressivism of business-as-usual and marching to the orders of government-as-usual. Major oil companies wasted their stockholders' money advertising admonitions to consumers to conserve the country's supposedly depleting energy assets, while ignoring the waste of crude they themselves were tolerating in their own refineries. They vehemently denied the feasibility of recovering the prodigious drain of these gases from their refineries for recycling into new supplies of motor fuel.

To West Germany and her EEC partners, the obvious incentive to go forward with this large-scale, long-term arrangement to tie their industries into Russia's remote new gas field was economic. The implied side benefit of buying a decade of political accommodation with Russia, however attractive, seemed incidental at the outset. Though it appeared that Russia was selling peace plus insurance against depression and that Western Europe was buying the package as a fair trade, the political reality brought a bonus to Russia that the Kremlin had not really contemplated. With no risk on her part, with no cost, and with a double profit from the development and sale of her gas reserves, Russia's presence at the other end of the pipeline provoked Reagan to play an even harder game against his NATO allies than he had promised. The Kremlin had hoped that the pipeline would build a new economic bridge to Western Europe. Not only did it do so, it demolished the political bridge that had linked Western Europe to Washington.

Russia's domestic economy had been bottlenecked for lack of steel products as well as the machinery and skills needed for such a gigantic and exacting project; financing industrialization through barter had been her problem for over a decade. The West German connection was guaranteed to provide for all of these needs without diverting Russia's capacities from her overriding priority to maintain her armament industries. Russia's partnership with European capitalism will relieve the external and internal strains visibly hampering her economy and will enable her to project the fulfillment at long last of a five-year plan. The fact that the pipeline partnership happened to be a ten-year plan made it twice as valuable; it freed Russia to project plans even further ahead instead of just talking about her intention to do so.

But the combined strategic and economic benefits to Russia from the pipeline are by no means limited to the European front. This is where the shrewd and far-ranging thrust of a Russified global version of Mahanist theory comes in. The pipeline frees Russia to use her new Middle Eastern navy to turn off, turn down, destroy altogether, or take over the oil fields in the Persian Gulf area—and still leave Russia with a fuel supply adequate for her own needs and for rationing to a Europe that is sophisticated enough in using gas to cut back on oil use. By the same token, the project gives Moscow the leverage to deal with the sheiks from strength without resorting either to the expensive, elaborate, and, in the end, embarrassing approach of showing her hand militarily, which served her so poorly in Egypt, or to the messy paramilitary methods of the KGB, which President Yuri Andropov was more than familiar with but compelled to avoid on the eve of his elevation to power and, certainly, during the honeymoon that followed. In short, the economic offensive the Kremlin used to mount the pipeline in Western Europe fit hand-in-glove with the menacing naval posture Gorshkov equipped Russia to assume at South Yemen and with the political offensive she was mounting throughout the entire Moslem world. It was an intricate pincer play brought to bear on the sheiks, a perfect formula for blackmail.

The moment Russia opened Europe up to her gas and, therefore, put herself in a position to show the sheiks that an oil cutoff would not work, she freed herself to project her lines of force into the Caribbean. Cuba had been her first conquest in Western waters; she did not regard it as an isolated breakthrough or as an exposed forward base. From the day the Russians held their ground there against John Kennedy's effort to take it back in 1962, they had been consolidating Cuba into their worldwide system and aiming it at one carefully selected target: the narrow Straits of Florida, through which Venezuelan oil passes on its way to American waters. If a shooting match were to break out, interdicting the northern flow of Venezuelan oil, America would have another Vietnam on her hands—this time in her own backyard—and Russia would run no more risk than she did in Korea, in Vietnam, or in Iran/Iraq.

Finally, the strategy suggested that Russia would play another winning hand in the Sea of Japan by taking advantage of the depression that had hit Japan's mammoth tanker-building industry to offer her a waterborne gas deal that, like Germany, she could not refuse. Where Western Europe has some natural gas, Japan has none. But she does have the capacity and the need to go all-out for natural gas imports, liquefied or not. Russia's offer, which soon materialized, offered Japan the opportunity to turn her problem of finding demand for her heavy industries into a self-financing (because bartered) solution to her built-in energy-supply problem. It took the form of a Soviet-Japanese oil-gas development project on Sakhalin Island, supported by proprietary U.S. technology, for constructing ice-resistant deep-sea drilling rigs. The deal was announced without a peep of protest from Washington and under cover of bold, brave promises by Japan's dynamic new prime minister to seal off the Straits of Japan from the Soviet navy while peddling a brand-new shopping list of high-tech armament to the Pentagon. Japan's hand was strengthened in this game by Alaska's acute need to find a Far Eastern natural gas market since domestic outlets are still mysteriously but stubbornly denied the Alaskan producers. Japan can always use imported energy materials, and she always needs to chase after customers for her shipyards. Japan's skill in turning her energy and shipbuilding liabilities into corresponding assets confirms the age-old adage that "necessity is the mother of invention."

The background of the Russian-European pipeline is worth a glance. It is no new brainwave but a proposition that has been peddled for a decade. Ironically, it was offered to America first, when the mutterings of OPEC still sounded like empty slogans. Though Russia was not one of the cartel's members, she certainly had open lines of communication with many of them, and she had every incentive to encourage all of them. Planned or otherwise, one good turn always deserves another. The pipeline project gave Russia a simple, controllable way to use OPEC's price push in order to cash in her own gas reserves. When she broached the proposition to the Nixon administration in 1974, money was still relatively cheap; oil no longer was. Nevertheless, she demanded an incentive interest rate offered by the Export-Import Bank. The Nixon administration was tempted to buy Moscow's goodwill by going along with it; Secretary of the Treasury John Connally's objections were brushed off as hawkish Texas provincialism. But the project hit a snag in Congress in response to the complaint that money and technology were the two remaining proprietary assets that America had not managed to give away and that this was no time to start.

Senator Harry F. Byrd, Jr. of Virginia was chairman of the Senate Finance Committee's subcommittee on international trade, when he called to ask my opinion on the advisability of the deal. I told him that it showed Russia had enough nerve to justify changing her national mascot from a bear to a brass monkey, but I argued against the prudence or need to reject the proposal out of hand. Instead, I suggested going along with it on a "yes, but" basis aimed at developing bargaining leverage against her in return for locking her into long-term dependence on American engineering for follow-on replacement parts, exactly anticipating the line William Simon was to take on his own in his futile efforts to explain to Kissinger how to handle the shah (discussed in Chapter Four). I called Senator Byrd back to quantify this suggestion. He was at his Washington apartment entertaining his colleague, Senator James Buckley of New York (subsequently undersecretary of state in the Reagan Administration at the time it tried to block Europe's pipeline deal). I told him that, on reflection, I thought the most effective course of action for Congress would be to approve the request in principle but to limit the authorization of the Export-Import Bank to a token amount. This, I explained, would show Russia that meaningful amounts would follow in response to any willingness on her side to accommodate the demands that Senator Henry Jackson of Washington was putting forward for the liberalization of Moscow's policy toward requests by Jews and dissidents to emigrate. Byrd welcomed this approach and said that he would discuss it the next day with Jackson and ask him to cosponsor a resolution to this effect. They did, and it went through both houses unanimously, the only measure to do so during that troubled year.

Russia, of course, rejected the token offer—$300 million of cheap and slow credit versus the $12 billion requested—as well as the quid pro quo behind it. Then, however, she signaled her willingness to deal by liberalizing her stand on emigration significantly and for no consideration. Unfortunately, the Nixon administration failed to take advantage of Russia's promising response to the Senate's ploy, and the Senate, of course, cannot take over from the executive branch in negotiating with a foreign power. America then spent the next eight years getting nowhere on this top-priority project. Kissinger continued to pose as the expert who knew how to deal with Russia. By the time America exported her depression in 1981, Russia was the only market in sight still open to Europe. And her exercise in Mahanism put her in a much more formidable military stance than she had been able to show in 1974.

Thanks to the time America allowed to pass between the outbreak of the oil war early in the 1970s and the military turn the war took early in the 1980s, she lost track of her strategic priorities and failed to comprehend the interconnections between them, especially between her economic and military priorities. When General Jones described the business of the military as one of setting priorities, he showed that he knew not only the business of his own profession but the business of government as well. Contrary to radical libertarians in politics and monetarists in economics, the function of government is not just the two *P*'s: to print postage stamps (instead of just money) and to police the jails. It is to set the priorities of strategic purpose that, in turn, dictate the priorities of defense programming. This double function is the only basis on which any government can distinguish its long-term borrowing needs from the short-term borrowing load that a bustling economy automatically puts onto the banking system. In America, the securities and the commodities markets function with continuous sensitivity to this double calculation. As the strategic priority-setting system gave evidence of breakdown at the unhappy governmental policy-making summit in Versailles in June 1982, the process for setting military priorities, which operate between policy making and market making, clogged up. The chaos in the markets that same year, especially in the credit markets, and the collapse in the economy, especially in capital investment, proved it. Only the panicky abandonment by the Federal Reserve Board of its austere monetary guidelines and the forced injection of dollars of financial first aid into the credit system following the summit gave the securities markets their historic reprieve between the summer of 1982 and the summer of 1983.

Russia's success in reaching economic détente with Western Europe had the immediate effect of intensifying White House paranoia. The administration reacted as if Attila the Hun had been sighted crossing the Elbe and proceeded to unleash a one-man presidential campaign to save the Continent from another invasion by his hordes. The administration was ready and willing, if not necessarily able, to challenge Soviet economic incursion into Western Europe; it was anxious, though clearly unable, to challenge the outreach of Soviet expansion emanating from Cuba and the region of the Persian Gulf. But it failed to see the Mahanist connection between these three orchestrated movements of expansion. It did not identify the economic advantage Russia sought to gain under cover of her naval power and her political exploitation of it, nor was it initially sensitive to the economic disadvantage its reaction to the pipeline deal elicited at home. Overall reaction in the polls was positive to Reagan's anti-Russian fulminations, but he did not play well in Peoria, a cloth-coat Republican stronghold where Caterpillar machinery parts for the pipeline were to have been manufactured. Though Reagan's tune changed in time and the sanctions he invoked fell by the wayside, the gas project still clouded the future of America's traditional coal-export market in Europe, as Europe shifted more energy to gas. The cunning of history was playing a bitter joke on the Republican heirs of Theodore Roosevelt. "I took Panama while Congress talked," he had bragged. But while Reagan talked, the Kremlin cut the lines of power he was defending.

Slogans have an eerie way of leaving ghosts behind. "More bang for the buck" was the reassuring rallying cry of the Eisenhower years. Never mind that his administration wound up getting less bang for more bucks than anyone was then willing to admit. The same slogan evolved into an American priority for the 1980s, aimed at the well-publicized Soviet "threat" and emphasized by the government's need to stop pyramiding obligations to spend in the future and to start collecting revenue in the present. At first blush, America was even less likely to relieve the mounting pressures to identify her strategic political and military priorities than she had been to eliminate waste from the government. Not very much scrutiny, however, was needed to disclose the fact that the Reagan administration did indeed sport a priority. It was military, and it was the wrong one: the nuclear weapon. The unusability of the nuclear weapon was only half the reason it represented the wrong priority; the usability of automated high-tech conventional weaponry provided the other half.

The professional military perception of the distinction sharpened with public revulsion for the specter of nuclear devastation. The advocates of limitation in nuclear arms opted for a switch to conventional weapons, and the military were all for it. Everybody knew that high technology was required to put nuclear weapons in place, but not everybody involved in the public debate was aware that even higher technology was being employed in weapons still classified as conventional. Not everything short of The Bomb was a descendant of the handgun. The new high-powered conventional weaponry on the drawing boards posed a devastating threat to the most powerful forces the Russians could mobilize. It illustrated the basic axiom of military technology: The defense always catches up.

In addition, mobile concentrations of weaponry—in the air, on sea, and on land—were increasingly cross-pollenating nuclear and conventional strategies. By doing so, they offered new challenges to switch confrontations into negotiations. The British flotilla that steamed to the Falklands in the spring of 1982 enjoyed no conventional air cover, but it carried nuclear warheads in its ammunition racks. The slowest-flying sitting ducks in the U.S. Air Force, the B-52s of Korean War vintage, remained the chosen instruments throughout most of the 1980s for dropping the highest-powered bombs over Russian installations. As fast as conventional forces are seen to be traveling on nuclear power and bearing nuclear weapons, the antinuclear movement is likely to broaden its scope into an antiwar movement.

The rational response to the antinuclear movement, at least in the United States, was a call for a step-up in the levels of effective conventional forces stationed in Western Europe. Precisely this appeal was made in the spring of 1982 when Messrs. McNamara, Bundy, Kennan, and Smith, the Four Horsemen charging against nuclear apocalypse, two of them stalwart Kennedy alumni, made their appeal to America to abandon her first-strike nuclear option. They were careful to balance the unavoidable horror conjured up by visions of nuclear holocaust with the sober recognition that America's sense of responsibility called for renewed emphasis on conventional military strength to offset the recommended deemphasis on nuclear strength.

Under cover of the changes in military planning produced by the old nuclear weaponry, the striking power of the new conventional weaponry was increasing at a rate promising to make nuclear weapons obsolete. The speed of its development raised the question: Who will need nuclear weapons when conventional ones are so much more controllable and readily usable? And when they can rifle their targets instead of bird-shotting them? Ever since America lost her head start in the nuclear race, the military has been haunted by the worry over whether any nuclear interchange would be worth the effort. Moreover, the Jones regime at the Pentagon was all for negotiating nuclear deescalation with Moscow. The most frustrating consequence of the ideological zealotry that distinguished the Reagan administration arose from its insistence on budgetary priorities for still newer nuclear weapons and its acquiescence in the crowding out of advanced conventional weaponry. The nuclear weapons given priority were political hot potatoes in the present and cold consolation for the far-out future. The conventional weapons, ready to be put into production but crowded out of the military budget because their costs were seen as running wild, were kept on ice. The need to give incentive pay increases to key personnel in excess of anti-inflation guidelines was recognized, but the need to supply the forces with ammunition for training was not.

Planned or otherwise, the decision to downgrade future munitions production, though reckless in light of the administration's hawkish rhetoric, was not as impractical as it seemed. Military technology, like industrial technology, is haunted by the ongoing battle between the next generation and the present generation for claims on end products. Thanks to the whirlwind pace of technological progress in weapons development, conventional high-tech devices that had taken years to go into production and to be activated for combat were subject to instant obsolescence, as the bitter little wars of the early 1980s showed. The basic axiom governing all investment, whether for military or industrial use, is that durability is the test of effectiveness; the longer a standard end product can be used, the more efficient it is. Henry Ford's original Model T flivver provided the classic industrial illustration of this. The B-52 workhorse, though immeasurably more high powered, was its military counterpart. Suddenly, however, no new military weapons enjoy any insurable life expectancy. This fortifies the case for mobilizing the economy as the mercy weapon that is also the durable weapon.

In the middle of 1982, a series of coincidences forced an abrupt reassessment of the terms of cooperation and confrontation between the two superpowers and their trading partners. The American economy was in grievous decline. On the other side of the trenches in the Cold War, more gain at less risk, and certainly at less cost, was the systematic objective of the Soviet offensive strategy. Less cost, and more security, but at greater risk, was the corresponding defensive strategy forced on America. America was faced with the additional, and demoralizing, realization that Europe might no longer offer her forces an unmixed welcome, a realization made no less pleasanter by the fact that America would be hard pressed to modernize them. Notwithstanding the 17 percent surge in military procurement in the first half of 1982 over the same period in 1981, the Reagan defense program was failing to get off the ground, or even to take shape; nor did the U.S. economy feel any spur. At the same time, Israel watched Russia skirt any direct challenge to her ability to control Syrian air space when she invaded Lebanon. Meanwhile, Iran and Iraq demonstrated that their war could not bring the oil glut down to manageable proportions. Here the coincidences stopped and Russia's adoption of Mahanism asserted itself. From the Baltic to the Red Sea, from the Caribbean to the Pacific, and at choke points in between, her purpose was not to risk a confrontation but to play for time and to pick up bigger gain at falling cost, as in the pipeline deal.

Historically, America has been too lucky to be forced to set her own priorities; her enemies and her crises have spared her the trouble. Until Reagan went to Versailles and plunged America into a two-front crisis with Europe—over the need America felt to defend Europe militarily and over the need Europe felt to declare independence from America economically—the country seemed likely to flounder along in a fog of her own making. Providentially, however, the crisis in the Atlantic community brought the challenge in Washington to a head. Providentially, too, the suspicion of recession in 1981 simultaneously sharpened into the recognition of depression in 1982, with the overtones of a full-fledged banking crisis signaling the rumblings of panic and the retreat to the expedient of hyperinflation. The junction of the foreign political crisis and the domestic economic crunch forced the quest for priorities back to its source: the defense budget in general and its economic applications in particular.

Reenter Senator Nunn, again to the rescue, this time with a NATO-oriented proposal, paralleling his nuclear-oriented challenge, for Reagan to present to Russia. In a report he presented to the Senate Armed Services Committee in March 1982, based on his one-man inspection tour of NATO facilities the previous January, Nunn analyzed the diminishing returns of NATO's long-standing strategy of falling back upon nuclear weapons in the event of a conventional attack by Warsaw Pact forces. He noted that the strategy had evolved when NATO enjoyed clear nuclear superiority but when no means of containing a conventional attack from the East existed. He went on to argue that the 1970s had seen Russia "eliminate NATO's nuclear superiority at both the strategic and theater levels, while at the same time expanding its traditional advantages in conventional forces." NATO forces, while outmanned, outgunned, and outdeployed in 1982 (by a factor of 2 to 1, as the Department of Defense admitted), still relied on theater nuclear weapons deployed twenty years ago. NATO vulnerability in all these areas persisted despite the $122 billion American military contribution to the alliance made during the 1982 fiscal year. (That figure included projected costs for manpower, procurement, and equipment for strategic forces; reinforcements, intelligence, and communications; and the allocation for Asia-based NATO GI's.) Nunn suggested that "taxpayers in every NATO country should question why the Warsaw Pact is credited with substantially more conventional military capability than NATO when NATO spends more money." As shall be seen, he then laid out a plan that, after assessing NATO's problems, recommended strategically effective and economically viable solutions that were designed to cool nuclear fears and, at the same time, to impress Soviet strategists.

Distracting holdups in setting priorities for national policy, as well as in setting courses of action—whether to secure the national interest or to "hepp seff," as Senator Nunn's shrewd great-uncle, Carl Vinson, used to say—come from the temptation to play guessing games with slogans. The challenge is to improvise operational breakthroughs and, more difficult than it sounds when experiments clash with well-entrenched theories and practices, to go with the innovations. We have seen what has gone wrong. Let us see how to put it right. Once the practical questions about how to reactivate the American economy are hit upon, workable solutions about how to propel it at the foreign political targets in its range will fall into place. Identifying priorities, like an exercise in mathematics, does not call for political loyalty oaths or sharper party divisions. Americans who have been discouraged by Washington's floundering might do well to recall the terse polemic with which Lenin staked out his claim to leadership when Russia herself was floundering in 1905. The title he gave it—"What Is to Be Done"—said it all. Armed with the questions that fasten onto what needs to be done to see America through the revolution of the 1980s, let us try to see how to do it—for the country and, therefore, for the world and, not least, for ourselves.

PART II

PRESCRIPTIONS FOR NATIONAL PROSPERITY: THE STRATEGY OF THE QUICK FIX

THERE'S NO FIX like a quick fix—the quicker the fix, the better; the more of them, the bigger the lift from any one and from all of them together. The personal courage and ready wit of Ronald Reagan on the day he was shot provide an unforgettable reminder of the pragmatism of the "quick fix" solution to emergency problems. After the assassination attempt failed and the hapless Hinckley was disarmed, the president and his aides started back to the White House. Business-as-usual resumed as the order of the day—until the president's driver, scanning the rear view mirror, noticed a trickle of blood coming out of the president's mouth. Reagan, of all people, learned at firsthand what it meant to get a quick fix and what it would mean not to get one.

Because we have taken the government's power to grow for granted, without examining its performance as it has grown, we have invited it to engulf itself and us in a depression crisis recalling the disaster of 1929. Then, the solution was simply to force-feed the economy. The government stepped up its spending and taxed and borrowed more to finance it. All during the 1930s, the government grew while the economy stagnated, and the agents of aggression won the race against time. The Depression dragged on for eleven years after the 1929 crash. It took the trauma of World War II to break the deadlock between government spending and private saving.

This time, the task is trickier: to show the government how to convert a depression into a fast boom, how to defuse the preliminary rounds of a military bloodbath into a bloodless confrontation in the markets. Like it or not, the government is stuck with the responsibility for managing the markets and, consequently, we are stuck with the responsibility for giving the government the lead it needs to do so. Its efforts to abandon that responsibility and to concentrate on managing the war crisis instead have invited the war crisis to invade the markets.

It is time for us to insist that the government keep its part of the bargain it makes each time it collects a tax check or meets a military payroll. It will fail to do so as long as we assume that it knows what it is doing or can learn by itself. But we can teach it. This is the job the second section of this book sets out to do.

If I could think of one quick, simple fix for the Reagan depression, I would have spelled out how to implement it and would have tried to calculate how much relief it would have brought. Instead, the multi-pronged offensive I am recommending against the economic stagnation, the financial overload, and the war danger feeding on it is dedicated to the next best expedient: prescribing a number of special-purpose quick fixes—eighteen to be exact—each directed against a different affliction crippling our political economy. Not that I claim proprietary credit for having exhausted the list of feasible alternatives. On the contrary, Senator Sam Nunn is entitled to full credit for the ingenious and thoroughly practical solutions he has devised for the two most pressing single challenges endangering us: to harness the technology of space for policing the nuclear terror on earth, and to restore America's shattered relationship with her European allies with a sane vote of confidence in the renewal of NATO.

I believe that these proposals can stimulate consideration of the pragmatic approach they illustrate and that they will suggest many additional stratagems for waging economic warfare and avoiding military combat. But the faster quick fixes are tried, the faster they are used up and need to be replaced. This process of trial and error is frequently called progress. Sometimes, however, it works out as the exact opposite. World War II, lest we forget, was ended with a quick fix—the first nuclear bombs. The quick fixes recommended here are offered in the hope that they will buy time against the smoldering danger that glaring weaknesses in the world economy—particularly in the oil economy— will invite military power plays. Whether or not these particular suggestions produce expedients that will really be tried, as the realization spreads that the depression will not be self-curing, the strategies they describe illustrate the only serious alternative to "staying the course" with Reagan's commitment to the rhetoric of reaction and the recklessness of inaction.

I am respectfully and sympathetically aware of the political prohibitions against the four conventional governmental remedies for economic slumps, which have traditionally been more spending, more taxing, more borrowing, and more federal battening on the resources of state and local government. Accordingly, not one of these prescriptions calls for expenditures by the U.S. Treasury. Nor does any of them propose the levying of additional taxes on any participants of the private sector of the American economy, individual or corporate. On the contrary, several of them propose extending tax incentives to individuals, others propose incentives to small businesses, and still others offer trade-offs to bigger businesses in return for new investment commitments made by them. A key proposal targets capital spending by state and local governments as the only vibrant source of investment in durable goods and suggests a device for enlarging its contribution to activity and employment. True, several of these proposals envision taxes on foreign participants in the American economy (though one offers a tax incentive), yet none of them advocates either a retreat to protectionism or a dogmatic commitment to free trade.

The order in which the following prescriptions are presented follows the line of analysis developed in the preceding diagnostic section. The first series is directed at foreign political sources of the defense-budget inflation that has led to the breakdown of both our budgeting process and our sense of economic security. The second series of prescriptions is aimed at improvising props for the splintered structure of world finance, which has been hit by repercussions from miscalculations in our foreign political and defense budgeting. The third series is a battle plan for an economic end to the oil war with a bloodless defeat for the aggressors. My fourth series is reserved for the domestic economy and is offered on the assumption that after the first three sets of prescriptions start the economy on the road to recovery, the fourth will speed and stabilize it. The fifth series specifically addresses the revival of our real estate market. Consistent with my identification of time as the enemy, I have avoided any structured social prescriptions that would take time to implement—Social Security is the obvious omission. But if we were to be feckless enough to delay action on quick fixes that will speed recovery while we wrangle over "reforms" in Social Security, we would invite the depression to deepen and to undermine our defenses, including Social Security. In the long run, the way to make Social Security work is to put the economy back to work.

Failed administrations of recent decades have suffered from seeing America's domestic economic problems as divergent from her foreign political problems. The analysis in this book has focused on the interconnections between the two. My proposals for putting the domestic economy back to work begin with an effort to bring the foreign political crisis under control, commencing with the arms race. The takeoff point is the same as Reagan's was in his first presidential statement: the notion that Russia is our "adversary." My working premise has been the same too: that the way for America to deal with Russia is from strength, not by feeding her paranoia but, instead, by playing to her incentives to negotiate by dealing from our strength, universally recognized as economic and technological. My strategy, however, is the opposite of the Reagan administration's. Surely, the American people are endowed with enough common sense to prefer prescriptions for fighting a depression to bromides for living with it.

The way to stay the course is to use opportunities, not to endure difficulties. The way to get the government off the country's back is to switch it from a dead weight on the economy to a live wire sparking it. A necessary precondition is to give the country and the government it winds up with in 1984 a chance to buy time and to use ingenuity in improving expedients before a world financial crisis makes the exercise academic. Lord Lever of Manchester, who served Britain's Labour government under Harold Wilson and James Callaghan as financial treasury secretary and made his acknowledged financial expertise available to Margaret Thatcher on a nonpartisan basis, dramatized this danger in a memorable article in the July 9, 1983 issue of *The Economist*. The international banking situation, he said,

> continues to deteriorate alarmingly. We have neither relieved the damage to the functioning of the banking system resulting from the deadweight of nonperforming debt, nor devised any arrangements to provide a measured flow of funds for the future. Defaults, by an ever growing number of sovereign debtors, are being papered over by rescheduling arrangements, i.e., by substituting future promises to pay for those that have already been defaulted. These piecemeal arrangements leave the fundamental dangers and anomalies of the situation untouched.

(I took great personal gratification in this proclamation of emergency by Harold Lever, of all respected financial elder statesmen, because I had learned to respect his acumen in the early 1960s. In fact, when Wilson complained to me that Callaghan, as chancellor of the exchequer, was no help to him, I told him that the ablest financial brain in Britain was one of his back-benchers. Wilson, by coincidence or cause, appointed him the next day.)

The week before his article was published, I invited Lever, at the request of Robert Anderson, secretary of the Treasury under Eisenhower, to participate in the emergency conference Anderson was convening in Geneva during August 1983 to consider measures to head off the banking crisis that all three of us agreed had become a clear and present danger.

CHAPTER NINE

Defense

PRESCRIPTION #1
Defusing the Danger of Nuclear Warfare

The Complaint

The step-up in the Russo-American arms race, plus increasing vulnerability to nuclear proliferation.

The Cure

Senator Sam Nunn's proposal to establish a joint U.S.-USSR crisis communications control center to monitor the proliferation of global nuclear capabilities of countries other than the superpowers and terrorists around the world.

The History

America wrote the first chapter when she dropped the bomb on Hiroshima and Nagasaki—after Japan was beaten. Russia wrote the second chapter when she broke America's nuclear monopoly in 1949.

The next thirty years were dominated by the Soviet-American nuclear arms race, which ended in a dead heat. But it created complications. America stationed thousands of tactical (short-range) nuclear weapons in West Germany. Russia reciprocated in Cuba, although at the time of the Bay of Pigs episode she undertook to advertise the removal of her weapons from Cuba without pressing America to remove hers from Western Europe. She also agreed not to advertise America's withdrawal of weapons from the Russo-Turkish border as part of the bargain. But the deployment of American tactical nuclear weapons in Western Europe raised the sensitive question of whether West Germany would become the battlefield in any American-Soviet nuclear confrontation. America did negotiate two successive nuclear arms limitation treaties with Russia, one in 1972 and the other in 1979.

However, when the U.S. Senate rejected the second, the atmosphere was left more rather than less turbulent. It confirmed the universal foreign suspicion that any international agreement entered into by an American president would win high marks for effort but low marks for performance because the Senate would refuse to ratify it.

The problem remained relatively simple so long as America and Russia remained the only nuclear powers and West Germany remained the only likely theater of nuclear warfare. But membership in the nuclear club could not be restricted. Sometime in the 1970s, Israel developed her own nuclear capability; so did South Africa, with which Israel maintains a close collaborative relationship, along with Taiwan. Although nuclear weapons are essentially offensive, the motivation for all three minipowers no doubt has been defensive. But potential users of nuclear weapons with admittedly aggressive intent—notably Libya, Iran, Iraq, India, and Pakistan—soon began to crash the club. By the 1980s, the list of countries with nuclear capabilities and aggressive stances began to read like a roster of insecure Third World governments.

In the Middle East, for example, Iraq, scarcely the heavy hitter in the war-torn desert, would have had a nuclear capability by 1982 if Israel had not made her preemptive strike against the Iraqi reactor in the spring of 1981. The individual cliques running each South American country have been in the race to qualify as nuclear powers too. As fast as any of them ran out of credit to raise the cash to pay interest (forget the principal) on swollen foreign debt, they nevertheless found the money to develop nuclear weapons. Argentina became the first of the oligarchies to qualify, and America helped her to a running start by giving her sophisticated electronic control equipment for nuclear power application as a consolation prize for our supplying Britain in the Falklands war. Brazil is committed to the proposition that anything Argentina does she can do better. Cuba was ready to go before any of the others started.

The 1980s found Russia and America still locked in defensive stances against the other. But they each had developed a common defensive interest in neutralizing nuclear threats from countries at all points of the compass—from terrorists, "toughs," "crazies," mercenaries, and would-be superpowers. With reluctance and misgivings, the two existing superpowers were pushed into reappraisals of their simplistic views of one another as contestants in the nuclear arms race. So long as the nuclear arms race was limited to Russia and America, with each under pressure to placate Western Europe, it was readily controllable, even in the absence of a definitive U.S.-USSR agreement. The internationalization of the danger of nuclear war escalated it out of control.

The Symptoms

- The frustration with efforts at industrialization throughout the Third World.
- The collapse of the oil boom.
- The failure of the Iran-Iraq war to alleviate the worldwide oil glut.
- The indiscriminate spread of depression among oil-producing and nonoil-producing countries.
- The inability of Third World economies to find suitable employment for the students they have been training.
- The rise of terrorism as the result of social alienation.
- The experimentation with "rootless warfare" waged by megalomaniacal dictators, religious extremists, mercenaries, terrorists, and disaffected youth; endless credits for advanced arms.
- The portability of nuclear weaponry from the reactor to the suitcase.

The Treatment

The Nunn plan engineers a procedure for policing the perilous spread of nuclear capabilities by deploying joint Soviet-American weapons-detection stations in outer space. Senator Nunn's proposal puts together a strategy for resolving the Soviet-American nuclear arms impasse with a solution to the threat of third-party nuclear strikes. The Nunn plan draws on findings of a pioneering technical study he initiated under the direction of General Richard Ellis (Ret.), commander of the Strategic Air Command (SAC) at Omaha, Nebraska, in March 1981. The following questions were examined:

1. Is the U.S. system of communications, command, and control capable of discerning the source of a nuclear attack by a distinguished third country or party?
2. What capabilities do the Soviets have in this respect (warning and threat assessment)?
3. What other scenarios should be considered in terms of U.S.-USSR strategic interaction?
4. Are there electronic arms control innovations and initiatives that can be proposed in [the nuclear arms control] area as well as in the overall communications area?

On May 11, 1982, Senator Nunn briefed the Senate Foreign Relations Committee on the SAC analysis. Its thesis showed "that the United States and the Soviets must dramatically improve their warning and attack characterization to deal with the use of a nuclear device by a third party in either a peacetime or crisis situation." The contents of the Nunn-Ellis investigation are, of course, classified, but its conclusion is not. Its finding: At least twenty countries, not to mention a rabble of terrorists, will have their hands on nuclear triggers by 1990. Its recommendation: We, jointly with the Soviet Union, can reduce the likelihood of accidental nuclear war or war by miscalculation. Its clear implication: By taking precautions against the danger of war by miscalculation, the danger of calculated nuclear war is limited.

Out of the Nunn-Ellis initiative came the following recommendations:

1. Establish a joint U.S.-USSR military crisis control center, based in outer space, for the monitoring and containment of nuclear weapons used by third parties or terrorist groups. The technology to operate such a center is already in place.

2. Seize the initiative for the United States in the existing U.S.-USSR communications hot line.

3. Reduce the intolerable vulnerability of present U.S. command, control, and communications technology which is relied upon to monitor the U.S. nuclear defense window, and which extends into NATO and other overseas forward base commands. Invite the Soviets to do the same.

The Recovery

The Nunn-Ellis plan would provide the tangible evidence the world has been waiting for, namely, that the superpowers recognize and share the need to avoid a nuclear holocaust. It would formalize the reality that each country's retaliatory power secures it against any threat from the other. It would focus their sanitizing capabilities on the third-party "crazies," terrorists, and mercenaries. It would enable the two superpowers to quiet the fears of nuclear chaos throughout the Third World, which were dramatized by Israel's incisive demolition of Iraq's nuclear installation. The self-interest motivating the Kremlin to mount the joint effort would provide built-in insurance against any Soviet surrogate or agent making a nuclear strike. The technology at the disposal of the joint superpower command proposed by the Nunn plan would enable it to police the air waves for nuclear explosives and to defuse them instantaneously.

Collateral Advantages

The Nunn-Ellis proposal, by virtue of focusing on America's top priority—nuclear security—would free her to activate the chain reaction of prosperity. To wit:

- Bring the Pentagon's nuclear budget under manageable control as the condition for bringing the total Pentagon budget under control and freeing the private sector to resume its proper role of financing the public sector.
- Open avenues of escape for Russia from the arms race without fear of attack—at least by the United States—and without loss of face, a necessary condition for defusing the time bomb ticking in the Straits of Florida between Havana and Miami, not to mention the one ticking on the inter-German border.
- Reassure Europe and Japan that the United States is no nuclear threat to them but, on the contrary, offers them their only hope of peace with independence.
- Retain civilian control over military decision making, as prescribed in the original Atomic Energy Act of 1946.
- Remove U.S.-USSR nuclear arms control efforts from the sole jurisdiction of negotiators subject to political pressures and place them under the shared control of scientists qualified to assess conditions for nuclear security.
- Ease the tensions within American society by offering goals that can be supported by responsible ranking military students of the nuclear problem as well as nuclear disarmament activists.

PRESCRIPTION #2
Putting NATO Back into Business

The Complaint

The European revolt against the American nuclear presence as institutionalized by NATO.

The Cure

A first-stage unilateral withdrawal from Europe of America's militarily unusable and politically provocative short-range nuclear weapons. Simultaneous automation of America's conventional defenses in the European theater. *Warning:* A joint Washington-Moscow protective initiative against third-party nuclear aggression—especially in Europe —will not reverse the Kremlin's commitment to territorial aggression overnight, if at all. Quite the contrary, calling off the nuclear arms race will give Russia an incentive to step up the conventional arms race. It behooves America, therefore, to anticipate this global-to-local switch of aggressive Russian priorities by modernizing her own outmoded conventional defenses in Western Europe.

The History

It begins with the partition of Europe at the end of World War II. Set up in 1949, the North Atlantic Treaty Organization (NATO) aimed to prevent Russia from using her base in Central Europe to encroach upon Western Europe. In 1961, the NATO concept focused the defense of Europe on the Berlin Wall. Dedicated to the "trip-wire" strategy, it conceded superiority of conventional forces to the Red Army on the grounds of size, and it counted on bringing American nuclear superiority into play as a counterforce if the Red Army set off the alarm. This two-tiered military strategy put the Soviets on notice that any first strike by the Red Army would "trip the nuclear wire," that is, it would trigger a nuclear counterstrike by NATO.

The U.S.-dominated NATO stance remained realistic as long as America's nuclear superiority remained unchallenged. Within a decade and a half after the Vietnam escalation, however, the Soviet Union regained the advantage in the European theater, effectively nullifying both the NATO nuclear and nonnuclear defense postures. Nevertheless, long after Russia made obsolete the defensive nuclear strategy that put NATO in business, America continued to rely on her original war plan for the defense of Europe, supplementing it with elaborate schemes to fly reserves of conventional forces into Europe once the Red Army invaded. Ironically, it was a European general with formidable credentials, Charles De Gaulle, who put America on notice that she had locked herself into a bear trap. De Gaulle fortified his distinctive record for realism as a military prophet by pulling France out of the NATO military command in 1966. Tragically, however, America did not get the message that NATO was a paper tiger. Instead, increasingly distracted by involvement in the war France had abandoned in Vietnam a decade earlier, the United States continued to worship the alliance as a sacred cow, if an expensive one, for another two decades.

The significance of De Gaulle's withdrawal from NATO's forces was threefold: (1) it was a clear warning that the entire NATO strategy was becoming unworkable militarily and insupportable politically; (2) it signaled a new economic partnership inside Europe in the place of the military partnership De Gaulle had canceled; and (3) it invited the rest of Europe to sit still, subsidized by America inside NATO, while moving forward in a profitable relationship with France inside the Common Market.

Europe's two marriages of convenience—with France economically and with America militarily—drifted along until 1982. The Reagan administration would have been content to accept the fiction of NATO as a formidable military force for another two years, even though all it had to show for the alliance's exorbitant cost was Europe's willingness to accept more. The fiscal 1982 U.S. defense budget of $229 billion was burdened with a $122 billion commitment to NATO. As a practical matter, America's NATO partners decided that extending their economic arrangement with France to include Russia was not only safer than playing nuclear war games with America but also offered them a comfortable halfway house between their familiar dilemma of being Red or dead. Russia's coup in uniting Europe behind the gas pipeline agreement and America's blunder in alienating Europe with an insupportable export embargo brought America face to face with the recognition that NATO, in its mummified 1983 edition, was a failure she could no longer afford to live with. It took America twenty years to realize that De Gaulle had been a realist.

The Symptoms

• The revolt across party lines of the antinuclear activists known as Greens in West Germany signifying Germany's withdrawal of political hospitality to NATO's American contingent and suggesting that American nuclear bases in West Germany might no longer be safe from raids—whether by professionals or, more incendiary still, by amateurs.

• The deepening of the depression throughout Europe, despite the gas pipeline deal with Russia and despite NATO's contribution to the European economy.

• The interconnected depressions in Europe, Japan, and America, putting strains on currencies, forcing retreats to protectionism in all three market areas, and aggravating the differences between America and her presumed allies over military policy.

• The budget crisis in America and the pressure it provoked to give domestic job-making projects a priority over long-standing overseas dollar drains, like NATO.

• The hard military evidence that America could not count on NATO to defend Western Europe against Soviet armor.

• The hard political evidence that America's volunteer army would not give NATO the infusion of new blood it needed.

• Washington's cumulative failure to coordinate the foreign political commitments of the United States with her supporting defense capabilities and her economic interests.

• Europe's fear that America might divert forces earmarked for emergency NATO airlifting into full-fledged battle in Central America, unbalancing Continental defenses and inviting Russia to crash the gates presumably guarded by NATO.

The Treatment

The key to revitalizing America's relationship with Europe is to restructure the NATO alliance. This calls for removing the nuclear threat to Europe as well as making NATO cost effective to America. Granted that the NATO deterrent is merely the military extension of America's political and economic connection to Europe, the damage to the latter cannot be repaired until the foundations of the former have been rebuilt. America's progress with high-technology conventional weaponry offers her an historic opportunity to revitalize the European connection. Senator Nunn has come forward with a proposal that supplements the alarm he sounded over the need for a Soviet-American nuclear crisis control center.

In January 1982, Nunn undertook a one-man inspection tour of European NATO bases. He conducted two similar reviews in 1974 and 1977, monitoring the Soviet threat to the alliance during the decade in which time had been a U.S. ally. On May 13, 1982, in his report to Chairman John Tower of the Senate Armed Services Committee, Nunn recommended a comprehensive revision of NATO strategy, based on the substitution of high-tech conventional weaponry for outmoded and increasingly unacceptable short-range nuclear weapons. The Nunn report stated: "The Soviet buildup itself has been crafted to further the Kremlin military tactic of attacking in wave after wave after wave of powerful forces designed to break through NATO's forward defenses at points of Soviet choosing. Soviet military strategy essentially seeks to play offense in a football game with Soviet rules, so that many fullbacks can charge the defensive line one after another over the same position on the premise that sooner or later some fullbacks will get through. . . . NATO must change the rules of the game to prevent this possibility."

The action line of the Nunn plan calls for bringing into play a new generation of high-tech weaponry calculated to prevent the second wave of Soviet attackers from providing the backup for the first. Like all sensible efforts to come up with answers, it began with questions, these to be put to the Commander in Chief. To wit:

I. **A.** How can NATO military doctrine be changed to substantially improve the chance of successful conventional defense?
B. Is the "Airland Battle" concept (using inherent NATO military strengths to exploit fundamental Warsaw Pact weaknesses) official Department of Defense doctrine? If so:

1. Has this new doctrine been proposed by the United States to NATO?
2. How can NATO forces be operationally integrated to implement this doctrine?
3. What programmatic changes are necessary to underwrite this capability?
4. What conventional programs and weapons are in the current budgets and five-year plan to enhance the disruption and destruction of Soviet follow-on attack echelons?
5. What new weapons or systems are available for this purpose that are not in the current budgets or five-year plan?

C. What opportunities exist to improve NATO conventional defense through improved use of European manpower reserves, organized and equipped for territorial defense?

D. If a viable conventional defense is achieved, how could NATO theater nuclear forces be redesigned and modernized to:

1. Deter Soviet first use of nuclear weapons;
2. Enhance conventional defense;
3. Provide options for major negotiated withdrawal of nuclear weapons from Europe?

II. Once the implementation of a viable conventional defense was firmly engaged, NATO could:

A. Propose a mutual U.S.-USSR negotiated withdrawal of several thousand battlefield nuclear weapons from Central Europe.

B. Seriously consider two joint and mutually dependent NATO–Warsaw Pact arms control pledges of:

1. No first use of nuclear weapons; and
2. No large concentration of conventional ground forces, with special emphasis on armor forces, within a specified distance of the inter-German border:

    a. A breach of the "conventional concentration pledge" would render null and void the no-first-use pledge;

    b. The effective date of any such arms control proposal must be geared to the implementation of a viable NATO conventional defense; and

    c. Any such arms control agreement must be verifiable.

III. Until the alliance agrees on a new doctrine and dedicates itself to its implementation, the president would instruct the secretary of defense to permit no net increase in the present number of U.S. troops deployed in Europe.

The president would also ask the secretary of defense to examine the five-year defense plan and, beginning in fiscal year 1984, to isolate the expenditures designed directly for NATO improvements and freeze those expenditures that exceed our NATO 3 percent (of GNP) commitment until the NATO political leaders reach a clear agreement on a military strategy for the coming decade.

IV. NATO leaders would agree to put their full weight behind renewed and vigorous efforts—including new or revised high-level NATO and Defense Department groups, if necessary—to accomplish the following objectives within specified deadlines:

A. Establish a cooperative defense-industrial effort within Europe and between Europe and North America;

B. Develop options for specialization and division of labor within the alliance so its members can share, equitably and efficiently, the financial burden as well as the economic benefits of NATO defense;

C. Promote increased integration and interoperability of NATO forces;

D. Identify weapons systems which could be standardized at an early stage of R&D and procurement; and

E. Monitor each NATO nation's defense budget at every stage of the budget process, providing information to NATO governments as to compliance with two-way-street and standardization agreements.

V. NATO would agree to use Western financial leverage, such as credits and taxes, to influence Soviet behavior, while sharing the burden among NATO's members. (Any benefits gained would attract France back into a cooperative stance with the alliance.)

A standing group in NATO would monitor all Western credits to the Soviet Union and the Warsaw Pact and keep its government leaders informed of current developments and long-range trends. This group would also be responsible for suggesting options on a continuing basis for reduction or suspension of credits and other financial measures, in response to NATO collective decisions.

My further discussions with Senator Nunn elicited two updated judgments from him with which I concur. The first relates to the hypersensitive issue of the withdrawal of tactical nuclear weapons: America would have nothing to lose and everything to gain by offering a first-phase unilateral withdrawal as she activates her strategy of modernization. The second relates to the thorny issue of economic and financial sanctions: The fiasco of Reagan's blunderbuss attack on the gas pipeline reflected America's loss of leverage as the depression became her principal export. But it did not preclude America's developing economic or financial leverage with Europe and against Russia under more effective leadership and more promising circumstances.

The Recovery

Adopting the Nunn plan would again lay out the welcome mat for NATO in Europe. Specifically, it would absolve America from responsibility for any nuclear threat to its survival; it would reequip NATO with the conventional weapons needed to fulfill its original mission of defending Western Europe; and it would cut manpower costs with their annual accruals of entitlements.

Defusing the danger of a nuclear disaster would not achieve a miracle of world peace. If Russia were to go along with the proposal for pooling detection and policing capabilities against third-party nuclear aggressors, she would not change her spots; she would merely use her collaboration with America to cover their joint exposure to a third-party nuclear strike, freeing herself to mobilize more strength against targets of her choice. The immediate effect of bringing the threat of random nuclear terror under control could well be to step up the conventional arms race to an even more frantic pace.

Collateral Advantages

• Relieve the Pentagon's cash shortage and chronic reliance on indiscriminate export sales to raise the cash it needs for usable end products and replacement parts.

• Put into overtime production the long shopping list of new military end products able to destroy Soviet armor on aggressive forays.

Appendix

While I try to function as a policy engineer, I am certainly not a weapons engineer. Over the years, however, I have kept abreast of the economic consequences of defense engineering problems and developments. During the Korean War, I served as an unofficial economic adviser to Lieutenant General Edwin Rawlings, the commanding general of the Air Materiel Command at Wright-Patterson Air Force Base in Dayton, Ohio. General Rawlings pioneered, among other innovations, the application of computers to defense production programming. During World War II, I enjoyed a similar connection with General Georges Doriot, the one-man brain trust behind the quartermaster general of the Army who, among other distinctions, was responsible for the remarkable speed with which the requirements for the first nuclear project at Los Alamos were met. After the war, when General Doriot returned to the faculty of the Harvard Graduate School of Business Administration, I was privileged to be a guest lecturer in his famous course in advanced management. Doriot was a pioneer in the venture capital business in America, and he singlehandedly bullied and cajoled major financial interests into backing the American Research and Development Corporation. The success Doriot made of this imaginative new venture established him as a triple rarity—not only a professor but also a general and a brilliant executive.

From both these remarkable men I have learned a great deal about the need for functional connections between the defense engineering production apparatus and the industrial mechanism. The awareness of this need led me to draw upon my friend and client, George McNamee, Jr., the head of the First Albany Corporation, for the following shopping list of high-technology defense products, which are needed and available to add a new dimension of modernized firepower to America's arsenal of conventional military firepower. I regard McNamee as the brokerage business's leading student of defense products and defense skills. This glossary is offered as an appendix to the above prescription, not because America needs more defense spending as a prop to her prosperity but, on the contrary, because America will have no chance to recover her prosperity until she has first settled on her defense needs and then arranged to fund them. This list is by no means complete.

Advanced Terminal Homing (ATH)—A program to develop an all-weather cruise missile precision-guidance system that will use scene matching and advanced sensor technologies.

Assault Breaker—A joint Army and Air Force system designed to attack tank formations. It consists of a single large missile carrying a large number of smaller submunitions programmed to locate and hit enemy tanks.

Electronic Countermeasure (ECM)—In all shapes and sizes, they perform a vast array of missions. The strategic bomber force and tactical fighter planes employ several of these devices. Here are a few examples:

AN/ALQ-77—A noise jammer that confuses enemy radar by emitting its own signals.

AN/ALQ-131—A fourteen-foot-long jamming pod that can be mounted in a variety of fighter and attack planes. It employs both noise and deception techniques over five radar frequency bands.

AN/APS-105—A radar homing and warning receiver to alert crew to enemy aircraft.

Flight Training Simulators—Have become more and more important for the services as actual flight time becomes more expensive. Flight simulators employ computer-aided design and manufacturing (CAD/CAM) and related technology.

Forward Swept Wing (FSW)—A wing shape concept becoming

feasible with the use of advanced composite structures. The FSW allows improved maneuverability, better angle control, and higher aerodynamic efficiency.

Harpoon—The Navy's long-range antiship missile, equipped with a sophisticated inertial and active terminal homing guidance system. With a turbojet cruise motor, it can reach targets at a range of seventy miles under all weather conditions.

Lantern—(Low Altitude Navigation and Infrared System for Night) employs millimeter-wave radar to achieve high resolution and control. This pod includes an air-to-ground, electro-optical firing system, allowing pilots to fly at low altitudes while identifying and firing at targets.

NAVSTAR Global Positioning System—Provides navigational information from its multiple satellite facilities. The three-dimensional effect achieved by satellite positioning allows highly accurate information to be relayed to pilots for air maneuvers and to commanders in the field.

Particle Beam Technology—Has applications for advanced weapons systems, space-based and ballistic missile defense. The capability to propagate the electron beams in the atmosphere is the technology to overcome. Developing a high-energy accelerator to test powerful electron beams is the focus of current military research.

Remotely Piloted Vehicles (RPV)—Used as air defense targets and decoys, certain types of these unmanned planes have the same radar signatures as the F-16 fighter. The drones expose enemy radar stations to antiradiation missiles.

Sonobuoys—Serve in several key areas of antisubmarine warfare: tracking, locating, and identifying enemy submarines. Using active sonar and a variety of oceanographic measuring techniques, sonobuoys relay information to antisubmarine helicopters or antisubmarine aircraft.

Space Defense—An area on the frontier of technology. Space defense programs include procurement of high-efficiency chemical lasers, along with large-scale optics. Feasibility of high-energy, space-based lasers is receiving new and broader attention:

Advance Laser Optics include development of mirrors with suitable quality and resolution for proper beam control.

The Chemical Laser Technology program seeks to resolve the efficiency, wavelength, and waveform problems of chemical lasers.

The Visible Laser program has many potential uses in air defense, satellite defense, and finally as ballistic missile defense. This program attempts to increase the energy or power and accuracy of the laser.

Stealth Technology—Primarily associated with the Advanced Technology Bomber (ATB) and air-launched cruise missiles. Features of stealth include a reduced radar signature, radar-absorbing materials and structures, optical absorbers, active radar jammers, and advanced design.

Stinger Missile—A programmable antiaircraft missile carried by the soldier. It has a disposable launch tube and a guidance unit called "identification friend or foe" (IFF).

Vertical Launch System—A contained missile launch system allowing multiple firing of various missiles from frigates, submarines, and other ships.

Very High Speed Integrated Circuits (VHSIC)—Technology has advanced because of military funding for research and development. Smaller volume, power, and weight requirements for microchips combined with greatly increased processing speed and efficiency have resulted from this technological breakthrough. Commercial and military applications are widespread in areas such as communications, electronic warfare, precision, and guided munitions.

PRESCRIPTION #3
Protecting the Middle East

The Complaint

America's military vulnerability in the Middle East.

The Cure

Assign NATO the mission of providing a network of European bases to support an airlift service to and from the eastern Mediterranean and the Persian Gulf.

The History

It begins with the Yom Kippur War of 1973. Two authoritative testimonials bear witness to American airlift capability in behalf of a Middle Eastern ally or client under attack. The first came from Anwar Sadat, explaining his defeat in the war: "Colossal U.S. transport aircraft landed, loaded with tanks and sophisticated equipment. . . . The United States was now taking part in the fighting by supplying Israel. . . . I did not intend to fight the entire United States of America." The second came from his victorious antagonist, Golda Meir: "For generations to come, all will be told of the miracle of the immense planes from the United States bringing in the material that meant life to our people."

Of course, the economic way to dispatch combat equipment to war zones is the old way: by ships loaded with complements of spare parts, supplies in bulk, and maintenance crews. But the only practical way America could hope to rush support equipment to hot spots on the outer rim of her overseas security umbrella is by airlift, with the problem compounded by the need for shuttle replacement parts and manpower. The U.S. military require an eighteen-day load-ship-unload-activate period for any sea-rescue mission. No cargo ships could meet it— not that the United States has any cargo fleet in service or on the waves, or, if it did, any defenses against the very formidable Soviet submarine pack. Either America will outfit her equipment with outsize, high-speed, high-flying wing power, supported by escort fire power, or a surrounded Fortress America will enter a permanent state of siege established by a new self-imposed isolationism.

The second phase began with President Jimmy Carter's frantic realization in 1977 that he had overextended America's lines of logistical support when he committed instant military support to the Saudis. White House decision makers since Eisenhower had been casual about the pressures of space and time in reckoning with Russia. Trapped into a two-front test of strength in Western Europe and the Middle East before she tackled her top-priority need to modernize her defense capability in Western Europe, America was sentenced by impulsiveness in the Middle East and inertia in Europe to glaring vulnerability on both fronts. Her air-shuttle capability did not exist. This weakness was economic rather than military.

When Carter woke up to the need to protect the flank he had exposed on the Persian Gulf, he asked Sadat to find the United States a refueling station within easy range of Saudi Arabia. Sadat arranged the necessary details with the Sultan of Oman. Oman, under nominal British control, offers air control over the mouth of the Persian Gulf, and Sadat was shrewd enough to select it as America's pied-à-terre in the Persian Gulf zone because it is an Arab oil principality but not a member of OPEC. Sadat subsequently paid with his life for this and other accommodations to Carter. The Moslem extremists who executed him showed no gratitude for the Oman transaction, the purpose of which was to protect the Saudi regime and, therefore, to keep its cash subsidies coming to them.

Once Washington took the first step toward negotiating a second front to hold, it put its adversary in Moscow in a familiar and comfortable position. No less than four separate but interrelated considerations argued for Admiral Mahan's well-schooled disciples in the Kremlin to invite his ignorant heirs in the White House to plunge further and deeper into the trap awaiting them in the Middle East. The first consideration making America's new undertaking risky for her was geographic: Whereas Europe had been brought within range of America's domestic arsenal as early as the Berlin Airlift crisis of 1948, the Middle East was still well beyond it in the 1980s. The second was military: Whereas America's first front in Western Europe was potentially defensible, subject to the modernization of her original war plan of the late 1940s, she had opened her second front in the Persian Gulf with no war plan at all, as Carter's bungled foray to rescue the hostages from Iran showed. The third was political: Whereas America's involvement in the defense of Western Europe was backed by unifying political support within the country among vocal and cohesive ethnic and opinion groups, even a token military deployment in the Middle East, let alone actual combat there, was bound to flare up into a divisive issue inside America. The fourth problem was logistical, and it was the one promising to be the most troublesome for America to manage and the most profitable for Russia to exploit: Whereas America's NATO war plan for the defense of Europe was chancy enough even in the event of an emergency limited only to Europe, it became subject to hopeless muddling in the event of a two-front emergency calling for battle-ready troops to be rushed simultaneously northwest from Italy and Turkey into Germany and southeast to the Middle East. In all probability, such a two-front emergency would also call for battle-ready troops to be rushed to the Middle East by way of European bases, with very little assurance that those bases could be held.

Russia approached her confrontation with America fortified by her history. For centuries adversaries had divided their forces before plunging into attacks on her western border and the vast space for blundering overextension that lay beyond it. America's insistence on leaping into the Middle East before looking awoke Russian memories of the military misadventures of Napoleon, the kaiser, and Hitler.

This exercise in recklessness was thoroughly bipartisan. Carter started it, and Reagan extended it. A glaring social weakness surfaced with it: America's loss of any functional sense of connection with her own history. As recently as 1941–1945, America had fought a two-front war but one in which the second front at Pearl Harbor had been forced upon her. Moreover, FDR, though not a self-proclaimed military genius like Hitler, had the good sense to sort out manageable priorities. He resolved to beat Germany first, and only then to concentrate the full force of American power against Japan. To conserve America's military resources, he gave the European front top priority for the land war and put the Navy on defensive antisubmarine and convoy duty in the Atlantic. Roosevelt bought time by respecting the logistical limitations of space.

The Symptoms

- Israel's refusal to permit American planes to use her military airfields for refueling en route to Carter's "Bay of Pigs in the Desert" in Iran.
- Secretary of State Cyrus Vance's citing his experience, as Johnson's secretary of the army, of the difficulty in conducting overseas military operations as reason for opposing the hostage rescue mission.
- The target of the Soviet push into Afghanistan: the link it provides to Pakistan and the corridors it opened to the blue-water ports of the Arabian Sea.
- The American rescue mission's need to refuel at the Oman base, which now operates subject to the sufferance of the Red Navy's Middle East fleet, thanks to its unobtrusive takeover of the region after the British pulled out of Aden in 1968.
- The fire-and-brimstone threats by the Iranian mullahs to mount an attack against Saudi Arabia and to support it by inciting a revolt by the kingdom's internal proletariat of Shiite Moslems.
- The intensification of internal strains and external conflicts shaking the regime of Hosni Mubarak in Egypt, exemplified by its refusal to harbor PLO refugees from Beirut.
- The overwhelming Soviet naval and air superiority at the eastern Mediterranean choke point and the temptation to use it against America's weak presence there, rather than against Israel's strong presence.
- The intensification of frictions inside the Soviet Union arising from the Moslem population explosion and the temptation to externalize them by establishing Soviet satellites in the Moslem world and, more than incidentally, by tying up Moslem allies likely to be useful in Afghanistan.
- Yuri Andropov's incisive promotion of the KGB's ranking Moslem apparatchiks.
- The deepening of the oil depression and the resultant loss of cash flows needed by the sheiks to buy off radical denizens of Arab slums or at least to prevent them from joining forces with the mullahs.
- Moscow's active encouragement of a radical Moslem united front between the mullahs and the PLO, as a higher-leverage, lower-risk strategy than a direct attack on Saudi Arabia.

• The waiting game Moscow has been playing inside Iran politically and along her frontier militarily while waiting for Ayatollah
Khomeini to die.

The Treatment

Supplement moves to reunite NATO, to modernize it, and to defuse
the nuclear threat it poses for Europe by equipping the alliance with
a high-speed, high-powered Middle Eastern airlift capability. Europe's
depressed aircraft and airline industries could participate in the project
with their American counterparts. NATO could avoid any additional
cost for broadening its mission logistically and free itself from some of
the cost pressure burdening it militarily by informing the sheikdoms
that the airlift will be a client service rendered at no profit to the NATO
partners but also at no cost, that is, paid for by the sheikdoms needing
the protection. America has no other way of fulfilling her unilateral
obligation to protect the sheikdoms, which have no way of protecting
themselves. The NATO countries, as well as France, and no doubt the
Scandinavian countries, are already in pawn to Russia for a considerable
portion of their employment and fuel needs. The sheikdoms' payment
for the military airlift service could be payable, of course, in the form
of crude oil for jet fuel, over and above payment for equipment and
operating costs. Customary practice among OPEC members in such
bartering of crude oil for refined products calls for the crude to be
booked at discounts under the fictitious market price and for toll to be
paid on the refined products at a premium.

Whether America meets its self-imposed obligation to protect the
Persian Gulf by involving NATO or by going it alone with her highly
touted Rapid Deployment Force (RDF), a military base will be needed
in a politically reliable country within striking distance of the Gulf.
Senator Ernest F. Hollings of South Carolina has complained that
Washington has been shopping in Kenya, Somalia, Oman, and
Egypt for a home for the RDF but has ignored Israel. As he argues,
Israel is

> the logical storage depot for the equipment. Israel is close to the scene
> of possible military action. It is the only country in the region where we
> could land military aircraft. It is the only country with air and ground
> defenses that can protect the equipment. There is no other country
> remotely comparable to Israel in its ability to help us project our strength
> in the Persian Gulf, the Mediterranean, and in Southwest Asia.

True, Israel once did extend an invitation to America to use her airfields
for refueling, but President Carter never brought the offer to a head,
and no doubt the failure of his hostage "rescue" mission could be at-

tributed to this error of omission. In 1981, the Reagan administration took the initiative of reviving the U.S.-Israeli project but then abandoned it. Israel could be approached again in NATO's behalf (and, hopefully, the arrangement would be expanded to include the inventorying of parts as well). Israel's tiny but technologically advanced and commercially aggressive military products industry would fit perfectly into a NATO airlift system.

The Recovery

NATO would start to regain its lost plausibility the moment it found a unifying strategic purpose to enlarge the original economic purpose of the Common Market. Europe was flung into the 1980s with keen and painful memories of the prosperous decade of the oil boom when her industrial export business to the Middle East flourished. She struggled into the 1980s with this Middle Eastern market gone, barely subsisting on what was left of her American market, petrified that American protectionism would shut it altogether, and defeatist about her chances of persuading her bankrupt customers and debtors in Latin America to provide any comfort for either her factories or her banks. Moreover, she no longer had any lingering illusions about keeping Japanese competition out of Europe. She had deep misgivings about the political squeeze Russia was likely to put on her as the depression sharpened the economic squeeze. Last but not least, she had learned from her own bitter experiences with irresponsible rulers to share Russia's view of the potential for disaster invited by any power undertaking a two-front military operation, and she shared the dim view Russia took of the war games played first by Carter and then by Reagan.

The rudiments of investment accounting explain why a NATO airlift originating in the United States, relying on European fueling and repair bases, and terminating in the Middle East, with intermediate fallback fueling/repair facilities in Israel (and hopefully Egypt), would be an engine of profit as well as of power from the moment it was launched. No investment projects are ever more profitable than those developed as by-products of an existing infrastructure, offering incremental returns on investment already made—especially when customer financing is provided for a portion of the overhead. No advanced technological industry big enough to be a major claimant for investment funds comes close to making the recovery impact on a depressed world economy that the aircraft manufacturing and transportation industries do. Unlike the high-tech industries, they spring into action as quick and continuous employers of labor, consumers of materials, capital-intensive buyers of equipment, and cost-plus users of technical services doing the same—especially when no time-consuming delays for the construction cycle are needed to activate operations.

Moreover, the expedient of layering this particular economic activity on top of NATO's elaborate military structure would endow it with an earned cash flow from (for once!) a cash-on-the-barrelhead source. No high-cost, large-scale military installation in history has ever enjoyed anything like this. The allied armies of occupation in Germany after World War I were supported by borrowings so big that the loans went bad. The reconstruction of Europe and Japan after World War II was financed by nonrecurring gifts. Vendors of mercenaries from ancient times through the first Prussian kaisers down to Fidel Castro have rented out bodies only, not high-cost military overheads. The cost-accounting effect of basing a trans-Atlantic and trans-Mediterranean airlift on NATO would draw on OPEC's capital for NATO's income.

Andrew Mellon, Hoover's all-powerful secretary of the Treasury, was given to referring to "property passing back to its rightful owners." He used it to describe the depression phenomenon of mortgage lenders foreclosing on unsuccessful speculations. A NATO-based airlift to the Middle East would effect the same financial shift, but as a signal that the economic engines would be started up again, not slowed down; this on top of the neglected military support function it would fill.

Collateral Advantages

• Make France an offer she could not refuse: to rejoin NATO, newly established as the only new recovery game in sight.

• Use America's European partners in NATO to mend Washington's fences with Israel at the functional level, where basic mutual interests meet.

• Provide a well-covered bridge under which the sheikdoms as well as the poor, heavily populated Moslem countries (Egypt, Pakistan) could formalize their practical dependence on Israel (and on Israel's military connection with the United States via NATO) for their national security, extending NATO's mission from peace keeping in Europe to peace making between Israel and her Arab neighbors.

• Preserve and extend the Camp David process.

• Resolve the anomaly of trillion-dollar defense budgeting and double-digit unemployment by sending the depressed aeronautical sector of the U.S. economy into another of its roaring takeoffs.

• A fast takeoff for a long flight by the aeronautical sector of the U.S. economy, which has never yet failed to send the stock market flying ahead of it. Once insured against a crash landing of the market move of late 1982, the aeronautical sector's leadership is more likely to inspire a broader, more sustained market advance than the high-tech market leadership has done in post-bull market years, which have been selective and volatile.

• Develop a profit-and-security building alternative to high-powered arms peddling to the political "crazies" and the financially bankrupt.

CHAPTER TEN

International Finance

PRESCRIPTION #4
Recapitalizing the Banks

The Complaint

The chain reaction of credit collapse and the bankruptcy boom.

The Cure

A massive injection of patient, powerful new capital into the U.S. banking system.

The History

The complaint goes back to the oil inflation of the 1970s and America's failure to control it. The oil inflation was welcomed as the source of an income gusher. But the income gusher was turned into a base for bank borrowings on the bet—which seemed riskless all during the 1970s—that the oil-price inflation would be topless. The collapse of the pyramided world oil-price structure in the 1980s capsized the world bank-credit structure at the top of it and issued an enormous floating margin call on the world banking system; as fast as banks saw their oil loans go bad, their depositors, stockholders, and regulators saw their capital eaten into or wiped out altogether.

Predictably, as the oil boom went bad, the oil war went military. Predictably, too, as the competition inside the oil cartel sharpened, the confrontation between the superpowers heated up. The rest of the world economy was caught in a withering cross fire between the oil bust and the arms boom. Soon depression replaced dollars as America's number-one export, a grim reminder that, like it or not, the direction of the American economy determines the economic direction of every country in the world.

Inside the American economy, the banks were flooded with U.S.

Treasury bills and notes. The paper itself was riskless. But the retirement of private bank debt slowed down with each step-up in the flotation of public debt; the creditworthiness of the private debt load was an inevitable casualty. Meanwhile, the arms buildup guaranteed the pileup of new governmental debt on top of old oil debt. But its failure to heat up the economy, as arms buildups are supposed to do, had a chilling effect on the liquidity of bank borrowers and, consequently, on the liquidity of banks as well. Bank liquidity problems were compounded by one default after another, starting with world oil loans but by no means limited to them.

Banks are in the classic position of Caesar's wife, either above suspicion or beyond redemption. Their cash on hand can never meet a depositors' run. Federal deposit insurance has freed them from this historic risk at the hands of retail depositors. But it has not guaranteed their ability to operate as going concerns with their business borrowers. The danger that came to a head for the banking system as the depression deepened in mid-1982 was not that the banks would fail to meet calls for cash from their depositors, as they had during the classic panics that dominated America's financial and political history all during the nineteenth century and into the twentieth. It was the more sinister and no less deadly danger that their loss of capital reserves would panic them into shutting off credit advances to their commercial customers, forcing their customers to shut off credit repayments to them.

This danger of a repeat performance of 1929, in turn, recalled the original purpose of the Federal Reserve Act of 1913. Its passage was provoked by the felt need to avoid the cyclical recurrence of bank panics. Its purpose was to establish the Federal Reserve Board as the lender of last resort to the domestic banking system. The 1929–1932 banking crisis, however, revealed the fatal limitations of any domestic banking safety net. The credit collapse that touched it off originated in the political structure of Central Europe, whose decay dominated the interwar years. Because the banking crisis of 1929 swept into America from across the Atlantic, it toppled the domestic banking system as if Washington had failed to provide a central bank defense. Nevertheless, in 1933, the banking system, with the Federal Reserve Board still behind it but not modernized to extend its safety net across the Atlantic, was floated back into the recovery stream. True, it was outfitted with a new auxiliary safety net in the form of Federal Deposit Insurance. But this was just another domestic defense. It was deemed sufficient protection for a future deemed safe, as indeed it was from the domestic commercial banking standpoint, for a full half century. Yet the eruption of the world banking crisis of the 1980s caught the domestic banking system overlent at long-term and undercapitalized to meet short-term emergencies. The oil-credit collapse put the system in the exact same untenable position as the Reagan administration had created for itself:

with an open checkbook for foreign borrowers going bad but with a closed checkbook for borrowers at home struggling to stay afloat. Ronald Reagan retained his popularity long after his performance gave Reaganomics a bad name and rehabilitated inflation. But hard times always turn even the friendly banker around the corner into a figure of menace. By 1983, the domestic banking system was in acute need of a capital infusion and a facelift.

The Symptoms

• The real estate crash in Hong Kong, the world's "swingingest" financial growth center, tumbling pyramids of debt higher than the skyscraper headquarters of its 360 banks of deposit and spreading panic as it revealed the absence of an official lender of last resort.

• The chain reaction of banking crashes and governmental defaults in Mexico, Argentina, Venezuela, and Brazil wiping out overnight most or all of the capital of U.S. banks caught on the handout side of the no-payback deals.

• Canada surfacing in its new role as "Mexico North," with cash flows drying up throughout her economy, Canadian banks holding bad loans and calling good loans, and Ottawa teetering on the verge of exchange controls.

• The U.S. comptroller of the currency's growing list of sick banks, including not just the Penn Squares but major ones as well, and *The Japan Economic Journal*'s list of twenty-two countries "Penn Squared" nationally.

• The comptroller's other list of sick loans in bank portfolios comprising up to 30 percent of the total outstanding.

• The public suspicion aroused by assurances from bank spokesmen that their foreign loan losses were just petty-cash portions of their total loans, as if their loan portfolios were not 400 times greater than their capital, and as if their capital losses were not the carrier of the panic virus.

• The step-up of foreign oil-producer liquidation of U.S. bank deposits and U.S. Treasury holdings contributing to the return to the United States of a balance-of-payments deficit.

The Treatment

If just banks were on the sick list again, the treatment would simply be to send them to the market for new capital, giving their stockholders first call on new issues. But standard cures became academic as the float of bad foreign debt surged uncomfortably close to the trillion-dollar peril point. The banks on the sick list have had their hands full raising cash by placing their paper in the overnight market, and the sick list has been growing. They need a private placement, and on a scale more massive than any market within their reach could supply. By definition, realistic calls for recapitalization never appeal to the profit motive; the incentive to put up the money is to avoid the compounding of losses, and no fast talk about turning over a fast buck. True, private-sector investors and creditors enjoy the option of cutting their losses instead of throwing good money after bad. But the banking system is hardly manned by private operators. If it were, the banks would not enjoy the three-ply safety net the government gives them of deposit insurance, the discount window, and unlimited ordinary income deductions against any capital losses in government paper. Only Washington can provide the new capital banks need. Only a Washington investment source can afford to sit with billions invested, collecting neither interest nor dividends and waiving any repayment or redemption rights.

The bankruptcy boom of 1982 provoked understandable calls for the creation of a new government agency modeled after the Reconstruction Finance Corporation, which Hoover launched before the banking crisis came to a head and which Roosevelt expanded into a major arm of his New Deal administration and, after that, of his war administration. (In fact, Tommy Corcoran, who emerged as the spark plug of the New Deal, was a holdover from Hoover's RFC). But three considerations militate against a new executive-branch agency (which the RFC was) as a reliable means to recapitalize troubled banks: (1) The government has long since accumulated more executive agencies than it can manage or than Congress can oversee. (2) Compromising on the legislation needed to launch a new government agency takes time, and the troublesome evidence of banks running out of capital is proof that the government is running out of time. (3) The government, the banks, and their customers will all be better off with the government continuing to regulate them through the front door rather than trying to control them around the back door.

One consideration is reason enough for the Federal Reserve System to be the "designated hitter" in the banking crisis. Its capital is owned by its member banks, and their reserve deposits are its reserves. The treatment, accordingly, calls for designating the Federal Reserve as the chosen instrument for refinancing the banks. The way for it to do so is to buy convertible preferred stock, paying no dividends, in all banks on the comptroller's official sick list. The amount: up to 5 percent of the lending power any bank, large or small, had before it was hit by write-offs for bad loans and/or deposit losses. Capital advances on this scale would restore viability to any bank suffering from the loss of capital. Fair play for the Federal Reserve from banks recouping capital losses calls for them to pay something like a 10 percent compounded annual premium to the Federal Reserve for the accommodation if, when, and as they put their troubles behind them and call Fed-held preferred stock for redemption. But turnabout being fair play, prudence calls for the Fed to exercise the right to vote the removal of any managements unwilling or unable to change their ways or their luck. At that point, of course, the stockholders' equity in any bank jumped by the Fed would be nil, and its management would be targeted for stockholders' suits, a fate more costly than even the forfeiture of a chief executive officer's expense account.

The Recovery

Its return would be signaled by evidence that the banks had been restored to a comfortable capital position. They would be freed from the need to put violent pressure on credit markets and the Federal Reserve to meet emergency calls for overnight borrowings in the Fed funds market. They would be relieved of the exorbitant cash drain resulting from high interest payments for emergency accommodation; inasmuch as many banks—including most of those with foreign branches and capital losses—enjoy income tax exemption, their interest charges are not deductible and cause further capital drains. The substitution of permanent capital for short-term bank borrowings would have the immediate, electric effect of reducing interest rates, regardless of the rate of inflation.

On the Federal Reserve System's side of the bargain, it is the only source of permanent capital for troubled banks that could afford to waive current interest or dividend charges for accommodation on a massive scale; it pays no interest on the banking system's reserve deposits. Moreover, its management of the credit markets and of short-term interest rates is again and again frustrated by distress bank borrowing in the Fed funds market. A massive cure for the capital shortages of big banks would eliminate distortions in the Fed funds market that result in transactions at 30 percent when the Fed is signaling a 15 percent rate.

Politically, the effect of the Fed supplementing the role assigned to it in the 1913 act as the lender of last resort by doing double duty as the investor of last resort, and at no charge, would go far to quiet the bipartisan chorus of its congressional critics. This accommodation would offset the accusation that it pays no compensation to the Treasury for the balances the Treasury carries with it. Once the Fed did restore capital viability to the troubled banks, it would free itself from a great deal of the pressure to fine-tune the economy by manipulating the credit markets and, therefore, from the criticism it invites for mismanaging both. It would be forced to concentrate on the business of bank supervision, which it understands, and would be relieved of the job of managing the economy, which it does not understand, as its record clearly shows.

The Federal Reserve is also overdue to extend its regulatory duties to the supervision of the foreign branches of American banks, which, by virtue of their participation in the Eurodollar and Asiadollar markets, are under competitive pressure to adopt wild and wooly lending practices. The Federal Reserve Bank of New York is the foreign agent of the U.S. Treasury. The effective way to force foreign banks and the governments behind them to enter into direct government-to-government negotiations with Washington over the problems responsible for the foreign-loan crisis, as well as for those resulting from it, is for that branch of the Federal Reserve to assume regulatory responsibility for foreign branches of the banks. The opportunism the Federal Reserve has shown in pressing the banks to throw good money after bad has fed the crisis and deferred the day of government-to-government negotiation until irresponsible debtors break weakened creditors.

Once the Fed has established voting beachheads in the councils of banks suffering indigestion in the Eurodollar and/or Asiadollar market, it would be forced out from under the protective cover of any claim that it lacks jurisdiction to extend its regulatory operations to overseas branches. Its then dominant position would give it the incentive as well as the power to require foreign branches of U.S. banks to post reserves with it against deposits, just as domestic branches do, and to insure their dollar deposits up to $100,000, exactly as it does domestic deposits. The result would be salutary: A torrential flow of deposits would flood foreign branches. Every sheik could open deposit accounts for his extended family, and the respective foreign banking systems, which have spent the last thirty years exploiting the naïveté and irresponsibility of the U.S. government, would be forced to follow the lead of the U.S. banks.

Collateral Advantages

• Lower domestic interest rates due to less short-term borrowing by banks with foreign-loan problems.

• An end to the anomaly that has put the Federal Reserve Board in the untenable position of encouraging continued foreign lending by banks with staggering capital losses abroad, while simultaneously discouraging domestic lending by those same banks.

• An ultimate sanction against irresponsible managements refusing to benefit from matriculation in the school of hard knocks. Once the Federal Reserve authorities exercised their voting rights to convert their preferred stockholdings and to vote a management out, the common stockholders would be left with no equity—except for any damages they might recover from ousted managements.

PRESCRIPTION #5
Bartering Food for Fuel

The Complaint

The failure of the world market to satisfy America's twin need for high farm income and low fuel cost.

The Cure

Negotiating long-term government-to-government deals that sidestep the market and yield annual oil-cost cuts and farm-income increases.

The History

Agriculture accounts for America's principal foreign trade problem. Its periodic booms have resulted from cycles of war justifying gifts, loans, gold movements, and all the other forms of emergency buying. Its recurrent depressions have been precipitated by the repeated failure of its cash-export markets. These failures have repeatedly aroused demands for and recourse to domestic cash subsidies. Not until the oil war emblazoned the bumper-sticker slogan I suggested—"Bushels for Barrels"—did our crop-export failures provoke calls to switch our crop-export business from a cash to a barter basis.

Farm radicalism in America has always been seen as progressive, but its intellectual roots are actually reactionary. Its simplistic strategy has been to compensate for the shrinkage of cash-export markets by paying farmers to take land out of production or, alternatively, by buying up their unexportable crops. An early and famous slogan of the farm revolt is still remembered from the panic of 1873: "It's time to raise less corn and more hell." But it was not until the farm depression of the mid-1920s staged its ugly preview of 1929 that the Grain Belt's demand for export subsidies split the Republican party. And it was not until FDR's first term that this demand evolved into a priority governmental operation—with cash paid out in subsidies to U.S. farmers for grain and cotton supplied to needy countries like Brazil and China. Nothing was requested or received in return.

Because the Republican farm rebels of the 1920s had demanded export subsidies, FDR borrowed the idea and used it to discredit the Republican establishment. Then he polished this Republican legacy into a prime asset of the New Deal and boasted of it as a "domestic tariff." First he paid the farmers to take acreage out of production. Then he paid them again to put the surplus they were still producing into storage. Finally, he paid them all over again in the form of export subsidies. Though FDR was courageous and wise in making the case for internationalism against a strong isolationalistic program, he was influenced by his choice for secretary of agriculture, Henry Wallace, who became his second vice president in 1941. Wallace spearheaded the drive to subsidize farm exports to South America, a program I opposed on the grounds that it would undercut farm economies in the Americas that the New Deal was supporting out of other pockets.

Agriculture had promised—on paper at least—to be America's strongest industry; it proved to be her weakest. From the perspective of half a century of history, the current depression revived the early warning of the mid-1920s that Wall Street's troubles blow in from the Farm Belt. In the 1980s, American agriculture started to go broke waiting for export demand to materialize at acceptable prices in a supposedly free market. But it refrained from blaming the government for its failure to negotiate the favorable terms of trade the market was not providing. By virtue of intensifying its mechanical and chemical productivity, American agriculture ran itself into a vicious circle: The more high-powered its machinery, the more land it needed to absorb the cost of working the machinery. Farmers are not habitual buyers of land for cash. They are unconventional enough to borrow cash equivalents from banks to pay for it, but conventional enough to depend on cash income to carry the loan instead of relying on noncash assets received in barter. Therefore, the more insolvent they made themselves buying land for paper on which they owed cash, the higher they drove land prices and the lower they ran their own liquidity. Meanwhile, with characteristic perversity, farm owners bit the hand that fed them. They stirred up a storm of protest against foreigners buying American farms and put restrictions on their purchases, even though foreigners are known to make large-scale land purchases for cash and to overpay for them.

The Carter administration, to make a bad situation worse, belied its dedication to free enterprise by underwriting an elaborate scheme for providing for storage bins on farms and paying farmers for the "service" of putting their surplus crops into the "loan," as it was called. This was no substitute for a return to market viability, but the farmers, in the name of free enterprise, took the government-surplus bins as a better outlet than the market could offer. Soon the grain storage bins matched the oil storage tanks in surplus spillage.

If the government had known how to operate in the real world, it would have seized on the surpluses as an excuse for developing barter alternatives. By the 1980s, this policy move offered the only hope of relief from the double cost of piling up farm surpluses and simultaneously going through the charade of paying farmers to carry them while they rotted. Damming up U.S. surpluses at the point of production also ignored the endless opportunities to use them as a bargaining lever at points of consumption. Instead, at the height of Reagan's row with Europe over the Soviet gas pipeline, and with no sensitivity to the connection between energy and food, the White House permitted Secretary of Agriculture John Block to declare economic war against Europe on the farm front. Backed up by the conservative spokesman Senator Jesse Helms, chairman of the Senate Agriculture Committee, Block went to the unbelievable extreme of exclaiming, "We have only one alternative . . . to deviate temporarily from our free market stance and engage in costly, short-term trade wars." Presumably, the blessings of the administration's "free market stance" were to be reserved for the domestic economy. To leave no doubt that America's alienated ally, Europe, was the target of this offensive, Block told a congressional committee: "We are going to do battle with the [European Economic Community] wherever and whenever it is necessary." Helms added: "It's time we gave them a dose of their own medicine." The administration seemed blind to the fact, when it rechanneled its farm war from Russia to Europe, that Europe was America's number-one farm customer. Due to the ignorance, the obstinacy, and the cowardice of the American government, however, the prevailing policy called for producing, subsidizing, and waiting for the export market to come back to life.

It was not until after the Reagan administration suffered its defeat in the Farm Belt during the 1982 midterm elections that it gave up on any hope of revival for America's farm-export markets (in a world convulsed with malnutrition). Then it came up with another harebrained scheme hashed out of the most impractical of FDR's hand-me-downs and Reagan's hangups. (*The Wall Street Journal* even reported that the program "was suggested by Assistant Agriculture Secretary William Lesher, who wasn't aware of the earlier program," a nice case of decision making colliding with history.) The new New Deal it offered the farmers called for the government to pay them to take land out of production—as if the government had not been down that road before —only to discover that the land kept in production would still produce enough to offset "savings" from the idled land. But the most asinine part of the new New Deal was the payment feature: not cash this time but crops paid in kind from the government's overflowing bins. This offer showed no appreciation of what farmers would do with any windfall gift of surplus crops: They would dump it for cash, sending market prices to still lower levels. When the Reagan administration was finally driven to adopt the barter approach, it confined its efforts to the domestic economy, ignoring the world economy.

Oil is on the other side of the barter problem. America—that is, in the beginning, Texas—gave OPEC the idea for holding back oil production in order to hold up prices. In the days when oil was still going for pennies (less than $1 per barrel), the legislature in Austin delegated regulatory power to the Texas Railroad Commission. "Prorationing" was the ingenious word coined to describe the procedure. Each month the Texas Railroad Commission told the Texas oil-well operators how many days they could run their rigs the following month. As it happened, the less oil they took out, the more money they poured into Louisiana, a move which spared its growing army of producers the discipline of "prorationing." The game Texas and Louisiana played together when oil producers were happy to lift oil out of the ground for less than a dollar a barrel is the same game that OPEC played with its weaker members: limiting their production, bankrolling them, and trading a piece of their action for protection of their price structure.

The irony implicit in America's failure to put her oil imports on a bartered basis is that the oil companies, whose thinking has dominated Washington, habitually rely on barter in their commercial dealings with one another. Their cash-rich positions have freed them from any pressure to see how business practices of the oil industry could apply on the political front. The oil companies have not even bothered to learn from the tactics other American businesses have often employed to move the goods they produce. In the early 1970s, Coca-Cola, whose name is synonymous with hard-hitting managerial procedures, especially in dealing with governments, took the barter route. (For reasons of its own, it prefers to describe its method of dealing with the blocked-currency countries as "counterpurchasing," meaning two-way, balancing cash transactions.) Headquartered in Essen in the German industrial heartland, Coca-Cola's bartering arm will buy any product it can sell for cash anywhere in the world to any government willing to take its syrup but unwilling or unable to pay in currency convertible to dollars. Its swaps have included forklifts from Bulgaria, Avea wine from Yugoslavia, martini toothpicks from Korea, and Krakus beer from Poland. To make sure that the products it takes on pass muster as cash merchandise, Coke sends its quality-control engineers into its barter partners' plants as part of the deal. No discussions about free markets.

Northrop is one government contractor that has made close use of my thinking over the years. Northrop made headlines in 1982 when it announced a barter deal with Turkey. The deal called for Turkey to receive new Northrop fighter planes, the F-5G and the F-18L, and to pay for them with wine, refrigerators, and other products to be distributed throughout the Third World by Northrop. Any American exporter of a manufactured product—and an advanced manufactured product at that—willing to peddle Turkish wine instead of collecting cash is a convert to the principle of barter. Northrop put this same principle to work with Canada. As part of its sale of F-18s to Ottawa, Northrop helped line up a customer in Liberia for a Canadian maker of paper cups. And as part of its 1976 deal with Switzerland for 72 F-5Es, the firm helped Swiss companies sell elevators to Egypt and precision tools to Spain. Fighter planes are obviously more sophisticated than paper cups, wine, and elevators, or precision drills, yet the Northrop management had the good sense to see the connection between them and to exploit it.

What is new about Northrop's breakthrough is that it has discovered what every company of consequence in Europe and Japan has always known: There is money in barter and, what is more, it offers the formula for growth in a shrinking world economy caught between galloping needs and crippled solvency. The list of companies committed to barter and/or countertrade is a roster of blue-chip success stories, headed by General Electric and Sears, Roebuck, and includes America's most flamboyant corporate resurrection, Chrysler. The innovative cars-for-alumina swap with Jamaica that Chrysler announced in 1983 was a case of necessity rediscovering history: Walter Chrysler built the company on export barter deals in minor markets during the 1920s. Increasingly important during a depression, there is overhead absorption and employment through barter too, not to mention the wherewithal to support the continuous research and development that the U.S. government interrupts at the start of each cash squeeze.

Israel caught the Reagan administration's attention at the height of the anti-Israel tide after the Beirut massacre in the fall of 1982. Defense Minister Ariel Sharon, no visionary free-trade reformer, picked Honduras, the CIA's staging area for military countermoves against "Marxist" power clusters in the Caribbean, as a far from conspicuous barter partner. On the safe assumption that any American client offers a growth market for arms, he put on his salesman suit and launched a whirlwind invasion of this banana republic. His coup dramatized Israel's formal challenge to America's remaining export industry: arms. It revealed Israel's adeptness at barter as an arms sales tool. Honduras' most expensive export staple, mahogany, fit neatly with Israel's most conspicuous basic shortage, wood. It also demolished the Reagan administration's set response that using barter would put the U.S. government into the business of foreign trade. The government is in it but with characteristic inefficiency and indirection: With cash diverted from deeper, freer pockets than the Pentagon boasts, it lends to the Pentagon's foreign customers as a subterfuge less politically abrasive than funding the Pentagon's true budget needs. Bartering for hard goods pays better than lavishing hard cash on cynical customers.

America has simply refused to participate in the barter game, which the OPEC countries, Russia, Japan, Germany, and especially well-run U.S. firms, to name just a few, have played so profitably. (Even New

Zealand, so far from the action at the world's crossroads, has been drawn into it, selling lamb to Iran through a broker in exchange for Iranian oil, which, true to form in barter, was peddled off to a third party outside New Zealand.) She has underestimated the strength and importance of agripower and the bonus it offers of complete immunity from a national crop failure: a first in history. She has been naïve enough to give away her reliability as a volume supplier, instead of exacting a premium for guaranteeing it.

America's self-defeating oil strategy has run into its most glaring reversal in Mexico. Mexico is plagued by a high infant mortality rate, a growing and impoverished population, malnutrition, and deficient health and sanitation facilities. Her only hope of achieving a decent living standard has been to export surplus population north to the United States as illegal immigrants. Yet America has acquiesced in Mexican price gouges for oil and gas that Mexico will not be able to deliver for at least a decade. In the process of going broke, Mexico all but broke the major U.S. banks that met her demands for advances with no questions asked. The Mexican default also showed history repeating itself. After his part in the Vietnam debacle, Secretary of Defense Robert McNamara was rewarded for his signal contribution to the American economy with the chairmanship of the World Bank. On a smaller scale, A. W. Clausen, the head of the Bank of America, had the dubious distinction of elbowing his bank ahead of Chase Manhattan into the number-one position among Mexico's lenders. He was rewarded with elevation into McNamara's old bank job. When Mexico went broke, the spotlight that went with this honor prompted Clausen's successors at the Bank of America to put a statement over the news ticker announcing that "the Bank of America is not broke."

When Mexico's third devaluation in 1982 finally plunged her into bankruptcy and chaos, Washington panicked and offered to throw still more dollars into the bottomless pit of the Mexican economy through the $1 billion Reagan gave to Mexico for an oil reserve America did not need. But it was a bitter irritant for domestic claimants low on cash for necessities, beginning with the American farmers who found themselves on short rations for carrying grain that could have fed Mexico on better than a subsistence level. The Reagan administration was ready with an explanation for its habit of finding business-as-usual responses to emergency problems, claiming that it was good business to lock Mexico into a promise to deliver the oil at no more than $35 a barrel as insurance against subsequent price increases. Out in the real world, however, the world spot-market price was slipping. One of the major unintegrated refiners systematically arranged tanker deals with Iran at significant discounts under the cartel price, paying with foodstuffs. At the end of May 1983, this company had chiseled the barter price down to $23.42 a barrel in a $28–$29 market.

Mexico, meanwhile, remained calm and turned her own admitted weakness into a source of strength at the bargaining table. She needed the giveaways to buy the proprietary American oil-field equipment to produce oil that she could sell for the announced price increases. She speeded up the vicious circle by paying for the equipment with promises to deliver marked-up oil and gas and by servicing her inflated debt with pesos that were devalued and then frozen.

The Symptoms

- The disintegration of OPEC.
- The backlash from OPEC's loss of control over oil prices on the loan portfolios and capital positions of the banks stuck with oil loans.
- The desperate need of the banks and their examiners to find a nonmarket price basis for valuing their loans on oil cargoes, reserves, equipment, and tankers.
- Seizure of oil cargoes en route to defaulting refineries, and arson of same.
- The spectacle of Iran, despite her membership in OPEC, relying on barter to move 70 percent of its oil.
- The step-up of three-way barter deals packaged together with shipments of cheap Soviet oil, among Russia, her satellites, and third-party governments.
- The stubborn insistence of the major international oil companies on paying their original contract prices of $34 to $40 a barrel in cash in a market that was already broken to $28 without finding bottom, at a 1982 cost to the four Aramco partners alone of $7 billion to $8 billion. (According to the prestigious international oil consultant Walter J. Levy, OPEC's loss of control threatened to take prices on a further tumble to $20 or even $15.)
- Indications that the oil glut might cost even the Saudis the remnants of their trade surplus.
- The Reagan administration's abandonment of its once fervent commitment to free-market principles and policies in coping with the farm depression.
- Its embarrassed, rapid-fire substitution of one farm-subsidy program for another.
- The building boom in grain storage bins.
- The failure of the farm futures markets to participate in the 1982 recovery in the gold and silver markets, as they normally do when the latter benefit from inflationary stimulus.
- The chain reaction of farm insolvency and bankruptcy.
- The pursuit of bartered farm deals by farm organizations traditionally opposed to them.
- Starvation spreading with the American farm depression.

• The rise of the U.S. foreign trade deficit toward the $100 billion-a-year level.

• The contraction in the world shipping fleet reflected in Hong Kong's banking crisis and London's insurance scandal.

• Israel's successful penetration of the Latin American growth market for arms, traditionally a U.S. market preserve.

The Treatment

Convene a White House conference of all private-sector participants in foreign barter deals to instruct all Cabinet-level officials on how the birds and the bees do it in world trade. A congressional initiative in this direction is in line with the pattern set by the Senate Armed Services Committee's request to the President for a report on weaponry. Congress is armed with constitutional powers over foreign trade, parallel to its powers over appropriations for weapons. To broaden the effect of any such action-oriented White House briefing session, the Federal Reserve Bank of New York could summon member banks from around the country to an emergency conference. It is the chosen agent of the U.S. government in financial dealings with foreign governments and their central banks and their custodianship of holdings of gold and U.S. Treasury securities.

The key to barter dealings is the bilateral and trilateral approach: government-to-government, central-bank-to-central-bank, and with foreign government-controlled corporations. The rule abroad is that government corporations, notably Pemex in Mexico, are the chosen instruments for national oil dealings. The more realistic operations, notably Russia's, have operated on a barter basis for years. The less realistic, like Mexico's, have resorted to barter after they have run out of money. This practical consideration—that governments and their agencies are the principals on the other side of the table in barter dealings—calls for the government to learn to play the game professionally, with no apologies for crimping the style of the market.

The first step would be for the White House to instruct the State and Treasury departments to initiate bilateral discussions with all governments identified as suppliers of oil to the United States and with all those of interest to U.S. exporters of surplus products accounting for either governmental relief payments (e.g., agriculture) or governmental unemployment benefits (e.g., heavy machinery). The bilateral-trade-agreement approach worked well in the early days of the Roosevelt administration as a booster on the road of recovery.

The moment the White House designated the first government on the barter list, every other government needing to move oil out or take food or machinery in would join the stampede to get into the number-two position. This approach fits the quick-fix-and-lots-of-them approach to prosperity, in contrast with the simplistic cure-all approach, which is nonfunctional, like a world economic conference doomed to talk about generalities. Pragmatism would call for choosing a barter partner with relatively little oil to offer but needing a great deal of food. This choice would set the pattern for the terms of trade in America's favor. The farm cooperatives could play an invaluable role as negotiating agents for the government.

Mexico's geography and needs make her the obvious first choice for lead-off batter. Thanks to her distressed debtor position, any announcement that America was going the barter route would whet Mexico's appetite for an oil-and-gas market. The fact that Mexico is richer in future oil and gas reserves than in present production would strengthen America's trading position: Mexico needs American machinery to bring those reserves into production, and America needs to get more job-creating export sales. Cash advances do no one any good.

Once Mexico agreed to sell her oil and gas at long-term fixed prices payable in U.S. food and equipment, she would buy herself protection against falling oil export prices. She would also give the United States an irresistible financial motive to expedite long-term credits for oil-field equipment as well as for food. Politically, once Mexico, in her dire straits, saw who was meeting her food and oil-field equipment needs and how they were being paid for, her defenses against Cuba would rise. She certainly would be better off trying to pay for her imports of food and industrial equipment with fixed amounts of oil than with pesos worth less by the day. The exchange value of oil would be easier for the two countries to peg than the buying power of the peso. The irony of the Mexican-American financial crisis is that Mexico needs to put her dealings with America on a barter basis more desperately than America does; yet America would profit more from the switch than Mexico.

America could make a strong start toward helping Mexico out of her misery and aiding herself as well by setting up a process to control and legalize immigration of Mexican refugees. In a May 1983 interview in *The Washington Post,* former West German chancellor Helmut Schmidt said, "If you do not put Mexico on a sound economic basis, the United States will soon be flooded by Mexicans pouring across the border." A first step would call for putting tax withholdings from their earnings on a business basis. In that case, special tax credits could be offered to newly arrived Mexicans as an incentive to attract them out of the moonlighting economy into the legal, tax-paying economy. The condition would be an agreement on their part to earmark the withholdings for payment in pesos to their relatives in Mexico. In that case, guarantees would be needed from Mexico not to tax the pesos owned by the relatives. The U.S. Treasury would withhold the dollars and give the Mexican treasury an export credit in consideration of handling the peso commission for the naturalized immigrants. The American government could then be sure of recapturing the Mexican market for its exports and, incidentally, of controlling a long-term option on Mexican oil and gas.

Washington could invite Mexico to offer her oil to all of OPEC's customers at $10 a barrel, well under the world price, and to guarantee to make up the discount by shipping food to Mexico. This would disarm OPEC and bring some relief to Mexico. It certainly would have been better business than rewarding Mexico for going broke and jeopardizing her already wounded bank creditors, while Washington refused to take advantage of the overpriced dollar to cut the price of the oil we were stuck with by even a penny.

This same device of bartering fixed amounts of oil for food could be applied to deals elsewhere, including three countries in the dynamite belt of the Moslem world—Egypt, Iran, and Pakistan—but the most obvious candidate after Mexico is Nigeria, America's number-one foreign supplier. *The Wall Street Journal* in September 1982 reported that Sheik Ali Khalifa al-Sabih of Kuwait, a key OPEC official, had singled out Nigeria as the weakest link in OPEC. He also warned that OPEC would stop at nothing to peg the price of oil at $34 per barrel in a market that Libya was already demoralizing at $28. Nigeria needs, said the *Journal*, "to produce at least 1.3 million barrels a day [presumably at OPEC's ceiling price] to stay afloat financially." Yet Nigeria's production was down to 600,000 barrels a day at Libya's price—or lower. Nigeria was wide open for a U.S. bilateral barter bail-out; instead Washington concentrated its fire on opening a second front in the trade war with Europe, dumping farm products on the Continent after having tried to sabotage the pipeline deal.

The threat of doing oil barter business with China, which has vast oil reserves and is hungry for oil-field engineering skills, would force Russia into large-scale barter deals with America. By 1983, selling Russia on the idea was no longer the problem; resistance to it in Washington was. A major American international trading concern took the initiative in developing a dairy-products-for-nickel deal, but Washington rejected it as a matter of policy. True, Russia clearly represents America's most serious source of insecurity, as America does to Russia, but the solution to any problem between Russia and America is to get as far as possible from ideological differences and as close as possible to nuts, bolts, barns, and bins. I have found Russians of standing prepared to accept the suggestion that America knows a better, more mutually advantageous, and safer way for the two powers to deal than looking down each other's missile silos. Helmut Schmidt also recognized the economic prudence of dealing with the Russians: "My town of Hamburg has traded with Novgorod for at least six hundred years. If we traded only with democracies, we would ruin our economies very quickly." America can offer the Russians a technical advantage in return for a political compromise, heretofore considered nonnegotiable. If the political consideration is to calm down the Middle East—and Russia did recognize the case for restraint in limiting her participation in the battle of Beirut in the summer of 1982—Russia could keep her part of the bargain by delivering enough oil wherever America arranged to have it delivered (not necessarily to American ports). But barter could also offer a basis for another try at a more ambitious nuclear arms truce.

Russia's famous food problem is twofold: wheat for human consumption, and corn, soybeans, and other feed grains for herds and flocks. Russia is too far north and too short of water to grow her own feed crops; her most productive farmlands are on the same latitude as Ontario. She can rely on non-U.S. sources of wheat for a significant portion of her import needs, but she has a critical dependence on U.S. agriculture for feed crops. Though she appears to be meeting her feed-crop needs in European markets, the fodder she has been buying is American in origin, transshipped to European mills. Thanks to Washington's naïveté in giving other countries a free gift of the brokerage, processing, and freight of the grains she refuses to sell to Russia directly, America's mills are working part-time while Europe's are working overtime. America would have bargained more advantageously with both Russia and Europe if she had controlled both the work on the raw agricultural products and the negotiations for the sale of the end products. Without drawing on American feed crops, Russia will be doomed to slaughter her herds of cattle and flocks of poultry.

Over the years of my vigorous advocacy of food-for-oil barter with Russia, with nuclear arms negotiation as a fringe benefit, I have found no more sympathetic ear than that of Senator J. James Exon, Democrat of Nebraska. On June 5, 1982, Exon went to McCook, Nebraska, to issue his "call on the United States to sweeten our arms control and reduction initiatives by offering, in conjunction therewith, a guaranteed long-term contract for raw and finished food. Such an arrangement would obviously be mutually beneficial." It would apply a lesson learned from the successful Soviet gambit of seizing upon Western Europe's natural gas needs. Instead of wringing our hands in desperation, why don't we deal in long-term contracts with the Soviets for something we have that they need?

I was particularly gratified to note that Senator Exon broadened his historic call to apply not only to bulk grain but to finished, packaged, and sanitized meats and meat products, as well as dairy, vegetable, and fruit products. Ever since the Roosevelt recession of 1938 when I stated my opposition to the first campaign for dumping crop exports, launched by Secretary of Agriculture Wallace, I have consistently deplored the narrow view that has relegated American agriculture to be a hewer of wood and a drawer of water for its export customers. This view has cost America an uncountable inflation of domestic food costs and a correspondingly uncountable deflation of export income. Processing raw crops domestically and exporting the finished food products would be immeasurably more profitable for America; it would also be cheaper for her barter partners.

Poland offers another test case for the use of barter to bargain politically with governments in behalf of peoples America wants to help. Poland's needs offer an opportunity as far as American grain exports are concerned. The Polish crisis is in part a food crisis. Russia cannot afford to lose Poland as one of her neighboring breadbaskets. Dangling food in front of the desperate Warsaw and Moscow regimes offers Washington a means of asserting America's ideals and strength throughout satellite Europe, without military risk or political provocation, yet with obvious implications for the instability of the Polish dictatorship.

The Polish crisis gives America an opportunity to forge a direct Polish connection and to put it to effective use both with NATO countries and as a counter to Russia. First, America could move to direct large-scale food exports to Poland, whose cities are in need of direct shipments into their empty pipelines. If America were to fill them, she could not only move burdensome surpluses but could also mend her fences with West Germany, her other alienated NATO allies, and her non-NATO critics. All of them live in dread of the Polish crisis spreading across Europe. American food shipments to Poland, backed up with financial contributions from Germany and the others, would be cheaper than paying America's farmers all over again to cut back on acreage use while hunger strikes abroad and budget deficits at home rise. Helping to pay for American food shipments to Poland would be cheaper for Western European countries than living in dread of igniting the Polish crisis, or increasing their assessments to NATO, or cutting back their imports into the United States. Secondly, America could designate Poland her food agent in dealing with Russia. This would make more sense than continuing to permit Russia to manipulate America's crop futures markets. (See Prescription #15.) But until Washington takes some initiative, Russia will continue to angle for a cheap option on American food all during the 1980s, and America will remain frustrated in her desire to strengthen Poland's hand in her dispute with Russia. The way to solve both problems is to dangle American food before Russia while showing Western Europe that food can be a bargaining weapon against the Kremlin and, by virtue of being America's distinctive weapon, a credible reason to repose trust in America again.

The Arab world is even more susceptible to bombardment by America's wealth of finished products. No Moslem country has facilities for processing, much less storing, such products as soya bacon and soya milk. The Moslem ban on pork products and the absence of food hygiene are restrictive. In 1982, for example, Egypt, the most advanced of the Arab countries, as well as the one most richly endowed by nature, was forced to mobilize her controlled media for an all-out, three-year offensive against her well-fed rat population, admitting that its rodent population explosion had outrun the supply of chemical eradicants and charging it with the destruction and spoilage of food supplies. American food technology can build bridges for Moslems to the modern world. Such a commercial windfall offers a by-product for the military budget: Where grain goes by ship, packaged food products can go by air. America's export transportation revenue has been dwindling for years. Air-cargo carriers needed for military purposes are expensive, but would be less so if a bona fide commercial need for them were found.

Washington has little to show for its dealings with the poor and populous Moslem countries. It would do better to forgo the dubious advantage of cash advances from the sheikdoms. These cash advances now cost a maximum in money and buy a minimum in nutrition—farmers in the supplying countries go broke, and beneficiaries on the sheiks' lists of clients go hungry. Reducing graft throughout the Moslem world is not a moral issue but one of efficiency. Barter would move more food into channels of consumption than cash grants have a chance of doing.

After the Moslem world went broke in the collapse of the oil boom, the Korean economy remained the only dynamic national operation on all five continents. "Giving feed grains to an animal," the Seoul spokesman of the U.S. Feed Grains Council told *Farmfutures* magazine, "was against the Korean concept that viewed grains as only good for human beings." But Korea has become a major market for U.S. feed grains, and Japan, beef-conscious but not beef-eating, turned to Korea as a feedlot as her export-dependent industries ran out of cash customers. Korea and Japan made a good thing between them of bartering Korean food and products derived from U.S. farm raw materials for Japanese industrial products, mainly capital goods with nowhere else to go. Typically, America furnished the bait without, however, being set up to haul in any catch.

The Recovery

Moving America's wasted food surplus for value received, either from barter partners or from third-party sources, would get recovery started. Giving the food-processing functions to American industry and exporting the end products would speed the recovery at both ends of the line. It would unwind the oil inflation by ensuring supplies of cheap imported oil, not so much to America as to other industrial countries cooperating with her and short of their own oil.

Recovery would benefit from getting an economic handle on Russia and exploiting it to get a political handle on her too. Doing a barter business with Russia that would strengthen America's hand and establish Russia's economic dependence on us would effect substantial military economies, while getting American agriculture back on its feet. It would open the way to significant avoidance of wasteful, large-scale, future-year burdens on the budget for nuclear arms and for farm aid.

America's unique agricultural economy is an arsenal of power almost entirely unmobilized. Incidentally, it is also a source of emergency first aid for the Third World, which presents a frustrating paradox unparalleled in world history: All of its members are as undernourished as they are underdeveloped, yet all of them are ambitious to industrialize rather than to improve agriculturally. None of them, however, has yet been willing to heed the advice given by Sir Arthur Lewis in *The Janeway Lectures* at Princeton in 1977 (which won him the Nobel Prize); namely, that the route to industrialization for an agricultural country is through the development of its agriculture. Moral posturing against mobilizing food as a weapon ignores its role as a promoter of peace. Utilization of this tactic can spare millions of innocent people the agony of killer weapons that will go off if the mercy weapons that are ready are not brought into play in time.

Collateral Advantages

• Development of a commercial source of freight revenue to help pay the cost of the air-cargo carriers America needs to supply her advanced bases in the Middle East.

• An incentive to Western Europe to tilt toward America and to reactivate her considerable bargaining power against Russia.

• Relief for the American government from reviving the grain embargo against Russia and wondering what to do after it fails again.

PRESCRIPTION #6
Exporting the Federal Deficit

The Complaint

The extortionate interest rates resulting from astronomic deficits.

The Cure

Export the deficit by selling to dollar-rich OPEC governments long-term, nonmarketable Treasury paper subject to no interest charges until maturity.

The History

No exercise in rediscovering the wheel is needed; fiddling with its old spokes will do the trick. The movement of money follows the movement of ideas. In the first chapter of American financial history, Alexander Hamilton imported from London Robert Walpole's thinking about how to re-fund a mountain of short-term debt into comfortable long-term paper. Hamilton's market operations then attracted the money of shrewd British speculators, who joined his Tory constituents in buying up the debt of the Continental Congress at deep discounts and converting it into his brand-new, gilt-edged "funded debt." During the Civil War, J. P. Morgan made his reputation by finding hard European money to relieve the Treasury of the pressure to place short-term paper. These two episodes, celebrated in forgotten tomes, illustrate the axiom that battles to defend currencies from deficits, like battles between armies, are best fought overseas. Hindsight has associated both victories with the growing pains of a young republic, but as America came of age she ignored the applicability of her struggle to remain maturely productive and avoid sliding into decadence.

More recently, in 1962, the Kennedy administration revived this approach without recalling its hoary tradition. It pioneered a device for placing nonmarketable, long-term Treasury bonds with governments that were dependent on the United States, friendly enough to admit it, and rich enough to help her. These instruments bear the official designation of Roosa Bonds. They were the creation of Robert Roosa, then the undersecretary of the Treasury for monetary affairs. A superb technician, Roosa designed these private placements to ease the pressure on the dollar that had developed with the rise in the U.S. balance-of-payments deficit. During 1961 and 1962, the deficit had jumped to $3 billion, which at that time seemed big enough to be troublesome; it put the dollar under a cloud, even though the United States was still running a comfortable trade surplus.

Beginning in 1962, the U.S. Treasury placed a total of $10 billion to $15 billion of Roosa Bonds with the three dollar-rich central banks. The West German Bundesbank took the lion's share. The Swiss authorities put their good housekeeping seal of approval on Roosa Bonds by buying some, and the Japanese authorities advertised their country's new status as a dollar power by following suit. This impressive achievement psychologically displaced an overwhelming amount of selling pressure on the dollar. Even more, it advertised the solidity of America's partnership with both her defeated former enemies and called attention to their financial strength and Washington's political determination to ensure the stability of the dollar. Interest rates were not a problem then, and Roosa Bonds carried coupons approximately equal to going market rates.

In any case, the consideration in this intergovernmental transaction was not yield but management of the dollar deficit. The maturities ran for two to five years. Moreover, the fine print made them readily extendable, if needed or even desired. More providential still as a token of the cooperative spirit Roosa inspired, they protected the United States against an exchange-rate penalty in the event of dollar weakness. However, as in the case of Hamilton's historic achievement and of Morgan's, Roosa's was shrugged off as relevant only to the specific problem he solved. Its applicability to the recurrence of the same problem in different form was forgotten, although the Treasury still routinely lists its nonmarketable debt in a special category.

Reagan had spent six full years on the campaign trail spouting slogans extolling the sanitizing, invigorating wisdom of "free-market forces" and deploring the government's heavy-handed intervention into their "miraculous workings." These same markets, supposedly straitjacketed by government interference, had by 1982 improvised a characteristically safe and shrewd defense against the erosive effect of insupportable interest rates in credit standings. This improvisation was simple enough to become an instant success in the Eurodollar bond market.

The new device was the "zero-coupon" bond. It was exactly what this descriptive tag suggested: a noninterest-bearing bond issued at a more or less deep discount (deeper if the credit rating of the issuer was lower but in any case redeemable at maturity for par). Corporations in need of long-term money and/or under pressure to raise cash easily placed bonds by the billions all through 1982. To be sure, some corporations with credit ratings less lustrous than Exxon's, let alone the U.S. Treasury's, accepted discounts of over 50 percent; others settled for maturities of no more than five years. So buying the Reagan prospectus and trusting the workings of the free market (which the Eurodollar market certainly is) calls for the U.S. Treasury to follow where corporate treasuries have led: into selling U.S. Treasury zero-coupon bonds to foreign buyers, subject to three caveats—that the buyers be governments, that the issues be nonmarketable, and that the discounts be nominal.

The Symptoms

• Interest rates remaining unacceptably high, even when dropping drastically.

• Drops in interest rates—even temporary ones—destabilizing markets.

• Collapse of the economy becoming the condition for drops in interest rates.

• Pervasive fears, not just inside the securities market but throughout the economy, that insatiable governmental demands for credit would crowd out private claimants for the productive borrowings needed to produce the earnings needed to produce the tax revenues needed, finally, to reduce the deficit: a Catch-22.

• Another Catch-22 of the collapsed economy: collapsing tax collections and inflating tax refunds (to the point at which fiscal 1983 tax refunds of $112 billion, if avoided by a vigorous economic recovery, would have converted the $110 billion deficit into a $2 billion surplus).

• Volatility in the securities markets incited by speculation over Treasury/Federal Reserve maneuvers and manipulations for financing the debt, with market offerings inflating rates, and/or bank placements inflating the money supply.

• The paradox of hyped-up dollar strength resulting from foreign money alternately chasing usurious interest rates and speculative market profits; contributing to the collapse in the economy by overpricing American exports while inviting cheap imports.

• Early warnings of hyperinflation, Continental Congress style.

The Treatment

In correspondence with Senator Slade Gorton of Washington in April 1982, I put forward a proposal for the United States to offer no-interest, nonmarketable, long-term bonds carrying a modest premium at maturity to Arab central banks in exchange for the guarantee of American protection. This approach recognizes that the sheiks continue to control the largest single foreign pool of dollar power, despite the political disaster they had engineered for themselves. The fact of their political impotence accentuates their need to use dollar power to buy protection. Terms: coupon, zero; maturity, twenty to forty years; discount, 10 percent; paydowns, none; face value, par. Alternatively, such a debt instrument could be issued at par but redeemed at par plus a 10 percent premium at maturity.

There is a political consideration for offering such a security to a Moslem country where receiving interest income is prohibited, though conspicuously flaunted by the sheiks. The usury issue is a provocation in the inflammatory world of Moslem politics. Profit made by cashing premiums paid by no-interest bonds at maturity, however, is permitted according to the Prophet. The no-interest feature would be an advantage to both parties in the transaction.

An alternative strategy would be to sell the Saudis the Federal Home Loan Mortgage inventory, for example, which consists of $100 billion of first mortgages, by offering them forty-year nonnegotiable U.S. government bonds at a discount but bearing no interest. These terms would relieve the Treasury of the cash drain from the debt and, in the process, reliquify the mortgage agency to resume home mortgage financing without a new appropriation by Congress and/or without burdening the market with new issues of its own. This is no idle theory. Such a deal was all but made by a consortium of American banks through my old friend Wilbur Mills in 1981, but Treasury Secretary Donald Regan successfully opposed it.

A second alternate strategy is to require foreigners buying American fixed assets to buy a limited number of zero-coupon, nonnegotiable bonds per dollar of assets acquired (allowing them, however, the right to borrow up to 70 percent of the face amount of such bonds at U.S. banks). "Funk" money from all over the world has been pouring into the United States, not for the purpose of yield or profit but for safety. Foreigners sinking their money into American fixed assets (real estate or businesses) have been buying a fringe benefit in the form of an equity in the continuing existence of the United States as the last safe harbor for property. But they have not been obliged to pay an entry fee in the form of nonmarketable bonds, which would be cheaper than an entry tax because it would be a portfolio asset held until maturity.

For all the local authorities in any American community may know, when title to a piece of property in their jurisdiction passes to the custodianship of a bank from Frankfurt to Singapore or, for that matter, New York, the owners of record behind the veil of anonymity may be Soviet purchasing agents buying their kickbacks from American grain dealers or incumbents of the Kremlin buying insurance against an unlucky roll of the political dice. (When the nuclear arms race heated up in Europe, the Soviet fat cats began to favor Hong Kong as their favorite depository over Zurich, which was too close to the potential firing line.)

The United States has been slow to cash in on its monopoly as the world's money haven. Where else can money go? Japan denies foreigners the free right to purchase fixed Japanese assets, particularly to take title to land. The Arabs still impose the same prohibition, though anyone trying after the oil war went military would have been in the well-known position of trying to break into jail. Foreigners have become accustomed to routine closeouts elsewhere—devaluation, taxation, confiscation, exchange freezing, labor trouble—and increasingly attracted to U.S. havens.

The incentive feature for private investors would be the right to use such packaged bonds as collateral for borrowing 100 percent of their face amount in the Eurodollar market. The purchase of a $100,000 long-term, noninterest-bearing T-bond could be made the quid pro quo for every $1 million invested in the United States by a foreigner. Why give all the money seeking sanctuary free protection? No one complains about paying fees to enter Switzerland as a visitor commercially. Packaged with the zero-coupon bonds could be gold and silver "dollar eagle" coins, priced at a premium over the bullion market, as is done by South Africa, Mexico, Canada, and Peru. The bonds could be priced at par but with no premium at maturity; the price of the coins would offer sufficient incentive. "Dirty money" on a scale too large to count is routinely bidding to be laundered on terms less attractive.

The Recovery

The condition of a stable recovery, first in the securities markets and then in the economy, is a drop in interest rates sustained long enough to break the Catch-22 chain reaction deflating the economy and inflating the deficit. The drop in interest rates manipulated by the Fed in the market vacuum of the summer of 1982 served as a short-run market tonic. While it lasted, however, Treasury spokesmen were quick to claim that the cost to the Treasury on interest paid while the deficit was rising was being reduced as substantially as if the deficit had been lowered.

Collateral Advantages

• Help the Federal Reserve Bank of New York with its new mission of policing the Eurodollar market.

• Resurrect the unknown soldier of America's money battles, the old-time Yankee trader, and show that he is alive, well, and haggling again.

• Cut the spending side of the budget at its only flexible point: interest expense. At, say, a 15 percent rate for T-bills—a rate difficult to figure but easy to anticipate—every $100 million of debt frozen in the hands of client governments saves $15 billion of annual interest expense plus the cost of interest on borrowings to pay that interest.

• Bring down long-term U.S. interest rates in response to successful long-term debt financing.

• Provide a durable boon to the bond market.

PRESCRIPTION #7
The Profitable Alternative to Protectionism

The Complaint

U.S. industry losing its domestic markets to subsidized foreign competitors.

The Cure

Investment in the modernization of American industry by the foreign competitors who have been profiting from its obsolescence.

The History

Tariffs have offered the traditional form of protection against import dumping; the alternative has been quotas against targeted foreign producers. But protective tariffs and quotas miss the mark as defensive measures against import offensives financed by foreign governments intent on "buying" decisive slices of American markets with no cost restraint. Cost is never a restraint for governments (other than the U.S.) that perceive an advantage abroad. In the past, both mechanisms have proved reliable against private competitors, but both have become obsolete in the modern era.

The price penalties imposed by tariffs once deterred foreign exporters from operating on their own. Since World War II, however, foreign governments intent on buying market penetration have ignored them. By the same token, quotas that limit imports coming in from one country do not bar imports that are financed by that same country (and benefiting it) but enter the American market through subsidiaries or affiliates based in other countries not on the quota list. Over the years, the successful industrial exporting countries have accumulated no end of foreign currencies from "sick-sister" countries not seen by Washington as import threats. They have also accumulated no end of dollars. The simple expedient of inviting aggressive exporting industries to use third-country currencies to invest in the construction of manufacturing facilities in those third countries has enabled Japan and the principal European industrial exporting countries to stay one step ahead of American crackdowns. America has not been under any pressure to refuse imports from such countries as Korea or Brazil.

Similarly, foreign manufacturers achieving a massive breakthrough into a domestic market, and anticipating a protective response in the form of quotas, have easily ducked under the domestic umbrella. Such firms as Volkswagen and Mitsubishi have built assembly plants inside the United States and imported parts. They have bought into a domestic company, as Renault did into American Motors. They have sold company names, as Mitsubishi did with Chrysler. They have sold parts to American companies, which do their own manufacturing, to assemble and market for them. Whichever course they have taken, cost has been no object, because the subsidy never runs dry. Governments have no problem using the miraculous workings of the Eurodollar market to clone all the dollars they need for the purpose.

Historically, market wars fought by competing manufacturers operating under rival flags have often been resolved by fighting wars, calculated to bring prosperity to all competitors. The Korean War was fought on a small scale militarily but programmed on a mammoth scale industrially by Washington in the name of national security. Consequently, the investment boom triggered by the Korean War in the "defense-support" industries cleared bottlenecks that had left American industry dependent upon European imports, for which it paid through the nose. The war deferred the issue of protectionist restraints against manufactured imports.

Since the Korean War, however, wars have outgrown their traditional role as economic stimulants, thanks to the revolution in military technology, which we examined in Chapter Seven. In the era of military high technology, governments have come to rely on munitions for their export growth. America has run up record deficits budgeting defense programs, but she has still suffered depression—a startling departure from historical experience. Complaints that American industry has priced itself out of world markets certainly do not apply to her munitions industries, which bring in a cash export "take" of $17 billion in a slow year, without, however, avoiding layoffs or supporting the defense industry in the style to which it was accustomed when the old rules applied. America has indulged in levels of consumption above levels of production, and she has taken pride in her evolution from a "goods" economy into a "service" economy. Even her "merchants of death" have become ripe targets for competitors who are on the rise and, so to speak, traveling light.

America began to pay for her anachronistic illusions during the 1980s. The Reaganites went charging off in three directions at once, promoting a big defense buildup, a capital investment revival spurred by a reduction in taxes, and a return to the credo of free trade. They thought they had a formula for a boom and relied on imports to prevent the economy from exploding into runaway inflation. Instead, the slump they started exposed the American economy to subsidized import raids from all over the world. The smaller, export-dependent industries abroad built up their volumes and cut down their unit costs as they staked out wider segments of the American market, which was the only free one open to them and the one where they could earn premium currency. As American industry yielded progressively higher proportions of its domestic markets to imports, its volume shrank and its unit costs rose. By the end of Reagan's second year, the goals of capital-investment expansion and an open door to imports, which the Reaganites saw as compatible, turned out to be at variance. The rich premiums on the dollar created irresistible incentives for foreign banking systems to dump goods produced under cost in their own cheap currencies in order to book premium dollar receivables. The American manufacturers who suffered took a surprisingly long time to realize that volume at any price rather than profit at comfortable prices was the foreign competitors' objective.

The Symptoms

• Stepped-up foreign investment in U.S. capacity to anticipate protectionist bans on imports.
• Japanese banks bailing out the State of Michigan.
• A major Japanese steel mill moving to take over control of Ford's River Rouge steel complex and offering to modernize it.
• Mitsubishi emerging as the winning horse in Chrysler's stable.
• The United Auto Workers giving General Motors concessions, and General Motors thanking the union by importing Toyotas.
• Both political parties scrambling to take protectionist positions.
• Calls for the reactivation of the Reconstruction Finance Corporation to provide government advances to finance industrial modernization.
• Unemployment and shrinkage undoing a generation of expansion in the South.
• America's sophisticated growth industries—semiconductors, computers—added to the casualty list of import victims.
• Transportation equipment, the workhorse sector for capital investment, becoming a prime import preserve, even in the public sector.

The Treatment

The treatment calls for making investment in America the condition for selling in America. It calls for recognizing that the ruins of America's productive base formalize the victory of foreign manufacturers in the

sales war, and for giving them the opportunity to assume the responsibilities for reconstruction. The way to do this is to require successful
importers to file plans of investment in the securities of the companies
they have beaten in the market.

The marketplace has been providing the clue to the treatment.
Industrial imports have risen to the point where successful foreign
competitors have found themselves in need of a broad industrial base
from which to serve the markets they have won. The decision to invest
in American productive facilities is theirs. Their success can be America's opportunity to modernize her own crumbling and obsolete arsenal
of productive assets. Schemes calculated to persuade or oblige the successful industrial importers to expand their operations cannot be discounted as visionary or wishful. This wave of foreign industrial investment has already been launched. It is the only vibrant source of
industrial investment in America, apart from defense and state and
local governmental investment in infrastructure and transportation
equipment.

But where those infrastructure investments are subject to increases
in taxes and debt, the foreign manufacturers enjoy three sources of
self-financing. The first comes from their customers in the form of cash
flow, the second from their own governments in the form of subsidies,
and the third from the attraction of the world's capital markets, particularly the American banks. The treatment I am recommending would
invite successful foreign manufacturers to draw on the American banks
for large-scale capital loans for productive purposes, which their beaten
American rivals are no longer making. These loans would be mercies
to the banks as well as boons to the economy because they would be
domestic loans. These major foreign competitors have the incentive
and the resources to be persuaded to launch a significant step-up in the
scale and the tempo of their industrial investment. They have the
money; Washington needs to find the method to persuade them to use
more of it. Putting private foreign capital to work in failing corporations
offers a more promising avenue to recovery than the government guarantees relied on in the Chrysler crisis.

The Chrysler case provides a perfect case history. As early as 1979,
before the American auto market fell apart, I had dealt repeatedly with
Nomura Securities, Mitsubishi's investment arm, at its initiative, in an
effort to explain how beneficial a Mitsubishi bid for working control of
Chrysler would be to all concerned. When I went to Tokyo in February
1980, I discussed these conversations with Ambassador Mike Mansfield.
He was quick to see the neatness of the Mitsubishi-Chrysler fit and the
pressure it would remove from the Treasury, as well as the static it
would remove from the political atmosphere. In fact, he expressed
irritation toward the Carter administration, which I had briefed on this
idea, for failing to discuss it with him.

I told Mansfield that the alibi offered by Mitsubishi and by the Carter administration for not moving to make a takeover bid had been to cite Chrysler's tank arsenal as an insuperable obstacle to Japanese control of the company. Three facts, as I explained to Mansfield, revealed the administration's shyness as the sham it was. The first was that the Carter Pentagon was pressing Japan to join it in the arms race (as the Reagan administration subsequently persuaded it to do). The second was that the Army was embarrassed by the cumulative obsolescence overtaking the Chrysler tank arsenal but was too tight for cash to make even the most modest and belated start at modernization. The third was that Chrysler's shaky financial condition would eventually force it to dispose of this dubious asset (as, in fact, it did, selling it to General Dynamics in the spring of 1982).

The most frustrating part of it all, as my memo to Nomura showed, was that Mitsubishi would have made a fortune out of assuming responsibility for modernizing Chrysler, if it had only made a public offer for 20 percent of Chrysler's outstanding shares at $25 a share in a market of just under $10. (Chrysler then had a live book value of $48 a share, before it emerged as the breakaway leader of the 1982–1983 market move, jumping to a high of 35%.) In that case Mitsubishi would have shared the newly created wealth with Chrysler, its stockholders, its market in general, and America. So far as my failed effort of 1979–1980 to be helpful to the cause of reciprocal Japanese-American dealings was concerned, it fell afoul of the "dog-in-the-manger" rights Mitsubishi enjoyed over the Chrysler franchise inside the Japanese power structure. The right of first refusal it enjoyed in Tokyo to take over control of Chrysler's finances carried the power to veto any such move by a rival Japanese combination. One good reason the Japanese compete with such deadly effectiveness against America is that they always present a united front. For them, competition ends at the water's edge.

The Recovery

It would begin by reversing the normal business-cycle recovery sequence of inventorying followed by investment after industrial operations approach capacity. Once investment starts the recovery cycle and inventorying follows, its longevity is assured. By contrast, recovery cycles that begin with inventorying are often too short and too weak to trigger any investment follow-through.

The late, great Walter Reuther is the most authoritative source I know of on the overdiscussed but underimplemented subject of productivity. "When the guy working on the line gets the idea that he may be punching himself into a layoff," Reuther once told me in a discussion of the conversion of auto plants to war production after Pearl Harbor, "he stops punching as hard or as fast as he does when he smells overtime pay." Reuther's practical sense of the motivation of working people shows up the delusions of the monetarists, who labor under the quaint misimpression that fear of unemployment will put the fear of the foreman into the clock watcher waiting for the coffee break. If any single source is guaranteed to establish a quantum leap in productivity it is long-range investment programs launched by new financial interests able to assure continuity of employment.

The third source of recovery will come into play with the movement of foreign money from stagnant pools of excess liquidity in New York or from underfinanced—that is, unmortgaged—real estate into productive investment channels. Of all the paradoxes of idleness amid need contributing to the failure of recovery around the world, none is more counterproductive than the phenomenon of foreign manufacturers mistrustful of their own countries and dependent on their American markets.

The fourth source of recovery would surface with a bang in the securities markets. It is standard Wall Street wisdom that foreign money always guesses wrong about U.S. bonds and stocks. The floor always buys when it sees concerted foreign sell orders piled up in the early morning telex orders, and it always sells in response to a buildup of foreign buy orders. But the moment it saw massive foreign investment in the basic smokestack industries that failed to participate in the abortive recovery of late 1982, it would reverse its habits and scramble to bid for the equity the foreigners would be under pressure to accumulate for long-term investment. There is no knowledge more confidence-inspiring to the first wave of stock buyers than that a second move of stronger and more patient buyers with a vested interest in holding for the long pull will be waiting to take them out at a profit. The old political adage, "If you can't lick 'em, join 'em," has its uses in the investment world. Instead of bemoaning the inroads of foreign competition, America will help herself by turning the competitors of her failed managements into the customers of her aggressive financiers. It is worth remembering that the American securities industry is the only major American industry that, far from succumbing to foreign competition, remains dominant in the world and is a major earner of foreign income. It has an important role to play in the implementation of a new American policy that requires foreign investment to follow import sales.

The fifth source of recovery would be fiscal. Reaganomics was on the right track in pushing for a revival of capital investment. It went wrong in its impractical effort to get the flow started. Once captive importers were directed to do so, however, the drain of refunds from the Treasury would be staunched, with resultant relief for the credit markets.

Collateral Advantages

- Avoidance of economic warfare with America's industrial competitors, who are also her political and military clients.
- Standardization of American, European, and Japanese military equipment.
- Revitalization and broadening of America's industrial base in time to buy insurance against inflationary bottlenecking when recovery does start and to support a surge of industrialization in the event of a national emergency.
- Insurance for American users of domestic industrial products that spare parts will not run out and that domestic bankruptcies will not leave American cost levels exposed to the tender mercies of foreign cartel pricing.
- Relief from the twin burden of a ruinous trade deficit and a cancerous payments deficit.

PRESCRIPTION #8
Housing on Wheels for Russia and the Third World

The Complaint

America's auto/truck depression and the housing shortage throughout Russia and the Third World.

The Cure

Exporting mobile homes.

The History

The U.S. automobile business evolved with a powerful assist from export breakthroughs. When it was taking over as America's premier growth business in the 1920s, up to 10 percent of America's vehicle production found markets abroad, and that was before the days of the Export-Import Bank, the World Bank, or America's awareness of the wonders of barter. The percentage of America's industrial product that reaches the export market had, for the auto industry, been reduced to a statistical zero by 1982.

The Symptoms

- Russia's endemic housing crisis.
- Russia's hopeless road deficiencies.
- China's deficiencies in both respects.
- The absence of vehicles and roads throughout the Third World.
- Extremes of heat and cold complicating the housing shortage in countries of critical concern to America.
- America's loss of export prices for manufactured products.
- The inability of new "mini" auto models—enclosed motorcycles—to provide mass production outlets for stricken U.S. producers of steel and other basic supply industries; the same for the growth market for "mini" housing units in multidwelling complexes.

The Treatment

Negotiate the mass export of mobile homes and campers, equipping them with heavy-duty axles and tires and dual-purpose heating/air-conditioning systems. Russia and China have endless demand for off-road vehicles outfitted with built-in defenses against extreme climates and deficiencies of light and plumbing. So do leading oil-producing countries.

In America, projections for economic recovery begin with revival of the housing and automobile sectors. But recovery prospects are counted in the number of units, not in the size of the units likely to enjoy recovery demand. Admittedly, however, the residential/vehicle units will be light and cheap, therefore bringing a disappointingly low measure of relief to America's depressed basic supply industries. But the glaring gap America's mobile home industry could fill in Russia, China, and throughout the Third World calls for precisely the heavy-duty, appliance-bearing homes on wheels needed to revive America's stricken workshop industries. To take just one obvious example, American mobile homes, to be serviceable under Russian environmental conditions, would carry enough steel, rubber, and glass to bring Youngstown, Akron, and Toledo back to viability.

In America's commercial economy, mobile homes and campers are built on commercial speculation and offered through dealers. The first step toward developing any export volume to state-directed economies would be government-to-government negotiation and, as a practical matter, it would entail U.S. Export-Import Bank financing. Congress would undoubtedly insist on offsetting considerations advantageous to the United States as a condition. America is the only industrial power in the world with the capacity to break this all-weather double bottleneck in Russia and the Third World.

The Recovery

The American economy needs an export-volume breakthrough in a proprietary industry capable of generating momentum, of asserting her proprietary design leadership, and of absorbing a significant volume of raw materials whose fabrication will generate enough jobs to matter. In today's world, recovery hinges on negotiations between governments, not on mere market adjustments. Consequently, the U.S. economy will either suffer from a lack of any significant export recovery, or its achievement will produce a double dividend: markets blasted open and tangible evidence of Washington's new ability to deal in behalf of her wounded industrial centers.

On the export-market side of this calculation, talk about industrial development will remain largely talk until the national economies that need mobile homes develop housing facilities offering privacy, sanitation, and modern creature comforts. Any hope among oil producers of soaking up the worldwide glut of petroleum products depends upon their willingness and ability to increase their domestic consumption of gasoline and heating oil. Any effort to do so would spark a joint incentive with the industrial world to keep oil prices down. By virtue of being gas guzzlers, America's mobile homes are tailor-made to contribute to this worthy purpose.

Collateral Advantages

• Opening a mobile-home market in Russia would be a more tangible form of collaboration than even space surveillance.

• The arms export boom is providing daily evidence that, contrary to sloganizing about free markets doing their thing, government-to-government dealing is the rule in arranging export deals. Opening an export market in mobile homes would demonstrate America's ability to develop peaceful commerce with her adversaries.

• Offering the successors of the young lovers, whom Turgenev immortalized, their first flings at indoor winter-time romance. Young lovers in Russia are reduced to waiting for the spring thaw to wander out into the fields with their blankets. When America came to Russia's rescue during World War II, legend has it that the most popular American in Russia was not Roosevelt, who sent them weapons, but "Gillette," who introduced them to the wonders of the safety razor. How about the wonders of bunks on wheels?

CHAPTER ELEVEN

Energy

PRESCRIPTION #9
Selling Oil Licenses to Importers

The Complaint

The failure of the oil glut to break oil prices.

The Cure

Forcing all the governments inside and outside OPEC, which need the U.S. oil market, to cut prices by bidding against one another for oil-import licenses.

The History

Everyone has been conditioned to believe that oil is subject to short-age, but with the development of the oil glut the oil market is seen to be dripping with surpluses. Examine the seemingly irrelevant case history of sugar: Sugar politics in Washington are bitter, with higher-cost domestic producers pitted against lower-cost foreign producers. Historically, domestic producers got protection against imports; foreign producers got import quotas. All needed some piece of the American market. Several of the more obscure ones had only one reason for producing: to win a U.S. sugar-quota award. The cards were stacked so heavily against the foreign producing governments that Washington wiseacres kept lists of the favored lawyers with political "ins" whom the sugar governments had to hire before the bidding could begin. The annual import license auction gave successive administrations one golden opportunity after another to reward laborers in the political vineyard by palming them off on the governments bidding for import quotas. Just as Americans need foreigners to tell us how to sell American products in their countries, hiring shepherds was part of the cost of dumping sugar into America. When Cuba lost her American market and hired her "Hessians" out to Russia, Moscow took over Washington's role as Cuba's sugar daddy.

The Symptoms

- Frozen oil-import prices.
- Inability of even the major American oil companies to bargain on equal terms with surplus-ridden governments desperate for a piece of the American market.
- Banks in Venezuela, America's chief supplier of boiler fuel (heating oil), going under, while U.S. boiler-fuel prices were pushed up during warm weather.
- The unseemly spectacle during the lame-duck session of 1982 of the President and Congress burying their hatchets in the backs of American users of motor fuel by sticking them with a 5¢-per-gallon excise tax.
- Pressure on Congress to deny consumers the right to take excise-tax payments as tax deductions.

The Treatment

Notify all foreign oil-producing governments that the United States intends to be equitable in assuring all of them continued access to the American market. Explain that this access is necessarily limited by the very considerable availability of domestic supplies, which satisfy 60 percent of demand. Warn, in the spirit of candor to which all trading partners are entitled, that this domestic supply is elastic and subject to expansion and that, as a matter of prudent national policy, the United States is embarking on an energetic campaign to expand its domestic sources of supply. Assure foreign producers that, for their protection, Washington has decided to take its sugar-quota experience as a model and to offer them the right to participate in annual bidding for oil-import quotas. Note that an interesting number of anxious oil-producing governments have also been regulars among the sugar-import supplicants: Mexico, Canada, Venezuela, Ecuador, Trinidad and Tobago, Nigeria, and Indonesia, among others. Remind the lot that any government participating in actions deemed unfriendly will be subject to loss of bidding rights. Not a word about prices; leave them to the tender mercies of the bidding process.

The Recovery

The big losers will be the oil-producing governments bidding for a share of the U.S. market and no longer able to divide it among themselves at fixed prices. They will not be able to pass the cost of their import-licenses on to their customers, nor will they be able to find alternative markets. This is one case of an import-licensing fee whose immediate market impact would be to deflate a basic ingredient in the cost of living and doing business.

One winner will be the U.S. government. Its winnings: the collection of oil-import license fees on approximately one half of U.S. fuel consumption, plus the confidence that it can open up one additional source of revenue without putting another crimp in the economy or inviting taxpayers to take more deductions. An even bigger winner will be the U.S. motor-fuel consumers, who have been blackjacked by "do-gooders" and the special interests alike since the start of the oil war. They will enjoy the use of their cars at much lower cost, with the added satisfaction of seeing their government collecting revenue from governments that have been ripping off the public but will now be absorbing the cost of their import-license fees. The domestic American oil producers would be winners, too, thanks to the tactic of limiting the share of the market the importing governments would be allowed to break with their competitive bids. American producers of consumer products subject to excise tax always benefit to the extent that they are free to charge solely for their products, instead of for their products plus the taxes they collect for the government.

The simple way to unleash an offshore oil-price war is to award every bidder the quota requested. No complaints would be heard from other import-dependent countries that generous import-license awards were exposing them to any renewal of shortage pressures. Senator David Boren of Oklahoma, a member of the Senate Finance Committee and that state's former governor, wrote me that this is "a striking idea well worth pursuing." More than incidentally, Senator Boren sits on the Senate Committee on Agriculture, Nutrition, and Forestry and, therefore, is concerned with any opportunities to exploit America's oil-bargaining power to maximize farm exports.

Collateral Advantages

• The opportunity to mousetrap the foreign oil-producing governments into bidding against themselves and to direct an export bonus to America's sick industries by reserving the right to have Iran, for example, paid for a cargo of oil with a cargo of trucks or tractors, in which case manufacturers participating in the export award would be given a free choice of either avoiding oil costs or selling the imported oil to any third-party customer they could find. (See Prescription #5 for details.)

• A practical initiation for cash-happy Americans into the workings of the wonderful world of barter.

PRESCRIPTION #10
Plentiful Motor Fuel

The Complaint

The high cost of cars engineered to fit preconceptions about shortages of high-cost, dirty gasoline.

The Cure

Get more clean-burning motor fuel out of the same amount of crude by adding alcohol reclaimed from the country's neglected by-product refinery capacity.

The History

The argument over gasohol has played a dual role: as a beacon and as a distraction. One of the original sponsors of this idea was Henry Ford. His notion, always considered cranky because it was his, was to derive alcohol from grain. This makes perfect sense chemically, but it will not produce one dollar of windfall economically. In the early 1920s, Ford's original gasohol initiative was blocked by a corporate alliance between du Pont, which then controlled General Motors, and Standard Oil of New Jersey, with which it had a working alliance. Nevertheless, all three recognized the need and the desirability of an additive to stretch the gasoline supply.

From the day the automobile industry was born, the world has been subjected to a series of oil-shortage scares. In fact, the original project to lay out the city of Los Angeles as the new frontier of the automobile was blocked on the grounds that there would never be enough oil in the world to supply the gasoline that the Los Angeles sprawl would need to keep cars moving. The du Pont–Standard Oil combine seized on the idea that the gasoline-refining industry would need a chemical additive to stretch the oil supply coming out of the refinery. It hit upon lead, which is an economical chemical additive but an air pollutant and a carcinogen.

Enter the Organization of Petroleum Exporting Countries (OPEC), which focused attention on the volatility of oil as a standard commodity with fixed characteristics in the marketplace but ignored its versatility as a chemical raw material in the laboratory. America bought this narrow view, kowtowing to OPEC as the Mecca of marketing wisdom but shutting her eyes to the rise of Houston as a monument to the infinite elasticity of petrochemical by-product uses. OPEC's financial and commercial interests were well served by America's fear that her potential for recovering gasoline from each barrel of oil was limited and that access to a dwindling flow of oil imports at ever higher prices would condemn the country to ration a falling supply of gasoline. More myopic still, and more susceptible to loudly repeated ignorant sloganizing, America bought hook, line, and sinker the canard that all gasoline additives are pollutants or are carcinogenic because leaded additives are.

Enter President Jimmy Carter, who gave the advocacy of redemption through abstinence a powerful push when he simultaneously launched his campaigns for oil conservation and a clean environment. He lent plausibility to his administration's unique combination of voodoo economics and voodoo chemistry with his claim to expertise as an engineer and efficiency as an administrator. Hence the false dilemma between effective environmentalism and practical economics. Neither the oil companies nor the auto companies had any fight in them against OPEC or against Washington. After their fashion, they went along with whatever Washington decreed. The oil companies at least had a commercial motive in going along with OPEC's blackmail; they continued to mark up the price of crude oil as a trade-off against recovering fewer commercial products from each barrel of crude oil refined into unleaded gasoline.

The auto companies had every reason to resist accepting Carter's technical decrees. The huge costs they ran up retooling their plants to conform to the Environmental Protection Agency's new rules helped price their new models out of the market, although foreign manufacturers managed to comply with the rules too and still remain competitive. Admittedly, the Japanese did so with a large assist from governmental subsidies. The reduced yields from unleaded gasoline contributed to consumer resistance against high-priced American models. Nevertheless, the auto companies showed no more interest than the oil companies in developing alternative chemical methods to put more horsepower back into their gas tanks in compensation for the loss of lead in gasoline. Nor did they show any more appetite than did the oil companies for explaining the chemical facts of life to the Carter administration.

The need to compensate for the loss of lead was critical to the problem. I wrote in the November 1979 *Atlantic:* "We were getting 14 percent less gasoline out of a given amount of crude flowing out of the refineries. For the previous fifty years, an average dose of lead additive (just a few grams per gallon) had been relied on to raise the base octane rating of gasoline by eight points. Consequently, refineries were able to produce a base of only 80 octane and still market an 88 octane gasoline.

Thanks to the lead additive, the oil companies used less oil to make more gasoline, and this was when oil was still cheap."

Clearly the problem was not to stop the phase-out of the lead but to find another high-powered additive that burned clean. As I noted in the *Atlantic* article, "By a fateful coincidence, the environmentalists won their fight to take lead out of the refining process at the same time that OPEC declared its war against the United States. However, while the environmentalists were concentrating on their anti-lead crusade, they were not alert to the need to substitute an alternative additive or to the availability of alcohol for the role." The subsequent quest proved that Henry Ford had been right in his feud with General Motors, du Pont, and Standard Oil but for the wrong reason. Alcohol was indeed the answer, not for the economic angle that Ford saw but for the chemical angle that du Pont and Standard Oil, of all people, ignored. Alcohol serves the same purpose as lead as a chemical additive. It is just as efficient, but it neither pollutes the air nor causes cancer.

So long as the Carter administration opposed any engineering innovation that provided insurance against overblown fears of an oil shortage, and so long as the oil and automobile lobbies refused to support any idea the Carter administration was against, the only hope for gasohol rested with the only group with the political clout and the incentive to be for it—the farmers. Although the economic cards were stacked against them, they had enough political muscle to open a commercial market for gasohol. The way they did it was to mobilize Congress to force the Carter administration to accept a 4¢-a-gallon exemption from the federal excise tax on alcohol derived from domestic crops. This cut was not enough to make gasohol competitive in price with unleaded gasoline until Robert Ray, the progressive Republican governor of Iowa, initiated an additional 8¢-a-gallon exemption from the state's excise tax, enabling gasohol to sell there within pennies of the price of regular gasoline. Other governors followed suit, and gasohol usage soon spread from the Corn Belt to New England.

The Wall Street Journal quoted the well-known oil industry analyst Dan Lundberg as reporting that consumer acceptance of gasohol in Iowa showed a 1982 increase of nearly 200 percent, not surprising in light of that state's acute need for an industrial outlet for its corn surplus and Governor Ray's leading role in the gasohol movement. But the nearly 300 percent increase in California was surprising, in view of that state's freedom from any corn-surplus pressures and the absence of any state sponsorship of the idea. The concentration of oil refineries in California (and its grim experience with refinery fires resulting from explosions of waste gases and refinery waste-gas smog) suggests that the state would be more than receptive to the spreading popularity of gasohol, which involves no freight costs incidental to moving bulk crops or product from the Corn Belt.

The agricultural tax exemption started the gasohol movement rolling; the peaking of gasoline prices stopped it. The Carter administration chose to ignore the endless economical source of gasohol that was already being burned off as waste gases at the country's refineries. The basic gaseous by-product in all oil-refining and petrochemical operations is ethylene. When hydrated (that is, when it reacts with water), it produces ethyl alcohol ready for mixing with unleaded gasoline. In 1978, when refinery operations were still running at capacity, the oil industry flared off 10 billion pounds of ethylene (which might have been converted into 2.5 billion gallons of alcohol) into the smog above its fractionating towers.

The Carter environmentalists would have scored their breakthrough in 1979, at no cost to the American economy and with no political risk to the United States, if they had done their technical homework and used their clout to promote the substitution of chemically derived alcohol for lead additives. Theoretically, the chemical industry, the country's largest producer of ethyl alcohol, had the technical capability to fill the alcohol gap, but its commercial capacity fell far short of the gallonage that would have been needed. Moreover, the interrelationships of the chemical and oil industries were too incestuous for the chemical industry to see any opportunity for itself, short of an all-out emergency in which the government would have drafted and, therefore, subsidized it. But the government saw no problem and did not even have a contingency plan to assist in the expansion of chemically produced alcohol. It ended up assisting the sale of agriculturally produced alcohol; it invited the public to continue assuming that gasohol was agriculturally produced alcohol and nothing but agriculturally produced alcohol.

Ronald Reagan greeted the lame-duck session of 1982 by swinging his support to one of Carter's pet projects, the 5¢-per-gallon gasoline tax —Reagan's first conversion to a Carter belief. A switch in calculation, however, was evident: Whereas Carter had plumped for the tax in the hope of cutting gasoline consumption, Reagan's purpose was to raise revenue, that is, to hope consumption would rise as the commercial price of the product fell and in spite of the offsetting tax increase. A political reality with profoundly educational implications surfaced with Reagan's emergency gasoline-tax legislation. It was sponsored by Senator Bob Dole of Kansas, a ranking member of the Senate farm bloc. His proposal advocated an extension of the exemption from the basic gasoline excise tax already enjoyed by agriculturally based gasohol. The successive drops in the commercial price of gasoline had not dampened the enthusiasm of the Middle West for the home-brewed product, but the Dole proposal perpetuated the myth that the farm was the only source of America's answer to OPEC.

The Symptoms

• Japan's shutdown of eight ethanol refineries, flaunting her freedom from fear of any eventual shortage of imported crude oil, and her notorious insensitivity to pollution worries.

• Brazil's aggressive American advertising campaign proclaiming world leadership in gasohol conversion; she was a fuel have-not at the outset of the oil war.

• The consuming public's pronounced preference for gas guzzlers, as recorded by the insurance industry's rate schedule.

• The inability of the new crop of enclosed motorcycles, uneconomically engineered by Detroit, to stimulate enough tonnage demand for steel, aluminum, copper, nickel, zinc, rubber, glass, plastic, paint, machine tools, and transportation to revive these depressed basic industries even if the auto assembly lines were running three shifts a day.

• The worldwide price war in the ethanol market, turning this high-powered source of clean-burning fuel into another drug on the glutted chemical market.

The Treatment

Here is the formula for the cure developed by my late brother, R. N. Janeway, whom Professor A. R. George, director of the Sibley School of Mechanical and Aerospace Engineering at Cornell University, called "one of the great engineers of our time." Just 4 billion gallons of alcohol would displace 28 billion gallons, or 667 million barrels, of crude oil per year. Here is how the calculation works: Each gallon of alcohol would replace 2.35 gallons of crude that would otherwise be needed to produce unleaded gasoline. In addition, because alcohol improves the yield of unleaded gasoline from crude oil by raising its octane rating, only 1.83 gallons of crude instead of 2.35 would be needed to produce a gallon of gas. Since alcohol improves the gasoline yield by a factor of .52 gallons of crude per gallon (2.35 − 1.83 = .52), one gallon of alcohol added to nine gallons of unleaded fuel would save an additional 9 × .52, or 4.68 gallons of crude oil; 4.68 added to 2.35 equals 7.03 gallons of crude oil saved for every gallon of alcohol added to nine gallons of unleaded gasoline to make gasohol. Four billion gallons of by-product alcohol, reclaimed from the refining process, could therefore effect a 28 billion-gallon yearly reduction in crude oil consumption—approximately a 15 percent savings in total consumption. That could enable the country to cut imports by one-third, over and above the imports that would be displaced by conversion of boiler fuel to natural gas. (See Prescription 11.) So much for the myth of America's dependence on

Middle Eastern oil and the bogus form of foreign aid known as import dependence on Nigeria, Venezuela, Indonesia, and Canada.

Alcohol can be produced more cheaply from the chemical by-products of oil and gas than from fermented corn, provided the tax is right. At $2.80 a bushel, the raw-material cost for making a gallon of alcohol from corn is $1.10, while the cost of a gallon of alcohol from ethylene is only about 52¢. Chemically derived alcohol is cheaper and more energy-efficient than agriculturally derived alcohol, as every country experimenting with both already knows. If corn alcohol is a sellout for the fields in Iowa, chemical alcohol is bound to be a bargain in the backyards of refineries in New Jersey or Texas, given the same excise tax.

Wherever I go, people are always asking me to suggest esoteric publications guaranteed to give them a peek at the cards that the big players hold. I always invite them to scan the advertisements in the major media for serious insight into the trend of events. On August 10, 1982, the Ford Motor Company, not the most technically advanced of the Fortune 500 but by no means the least, ran a two-page ad in *The New York Times*. Its headline trumpeted the claim: "Ford automobiles do not run on gasoline alone." To support it, the copy said: "Since 1979 alone, Ford has manufactured and sold over 80,000 ethanol-fueled automobiles to the people of Brazil. In fact, 37% of all Fords sold in Brazil in 1981 ran on ethanol." On September 28, *The New York Times* ran another ad, this one by Petrobras, Brazil's state-owned oil company. The copy recites Brazil's breakthrough "with locally produced sources, such as ethyl alcohol, for internal combustion engines." The ad quantifies the progress report with this table:

Period	Internal consumption (barrels per day)	Brazilian production petroleum + gas + alcohol (barrels per day)	Imports (barrels per day)	External dependence on petroleum
July '79	1,225,000	211,000	1,014,000	82.8%
July '80	1,197,000	253,000	944,000	78.9%
July '81	1,093,000	255,000	838,000	76.7%
July '82	1,064,000	341,000	723,000	68.0%

On the same day, the *Times* published a front-page story quoting the president of Brazil as charging that the world was facing a depression of 1930's magnitude and accusing the major powers of destroying, not creating, wealth. No serious voices were heard chiding him for being an alarmist, another "Mr. Gloom Boy." If events turned out to prove him realistic, no reason for the debacle would be more commanding than Washington's achievement in proving that where Brasilia (with a booster shot from Dearborn, Michigan) could lead, America did not even know how to follow.

The Recovery

Reliance on chemically produced alcohol would guarantee freedom from fear of gas lines in the long run and would bring back cheaper gasoline in the short run. It would reproduce the atmosphere in which Henry Ford improvised the building blocks of America's prosperity in the 1920s. It would also free the automobile manufacturers and the driving public from the unproductive costs run up by loading antipollution equipment onto cars. It would use the popular but fiscally responsible device of excise tax relief to help revive America's sickest manufacturing industry, whose troubles have infected every other basic industry in the American economy. The cash flow into the Treasury from paychecks earned from a revived American automobile industry and the industries serving it would more than offset the revenue loss to the Treasury due to excise taxes forgiven to invite the use of chemically produced gasohol. Value added in domestic facilities to domestic raw materials always harvests more tax revenue, even allowing for the additional revenue losses that, in this case, would be forced on the Treasury as the result of the political necessity of offering the farm bloc comparable tax relief for agriculturally produced alcohol. Significant increases in domestic industrial use of America's exportable corn surpluses would prod foreign fear buying. This move would pay the Treasury, the economy, and the country even if the oil industry were given tax credits as inducements to expedite the adaptation of refineries to reclaim and cycle waste gases into ethanol. The answer to oil-management grumbling that gasohol in any form is inefficient is that it is a form of insurance—in this case national insurance—and that all insurance runs up costs. Oil-company managements do not grumble when they pay insurance premiums on refineries that do not blow up, nor are we heard complaining when we pay term insurance premiums but fail to cash in on our unearned death benefits. The oil-company propaganda against gasohol as uncompetitive has invited the consuming public to confuse the price it pays with the cost of the commercial product it buys, as if it were not charged for the cost of government in the form of excise taxes along with the cost of the gasoline. If the product mix at the gas pump costs the public more in price for better fuel containing less in crude oil but less in tax for worse government, consumers would wind up paying no more money but getting better value.

Collateral Advantages

• Achievement of national oil independence without loss of national economic viability.

• Quick creation of private-sector jobs to adapt and add refinery capability for producing by-product ethanol after the ocean of surplus built up during the depression has been soaked up.

PRESCRIPTION #11
Cheap Heating Fuel

The Complaint

The phony natural-gas shortage and the real risk of importing high-cost, high-pollutant heating oil.

The Cure

Flushing out the full extent of the literally limitless and uncountable U.S. surplus of natural gas (excluding Alaska) and mandating high-speed, top-priority conversion of boiler fuel from liquid petroleum to domestic natural gas.

The History

The movement of domestic natural gas into interstate commerce has triggered a second war between the states over the terms of trade. Long before OPEC jumped the price of liquid petroleum imports, the federal regulation of interstate gas prices gave producers an incentive to understate their reserves and to hold back their production. The gas-price tug-of-war between Sun Belt producing states and Frost Belt consuming states distracted attention from America's need to get a count on her gargantuan reserves of domestic natural gas, to maximize the use of it, and to minimize her dependence on imported liquid petroleum for boiler fuel. The popular impression, fostered by governmental bungling and complicity, assumes a supply shortage and expects a price gouge during any cold snap, a scenario as phony as the 1973 OPEC embargo. The reality, however, is not saturated with gloom and doom about the basic, all-purpose, clean-burning fuel. The talk in America's mid-continent gas fields suggested a cigarette-smoking ban for reasons entirely unrelated to fears of cancer—light a match to have a smoke, and you're apt to blow up the state of Oklahoma. The same holds true for the region around Prudhoe Bay, Alaska, where, as *The Wall Street Journal* reported, the oil companies "have been producing one billion cubic feet a day of natural gas and . . . painstakingly [compressing it to] inject it hundreds of feet back into the frozen earth." The popular statistics calculating U.S. dependence on foreign oil invariably jumble imports of heating oil, a refined product, with imports of crude oil for motor fuel, the alternative use, and therefore exaggerate America's supposed dependence on overseas sources. Gas producers cannot be any more comfortable with the adverse publicity and congressional scrutiny that each winter's freeze brings them than their Frost Belt customers are with their gas bills.

Venezuela is America's number-one source of imported boiler fuel. Venezuela is also number one in the export of pollution. So long as Nelson Rockefeller exercised meddling rights on America's oil-import and oil-lending policies—which he did from the 1940s as Roosevelt's assistant secretary of state for Latin America until the 1970s as governor of New York and then vice president—everything Venezuelan was beyond the reach of criticism. Venezuela put the franchise her Rockefeller connection gave her to shrewd use when she surfaced as an instigator of OPEC. In the first phase of the oil-price gouge of the 1970s, the Venezuelan oil minister confided to me that the sky was the limit on the money Venezuela could count on drawing out of America, not only from current sales at high prices in store for Americans but even more by borrowing on anticipated sales revenues. This look into the crystal ball did not show what happened: Venezuela managed to go broke right behind Iran.

Enter the Carter Energy Act of 1978. It typified the worst kind of legislative abomination: one calculated to accomplish the exact opposite of the purpose advertised. Its official aim was to produce the conversion of boiler fuel from liquid petroleum to coal by 1990. This was a safe goal to advertise as a cover-up of the real purpose revealed in its fine print: to forbid any switch from liquid petroleum to domestic natural gas.

The Symptoms

• Annual winter trauma over gas "shortages" and price rip-offs across the entire Frost Belt where gas charges have gone up in the wake of the price gouge invited by the oil "shortage"; mysteriously, the huge domestic gas surplus has exerted no restraining influence.

• Continued feuding between gas-producing and gas-consuming

states over the right of the former to raise prices and the need of the latter to receive supplies.

• Systematic reversal of normal "free-market" functions, with prices inflating responsively to demand pressures at the retail end of the pipeline but deflating unresponsively to supply pressures at the production end of the pipeline.

• New domestic natural gas finds in an admitted "landmark" surge over usage.

• Regional associations of heating-oil marketers buying radio time to exploit claims of gas shortages.

• Indications that not even a depression flaring up into mass unemployment would deflect public opinion from its pursuit of environmental clean-up goals; gas burns clean, as oil and coal do not.

• The heating up of America's potential new Vietnam in Central America, accentuating the geographical reality that the bulk of America's intake of boiler fuel travels across sea lanes too narrow and too close to Castro's guns to be permanently assured of safe passage. It put America on notice that hawkishness in the Straits of Florida calls for boiler-fuel self-sufficiency.

The Treatment

A simultaneous two-step move is overdue. America's first need is to repeal the covert prohibition in the 1978 Energy Act against conversion of boiler-fuel use from liquid petroleum to natural gas. Her second need is for positive legislation to order this same overdue conversion. Most utilities' boilers operate on a dual-fired—that is, oil or gas—basis.

In testimony submitted to the Senate Judiciary Committee in December 1981, I suggested the following steps to reverse the Carter gas prohibition:

• Declaration of an amnesty from tax (and perjury) penalties for all owners of gas reserves to encourage full disclosure of the extent and value of their holdings. When De Gaulle took over in France in 1945, he announced just such an amnesty to all Frenchmen who would repatriate their gold and help mitigate the country's problems. It worked like a charm.

• Modification of the current provisions in the tax code banning the right of borrowers who claim an interest deduction to receive tax-exempt income. The U.S. gas economy would receive a long-needed shot in the arm once easing of these tax restrictions opened up the securities markets to new offerings of productive capital by gas utilities and municipalities paying tax-sheltered income. Precedent for giving the public access to market securities paying tax-sheltered income (a market sector normally reserved for state and local governments) was set during the Korean War when stockholders did not have to report dividend income.

• Initiation of an eighteen-month, across-the-board, mass-conversion effort to maximize new investment in the gas economy. To ensure responsiveness by owners of gas reserves, I recommended the appointment of a blue-ribbon presidential board whose sole duty would be to certify projects for investment in the production, transmission, manufacture, and marketing of natural gas. The certification of gas companies would exempt them from the windfall profits tax, provided they plowed back gas-related profits into new facilities and supplies, and would entitle them to pay tax-sheltered dividends.

The Recovery

President Reagan's exhortations against a quick fix have given a bad name to all emergency actions that stimulate activity and create jobs. The unspoken assumption behind his rhetoric has promulgated the prejudice that all quick fixes call for subsidies in the form of government spending. This is simply not so in the case of legislation that eliminates roadblocks in the way of conversion of boiler fuel to natural gas and orders the conversion expedited. All the additions to payrolls would be accounted for by private utilities and their suppliers. Any investment tax incentives legislated would more than compensate the Treasury in income taxes withheld for corporate income taxes and unearned incomes deferred. Accelerated depreciation never avoids taxes but merely defers them; in the case of individuals, it subjects subsequent profits to ordinary income tax, which accrues at the 50 percent rate rather than the 20 percent capital-gains rate.

The popular bogey of inflation speeding up with activity would not apply to gas conversion. Thanks to the providence of nature in endowing the continental United States with literally limitless reserves of natural gas and to the advances of technology in facilitating its extraction and transmission, heating and cooling costs would be lowered. Extensions to existing facilities are less costly and act more as antidepression stimulants than do massive new "green field" projects. Gas presents no problems of bulk storage, as oil and gasoline do in requiring the acquisition of adjacent land, which costs time and money disproportionate to jobs created and supplies ordered.

Collateral Advantages

• Split OPEC at its weakest link: Venezuela. Mobilize American industry to debunk OPEC's oil-shortage propaganda.

• Show that America is as ready to use her own natural gas as Europe is to pay up for the privilege of using Russia's.

• Give America time to plan effective technical schemes tapping its coal reserves, perhaps for gasification and liquification at the pithead but, in any case, for coping with the enormous transportation problem involved.

• Mediate the impasse between investment and conservation. Gas is the one basic energy resource that poses no environmental problem and still delivers energy for high-powered industrial use (as, for example, solar energy does not).

CHAPTER TWELVE

Domestic Finance

PRESCRIPTION #12
Refinancing the Public Sector

The Complaint

The splintered productive base of the U.S. economy.

The Cure

Transfer the public sector's high demand levels for goods and services into high supply levels furnished by the private sector.

The History

It started with Pearl Harbor. The "shotgun wedding" forced upon business and government by the war mobilized the United States to fight a war of production; business was drafted to serve as the government's helpmate. With Japan's defeat, the marriage ended in divorce. Thanks, however, to the large two-way, ongoing postwar cash flows between business taxpayers and the federal tax collector, the two wartime collaborators remained dependent on one another. Procurement funds flowed out to contractors, and tax payments flowed back to the Internal Revenue Service.

America went on from her victory in World War II to lose two other wars. While Harry Truman was losing the first one in Korea, he was smart enough to figure out that he was not up to improvising a new approach to war mobilization, and therefore he simply ordered a reenactment of FDR's World War II program, including the Victory Loan. Its original use had been suggested by a client of mine, Thomas A. Morgan, the president of the old Sperry Gyroscope Company, a prime Navy contractor. Morgan resisted Navy pressure to place Sperry's credit behind a loan to build a special-purpose ordnance plant. But he and I worked out the eventual V-Loan idea with Thomas G. ("Tommy the Cork") Corcoran, the New Deal's mercurial ambassador-at-large, and it passed muster with Carl Vinson, the chairman of the old House Naval Affairs Committee. Truman's revival of the V-Loan reconciled business and government for close to three years, after which time they went their separate ways again, and the country returned to business-as-usual. Until Vietnam.

As we saw in Chapter Three, the tactics Lyndon Johnson improvised for financing this jungle war suggested that, as he might have said in his own patois, he "had gone to business school with the Vietcong." When his congressional opponents finally cornered him, he ordered a wartime surtax to finance a major military escalation. The financing problem presented by the Vietnam War was entirely different from that dictated by the circumstances common to World War II and the Korean War. In both earlier war emergencies, Washington mandated the shutdown of the entire civilian economy, leaving the banking system flush with excess cash and industry with only war work. Vietnam, by contrast, was an exercise in guns and butter, which at one and the same time diverted secret funds to the war economy and inflated cash flows throughout the overstretched civilian economy. Johnson had the V-Loan technique at his fingertips but was barred from reviving it by his strategy to escalate the war by stealth. So Vietnam, by virtue of gunning the private economy and flooding the private sector with cash, was not relevant to the problem of refinancing the public sector and using it to revive the private sector, which the V-Loan is uniquely equipped to solve.

The impact of Ronald Reagan's various programs inflated the military budget but collapsed the economy, recreating the lopsided relationship between the public and private sectors that prevailed—at least so far as the demand for credit was concerned—between 1941 and 1945 and again between 1950 and 1953, without a shot being fired, without a shortage being created, and without a specific confrontation between adversaries. Despite the failure of the Reagan administration's trillion-dollar defense program to provide a safety net for the collapsing economy—or perhaps because of it—the Pentagon's contractors and their suppliers can be important enough as money users to make the difference between depression and boom. The lower the economy falls, the more important the role of defense contracting and contractors is bound to be. The fact that fiscal year 1982 defense procurement awards rose by 17 percent a month over the corresponding periods of fiscal year 1981 provides disturbing evidence that not even a direct surge of these proportions in start-up disbursements for defense proved sufficient to revive business investment.

The fiasco of dashed recovery hopes in 1982, moreover, left total public-sector procurement awards by state and local governments, as well as by the federal government, bulking larger in the total cash flows for investment purposes than during any period of normal activity up to acceptable recovery levels. The 1982 depression, however, aggravated problems that had been festering in the defense industries since Vietnam began to wind down. According to Jacques S. Gansler in his 1980 study, *The Defense Industry,* the number of aerospace subcontractors decreased 35 percent between 1968 and 1975. Gansler noted that many defense contractors, subcontractors, and suppliers were vulnerable to being forced out of military business simply by the Department of Defense's paperwork requirements. The overhead required to churn out forms, technical manuals, and other records to comply with the department's testing and legal requirements, or even to qualify to bill the government and get paid, is prohibitive to many small, high-tech outfits (with minimal overhead) that also rely on commercial business to survive. The basis on which the government accepts billing is time spent, documented by time sheets, that is, by overhead, which is also the basis on which big law firms bill their clients. But small businesses get paid on a products-shipped basis, which is exactly what the armed services need but cannot get from firms that don't have the money needed to deal with the Pentagon. An interagency group in the Reagan administration determined in April 1983 that fifteen of twenty-four key industries supplying defense-related hardware had suffered serious erosion of their production bases at the hands of import competitors.

The bottom line is that recovery requires borrowings and borrowers willing and, what is by no means the same thing, able to use the new money for productive purposes. In 1982, private sector bank loans were at a new high, while business liquidity was at a new low. Only the notes signed were new. The money borrowed went to roll over old loans plus interest, not to finance new buying and new hiring, as bank loans classified as "productive" are supposed to do.

The Symptoms

- Crumbling U.S. infrastructure (roads; bridges; railroads; transit, water, and sewage systems; prisons; all other public works).
- Torrent of new tax-exempt bond issues to finance public-service projects.
- Galloping state and local tax increases.
- Federal cutbacks in basic social support facilities, especially in those jointly financed with state and local governments.
- Pentagon cash shortages crowding munitions production out of defense commitments.
- Shutdowns of basic materials and facilities (copper, steel, nickel, etc.).

• Scrapping of basic industries furnishing common components of production (machine tools, foundries, forgings, valves, pumps, etc.).

The Treatment

Reactivate the V-Loan, the emergency expedient for financing war production facilities between 1941 and 1945 and again between 1950 and 1953. It can be easily and economically applied during peacetime to any public-service construction project undertaken by any governmental entity armed with the taxing power, without risk of abusing federal credit, as with the case of student loans, and without overburdening the tax-exempt bond market, as conventional financing does.

Here is how it worked during the two wars it financed and how its reach could be expanded again to win a peacetime war against a new depression: Companies with wartime contracts and with what were called defense-support contracts (to build power plants, foundries, etc.) were authorized to liquify them with bank borrowings needed to launch construction. The practical innovation achieved by the V-Loan technique was the wrinkle that turned direct governmental defense contracts into gilt-edged collateral good for "productive" borrowing purposes at any bank, not just the bank of the borrowing company, and therefore not chargeable against the borrower's credit entitlement. The same right of liquifying on the credit of the governmental customer was also extended via the banks to private corporations awarded federal "certificates of necessity," which authorized them to take specified rates of accelerated depreciation on their new investments in plant and equipment deemed necessary for munitions production and/or for "defense-support facilities." The V-Loan procedure channeled short-term bank money into long-term investment projects without sticking the banks with bad paper or leaving them with no money. It deferred the need of the Treasury to spend money before the armed services received deliveries on their contracts, but it enabled the Treasury to start collecting withholding taxes the moment bank advances to contractors entered the spending stream.

Admittedly, the V-Loan was put to work under circumstances different from those in force during the 1982 depression. The most obvious difference was that the cost of money was then only one percent; the other was that all halfway well-run banks were in excellent shape. Nevertheless, the V-Loan is an expedient for all seasons. In fact, its uses promise to be most beneficial during the bank-crisis phase of a depression, when stimulus and reliquifying are both rarities and urgencies.

But the simple device that financed America's last two legal war emergencies has been mothballed along with the ships and plants it financed. The V-Loan could be reactivated at no expense for the explicit purpose of putting idled bank money to work financing projects that the public sector needs to finish but lacks the money to start. No precedent exists in the challenge to finance a depression emergency, made all the more dangerous because it is complicated by a defense-finance emergency. The V-Loan could be used to bring both facets of this emergency under manageable control: endowing borrowers in the red with a flood of riskless receivables in the form of public-sector contracts, which they could put up as collateral to support bank loans. This procedure would reinstate their lost credit ratings and, therefore, cut their interest-rate charges as they increase their borrowings. These same receivables would also serve to upgrade the loan portfolios of banks that are aggravated by "nonproductive" loans. Top-quality loans generate the ongoing flows of deposits that banks with capital-deficiency and liquidity problems need.

If the V-Loan expedient had been in force in the troubled summer of 1982, a foundry with no access to credit and subject to interest charges significantly above prime would have been able to finance modernization along with a flood of "money-good" orders for castings. The armed services and any number of sick cities would have been anxious to put out orders backed by their guarantees in lieu of the cash they did not have. The embattled foundry in such circumstances could have cashed out its receivables on shipments, as well as its backup payables on purchases financed at some discount under prime, and settled for cash on new sales at wider discounts under list prices. The effect of saving interest charges for companies in the red is to enable them to cut their prices and vault into the black.

The salvaged foundry, which had been laying people off and running up its unit costs working only a few days a month, would be enjoying and spreading benefits because it would be paying taxes again. A cut from higher nondeductible interest charges to lower deductible charges would enable the foundry to generate cash on a scale large enough to reliquify its financial arteries instead of continuing to drain them, while resuming tax payments to the Treasury.

Only one incidental change would be needed: for the Federal Reserve Board to agree to accept public-sector term notes from member banks for duly authorized productive purposes and to hold them for more than a couple of days at a time, as it normally does with loans subject to private-sector credit risks. When the crisis of the savings and loan associations (S&Ls) turned acute in the summer of 1981, the Federal Reserve Board actually provided such emergency accommodation for embattled lending institutions that were not even under its jurisdiction.

Any V-Loans would be absolutely risk-free to the banking system because the guarantor of the loan behind the contract would always be another arm of the public sector that is the customer for the public work being financed. The thrust of the V-Loan, as I wrote to Senator Ted Stevens of Alaska, the assistant majority leader, in response to a reminder from him about congressional concern over abuses of government-guaranteed loans to third parties, "is to accelerate funding, via the banks, of transactions that would eventually be consummated anyway. There is no way in the world that the ultimate customer of these transactions would or could go bad; it is the U.S. Treasury disbursing on behalf of the Pentagon." I emphasized that in the case of federal contracting and borrowing, the V-Loan would perform the miracle needed to liquify the productive apparatus in the act of revving it up again. Where the normal procedure in governmental procurement is to spend first and to borrow afterwards, the V-Loan procedure calls for inviting the government contractors to borrow first by lending the government's credit to it, and for the government to start spending *after* it has begun to collect withholdings on the work done. No V-Loan financing is appropriate for disbursements for payrolls and interest, only on investment projects providing a durable asset.

The V-Loan principle can also be applied throughout the entire public sector, that is, where no third-party borrowers, private or foreign, are concerned. "All public-sector borrowers," I continued to Senator Stevens, "are of course armed with the taxing power and enjoy borrowing access to the tax-exempt market. Also, they are able to persuade banks in their jurisdictions to hold their obligations in investment portfolios, and, therefore, all state and local governmental units would qualify as money-good guarantors to the satisfaction of both the Treasury and Congress." Neither the lending banks nor the governmental entity involved would in such cases be subjected to the third-party risk that the government routinely accepts in guaranteeing private-sector loans to the Federal Housing Administration, the Veterans Administration, college students, the Chrysler Corporation, New York City, Poland, etc.

A final consideration prompted by the nationwide phenomenon of Kemp-Roth tax legislation, combined with the squeeze on states and cities to raise their income tax rates under cover of federal tax cuts, is that the recipient of a paycheck subject to withholding generally has eyes only for the bottom-line entry on the check stub showing his/her take-home pay, not the sources of the withholding. The ability and/or willingness of the American work force to spend freely in the retail market has always varied with its windfall income from overtime and bonuses, its base pay being absorbed by subsistence needs. When Reagan promulgated the promise of Kemp-Roth, he neglected to bind the states and the cities to his tax-cutting commitment to the work force. Congressman Jack Kemp, an original "back-when" Reagan supporter, won a nationwide constituency for himself with his eloquent preaching against the evils of "bracket creep." The federal government itself, however, will be powerless to stop bracket creep until it can persuade state and local authorities empowered to levy income taxes to stop accelerating it. The federal government would be entitled to a reciprocal agreement from state and city taxing authorities the moment it cut them in on the V-Loan privilege. The most constructive form such reciprocity could take in the interest of all concerned—the federal, state, and local tax authorities, the work force, and the country's retailing industries—would be an agreement to stop bracket creep at its source. The way to ensure it is to direct presidential jawboning at state and local governments, and urge them to join the IRS in putting a tax-rate freeze on the top bracket to which the last $1,000 of earned income is subject. This would encourage the work force to opt for the fringe benefits that accompany overtime and bonus pay and to resist the temptation to continue earning it in the moonlighting economy where the offset against withholding is the forfeiture of fringe benefits.

The Recovery

As a depression expedient, the extension of the V-Loan privilege to state and local governments would give the economy an urgently needed stimulus at a time when the pipelines of production are empty and suffering shrinkage. As was discussed in Chapter Five, what makes the difference in the overall trend and pace of activity and employment is always the prevailing impulse to accumulate or liquidate inventories. No prod sends purchasing agents chasing after materials more frantically than does word of machinery orders and plant construction starts after months of holdbacks on everything. General Electric bears impressive witness to the credo that investment in the modernization of manufacturing plant and equipment is not a lost cause. If any hoary, red brick pile looks like a monument to terminal obsolescence, it is GE's locomotive works in Erie, Pennsylvania, which dates back to 1900. Yet, its executive vice president of technical systems told *The Washington Post* "that the way to stay world-class competitive was not to whine and procrastinate and wait for better times and high volume, but to produce the world-class best locomotive at a competitive price." He expressed encouragement over the growing numbers of customers "willing to be born again in the waters of electronics. . . . Automation does work, it's practical, it can make old businesses tough and competitive, and it's good for the country." The effect of steel mills ordering generators after months of refusing to accept deliveries of coal, as they did in 1982, would be electrifying. Reactivation of the V-Loan procedure would accomplish this transformation overnight, not only reversing the normal business-cycle sequence of inventorying first and investing afterwards but also speeding it up.

A demand for V-Loans would simultaneously start up the engines of production of basic materials, which have been shut down tight, and of common components, which have been scrapped as obsolete in a "service" economy. The longer a depression is tolerated, the bigger the budget deficits and business bankruptcies it makes unavoidable. Tax collections are the only elastic ingredient of the fiscal equation offering hope of shrinking the deficit, and they swing with business activity and earnings. There is no way in the world that any president, however popular or strong, can survive politically while cutting the annual rate of spending increase—and that is all that Reagan ever promised to cut —but simultaneously tolerating a depression amid an arms buildup.

The Reagan administration's focus on the spending side of the budget is understandable, if only because the spending side is easier to project than the collection side. Projections of collections and refunds boil down to forecasts for the performance of the entire economy as well as for the financial condition of the federal government and its impact on the markets. Therefore, they are likely to be just as realistic as the incumbent administration's sense of direction about the economy. Revival of the V-Loan offers a golden opportunity to solve a number of problems at once: to speed up riskless business borrowing and buying; to raise withholding- and sales-tax collections without raising tax rates; to rely on bank loans instead of government spending to hit both interrelated accelerators at once; to enable the armed services to supplement their overhead cash drains by filling in their supply shortages; and to invite the government to restore excessive social-service cuts without increasing its spending.

Collateral Advantages

• Shrink the cycle of procurement, production, and delivery, while lengthening the lead time for payment, to buy time to prevent obvious basics from being squeezed out of the Pentagon budget, as they are year after year, and to slow down the rate of defense spending.

• Give interest rates a sharp downward push as the result of arming the country's insolvent heavy industries with the credit of their public-sector customers; the country's better-financed banks would respond by pressing large loans at below the prime rate on well-financed companies.

• Extension of the same technique to the utilities industry, until 1982 the reliable workhorse pacing all U.S. capital investment. Because the utilities are guaranteed a minimum rate of return on all capital outlays, their obligations are money-good. They are on a cost-and-cash squeeze and have curtailed their outlays sharply. Extension of the V-Loan to them would result in a sharp and swift capital and investment turnaround, motivated by utility-management perception of cost inflation and delivery bottlenecks coming with power shortages on day one of recovery.

PRESCRIPTION #13
Reprieves for Small Business

The Complaint

The bankruptcy epidemic among small business and the unemployment feeding on it.

The Cure

Emergency tax-relief measures helping small businesses stay solvent.

The History

One of the original cries of the Civil Rights movement, "Last to be hired, first to be fired," applies to small-businesses as well. Their troubles have always forecast those in store for the economy; economic recoveries have rarely progressed far enough or lasted long enough to eliminate what in politics is known as "the small-business problem." The first formal effort to do something for them was the New Deal's ill-fated move, under the auspices of the National Recovery Act (NRA), to make cartels of the entire structure of American business, large and small. Big business ran its "blue eagle" programs, as its price- and wage-fixing schedules were called, to suit itself. But the programs that covered industries comprising smaller businesses, like the garment industries, were run by the unions. This operation blew up when the Supreme Court threw out the NRA in 1935.

The second attempt to deal with the small-business problem was forced on Washington after Pearl Harbor, when it shut down the civilian economy and required every business, desperate due to the lack of materials, to apply for priorities to get them. The idea was that a governmental agency would be needed to plead the case of small businesses for priorities, to help small businesses qualify for defense procurement, and to get a hearing for new ideas offered to the armed services and their main contractors. The resultant wrangling gave FDR a flimsy public-relations defense against the charge that he had turned his third-term administration, his first war administration, over to the fat cats. It also institutionalized a place in the Washington scheme of things for a kind of administrative ghetto tending to the concerns of small business, culminating in the creation of the first peacetime Small Business Administration (SBA) as an independent agency.

If the idea of an SBA had not been around by 1960, the Kennedy administration would have invented it. Their laudable concern for civil rights unfortunately led the Kennedy people to devise a financial monstrosity for the purpose of providing first aid to smaller businesses, which they envisioned from their standpoint to be primarily Black and Hispanic. Predictably, the credit offered was easy to get but hard to pay for. Businesses that by definition needed the cost of money to be lower than their larger competitors, suppliers, and customers were soaked with usurious charges. Overnight, therefore, swarms of financing companies catering to the needs of small business were hatched with largesse from Washington and invited to pyramid bank credit. Banks with small-business customers formed small-business subsidiaries to get in on the party. Some of these ill-conceived financing vehicles were actually taken public. Their most useful function was as a job haven for political hangers-on and, increasingly, as a sop to those minority businesses that had "connections." Republican administrations, incidentally, have relied on the SBA gimmick as much as Democratic administrations. Neglect of the problem has been thoroughly bipartisan, as has its exploitation.

During the pretax era, Karl Marx blamed the capitalist system for widening the cleavage between bigger businesses in the black and smaller businesses in the hole. The age of apparent affluence has seen the government operate as a more efficient engine of bankruptcy for the weak than Marx had ever predicted. In the normal sequence of disaster, the government taxes business into the red and, once the damage has been done, regulates them out of deductions as they run out of earnings. Once they run out of credit, bankruptcy becomes the only way out. Small business is the biggest source of employment in good times and therefore the biggest source of unemployment in bad times. It gives America its economic base. Plants do not sell goods, people do; and the people who do, even for General Motors, Exxon, and General Electric, run small businesses. The same is true at the opposite end of the pipeline for the people who supply big businesses. The biggest businesses in the country depend on an army of suppliers, a good number of them quite small. So does the vast apparatus of defense contractors. Consequently, the squeeze on the biggest, the richest, and the best-run businesses in the country imposed the death sentence on small businesses en masse when the economy started to falter in 1981.

Specifically, the tax code became the engine of doom for small business. Its destructive impact paralleled the interrelated disaster in the real estate market and the mortgage banking business. The reason goes back to the two-tier basis on which businesses calculate their operating revenues and their tax accruals. Businesses in the black that owe money —and just about all of them do—take tax deductions for the interest they pay on the debt they owe. On the other side of the competitive fence, businesses in the red are obliged by circumstance to owe more money relative to their volume than well-financed businesses in the black. But as their operating losses mount, deficit corporations forfeit the right to claim interest charges paid as deductions against taxes owed. The relief from tax payments that comes with their losses is scant consolation. Losses, far from granting exemption from the interest burden, turn it into an ongoing capital levy. Loss corporations invariably overborrow. As they lose deductions along with their earnings, they run first out of cash, then out of credit, and soon after that fall into bankruptcy.

The Symptoms

- Delinquency in settling withholding taxes.
- Lapsing of insurance policies.
- Retreat from bank credit to supplier credit.
- Inability to carry inventories of either raw materials or finished products.

The Treatment

Create a new type of entitlement for small business, requiring no new cash drain on the Treasury, to stop the rash of bankruptcy among smaller businesses. Its purpose: to permit small businesses to use their tax losses as last-ditch alternatives to bankruptcy. Its modus operandi: to authorize the swapping of operating losses, dollar for dollar, with profit corporations able to use such losses as deductions. When in March 1982 I testified before the Senate Select Committee on Small Business, I recommended that businesses struggling for survival be allowed "to monetize tax losses in a free private market as a defensive strategy calculated to protect the economy and the Treasury against the danger . . . of bankruptcy splintering the base of the economy." The thrust of the proposal was to turn the tax-loss swap concept into a private economic asset and a public economic benefit.

Regrettably, however, this unabrasive effort at aiding small business was seized upon by lobbyists for some of the more predatory members of the Fortune 500 and incorporated into a program bearing the name "safe harbor." It was a travesty of the simple proposal I offered for fending off small-business bankruptcies. As I told the Small Business Committee, chaired by maverick Connecticut Republican Senator Lowell P. Weicker, Jr., "Glaring inequities are built into the ability to enjoy access to the safe-harbor mechanism. High-powered batteries of expensive lawyers and accountants are indispensable for entry. Megabucks of ready cash are the engine of discrimination inside safe-harbor deadlines. Under present conditions, the Treasury's case for standing pat excludes every small business in sight—if not by law, then by effect. This is a raw deal from a stacked deck, yet the Treasury is defending it on the grounds of equity."

As we saw earlier, pioneering ventures have already sprung up and are doing an active barter business by serving as clearing houses for cash-poor businesses. These entrepreneurs at the barter game function as small-scale equivalents of the Yellow Pages for private swappers of anything from loaded coal cars for airplanes, to bicycles for restaurant meals, or, to take a case of direct dealing without a barter broker as an intermediary, swapping Northrop fighter planes for Canadian paper cups and Turkish wine. Outfits in the barter business charge a cash fee for rendering this service. The SBA could too; and in the process of turning an honest dollar for the Treasury, as so many other financing arms of the government have done for so many years, it could be filling a bona fide functional need instead of filling a hack political role.

As I told the Small Business Committee, "No cost or burden to the government would result from entitling smaller loss corporations to engage in the free-market bartering of their tax losses with profit corporations, large and small. Any profitable business filing its tax return would merely append the tax returns of the loss corporations whose losses it had bought, claiming those losses as its deductions and stating what consideration it had paid for the privilege." Any tax-loss incentives that worked to avoid cutoffs in the flow of payroll dollars would earn their keep with the Treasury by bringing withholding dollars back into it.

The SBA would be charged with recommending guidelines to the IRS to ensure that businesses in the black, which get certification from the SBA to swap tax losses with businesses in the red, give benefits for value received—specifically, charging less if selling and paying in advance if buying. In any case, the tax losses offered up by small businesses in the red could serve as entitlements for them with the businesses in the black on the other side of the transaction: either to book sales orders or to place purchase orders. Monetized tax losses are as good as money in the bank. Why not start a free market in them?

Liberalization of the rules governing payroll-withholding payments would go far to ease another source of frustration and uneconomic cash drain on small businesses. They are required to deposit their withholding payments in custodial accounts at commercial banks within three days after payday. No experience can be more bitter, nor can any inequity be more devastating for the economy, than the experience of the small business that dutifully meets its payroll on a Friday by straining the personal credit of the proprietor and then deposits its withholding add-on in the custodial account, only to watch the bank get the use of its money prior to bouncing its next payroll and putting it out of business. More equity and efficiency would result if failing businesses were entitled to use withholding payments made during any previous quarter to qualify them for bank credit secured by prospective refunds from the Treasury during the next reporting quarter. The thrust of this simple proposal would be to accelerate refund payments and to qualify every business that had made its withholding payments as a good credit risk. Banks are more likely to extend credit to loss businesses during a period of general distress if the firms are building up refund entitlements from the Treasury.

Another simple expedient that would earn more cash for the Treasury in uninterrupted withholding receipts than it would lose in deductions claimed would be to raise the ceiling on the deduction of capital losses. Congress has been blurring the distinction between capital gains and ordinary income and seems intent on eliminating it altogether. A basic principle of the tax code entitles taxpayers to recapture their losses free of tax. This right, however, is severely limited on capital losses. Many a proprietorship is being forced to go under as the direct result of the nondeductibility of capital losses against all income beyond the $3,000 ceiling in force. This ceiling is overdue to be lifted.

Small businesses would receive another productive lift if the tax code allowed them to treat the premium payments they make on "key man" life insurance policies for their executives as tax deductible. This tax break would enhance a small firm's ability to get credit against the insurance policy without having to borrow at the bank or the financing company. Buying insurance is the first responsibility of anyone starting or taking over a business. It is the last alternative to insolvency for a proprietorship or partnership. It is a take-out for creditors, including the IRS, and an anchor for heirs.

The Recovery

Projecting a recovery without taking steps to preserve the viability of small businesses is as impractical as planning to put a machine tool to work without a cutting edge or putting an intercontinental missile into production without first deciding on a launching pad for it. Small business mans the base of the economy; big business is the pyramid built on it. The breadth of the base provides the equilibrium for the height of the pyramid. The depression splintered the small-business base at both ends simultaneously, as suppliers were decimated on the production side of the economy's flows of goods and dealers were decimated on the distribution side. The cheap and simple recommendations made to reduce the casualty rate among small business would cost the Treasury no revenue; on the contrary, they would earn the Treasury revenue by enabling small businesses to retain their role as the economy's largest source of employment and, therefore, of withholding taxes. As a practical matter, the hope of recovery hinges upon the start of an across-the-board reinventorying move by businesses. To trigger a bona fide, self-propelling recovery, such a move would need to meet a double requirement: to be big and broad enough to raise capacity utilization back above 90 percent and to pour enough production into the pipelines of distribution to prevent bottlenecking and costly inflation. The only way to accomplish both purposes at once is to drop the casualty rate among small businesses and to attract new entries. The top grades of executives in bigger businesses are always straining at the leash to strike out on their own—even during a depression when it pays better to be on a payroll than to meet one and is no safer.

Collateral Advantages

- Stem the tide of unemployment and the drain on the Treasury as well as the states, resulting from small-business bankruptcies.
- Establish an economic function for the Small Business Administration.
- Put a competitive prod onto big business.

PRESCRIPTION # 14
Fast Bucks and Comfortable Fallbacks in Savings Bonds

The Complaint

High withholding levies against take-home pay.

The Cure

The right to instant liquidity without penalty for U.S. savings bond holders.

The History

John Maynard Keynes, like him or not, was the innovator of the U.S. wartime savings bond. It fit neatly into the gap between the limit of wartime taxation and the risk of wartime inflation in both World War II and the Korean War. With the shutdown of residential construction and production of consumer durables between 1941 and 1945 and again between 1950 and 1953, money had no place to go except into savings for the duration of the Treasury's need to borrow beyond the limits of what it could tax and to keep the money borrowed at low cost.

So long as interest rates remained at their postdepression lows, as they did from 1941 to 1953, this presented no problem. With three-month Treasury bills yielding 1.0 percent during World War II and 1.5 percent during the Korean War, the device of deferring interest on savings proved irresistible to the work force, as did the incentive to waive the going rate of interest in return for the guarantee of receiving future gain at a higher rate. In subsequent years, after interest rates had risen, savers and investors found it hard to recognize what a popular instrument the war savings bond had originally been. The peculiar tax feature of the savings bond served as a testimony to its popularity. Though the deferred payout was clearly a capital gain to any saver/investor willing to hold it to maturity, the Treasury nevertheless managed to classify its cash return at maturity as ordinary income.

How come it worked? Payroll withholding was already institutionalized, and the popular outlets for spending money were shut down. The total collected for savings bonds between 1942 and 1945 averaged $28 billion a year, 66 percent of the admitted average deficit during that period. During the Korean War, the Treasury took in an average of no less than twice as much: $57 billion a year. With the deficit at $1.5 billion during the first spasm of red ink (fiscal year 1952) and at $6.5 billion the next year, the cash realized from savings bonds clearly made all the difference. Even with interest rates next to nothing, the wartime federal deficit would have been horrendous without this expedient.

During both wartime experiences, the claim for savings bond withholding came to 20 percent of taxable income. It accounted for the second 20 percent claim; withholding for income taxes clipped the first 20 percent from each paycheck. Payroll withholding plus savings bond investment therefore preempted 40 percent from each paycheck, a big bite, even with the civilian economy shut down. Total cash receipts for the Treasury came to 40 percent, though the 20 percent rate of payroll withholding remained the same. Each bond came in a denomination of $18.75, redeemable at $25 after ten years, with no interest along the way. This came to a gain of 33 percent, an eye-bulger in those days; never mind that this worked out to a swift 3.3 percent annual gain, less than the 5 percent wartime formula for wage increases.

By the 1980s, two-digit yields on Treasury bills changed the terms of trade between the Internal Revenue Service and its customers in the work force. The Treasury needed more withholdings, but it also needed to recapture more preempted pay. The problem crystallized into two parts: how to get the government more cash up front and how to let the members of the work force keep more in tax cuts from week to week. Taxation on a scale to cover those T-bill yields (not to mention federal borrowings on which interest had to be paid) caused a tax revolt by the public in the tradition of the Boston Tea Party.

More recently, the first two years of the Kemp-Roth tax cut returned 15 percent of pre-1981 income tax withholding to taxpayers; the third year promised another 10 percent. Statistically speaking, none of these cuts enabled the beneficiaries in the work force to keep enough to buy anything substantial. Nevertheless, the aggregate cost to the Treasury of passing out petty cash to the entire work force kept it shorter of cash than its beneficiaries were. Meanwhile, all taxpayers, even those not borrowing, were complaining about the sharpened bite of interest rates due to the heavier burden of governmental borrowings.

During World War II and Korea, an alternative program of taxation at politically acceptable rates, but *without* the attractive device of savings bonds, would have left enough of a shortfall to touch off inflationary dynamite. As it turned out, however, both a wartime taxpayer revolt and a wartime inflationary spiral were avoided. The savings bond accomplished three objectives: (1) it kept the Treasury's cash flow comfortable while meeting its wartime needs; (2) it minimized the pinch on the tax-sensitive nerve of the work force; and (3) it left the investor in savings bonds confident in the expectation that wartime withholdings would be recaptured with a generous guarantee of a profit.

Keynes, like all seminal thinkers, was controversial in his time and misunderstood in later years. Contrary to his posthumous reputation, he preached fiscal austerity and advocated financial puritanism. His prescription for the original savings bond stipulated that it be nontransferable and nonborrowable. His device left members of the work force in need of borrowing, and when they did borrow, they were unable to raise cash on their bona fide investments in war savings bonds in order to meet their interest bills. Not only was borrowing on savings bonds forbidden, but the expedient of liquidation was too. The ban on spending, made enforceable by the conversion of facilities to war production, made these other prohibitions enforceable as well.

The Symptoms

- Erosion of savings reserves in the hands of the work force.
- High-pressure bidding contest for retail savings at uneconomic rates of interest.

- Work-force revolt against high withholding rates.
- Popular resistance to increases in withholding taxes to finance Social Security.
- Demographic disparity in the distribution of savings. Older savers, with investments (especially in tax-exempts) but no jobs, holding most of the savings, while younger people, with jobs but no investments, unable to save.

The Treatment

The run-up in interest rates during the pre-1980 years calls for a modification of both the rate structure and the holding period of the emergency savings bond. By the end of 1982, the runaway federal deficit, as well as the renewed fear of rampant inflation, emphasized the urgency of popularizing the purchase of savings bonds once again—this time with a variable rate of interest and a flexible maturity. By the same token, the threat of compulsory withholding called for a sensitive application with consideration for the work force and practicality in setting terms, conditions, and, not least, investment incentives.

The technique calls for using withholdings from savings bonds to protect the Treasury from the need to borrow more in lieu of collecting more; and to free the taxpayer, obliged to "invest" in savings bonds, from being taxed more. A fair trade, if workable. And workable, if made intelligible.

The first step is to reset a payroll withholding rate of 20 percent for investment in savings bonds, subject to two exclusive new features: marketability and marginability, or the rights to sell and to borrow on them. The Treasury collected $397 billion in withholding during the 1982 fiscal year, despite the shortfall due to double-digit unemployment and the de facto ceiling on pay increases imposed by the depression in the economy. Rounding out the withholding figure to $400 billion and assuming no improvement in the economy, a 20 percent withholding for savings-bond investment would net the Treasury $80 billion annually, equal to more than 33 percent of the deficit for fiscal year 1983 ($225 billion plus)—enough to make a respectable contribution in limiting it and, along with other prescriptions presented here, an adequate one. Assuming finally that inflation, new tax increases, catch-up pay increases, or cost-of-living adjustments upgraded every taxpayer into the 50 percent bracket, and that all taxpayers liquified their savings bonds by borrowing on them, say at 12 percent per year, they would run up an annual interest bill of $9.6 billion. The after-tax damage to the work force, therefore, would amount to only $4.8 billion on the $80 billion earned. The effect of borrowing on these bonds would endow the work force with disposable income of $75.2 billion on debt its members would never have to repay; the bonds would pay off the banks. Everyone borrowing to buy these new bonds would still own them and benefit from the built-in annual increment.

THE MARGINABILITY MODIFICATION

The right to borrow to buy savings bonds would be automatic on payday, just like the withholding. A terminal installed at payroll points would give all members of the work force not free or willing to sit on their savings bonds the right to collateralize them at the prime rate with the use of a credit card. Interest for the first year would be prepaid on each bond borrowed, so that the loan proceeds would amount to the purchase price less a year's interest. Bondholders could do whatever they pleased with the cash borrowed. It would not be taxable income, and the prepaid interest would be a tax deduction. The bank favored with the payroll account would take the savings bond back as collateral, and savings-bond holders, not feeling the need or desire to borrow on their bonds, would be free to hold them until maturity or, alternatively, to sell them at any time. Bonds and brokers would be authorized to make markets in them. The annual appreciation built into each bond would invite dealers to price them each year at discounts measured by each successive year's step-up in capital values.

THE MARKETABILITY MODIFICATION

The banks would get the first aid they badly need in the form of new reserves in lieu of new capital, which they would be welcome to liquify by discounting at the Federal Reserve window or to post as reserves; government bonds are always usable for this purpose. This need was not felt in 1941–1945 or 1950–1953. Then, the banks were loaded with excess reserves and therefore were under no pressure to attract savings bonds from the hands of the work force. Today, with interest rates in double-digit territory, the luxury of sterilizing savings bonds in small denominations is uneconomic, when they could be made to do double duty as reserves the banking system needs—at no one's expense.

Everyone involved in the deal would benefit. Banks are already required to post reserves against deposits with their regional Federal Reserve banks. If they were also allowed to use as reserves savings bonds taken in as collateral on loans made to income holders subject to withholding, they would be able to add a steadily growing portion of the assets in their loan portfolios to their postal reserves.

THE LONG TAX FORM MODIFICATION

Members of the work force electing to borrow on the new savings bonds would have the right to take their cash interest payments as tax deductions. Qualifying for the right to use the long form for tax reporting would cut up-front interest charges in half, assuming that the work force is gravitating toward the 50 percent tax bracket on additions to income after salary. Assuming such a bracket, a 15 percent rate of interest prepaid on borrowings at the time of investment comes to a posttax cost of 7.5 percent. By contrast, the annual markup in the face amount of the savings bonds purchased would accrue to investors tax-free until the bonds were cashed in at maturity. For anyone electing to hold them that long instead of cashing them in, the gain would be taxable at the going rate for ordinary income.

THE CAPITAL GAINS MODIFICATION

Where the original wartime savings bonds trapped the unwary investor into paying taxes on accrued capital-gains at ordinary income tax rates at maturity, the equitable and practical rate at which to tax a newly designed savings bond is at the capital-gains rate of 20 percent on redemption. After deducting annual interest costs on any borrowings, this tax would be inconsequential—even in the unlikely event that the capital gains rate is no longer 20 percent or eliminated altogether. If it were to be eliminated, interest paid on borrowings would still be deductible against taxes owed at ordinary income rates on earnings.

The Recovery

Everyone would benefit—from the Treasury to the wage earner. The Treasury would harvest a new cash crop equal to 20 percent of payrolls, which it could not hope to collect in taxes. The work force could come to the bargaining table armed with the righteous claim that its members had accepted a 20 percent cash surtax on their hard-earned incomes, but they could still reserve the right to liquify it, less only 7.5 percent for after-tax interest charges. But they would be compensated at the end of each year for this nominal cost by the guaranteed appreciation, free from any risk of market loss, in the face amount of each bond. The banks would be reliquified but without any pressure on the Fed to inflate the money supply and to accentuate the volatility of interest rates, the standard method and predictable result of its normal operations. The borrowings cashed out against savings bonds put up as collateral would provide an enormous stimulus to the economy.

Collateral Advantages

• Impact of the realization that money earned takes two forms: taxable income *and* appreciable assets.

• Democratization of tax benefits by ending the destructive argument over cutting or raising tax rates.

• Substituting gilt-edged, nondepreciating domestic reserves, in the form of savings bonds deposited as collateral for loans, for bad foreign loans that force write-downs in bank capital.

• Spurring the economy, without increasing government spending or taking inflationary risks, by slashing tax rates and/or gunning the money supply.

• Giving the work force an incentive to accumulate capital, instead of just complaining about "bracket creep," by working overtime after the siege of unemployment.

• Enabling the Treasury to collect cash free from interest charges years before incurring the obligation to pay it out; collecting first and paying later is always good business; ask the bankers.

PRESCRIPTION # 15
A Single Standard for Market Regulation

The Complaint

Inconsistent, inequitable, and impractical market regulations.

The Cure

Extension of the rules that work to the exchanges in need of them.

The History

All effective market regulation began with Joe Kennedy's pioneering operation as the first chairman of the Securities and Exchange Commission (SEC). The founding father of the Kennedy clan focused his regulatory powers on the single most glaring abuse responsible for the 1929 market crash: the freewheeling operations of the short-selling pools, especially those he himself had run. While the crash was taking its toll, the trapped and panicked public saw the calamitous drop in stock prices and the disaster caused by the forced liquidation of stocks owned on thin margins, but not the underlying abuses responsible.

As Kennedy knew better than anyone, the trip-wire effect of short-selling on margin calls was direct and devastating. The feedback from margin calls, which wiped out the amateurs, guaranteed princely windfalls to the professionals who ran the "short" pools. Margin calls forced desperate selling in wholesale lots, breaking stock prices and giving free rides to the "shorts." The hunting license the shorts enjoyed, until Kennedy cleaned up their act after the damage was done and the bottom was hit, put them in the inhospitable position of a crooked saloon bouncer who gets on the staircase one step above a drunk, fallen half way downstairs, and kicks him the rest of the way before picking his pocket.

To protect the market from further damage, Kennedy drew upon his earlier seamy and successful exploits. But by then the stock market had been driven too low to preserve the incentive to continue shorting. Nevertheless, Kennedy reformed short-selling practices by having the SEC institute two simple rules. First, he obliged the floor to list all short sales in all listed stocks separately, and second, the SEC prohibited brokers from executing orders to sell short until a previous uptick in each shorted stock had been registered.

Both worked like charms. Kennedy's first requirement transformed volume on the short side from the bearish force it had been to the bullish signal of a reinvigorated market. The market woke to the realization that shorts are a market's best friends. All speculators who sell stocks short become captive buyers. The reason is built into their shorting; they always borrow on margin to sell stocks they don't own but hope to buy back later at lower prices. Therefore, when they get lucky, the stocks they short go down, and they take their profits by buying the shorted stocks. When they guess wrong—and even in bear markets, shorts get caught in rallies—they get hit by margin calls and are faced with the choice of either putting up more money or getting out. Either way, whether to take profits or to take losses, today's freewheeling shorts are tomorrow's captive buyers.

Kennedy's second rule, requiring anxious shorts to hold their fire until an uptick had first been recorded, broke up the short pools. Its double impact was crystal clear. Shorts retained their freedom to take their chances anytime they decided that upticks were overpricing a stock or group of stocks, but their pre-1929 license to break already weakened stocks was revoked. Inside the special world of the stock market, these two rules have never been questioned or amended. They worked. Their joint success raises the question why they have never been applied to speculative futures markets. Because they worked?

As the corporate takeover game raged in the early 1980s, it added a new dimension to the regulatory problem. Specifically, the takeover game created a conflict between the responsibility of the SEC for equitable market practices and the regulatory irresponsibility of the Federal Reserve Board in policing takeovers. Thanks to the profit squeeze, corporations with spare cash and/or credit were coming to the realization that buying existing assets from companies with no interest in developing them made more sense than investing in new assets of their own. Since cash-rich companies had cut back their own investment programs, they were not making active use of their lines of credit. Nor were their banks making new loans to them for productive purposes. Accordingly, the corporations eyeing takeover targets followed the path of least resistance and used their credit lines to finance their takeover bids. In the process, they made a mockery of the Federal Reserve Board's margin rules by putting close to $100 billion ($40 billion in 1981 plus $55 billion in the first six months of 1982) of nonproductive takeover loans on the books.

Two separate and distinct complaints have contributed to the general malaise that then seized all the speculative and investment markets —not only the established speculative markets in commodity futures and the supposed investment markets in bonds and stocks but the constantly growing smorgasbord of casino-table offerings with volatile price tags as well. The abuses were institutionalized by the three-way division of regulatory responsibility among the Securities and Exchange Commission, the Federal Reserve Board, and the Commodity Futures Trading Commission (CFTC). The confusion was compounded by the rapid growth of unfamiliar trading practices and dynamite-loaded margining techniques on the list of speculative markets subject to regulation.

The first administrative lapse can be charged to the Federal Reserve Board. It had been given jurisdiction over margin regulations before the Great Crash, when Congress held that margin regulations are primarily a bank-credit problem. After the crash, when the New Deal put the SEC into business and charged it with cleaning out the stable and putting a lock on the door, "margining" was out of fashion with the public. Consequently, no one bothered to move this vital regulatory responsibility from the Fed to the SEC. During the salad days of the New Deal, when the SEC was its trailblazing agency, speculative activity and public participation in the markets were not issues. Besides, the SEC and the Fed operated closely together as policy-making agencies, and the split of responsibility was not a problem.

Misconceptions about what the Fed can and cannot do are numerous, beginning with the notion that it can control the money supply, which, in fact, it cannot even count, and ending with the conviction that it sets interest rates (see Chapter Five). The media and the public, awed by the mystique surrounding the Federal Reserve and, therefore, overestimating its powers, remain unaware of the endless time the board takes even to attempt to deal with these two responsibilities, which no other agency can handle. On top of this, the depression of the 1980s burdened it with the endless chore of managing "mergers" of banks in trouble. But the regulation of margin rules is a recurrent cause for public concern. When it does surface, the Fed becomes the focus of worry. It did so when it presided indulgently over flagrant breaches of its margin regulations by the blue chips on the Fortune 500 list. Their dealings touched off the takeover debate of 1981. By that time, take- over finance had become a major force, intensifying the destabilization that the markets were suffering in 1982. In fairness, the Fed never knew what hit it.

The second administrative bungle could be attributed to the CFTC, which Congress created in 1975. Common sense and less diligence than is required for a small-town CPA to file a simple tax return would have guided the agency from its first day to adopt the 1934 Kennedy rule governing the policing and disclosure of short sales. The rule was tailor- made for the CFTC, but the CFTC never adopted it. Such is the atti- tude of novice bureaucrats toward tried and tested rules improvised by veteran bureaucrats in older agencies. The mystery deepened in 1981 when the CFTC was given administrative jurisdiction over the new habit-forming fad of trading stock futures. The wiggle-waggling of this new index, with a large assist from undisclosed futures shorting, im- mediately began to influence the stock market in the way that dogs follow their tails. It also illustrated the principle that one arm of a schizoid octopus does not know what any of its other arms may be doing. The CFTC never bothered to find out how the SEC freed the securities markets from manipulation by short sellers.

SHORTING ABUSES

"Shorting" the market is a perfectly legitimate activity. The commodi- ties futures markets, by virtue of their volatility, have taught industrial processors of raw materials, as well as commercial marketers of their end products, to use the futures markets as hedge markets, that is, to short futures of commodities already owned as insurance against inven- tory losses. Managements routinely dealing in speculative commodities know enough not to tread in the tricky crosscurrents where speculators with eyes only for a fast buck always rush.

So far so good. No complaining about secrecy. No end of complaint, however, about the CFTC for its stubborn failure to adopt the SEC's disclosure rules. The CFTC in its dogmatic slumber has been content merely to publish all outstanding futures contracts traded on the futures exchanges. These totals are called the "open interest," which anyone can read in the newspapers. All concerned fulfill their legal obligations by disclosing the number of contracts outstanding on every trading day in every futures market. But this disclosure, in addition to wasting high-cost newsprint, fails because it makes no mention of the "short interest." Congress has operated under the impression that it has discharged its obligation to regulate the futures markets through the CFTC as effectively as it has regulated the securities markets through the SEC. The conflict between the SEC's effective regulation of stock shorting and the CFTC's default on regulating futures shorting was allowed to drift beyond the scope of congressional scrutiny.

The amateurish surveillance the CFTC exercised over the commodities futures markets, moreover, made the Kremlin an unwitting gift of the key to America's granary. At planting time each spring in Russia, the Kremlin's news managers take the precaution of leaking their necessarily chancy crop guesstimates to the U.S. Central Intelligence Agency, and these leaks about crop planting invariably make headlines. It goes without saying that all Soviet crop forecasters talk big at planting time and, as the record shows, lower their sights by harvest time. But statistical expertise is not the purpose of the exercise; price manipulation is, with the CIA unwittingly acting as the USSR's publicity agent.

Wheat futures prices are the top-priority targets of the ongoing Soviet press barrage. But wheat is not the main crop shortage Moscow relies on America to fill; feed crops are (see Prescription #5 on barter). Feed-crop prices fluctuate with wheat prices and, predictably, prices plunge in response to news coming from Moscow of bumper crops. The absence of any obligation to report short sales in the U.S. futures markets gives Soviet grain-market operators a golden opportunity to earn a fair share of each year's crop bill months before it comes due. All they need do is short futures prices just as they pass the good news about the size of their next crop on to the CIA and the media. Long before their forward buying comes due for payment and the admission of their current need has driven prices back up, they have had ample opportunity to cover their short positions and to contract to take delivery of the new crop at bargain-basement prices. So they manipulate American crop futures prices down in time for them to do their buying, and they manipulate prices up again afterwards to cover their tracks at no extra cost. Nice work to give a needy customer who has also been targeted for nuclear bombardment.

TAKEOVER LOAN ABUSES

Markets on their way up normally behave like a child with a sweet tooth. The stock market's gluttonous appetite for takeovers paid for at rich premiums ended with a fit of indigestion in the summer of 1982. The day of reckoning arrived in June, when Gulf Oil's ill-timed feat in outbidding the field for Cities Service ran into a hailstorm stirred up by the buildup of excesses that had gone unnoticed. Never mind that Occidental Petroleum sneaked in when Gulf moved out.

On the face of it, the original Gulf takeover bid made a sensible fit, as did the subsequent Occidental bid: Cities Service represented a treasure trove of energy assets and related land plays accumulated long before inflationary markups became à la mode. Better still, they were all domestic and therefore guaranteed to be worth more the moment the crisis demonstrated that all assets owned overseas were worth less because they stood in the path of the oncoming storm. Cash was no consideration, Gulf having arranged lines of credit with a group of banks to assure consummation of this marriage made in heaven. Gulf bid $4.8 billion—$55 a share—for control of Cities Service, which, despite the market's awareness of an impending takeover bid, was then selling for only $38 a share. To ward off a competitive bid, Gulf stoked the fires under the boiling takeover market by raising its bid and inviting the world to carry its stock on margin. Even at $63, Cities Service stockholders complained that Gulf was stealing the company out from under them, and they were right. But they had to reckon on being on their own with the Federal Trade Commission (FTC) against them.

In August 1981, Senator Howard Metzenbaum, Democrat of Ohio, in collaboration with Herman Schwartz, chief minority counsel of the Senate judiciary subcommittee on agency administration, published a scorcher of an article in *The New York Times*, entitled "Merger Madness." The article, which focused on du Pont's $3.9 billion nonproductive loan to finance its controversial takeover of Conoco, charged that the heads of the Justice Department's Antitrust Division and the FTC had "apparently decided to ignore Supreme Court decisions condemning vertical arrangements in the production and distribution chain and to ease guidelines in mergers between competitors." When Metzenbaum and I discussed his article, I pointed out that he had limited his strictures against the Justice Department and the FTC to the public policy implications of "merger madness" but had spared the Federal Reserve Board the much more specific criticism of having winked at actual violations of its own margin rules on the books. On August 7, I wrote him that "these loans, made as they are for the purpose of buying stock, are in flagrant violation of the margin rules . . . not only because they offer no visible means of repayment but also because of [du Pont's] failure to put up 50 percent of the purchase price as required by the margin rules and to borrow only half of it."

More heinous still, the hysterical counterproductive rush to convert equity accumulated in the preinflation era into short-term debt defeated and subverted the administration's promise to reactivate productive investment. Stockmanism makes it profitable to buy, especially by borrowing, and prohibitive to build, especially by putting up cash. It engraved a cynical new epitaph on Horatio Alger's tombstone.

That same August, Metzenbaum fired off a letter to Federal Reserve Board Chairman Paul Volcker raising these interrelated regulatory questions. Volcker replied that the board had been advised by counsel, after scrutiny of the specific facts related to the du Pont loan, "that it was not violative because most of it had been arranged with the offshore branches of the participating banks. Counsel had assured the Board that it had no jurisdiction over these offshore branches for the purpose of enforcing its margin regulations over them."

This disclaimer of responsibility on Volcker's part confirmed the remark I had written to Metzenbaum: "If some supporter of yours had been caught breaking the lending rules this flagrantly and the Fed had come after him, you would be reduced to having one of your staff people tell his lawyer that you could not interfere with the judicial process."

By the time Gulf made its bid for Cities Service, a steady drumbeat of criticism was being heard against the Reagan administration's indulgence of fat cats. Its abrupt turn from tax cutting to tax hiking (and punitive tax hiking, at that) did not stop with the tax-reform bill of 1982. The FTC felt the political heat, too. On July 29, 1982, it announced its intention—by a unanimous vote—to bring suit to block the Gulf takeover. Cities Service was selling at $60 a share on the day the FTC bombshell hit the market. The price collapse that followed, dismaying though it was for Cities Service stockholders, was the least of the damage it inflicted upon an already sick market. The worst surfaced as still another case of the octopus suffering from lack of hand coordination. The hapless stockholders were trapped between conflicting rules imposed separately by the SEC, the Fed, and the FTC. The SEC required the suspension of trading; the Fed required the maintenance of 50 percent margin by civilians (as distinguished from the big shots); and the FTC was working to block the merger. The owners of 69 million shares of Cities Service stock tendered to Gulf at $63 a share, who had been confidently awaiting payment, woke up to find themselves unable to get paid. They also faced the threat of a disastrous price collapse weeks after Gulf had acquiesced in the FTC's veto and had withdrawn its offer. No less than one quarter of these Cities Service stockholders had been carrying their positions on margin in their capacity as professional market makers and dealers. A sorry case history illustrating the caliber of management inhabiting executive suites.

While the Federal Reserve Board still required investors content to buy old-fashioned shares to put up a 50 percent margin in cash, the Federal Trade Commission was using its authority over trading and stock futures, calling for only a 10 percent margin to be put up by the new crop of swingers, who preferred to play stocks by the pre-1929 minimal margin rules. In fact, one reporter for a major publication found that at a Chicago futures exchange he could do even better than the front-door 10 percent margin. He was asked the routine "due diligence" question about whether he owned any stocks. He admitted to having 100 shares of nonmarketable stock in the company employing him but did not disclose his employer's identity. To his astonishment, he was told that this qualified him as a professional investor, allowing him to put up only a 4 percent margin. So it was 1929 revisited in the stock futures market, while the experts pronounced the Big Board safe from collapse because the action on it was so slow.

The new dimension to low-margin speculation added by the stock futures fad, including the stock-index trading fad, laid to rest a hoary hardheaded Wall Street rule, that the only way to make any money out of talking about the market averages is to figure out which stocks to buy. The premise behind this traditional thinking was that the purpose of buying stocks was to hold them for investment. The revolutionary takeover of the market by the options traders changed all that. By definition, the purpose in buying a contract in an option with an expiration date a few months or even a few weeks out is to get out of it before the expiration date—another telltale indication, and a powerful one, of speculation crowding out investment in the public markets. An institution owning a block of stock and selling a call on it for a 10 percent windfall cash fee will not benefit from its long-term appreciation but will buy a hedge against the likelihood of the market discovering that it was overpriced. In that case the windfall cash fee becomes a trade-off for losing control of the stock if its price does surprise its owner by rising. The growth of the fad exemplified a logic that was incompatible with confidence in the growth of stocks.

The Symptoms

- Excessive volatility in all the futures and options markets, undermining public confidence in them.
- Painful illiquidity inside public markets amid stagnant pools of liquidity outside them (e.g., money markets, Eurodollar market).
- Huge investment markets subjected to manipulation by relatively small speculative market adjuncts.
- Flagrant abuses of the disclosure rules in takeover raids.
- The double standard in margin privileges.
- The double standard in the treatment typified by the granting of an incentive entitlement for 40 percent of profits on futures contracts that qualify for capital gains treatment, while none of the profits on options trading do.
- Recognition of the gravity of the problem in the form of a 1982 agreement between the CFTC and the SEC to negotiate a merger

but—typically, with no sense of emergency—two to three years down the line.

• Standing invitation to Russia to manipulate U.S. crop futures markets to the detriment of U.S. producers.

• A spokesman for the Federal Reserve Board saying in February 1983 that "the issue has become so charged with emotion that I want to stress that the Board has not taken any position on the margin question, nor has Chairman Volcker, who has said he is keeping an open mind on the subject."

The Treatment

Regulatory uniformity is overdue in administering the margin and short-selling rules. Stern notice by Congress to the Fed, the SEC, the FTC, the CFTC—with copies shown to the Justice Department—that they all work for the same government would do the trick. Extension of the disclosure obligations enforced by the SEC to the commodities futures markets would work wonders, especially against foreign operators within them. (Never mind that the resultant reporting might suggest that brokers based in tiny Switzerland are buying on the scale needed to feed a population as large as Russia's.)

In October 1981, I submitted testimony to the Senate Judiciary Committee on the takeover issue, identifying oil and gas takeovers as the chief attraction and, therefore, also the chief irritant. I recalled the great debate of 1935–1940 over the breakup of the old public utility holding companies and suggested the application of that procedure to oil and gas takeovers. So bitter was the fight that it flared up into a prime domestic issue in the 1940 presidential race, which FDR won by a smaller-than-usual margin thanks to the whirlwind campaign staged by Wendell Willkie, who was catapulted into prominence by the holding-company issue.

The "Death Sentence Clause" of 1938 called for all public utility holding companies to file plans for reorganization. My 1981 recommendation called for reassuring all planners of oil and gas takeovers that the green light is flashing for those who play by the rules of the road; and for warning them that all acquisitions qualifying for approval will be subject to such rules. Specifically, I called for all takeover bids to be supplemented with the filing of plans scheduling the work needed to bring the necessary assets out of the deep freeze and into production, including plans for financing them. I proposed assuring bidders that productive loans would be available on incentive terms for the development of takeover properties whose financing plans win approval.

The fight over the breakup of the public utility companies has long since been forgotten. Healthy, publicly financed local utilities listed on the Big Board have long since become part of the scenery. On the surface, this analogy may seem irrelevant to the bitter debate about takeover finance, especially for the gas and oil companies, which are the big prizes. But the same rule requiring plans to be filed by companies with claims to residual assets applies to the takeover issue. To the complaint that this procedure would reduce the oil companies to the status of public utilities, one answer would be, "High time," and another, "Only if they sit on the assets they grab instead of working them."

The Recovery

Full disclosure of the extent of short selling would exert an immediate bullish impact on all public markets, in commodities as well as in securities, as large-scale short selling always does. This is an urgent prerequisite for recovery, especially in the depressed agricultural and mining sectors of the economy that the 1983 recovery never reached. It would serve a double recovery purpose. Its immediate effect would be to increase incomes and jobs in the primary extractive sectors. Its domino effect would be to raise demand pressures in the secondary processing industries, which would find themselves scrambling first to meet new orders, then to get ahead of them by inventorying. The point at which a sales improvement stimulates business buying ahead of new orders for the express purpose of increasing inventories in the hands of manufacturers and merchants is the point at which recovery takes hold. Not one new cent of governmental spending, borrowing, or taxing would be needed to make this basic market-oriented contribution to a genuine recovery—nothing but regulatory uniformity.

The simple regulatory requirement for companies seeking antitrust clearance for takeover bids to file investment plans would have a truly expansive impact on the economy. Where inventorying is at once the condition and measure of recovery, investment in the activation of idle reserve assets marks the spot at which recovery sparks prosperity. It is possible for a recovery stimulated by business inventorying and supported by consumer spending to chug along for two or three years without blossoming into prosperity, but it is impossible for business inventorying and consumer spending to peter out while business investment is picking up.

Back in 1938, the purpose of the legislation that broke up the public utility holding companies and put the local utility operating companies in business for themselves was equity and efficiency. Its long-term economic effect was to thrust these newly divested independents into the number-one investment position among America's basic industries for the next fifty years. In fact, the preeminence of the utility companies in productive investment is underscored by the domestic nature of their investments, in contrast to the investment of export-dependent capital industries. The regulatory reform recommended here would have the similar effect of stimulating long-term capital investment in bringing the country's considerable energy reserves to market.

Collateral Advantages

• Averting a market crash triggered by a repeat performance of 1929's margin abuses—more serious in the 1980s than in the 1920s because this time the excesses have been institutionalized by regulation and therefore have created immeasurably larger-scale vulnerability than in 1929.

• Elimination of redundant jobs in the regulatory agencies, making a token contribution to trimming governmental overhead without political theatrics or fiscal exaggeration.

PRESCRIPTION #16
A Fair Trade for Excise-Tax Relief

The Complaint

Excise taxes pricing consumer farm products off the domestic market, and unmanageable surpluses of grain backed up from the export market.

The Cure

A trailblazing offer by the brewers and distillers to take their future-year grain needs off the government's hands in return for excise-tax relief.

The History

The first relevant chapter began with the crusade for Prohibition. Do-good advocates of "The Noble Experiment" claimed that it would free the workingman from the temptation to dissipate his wages in drink. Its disastrous economic consequences for the brewing and distillery industries and the industries serving them went unnoticed during the prosperous 1920s, all of which contributed to the farm depression that struck halfway through the decade.

The second chapter punctuated the depression-era presidential campaign of 1932. Herbert Hoover, the worst politician who ever wandered out of an executive suite, was afraid to offend the "church" vote, and he waffled on the issue of Repeal. Franklin Roosevelt dramatized Hoover's decision by coming out foursquare against Prohibition. He even went a step further and seized on the unemployment in the beer business, promising to put the breweries in the vanguard of reemployment—and without resuscitating any government spending. A sidelight of this historic campaign was Roosevelt's charge that Hoover had spent the country into the depression and his own promise to lead the country back to prosperity by balancing the budget.

The third chapter of economic and fiscal history was acted out during World War II, when America simultaneously ran out of grain for beer and spirits, as well as for gasoline. Retail demand was diverted to rum, thanks to the Cuban and Puerto Rican sugar surpluses. The U.S. Treasury was collecting so much income tax that excise taxes were not the issue, especially with so many consumer industries subjected to draconic rationing. Senator Guy Gillette of Iowa, then chairman of the Senate Agriculture Committee, put forward the first serious political proposal to ration grain for gasoline, which was resisted even though the war had shut the grain-export markets.

The Symptoms

- The unmanageable proportions of the grain surplus.
- The desperate retreat of the Reagan administration from its original determination to "stay the course," as it waited for "market adjustments"—in plain English, lower prices and more bankruptcies—to mop up the surplus.
- The depression-deepening remedy offered by Secretary of Agriculture John Block to distribute government-held surpluses to farmers in exchange for their agreement to take acreage out of production, New Deal style: a Rube Goldberg caper.
- The broadening and acceleration of the fiscal war among the federal government, the states, and local governments, not just to switch the revenue burden and fight for the income-tax dollar but to fight for the excise-tax dollar as well.
- Consumer resistance to the rising prices of "luxuries" at the point of purchase due to excise-tax increases, despite cuts in the retail prices of those products packaged with the excise tax.
- The galloping depression and the resultant casualty rate in the brewing and distillery business, all the way from suppliers to plants to retail outlets.

The Treatment

I outlined a proposal in a speech before the National Beer Wholesalers Association in October 1982. I called for a new fair trade by the brewers and distillers with Washington in the form of a cash offer to buy future grain needs in exchange for negotiated relief in excise taxes. The depression in grain prices would make such an offer commercially attractive to the brewers and distillers. The falling ratio of product prices to excise tax levies would make the prospect of an excise-tax rollback financially attractive to the consuming public. The release from the burden of farm relief while paying for the surplus would be fiscally attractive to the government. The opportunity to direct more tax dollars to advertising would be economically attractive to the media.

The Recovery

At best, its contribution would be very limited, as Repeal was for the bank crisis of 1932–1933. But it would demonstrate how private industry, on its initiative, could deal with the government; it would add momentum to the precrisis initiative by the farm groups and the alcohol processors in winning excise-tax relief for gasohol and protecting it, despite the return of gasohol price wars. It would offer a lead to other processing industries drafted as unpaid tax collectors for the Treasury. It would give the consumer a break and give the small businesses manning the arteries of distribution a reprieve from the death sentence they are under.

Collateral Advantages

- A start toward a marginal increase in domestic processing of raw materials traditionally routed into export channels.
- A constructive recovery twist to the ongoing guerilla war between the commodity lobbies.

CHAPTER THIRTEEN

Real Estate

PRESCRIPTION #17
The Tax Advantage in Interest-Only Mortgages

The Complaint

High interest rates shutting down the market in homes but inviting rents to run away and property-tax collections to fall behind.

The Cure

Adoption of the "interest-only" second mortgage.

The History

Since the bank panic of 1933, more Americans have accumulated more capital from the appreciation of property values than from any other method. Median-income families that started out with nothing except jobs were able to finance residential property purchases with long-term, low-interest mortgages. Even at the worst of the 1982 depression, homes built in the 1930s for $15,000 to $20,000 and paid for with petty-cash down payments were still selling for $50,000 to $100,000. Though these investments worked out considerably better than most alternatives, they were not made as investment decisions. Necessity dictated the purchase of a roof over one's head; bargains invited these decisions. Paradoxically, while the economy was still expanding during the 1970s, the homeowners who put up the down payments and assumed the mortgage obligations that seemed burdensome at the time struck it rich simply by being in—that is, living in—the right place at the right time. But the combined impact of the oil-cost inflation and the interest-rate inflation that accelerated across the decade culminated in trouble for the home market. Ironically, the twin inflation made more trouble for developers at one end of the home-market pipeline and for the affluent home buyers at the other end than for the home market itself. The high casualty rate among developers closed the pipeline to new building starts. Consequently, buyers with high standards found themselves confronted with high prices and onerous carrying costs just when the depression began to threaten the entire work force with lower incomes or none at all. Yet as long as necessity dictated the terms of home buying, the owners of residential property could name their own selling prices, provided they could in turn find acceptable properties to buy. But the accelerating upward spiral in property values sent the discomfort index flying with it.

Splurging on homes to get rich quick, to show off to friends and family, or to participate in the growing market for vacation and weekend homes quickly turned the spotlight on a new phenomenon in American economic society: the high-living paupers. Their two conspicuous characteristics are big incomes and no capital. When the postwar economic boom was at its peak, the twin goals of keeping the cost of one's shelter within 25 percent of after-tax income and squirreling away six months' income in a savings account were still realistic. The home-market crisis that greeted the 1980s, and that the subsequent depression intensified, surfaced when people began to complain that homes bought in the confident expectation of accumulating capital were dissipating capital in carrying costs.

At the outset of the banking crisis in 1981, when President Reagan invited eight conservative Democratic senators, for whose support he had been lobbying, to discuss with Secretary of the Treasury Donald Regan and himself the problems suffered and created by the savings and loan associations (S&Ls), Senator Ernest Hollings of South Carolina asked what the Treasury proposed to do in the event of a run on the institutions. "Pay the depositors off," Secretary Regan replied unhesitatingly. As the eight senators left the Oval Office, they speculated with one another over whether Secretary Regan knew exactly how much new debt he had just committed the Treasury to take on without acquiring a cent of additional revenue, and, in that case, how he proposed to raise the debt ceiling by the better part of a second trillion above its first quantum leap over the trillion-dollar mark.

The Symptoms:

- Understandable shrieks of pain over the shutting of the real estate market.
- Angry echoes from builders and developers.
- The rapid rise of outstanding second mortgages as a method of liquifying increased equities in homes without disturbing cheap and slow first mortgages already in place; motivated by either the need to raise cash or the incentive to reinvest it, despite the costly practice of requiring amortization.

- Cities labeled disaster areas because of the collapse of property-tax collections, and the rise of foreclosures and abandonments over back taxes.
- The spread of unemployment and the drop in incomes compromising the credit entitlement of home buyers to mortgage accommodation.
- The surge in interest rates immobilizing S&Ls.
- Paradox of a famine of rental units and a runaway in rents amid a market glut of residential units.
- The ominous recurrence of onerous demands for "points" and closing fees by mortgage lenders during the tricky respite from inflationary interest rates in late 1982–early 1983.

The Treatment

In the drawing-room mysteries of G. K. Chesterton, the murder weapon invariably turns out to be an ordinary object under everyone's nose. The solution to the interrelated problems of uneconomic mortgage costs, unsalable property, lender illiquidity, tax nuisances, and home-building depression is just as easy to locate.

Start by limiting payments on new mortgage debt to interest. This would give the mortgage-lending institutions the earnings they need. Their interest income is income; their complaint is that they don't have enough of it. The second step would be to exempt new borrowings from amortization payments, which represent an accounting waste to the mortgage lenders.

The interest-only second mortgage invites taxpaying mortgage borrowers to use the long tax form, allowing them to take advantage of all the tax deductions to which they are entitled. To a borrower in the 50 percent bracket, an 18 percent rate of interest will work out as costing only 9 percent. (No less than 40 percent of all taxpayers were still waiving this right in 1982, while complaining of being overtaxed.)

The problem for the residential market has been complicated by the simultaneous squeeze on incomes, the "bracket creep" on taxpayers, and the shortening of maturities on mortgages written since the onset of the mortgage interest-rate spiral into double digits. The source of the complication is structured into the U.S. tax code, which treats interest payments as deductible and amortization payments as not. Consequently, while the cost of a dollar of interest expense to a taxpayer in the 50 percent bracket is only 50¢ of after-tax income, the cost of paying back a dollar of amortization on a mortgage is $2 of pre-tax income— thanks to the requirement that tax indebtedness on the income be incurred before a claim can be made. This means that the cost of paying a dollar of principal is four times greater than paying a dollar of interest.

In the states and cities that levy income as well as property taxes, this two-tiered taxation puts an even heavier burden on the taxpaying mortgage borrower. In New York City, for example, taxpayers are subject to a 50 percent top federal tax bracket, plus a 14 percent top state income tax and a 4 percent city income tax. The latter, being deductible, put the federal taxpayer in the 50 percent bracket in a net 59 percent bracket. In New Jersey, the state income tax has been raised from 2.5 percent on incomes over $40,000 to a graduated levy of 3.5 to 6.5 percent.

The mortgage-lending institutions, with a keen instinct for shooting themselves in the foot and their customers in the head, have responded to the rise in interest rates and the drop in their earnings by pressing for faster and bigger amortization payments. Their problems, however, are centered in their earnings. Faster pay-downs do not improve their earnings; they merely provide more cash for them to lose speculating on securities and financial futures. Besides, if forebodings of a new era of hyperinflation are justified, why would they want their money back? Earmarking all of their cash receipts from mortgages for interest payments would multiply their earnings. It would also help their hard-pressed mortgage borrowers stay current with them.

The lending institutions have been complaining about the unendurable cost of collecting interest on older mortgages all the way down to 5 percent. At the same time, the borrowers blessed with these low rates have been penalized by the high percentage of amortization payments relative to interest expense. Ironically, the older these low-yielding first mortgages get, the sooner they are scheduled to be paid off and, therefore, the safer they are for the mortgage-lending institutions. This means that no risk is involved in putting second mortgages on top of them. It also means that the cost of averaging up a higher interest charge on a new second mortgage will not be onerous. The first-mortgage rate is low enough to carry a second mortgage loaded on top of it and low enough to ease the burden of a more costly second mortgage. If, for example, a homeowner has a $30,000 first mortgage bearing a 6 percent rate and puts on a $50,000 second at 18 percent, the total debt owed will be $80,000 and the annual interest charge will be $10,000. Assuming an interest-only basis for both mortgages, the overall rate will be 14 percent. The first carries the second.

The proposition is as long as it is broad. To the mortgage-lending institutions, the profitability of averaging up an 18 percent return on top of a 6 percent return on the old first mortgage will be a windfall, all the more so because the balance on the old 6 percent will be comparatively insignificant, while the commitment to the new 18 percent will be big enough to provide meaningful income. Consequently, the more money the country's S&Ls lend on high-yielding second mortgages, the faster they will dig out of their earnings problems. The S&Ls

already have the right to make second-mortgage loans, but instead they are pressing their customers to pay off first mortgages in full. Supreme Court Justice Sandra O'Connor's "strict constructionist" decision giving lenders the right to insist on the "due on sale" clause when homes are sold, instead of allowing home buyers to assume old mortgages from the sellers, has encouraged the lending institutions in making this uneconomic, self-defeating demand.

Granted that the prescription for a return to prosperity in the mortgage markets is clear enough for bankers, regulators, and even judges to see, the missing link is the source of new funds to illiquid institutions for second-mortgage lending in anticipation of the higher interest rates bound to come with higher levels of federal borrowing. The Federal Reserve Board would produce less inflation, more liquidity, and more solvency if it were to provide discount facilities for three- to five-year second mortgages, subject to "interest-only" charges, instead of sticking with the expedients that precipitated the crisis in the first place. This three- to five-year breathing spell would give the economy a period for recuperation, provided its direction is set straight again.

Marketability is an essential ingredient of market value. The right to assume an attractive mortgage clearly has made the difference between the ability to sell homes and/or rental properties. Therefore, the value of the mortgages held as collateral by the lending institutions is as good as the marketability of the homes behind the mortgages. Perversely, when the S&Ls won their fight against the "right of assumption," they undermined the right of collateralization. The Mortgage Appraisers Professional Institute (MAPI) has validated a third method of property appraisal—cash flow—supplementing its two traditional alternatives of original cost and reproduction cost. In a high-interest era, any cash savings to the mortgage borrower will increase the appraised value of property. If this level of appraised values was handy enough to keep the sheriff away from the banks' doors in 1982, it is sturdy enough to give their borrowers a helping hand.

The Federal Reserve Board habitually uses the discount rate as a 3 percent to 4 percent under-market subsidy for the commercial banks. The commercial banks need this subsidy less than the S&Ls, though they too are stuck with the same negative mortgage-yield problems as the S&Ls and the savings banks (which are also under the direct jurisdiction of the Fed). It is unfair and impractical for the Federal Reserve to subsidize an under-market rate of interest for the commercial banks and to deny it to the S&Ls. Not even free-market extremists have demanded that the Fed cease and desist from maintaining its discount-rate spread under the prime rate. With the country's S&Ls owing the public over $750 billion in federally insured deposits, extending the discount rate to the S&Ls on new interest-only second mortgages at market rates would spare the government more fire-fighting exercises and would save it considerable expense in the cost of pyramiding new debt on top of old debt to bail out banks and S&Ls.

A final consideration: Come the happy day when the government of the United States again frees itself to offer a helping hand to the younger people on whom it will depend in the decades ahead to earn enough to pay their taxes to it and to lend their savings to it, the president will agree with the Congress on the appropriateness and the prudence of adding a new arm to the Federal Housing and Veterans administrations. Each agency would be empowered to extend its mortgage-insuring activities to incentive financing for tenants, enabling them to buy the apartments they rent with modest down payments. When recovery does come, it will unleash irresistible inflationary forces against immovable inflationary bottlenecks. At that point, hindsight will verify the bargain offered by tenant ownership of rental units. The alternatives will be the implicit inflation invited by rent controls and the explicit inflation fueled by the pay increases it makes worthless.

The Recovery

The home represents the most important investment any family makes, and it accounts for the biggest drain on the family's disposable income. Once the treatment succeeds in realigning the country's mortgage-debt structure to work with, instead of against, its tax structure, recovery will be assured. Mortgage-lending institutions will increase their earnings from their interest receipts as homeowners pay out more interest but keep more spendable, savable, and investable cash. Once mortgage applications by individuals are appraised by the same method as applications by commercial real estate operators—the "cash-flow" method—individuals obliged to pay only interest on their mortgages will qualify for bigger mortgages without exposure to overborrowing.

Collateral Advantages

- Use of the tax code to spur recovery instead of blocking it.
- Scotching of tax-reform proposals aimed at eliminating deductibility of home-mortgage interest charges.
- Improvement in the credit ratings of local governments whose sources of revenue have been pinched by the squeeze on the mortgage market and the stoppage of new construction.

PRESCRIPTION #18
A Tax Lure for Foreign
Real Estate Investors

The Complaint

The commercial real estate market remained as glutted as the oil market at the height of the 1983 recovery in business expectations.

The Cure

Offer foreigners a special tax advantage calculated to invite them to buy up the U.S. commercial real estate glut on an all-cash basis, that is, without putting any borrowing load on U.S. mortgage lenders.

The History

Wilbur Mills, during his last year as chairman of the powerful House Ways and Means Committee, was on the verge of writing a new chapter in the history of the pivotal commercial real estate market. Recycling Arab petrobillions was not then a public issue. Mills and I discussed the advantages of repealing the estate tax on foreign owners of American real property, that is, treating real property held by foreigners as free from federal estate taxes, though assessable for annual property-tax assessments levied by state and local governments. The Internal Revenue Service exempts foreigners from taxes on capital gains taken on investments in the United States. Mills argued that the advantages to America would be even greater if the same exemption on estate taxes were offered to foreigners owning real estate.

My discussions with Mills during the early 1970s anticipated a worldwide buildup of panic pressures bringing unprecedented amounts of foreign money into the United States for sanctuary. We saw that the money from around the world driven into U.S. commercial real estate was neither income while sitting nor gain on selling. Safety of capital was the motive that took over late in the 1970s; it has become more dominant every year since. Moreover, foreign money has been conditioned down through the ages to prefer the ownership of real property to securities or paper in any form.

Mills identified the Persian Gulf powers as the most eager new entries into the U.S. real estate market, catching up with the Germans,

252 • PRESCRIPTIONS FOR PROSPERITY

the Japanese, and the Hispanics. He also targeted a sociological inhibition most conspicuous among the Arabs (but influential with the Germans and others as well) against buying property subject to property or estate taxes on any change of title. Its source is the Arab custom of accumulating large holdings of property in the names of large numbers of related individuals on the scale of a clan. The risk of title change due to death or disaffection of younger generations rises with the number of participants, especially where the elders of the owning group insist upon imposing rigid moral standards on their presumptive heirs and where all members of the owning group are exposed to rising risks of political violence and ethnic intermingling (a trend that predictably follows educational intermingling).

The Symptoms

• Uneconomic vacancy rates in existing commercial income property, most notably office buildings but also shopping centers.

• The stoppage of new commercial construction.

• The failure of estate taxes to produce revenues on any significant scale. (Lawyers get more money showing their clients how to avoid this tax than the IRS does collecting it.)

• The reluctance of foreign investment syndicates to risk exposure to the U.S. estate tax by taking title to U.S. commercial property in multiple names, an exposure that increases upon the death of any syndicate participant.

• The clear preference of moneyed foreigners for top-quality commercial, rather than residential, properties to invest in, where money is no object and thus mortgaging unnecessary.

The Treatment

The removal of the federal estate tax on foreigners would invite a considerable new flow of foreign money to break the logjam in the property market. The Arabs in particular, but other wealthy foreigners as well, would take such a move as a sign that the welcome mat was out for them in the U.S. property markets.

The Recovery

Foreigners, who are always willing to pay up for property in any country outside their own, feel strongly that American property, with the land under it included in the purchase price, is a "giveaway" compared to property anywhere else in the world. Abroad, ownership of the land is usually retained by the landlord, who charges "ground rent" for the privilege of owning or renting and rebuilding the structure built upon the land.

State and local governments across the nation would benefit from the arrival of a flush new crop of buyers for prime real estate. American cities that are financially strapped—and the number is rising by the year —have a desperate bread-and-butter need to see property values marked up in order to avoid depression-time markdowns and the loss of revenue that accompanies them. Property taxes, like wages and fuel, are an operating cost in every community. U.S. cities would have a hunting license to raise property taxes on foreign owners of commercial and residential property (compensating for their inability to tax official, foreign-owned buildings). Banks would get windfall deposits from foreigners free from any offsetting pressure to make real estate loans: a sure formula for reliquifying insolvent banks.

Collateral Advantages

- What is good for any one sector of the American real estate market is good for the other sectors.
- Expediting title transfers is one sure way to open up construction, maintenance, and repair jobs; new owners always go in for face lifting.
- Capital improvements by new owners support higher tax assessments, besides making jobs and creating hard-cash, nonspeculative private-sector demand for construction equipment, appliances, and building materials.
- Capital inflows on the massive scale needed to buy prime commercial property would contribute offsets to America's troublesome deficits in foreign dealings.

PART III

POLITICAL STRATEGIES, THE ECONOMY, AND THE MARKETS

CHAPTER FOURTEEN

The Market Barometer of Political Confidence

WHEN FORMER Treasury Secretary William Simon explained that "markets are people," he was telling us a great deal about both markets and people. Markets, contrary to popular belief, are not leading indicators of what people think about money; they are lagging indicators reflecting what people have been doing with money and what governments have been doing with people. Consequently, behavior within the specialized world of the stock market is a response to events and attitudes in the larger world outside the market. The government is the commanding event maker and opinion former in that larger world in which people make their livings. Lest we forget, the government gets its money when and as people make theirs, and it gets its power from the automatic taxing process by which it dips into the income stream and from the continuous borrowing process by which it dips into the capital reservoir. The indirect influence the government exerts on Wall Street by way of Main Street is immeasurably greater than its direct influence. The government makes and changes markets every time it influences what people think and what they do with the money they have and the money they borrow—especially the latter.

The prime market maker is the president of the United States (functionally speaking, in the media age, it is the White House staff acting in behalf of the president), though he invariably thinks of himself as just another market watcher. The milestone episode illustrating this axiom erupted in the markets on August 6, 1982, when the Federal Reserve Board, acting at the behest of the White House, used the discount rate as the match that exploded the prices of bonds and stocks. The country wanted the government to "do something" to bring interest rates down. The Federal Reserve Board got the message when the White House picked it up in the polls and transmitted it. No such dynamite effect on bonds and stocks could have been initiated within the markets themselves. This presidential initiative in the markets harked back to

Wall Street's speculative boom between 1927 and 1929, when the Fed-stoked stock market doubled. But as monetary and market history can be seen repeating itself, the pattern of related political history can too. Halfway between the bottom and the top of the boom of the late 1920s, President Coolidge, preparatory to uttering the only historic declaration he ever made—"I do not choose to run"—had dispatched the Marines to Nicaragua. This history, however, did not quite repeat itself in the 1980s: America's confrontation with "Marxist power" in Central America coincided with the market making its top.

An old joke going back to pre-TV and pre-computer days explains how word of this presidential role seeped through to the markets. It concerns a literal-minded young census taker collecting the vital statistics of a hillbilly family. Disposing quickly of Paw and Maw, the interviewer moves methodically from number one in the litter, aged thirteen, to number two, aged twelve, and on down the line to number five, aged nine, only to discover that the line ends there. At that point Paw Hillbilly breaks in to exclaim, "We found out what made it happen." It took the government and the markets a long time to find out that they were in bed together and to figure out how the government, sometimes acting as predator and sometimes as protector, made the markets behave as they did. Even advocates of laissez-faire have come to explain market performance in terms of governmental decisions. This perception dominated Washington's dealings with the entire country early in 1982 when, with the government spreading the impression—which it shared—that it had turned the economy over to the tender mercies of the marketplace, the economy collapsed, and the markets followed. Both the executive branch and the Congress, despite the conflict raging between them, fell over each other in their anxiety to send "reassuring signals" to the markets as the economy plunged in the first half of 1982. They justified their compromises, all of which were fated to send contradictory signals to the markets, on the grounds that, as the federal budget went, so the markets would go. The hope expressed in the critical corollary behind this proposition was implicit: As the markets went, so the country would go. The government saw its job as spurring the feverish and treacherous market revival during the winter of 1982–1983. But the country refused to follow its lead. The economy continued to weaken; by the time it strengthened, interest rates did too.

The markets were even more surprised than the Reaganites by the failure of the unprecedently electrifying move they had made from August to December 1982, to get the economy moving again. By the 1980s, of course, Wall Street had been reconditioned to recognize that it had outgrown the comfortable cocoon of its traditional bilateral relationship with the economy. Once the government led the economy out of the Great Depression and into the three foreign wars that extended the short recovery of the 1930s into the long boom of the midcentury and the aimless and turbulent stagflation that followed, it turned a predictable bilateral relationship into more than a proverbially tricky triangle, with the government operating as the principal source of friction and motion. The failure of the explosive late 1982–early 1983 rally in Wall Street to move the economy effectively provided an unforgettable demonstration of how the relationship works. The governmental operations that gunned interest rates sky-high had the predictable effect of shooting the economy down. But no governmental signals that gulled the markets into dropping rates could repair the damage to the economy or, for that matter, in the absence of effective government actions, keep interest rates down long enough to prevent the structural damage to the economy from deepening.

The historical transition between the period when the markets had eyes only for the economy to when they became reliant on Washington took a generation to develop. True, the government had been a factor in the markets before then, but the economy had not responded to its experiments in stimulation until World War II eliminated its need to try. Dwight Eisenhower's magnetic appeal as a war hero gave him his chance at the presidency. But a solid achievement had consolidated his mandate: his switch of emphasis in defense programming from shot-and-shell and manpower to intercontinental missilery and the space race. The first year of his term provided the first trial run for the new three-way relationship among the government, the economy, and the markets as the cushioning force in the system, its source of equilibrium. It was launched under the most favorable of circumstances, with the government free from pressure to launch emergency programs and with the markets full of confidence in the future. So confident was the new administration in its welcome from the markets that it offered a long-term bond at 3.25 percent as a token of its determination to stop the inflationary signal flare sent up by the noble experiment's thundering failure.

Early in 1953, I made a presentation to a trend-setting group of institutional portfolio managers in Boston. The consensus in the audience assumed a deep postwar recession. My thesis that day targeted the Air Force, the old Atomic Energy Commission, and the then still new National Aeronautics and Space Administration (NASA) as the chosen instruments for what was then scheduled to be a breathtaking, decade-spanning breakout in government spending, from $5 billion to $20 billion. The next morning, back in New York, I received a querulous phone call from the outspoken leader of the group asking me from what set of tea leaves I had conjured up those explosive inflationary numbers. When I told him that the Eisenhower administration had already programmed those numbers and had decided to unveil them on the installment plan, assuming no more Koreas, he replied that he had the budget in his hand and that it called for the customary postwar decrease over

Harry Truman's last-year war budget. I invited him and his colleagues to join me on a Cook's tour of the policy-making circuit in Washington so that they could find out for themselves that a multibillion-dollar, multiyear gap was opening between the amount of defense spending the government was budgeting for fiscal 1954 and the even more enormous obligations it was incurring. In bond market calculations the term of maturity counts for more than current yield. The same distinction would eventually come to be recognized, I argued, between defense expenditures in the budget and defense obligations in the pipeline. The market was not yet alert to the parallel.

In that bygone era of market and political history, the portfolio managers who prided themselves on being the market makers still had a plausible professional excuse for being confused about the difference between the plain meaning of business statistics and the complicated meaning of governmental statistics. The dollar figures on retail sales, for example, mean exactly what they report about consumer spending. But governmental statistics invariably conceal a political motivation. Since then, Wall Street analysts have learned that when the government announces its annual spending figures, it is not telling the markets all they need to know about how present commitments will become minimum down payments on future spending obligations.

Between 1953 and 1981, portfolio managers who still trusted budgetary appearances asked for the same treatment that David Stockman gave the markets during the Reagan years. They were lured into treating intricate fiscal calculations as though they were simple industry reports, with no allowance for the political motivation behind the performance statistics. Coming into the 1980s, however, the portfolio-managing fraternity was belatedly jolted into asking realistic questions about governmental statistics. Even at the height of the speculative fashion for fathoming the money-supply figures, when Wall Street still programmed its buying and selling each week with the ups and downs in M-1 (the count of cash in circulation plus checking accounts, seasonally adjusted), the real questions it learned to ask were not statistical. They were: "What is Volcker up to?" "What discipline is he putting on the Treasury?" "What pressure is the White House transmitting from the country via Congress to him?"

The oldest rule in the market book tells us that the biggest money in the markets is made and lost on shocks. During the twenty years between 1963 and 1983, the big shocks to the markets were all political and hit Wall Street on a direct bounce from Washington. Before then, the shocks that moved the markets resulted from the introduction of revolutionary new products (the telephone, the automobile, the power generator) and the promotion of new financing techniques (the holding company, the reorganization of bankruptcies, takeovers). Since 1963, however, the whirlwind pace of technological progress absorbed more investment and speculative capital than ever. Yet no market takeoffs were triggered or sustained by any major new industries. True, high-technology industries have outperformed the markets as a whole; IBM has led their starts, their stops, and their turns. But the most influential of these political shocks, apart from wars and elections, have been monetary shocks—alternating sieges of and reprieves from credit tightening—which the markets have learned to recognize as political.

Confirming the transfer of the leadership role in Wall Street from industry and finance to politics, the ambitious and dazzling financial innovations of this same period struck the markets as what *Variety*, the newspaper of show business, calls yawn makers. In fact, the last purely financial move the market generated internally was a hot new-issue market in that same formative year, 1963. As Wall Street wits joked at the time, "Why go broke when you can go public?" Any new issue whose name ended in "ionics" (they named their favorite "falsie" during that craze "Ultrahistrionics") could be taken public, priced at $5, at infinity times earnings, and run up to $55. (The price multiplier on negative earnings is infinity, as any secondary school student of algebra knows.) The return to a hot new-issue market in 1982–1983 proved as much of a caution for the stock market as it had in 1963. It was the same drama, with different players; the danger signals were even more arresting because hot new stocks with no earnings and whose names most often ended with "ics" or "techs" were being gunned, while established companies were going under. The market mania of 1982, triggered by Paul Volcker's abrupt role-change from market ogre to market angel, put a new twist on the classic bottom-line definition of bankruptcy: "You won't go broke as long as you can borrow any interest not covered by income." This time around, the incentive became: "Go broke in order to boom your stock." Johns Manville, the staidest of old-line blue chips, quadrupled its stock from a 1982 low of $4 a share to a 1983 high of $16⅝, just after it entered Chapter 11 of the bankruptcy laws to shield itself from damage suits.

While in my own experience the first Eisenhower year, 1953, marks the real emergence of Washington's peacetime trend-making role in Wall Street, the market consensus no doubt saw this happening in John Kennedy's last year, 1963. It was not only the year the new-issue market failed, it was the year Kennedy forced U.S. Steel to roll back a price increase without asking Congress or the courts for their consent; and it was the year when this same President was assassinated. The shot that shocked the world, paralyzed the markets; the New York Stock Exchange was shut down at 2:23 P.M. on November 22. Over the next ten days, the injection of new life into the markets, which seemed dead, stands as a classic case illustrating the power that the presidency and the political shock waves it activates have developed over the markets.

In the market drama that followed, President Lyndon Johnson

designated Robert ("Bobby") Lehman, the head of Lehman Brothers, to be his personal emissary, via transatlantic telephone, to the European investment institutions. Lehman's mission was to ease foreign financial fears and to spark appetites for Johnson's plans, while the new President contrived to stretch out the mourning period from the Friday of the assassination until the second Monday after it. The guidance Johnson had sought from his advisers, principally Donald C. Cook, counsel of his Korean War Investigating Committee, steered him into a fail-safe, three-ply course of action. The first expedient called for keeping not only the markets but the post offices, the banks, and the brokerage firms closed, preventing the margin calls that had gone out the first business day after the assassination from serving official notice on anyone to put up more money on pain of being sold out of positions. The second step was to invite the short interest from all over the country to build up for posting with the brokers and dealers on the first morning of resumed trading. There is nothing more bullish for a market than a quick buildup of selling pressure, identifiable to the experienced market eye by a surge in the short interest. The third segment of the strategy exploited the standing of the Lehman name in Europe and Lehman's connection with Johnson to run up the prices of the big American stocks quoted in Europe before the New York markets were freed to open.

The effect was electric, demonstrating the dynamic impact of a double play engineered in Wall Street from the White House. But the bullish repercussions of this gambit of Johnson's were not limited to the ceremonial period of national mourning, which he had skillfully used as cover for the technical manipulation of the stock market. The momentum his ploy generated carried over from December 1963 to January 1965. If a tycoon had engineered such a manipulation, the SEC would have had him in stripes in short order. The only complaint heard was Bobby Lehman's surprise that LBJ had never thanked him.

By coincidence, I addressed the Detroit Economic Club the Monday after the assassination. The atmosphere was shrouded in gloom. The markets were thought lucky to be shut. The Detroit *Free Press*, expressing relief rather than belief, devoted a front-page headline to my assertion that the stock market was on its way to new highs, not because Wall Street knew where it was going but because Johnson would show it the way. I promised a market rendezvous with 1,000 on the Dow Jones industrial average within a year of the assassination. I erred on the side of optimism; it took thirteen months.

Market buffs, with their antennae tuned to nothing but dollar signs, had soon satisfied themselves that the irresistible surge from the panic over Kennedy's assassination to the climactic vault over the symbolic hurdle of 1,000 meant that all of the market's money gears were meshing. They were right. In fact, statistics showed that the market was accomplishing the impossible, squaring the circle. Interest rates were low and firm and the bond market was strong, yet corporate demand for funds to finance record capital investment was at a new high, as it is never supposed to be when interest rates are low and stable. At the same time, the work force was enjoying overtime, and no one was complaining about inflationary squeezes, even though Johnson was simultaneously passing the Kennedy tax cuts and pouring record appropriations into his Great Society welfare programs. Only one standard statistic seemed out of sync: The government's payments deficit was up to $6 billion, then still considered a big deficit number. But no one took alarm because none of the deficit was due to a profligate disregard for the dollar. The deficit accrued as the cost of sustaining the economies of Britain, Italy, and Brazil escalated—at the time all prudent uses for aid outflows. Besides, a healthy trade surplus still offset the payments deficit.

The policy engineering responsible for this unfamiliar "product mix" of traditionally irreconcilable statistics, beginning with a capital investment boom in the presence of low interest rates and the absence of inflationary pressures, demonstrated that the market would follow where the presidency led it. The equally remarkable combination of a first-year tax cut at the top of the income pyramid, dramatized by the elimination of the punitive 91 percent surtax on earned income, and a matching welfare increase for communities too disadvantaged even to qualify for inclusion in the income pyramid, confirmed the achievement that antedated the Vietnam ordeal. No one dreamed of the trauma that lay ahead. The market did not suspect that it was charging into a trap set in Vietnam, beyond the reach of the system of world finance. All that it knew or needed to know on its first trip to 1,000 was that a benevolent conductor in Washington was orchestrating its movements with a magic touch.

Between Johnson's honeymoon into 1965 and Reagan's honeymoon during 1981, the stock market made innumerable tries to vault the "Johnson barrier" of 1,000 on the Dow. The repeated market cycles of politically induced euphoria and despair coincided with four wrong turns made by four successive administrations. Each of them was allowed a second chance; each missed it. Each trial of the presidency took the stock market by surprise at a time when confidence was running high, yet none was able to maintain momentum in the face of political disillusionment. The moral of these blunders is that the market always reacts to the political barometer that registers the performance of the presidency. Exaggerated hopes for the success of the presidency start out by impressing the market as thoroughly as real achievement.

Johnson's challenge had been to perform on Kennedy's promises. Then he made his wrong turn into Vietnam. The war marked the turning point for both the presidency and the market. Bull markets roar on when they see evidence of international cooperation, but they sputter when they realize that isolation for the U.S. presidency means separation for the country and its markets from their natural allies abroad. At least Europe and Japan had made a good thing out of the Korean War; no one benefited from Vietnam. Therefore, it marked the end of the post-World War II stock-market boom. The relieved response of the market to Johnson's acceptance of defeat in Vietnam came as the unkindest cut of all. From the time his first unsuccessful run for the Senate had wired him into the big money, he had been a market hound. Billy Lee Brammer's minor masterpiece, *The Gay Place*, which transposes Johnson from the all-powerful *fenstermacher* (pidgin Anglo-German for fence mender), depicts him as pausing from his classic political labors in midmorning to call me to check the market. Nothing gave Johnson a stronger shot of adrenaline than a market rally that could be connected to some exploit of his; nothing, that is, except for a cheering crowd. He once came off a speaker's platform glowing, his applause meter in his hand, and told me, "It went off twenty-three times. Beats screwing."

Richard Nixon's challenge had been simply to get out of Vietnam, but he made his decisive wrong turn when he failed to stay out of trouble at home. The Watergate ordeal presented the stock market with its next test, but the market was foredoomed by the discrediting of the presidency. In his farewell appearance in his own soap opera, Nixon revealed what had gone wrong. Tears running down his cheeks, he told the media, "I lost my congressional base." No apologies. No second thoughts. No misgivings. No mention that the same fate was suffered by Johnson at Gene McCarthy's hands just six years before as punishment for the same breach of trust: lying about presidential operations. Just a simple recitation of the shift in the balance of power, again isolating the American presidency. As it happened, I was in a unique position at the time of Nixon's downfall to testify to the realism of his exit line. In response to an invitation from Senator Harry Byrd, Jr. of Virginia, Albert Sindlinger, the well-known sampler of consumer trends in the economy, and I met with a bipartisan group of conservative senators in July 1974 to forecast the likely size of the deficit for the new fiscal year. Byrd did not tell me, nor did I ask him, whether the concern of those conservative senators over the fiscal drift under Nixon was a cover for their growing political alarm and, therefore, whether they felt any inclination to put distance between themselves and the presumed conservative in the White House.

Sindlinger and I, although working separately, agreed that a fiscal 1975 deficit of $75 billion and a fiscal 1976 deficit of $100 billion seemed all too likely, based on the very different data we were accustomed to use. Both calculations seemed astronomic in the second month of fiscal 1975 (as August then was). We had an intensive discussion with the senators and staff aides whom Byrd had assembled at the Capitol City

Club. The atmosphere was grim. None present defended the fiscal record of the Nixon administration. Not a word was uttered about Watergate. That evening, Sindlinger and I compared impressions on the telephone. "Nixon's too hot for them," I said. "They'll have him out of there in a month." Sindlinger agreed, but we both miscalculated. It took only two weeks for a delegation of conservative Republican senators to hand him the abdication pen on August 9, 1974. When the curtain came down on his act, the stock market followed. Between the euphoria preceding Nixon's landslide victory over George McGovern and the mood of despair brought on by Watergate, the stock market fell from a reelection high of 1,051 in January 1973 to a Watergate low of 577 in December 1974. The cause was unmistakable; the market follows where the presidency leads. It falls when the presidency falls apart.

Two powerful new forces hit the stock market just after Watergate. Each was a judgment on the effectiveness of the presidency, though the market did not see either that way at the time. The first was the takeoff in oil prices; the second was the takeoff in gold prices. The White House acquiesced when the lid was blown off oil prices, which, in turn, helped trigger the run-up in gold prices. Both moves were profoundly inflationary. Each confirmed that the White House did not know how to manage the government, much less the economy. Therefore, both moves were bearish.

When Gerald Ford took over, finishing up for Nixon, he was too busy contending with Henry Kissinger's ambition to get into trouble. The market paid no attention to him; his presidency was a nonevent. The political sophisticates, who knew that it was Kissinger who was the power in the Ford administration, made no impression on the market. Ford had been appointed to the vice-presidency on the practical calculation that his standing as an inside member of the congressional club uniquely qualified him to hold the congressional pack at bay and prevent an impeachment. The only success he scored was unwitting—he failed to block the drive to oust Nixon and, with his subsequent elevation to the Oval Office, he changed his luck by pardoning him.

Jimmy Carter deserved full credit for engineering his own crisis, and his wrong turn in "invading" Iran capped the climax. His arrival on the scene had dangled new bait to the markets, which they took. Warming to the credo of a redneck fiscal conservative who promised to be progressive with the poor and firm with the Russians, market hopes were confirmed when, after only nine months in office, Office of Management and Budget Director Bert Lance produced a $9 billion surplus as a cash bonus to the credit markets. The stock market celebrated this achievement by making its first Carter high of 1,014 in September 1977. From then on it was all downhill. The Carter Cabinet cabal that hounded Lance out of office failed to prevent his start-up surplus from turning into an unmanageable deficit. The price of oil ran wild in the absence of any political effort to tame it; the price of property ran wild as a vote of no confidence in the advantages of owing debt over owning dollars; and the price of gold ran wild because the world saw Washington losing its leadership as well as its ability to manage its own money.

These three parallel price breakouts—in oil, property, and gold—raised a troublesome question about the failure of stocks to run wild as well. On the contrary, measured against the wide-open inflation in the prices of these commodities, prices of stocks, by virtue of having failed to keep pace with inflation over the decade, had fallen. Oil was up fourteen times, from $3 per barrel in 1972 to $42 in 1980. The price of property at all ends of the market, led by rental property, quintupled, to take a conservative multiplier. The price of gold went from $103 an ounce in June 1976 to $875 on January 20, 1980, a jump of nearly nine times. (The increase amounted to no less than twenty-five times the U.S. ceiling price of $35 an ounce in force until August 15, 1971.)

Ronald Reagan's wrong turn into a "quick-fix" tax cut, which was designed to stimulate the economy and to finance a long, drawn-out arms buildup, triggered the depression in 1982 and hit the markets with tax increases that same year, just as Johnson's Vietnam escalation had in 1967. Though Reagan took over with the promise to return the markets to their participants, his charismatic performance held the market world in his spell. As he set out to repeat Johnson's market miracle, our old friend the cunning of history set a cruel trap for Reagan. He set out to send inspirational signals to the markets, intoxicating them, as Johnson had in his honeymoon year. What Reagan reactivated instead was a vicious backlash from an undisclosed, unfunded, and unmanageable Pentagon budget onto an unsuspecting public, an unreliable Congress, an unstabilized economy, and an unsupportable structure of bond and stock prices. The country's refusal to stay the course in Vietnam had flushed out Johnson's failure to settle down to enjoy the promise of his gala honeymoon celebration. Its refusal to stay the course with the inflationary depression flushed out Reagan's choice of the wrong Johnson experiment—financing an arms buildup with a tax cut—to duplicate in his own glittering honeymoon year.

Entering the 1980s, Reagan was the first president since Franklin Roosevelt to take office amid simultaneous political, economic, financial, and military crises. Herbert Hoover had responded to the Great Depression with inaction or, at best, with action too little, too late, and too timid to win him credit for acting at all, as in fact he did. Despite inheriting a depression and failing to rid the country of its vestiges, Roosevelt remained popular because people were doing better, and he was given the benefit of the doubt for trying. They could scarcely have been doing worse than in 1933. FDR did not *ask* the voters of his time what action to take; he *told* them. And his programs were new and different enough to stir up a series of arguments, which he won by his skill as a communicator and which were fortified by his knowledge of the uses of patronage in a new era of big budgets. His victories and, even more, his political fights overshadowed the shortfalls of most of his economic programs. Reagan, like Roosevelt, won credit from the day of his inauguration as an action president. Reagan, by contrast, inherited a boom and remained personally popular despite inviting blame because people were doing worse; they could hardly have been doing better than they were in 1981, notwithstanding inflation, or perhaps because of it. The problem the President made for himself, and subsequently for the securities markets, was that the action he gave the voters was exactly what they wanted.

The voters never can see the cables pouring into the Situation Room of the White House from the embassies every morning. The IRS cannot give them a peek at all the tax returns. The White House cannot let the president read his own mail because there is too much of it. Members of Congress could not tell Reagan about their mail because they were not allowed to see him alone. While most voters are no doubt always ready with ideas about what they would like to see happen, they want a new president to come up with ideas of his own that he can sell with his voice, as FDR had, that he can make happen with Congress, as LBJ had, and that will work as quick fixes, as each of their bold new starts had. Reagan passed the first two tests with flying colors but flubbed his lines and flunked the third. When the president whips up enthusiasm by unveiling a hatful of new ideas, he inflames the markets. When it turns out, however, that the new ideas packaged for him are the old ideas that have been kicking around from boardrooms to campuses— and the fad of supply-side economics was a 200-year-old hoax by the time Reagan caught up with it—the markets suspect that they have been had. Nothing depresses believers in new gimmickry so much as the discovery that they have been sold snake oil out of old bottles dressed up with deceptive labels.

The famous French diplomat Talleyrand did not know anything about markets, but he knew a great deal about people. (On Bill Simon's premise that markets are people, he would have known plenty about markets if he had come on the scene later or if markets had come on the scene earlier.) Being a Frenchman, he also knew a great deal about what goes on in kitchens. When he delivered himself of his famous dictum, "The soufflé never rises twice," he might as well have been writing about markets, which are not apt to respond to the same stimulus twice, at least not for any significant holding period. By the summer of 1983, the stock market would satisfy itself of the wisdom of that warning.

The impact of a failed presidency on euphoric markets is invariably traumatic. It shocks investors who have been unknowingly speculating on presidential charisma into securing their own defenses. The hosannas stirred up in 1982 by the dramatic drop in interest rates neglected to focus on one pocketbook consideration vital to market confidence: The 50 percent drop in interest rates hit people dependent on unearned income with the force of a 50 percent pay cut. The financial demographics of the early 1980s left the markets unusually dependent on the fears of older people holding old blue chips paying yields that were high when reckoned against cost but seemed low when calculated against current market prices. The life expectancy of these investors had dramatically increased, but so had their financial obligations and needs. Their earning power, however, was nil. Therefore, they were the first investors to adopt a defensive stance toward market fluctuations. They defended themselves by selling stocks from the beginning of the late 1982 market move until its end. Thanks to the drop in interest rates, they did not reinvest the proceeds of their sales in stocks offering "kicks." Instead, they switched their hopes for investment income into utility stocks and municipal bonds; they built their cash reserves and ceded the market-making role to the institutions.

The departure of the sober, income-minded, "cloth-coat Republican" element deprived the institutions of the safety net they need after a period of accumulating blocs of high-priced stocks. The anticlimactic process of distribution, known as profit taking, calls for the retailing of overpriced blocs in small lots to buyers of brand-names content to sit out sieges of market indigestion. No forced market adjustment to Washington's loss of control over events is ever more destructive than one that starts with a handful of institutional managers under stress to outsmart one another in finding innocent income-minded private investors to whom to distribute blocs. The one that started in May 1983 was foredoomed by the worst conceivable combination of market circumstances: with market yields from dividends uncompetitively low and market yields from interest on the rise from levels speculatively depressed; with institutions downgrading their portfolios into concentrated positions in low-grade, volatile stocks difficult to liquidate under disturbed market conditions; with a weak public inflamed by exaggerated expectations; with low margins being stampeded out of those same stocks under barrages of margin calls; and, cruellest blow of all, with a government, trusted to protect the market, wrecking it under the impact of interest-rate increases incubated in Washington.

Contrary to popular belief, opportunities to make money do not end with booms. In fact, the people who lost confidence or, what comes to the same thing, maneuverability, and sold securities into the market boom of 1982–1983 were themselves prime examples of the extraordinary opportunities that depressions offer for putting money to work. Many of them were owners of the cheap Exxon, IBM, GM, and other old blue chips, which had been patiently accumulated during the early 1930s and held at progressively higher yields measured against their original cost, but which, of course, netted unacceptably lower yields measured against each new upward spiral of stock prices. Any time stock prices outrun cash yields on dividends, with interest rates developing an inflationary upward backlash and the need for investment income rising, the stock market will prove hell-bent on running itself into a collision with money pressures it cannot overcome, which it did during the summer of 1983.

All depressions culminate in new rounds of inflation. The question posed by any new depression is whether the inflation it will trigger will be deferred until after the government has presided over the liquidation of all but the hardiest survivors, as Hoover did in 1932, or whether the pressure for quick fixes will force the government to package prescriptions for prosperity in time to limit the damage. While the government is seen to be out of business as the country's pharmacist, the pressure is on each and every citizen to start devising prescriptions for personal prosperity. Following are the personal prescriptions that can be filled while the chief pharmacist in Washington is out to lunch.

PART IV

PRESCRIPTIONS FOR PERSONAL PROSPERITY: A FINANCIAL STRATEGY FOR ALL SEASONS

CHAPTER FIFTEEN

Main Street Puts Its Money to Work

PRESCRIPTION #1
Playing the Do-It-Yourself Money Game

SOON AFTER Lyndon Johnson assumed his duties as Senate Democratic leader, Elizabeth Janeway arranged to drop by his office on the always chancy calculation that she could enjoy a brief visit with him en route to joining me in the office of Senator Ed Johnson, Democrat of Colorado. LBJ, on ascertaining her next stop, came up with this typically gargantuan last story for the road (whose echo I have never picked up from any other LBJ collector): "Tell Ed that I told you that, in the beginning, everybody was named Johnson, but that only the good Johnsons kept the privilege, and that the bad Johnsons had to start going by all those other names." His colleague from Colorado, being nicer and also slower-witted, did not express surprise that LBJ had managed to keep the privilege.

One of the good Johnsons who did keep the privilege right into the eighteenth century was Dr. Samuel Johnson, whose sayings everyone still repeats. "Patriotism is the last refuge of a scoundrel" remains a pungent political gem; its applicability to his co-tenant in the Johnson hall of fame is prophetic. Another carries a grim message, useful for financial survivors: "When a man knows he is to be hanged in a fortnight, it concentrates his mind wonderfully." Those who find themselves apparently sentenced for life to endure an inflationary depression, and to agonize over where new money is coming from and where the money they had went, will be on notice to "concentrate their minds" too. But they at least can do something to influence their fate.

Most people fail to concentrate on the difference between making money and keeping it. They go through life working casually for themselves but diligently for the government as unpaid tax collectors. This has been the role of every American earning a paycheck since withholding taxes went into effect; everyone earning interest and dividends was threatened with it too when the 1982 tax bill caught up with savers and investors and authorized the Internal Revenue Service to get ahead of them—until their revolt forced its repeal. All businesses run up overhead doing this same job every time they meet a payroll, collect a sales tax, or collect income on spare cash and disburse the earnings to creditors or stockholders.

The arrival of the age of affluence, and its successive speedups with inflation and slowdowns with depression, reconditioned people to become matter-of-fact about three new financial sensations. They saw more money changing hands than they had ever tried to count; they felt more money going through their own hands than they had ever expected to spend; and they listened to more people talk about money with more frustration than they had ever heard whispered about sex. In fact, as sex became more casual, money began to replace it as popular fantasy. What sells in a media society is reflected in the advertising space and time that businesses buy. More dollars pass through the media telling people what to do with their money than how to enjoy their love lives or improve their minds.

When in doubt about the practicalities of life, it is wise to steer clear of accountants, lawyers, and financial advisers. Writers are apt to offer shrewder guidelines, especially writers with a flair for cynicism. Dr. Johnson is one. George Bernard Shaw is another. Shaw's play *Pygmalion* was adapted into the unforgettable Broadway musical *My Fair Lady;* everyone remembers its hit song, "The Rain in Spain." A whole new world opens up for the ragamuffin heroine, Eliza Doolittle, when she jumps the fence from cockney singsong to educated English, even though she does not have a shilling to her name. She can pass as a lady in Shaw's plot, a well-spoken, high-living pauper, but eligible in Shaw's world to enjoy access to the money that social position could attract.

The moral for Americans today? The same but with a dismaying difference. America's rising generation of MBAs and PhDs, scientists, mathematicians, computer whiz kids, engineers, doctors, dentists, psychologists, lawyers, accountants, and media stars, as well as assorted readers of *The Wall Street Journal* and viewers of TV stock-tipping shows, have evolved into a privileged caste of well-spoken, high-living paupers: Eliza Doolittles, tutored, like Shaw's but by professors whose specialties blind them to reality, and hyped up by our "pop-finance" media coverage of the money world. It is a sad commentary on the progress of capitalism since 1848, when Marx and Engels told the workers of the world that they had nothing to lose but their chains, that the elite brainworkers of the country have nothing to lose but their lifestyles.

Gradually and painfully, America's insecure upper-bracketeers are learning what every London cabdriver and Yorkshire coal miner has known since Shaw's day, when commercial gambling was introduced: The only way for an ambitious pauper, with or without a tennis court and a tax adviser, to prosper financially for the duration of a crisis is by gambling. Anyone born on the wrong side of the fence can make it big by betting and can strut like a duke who has been collecting rent on property owned by his family for centuries.

Wall Street used to dignify gambling by calling it speculation; "crap-shooting" has evolved into the technical term for it, exactly as in Las Vegas or Atlantic City. Still, speculating deserves a better reputation than it enjoys. Bernard Baruch, the legendary self-made market wizard and elder statesman of the first half of the twentieth century, when asked in a hostile Senate hearing to state his occupation, replied, "I am a speculator." The shocked reaction reflected the popular impression that it was, and remains, some kind of off-color activity. Yet even all conservative investing is impregnated with unstated speculative premises—not only the obvious bet on the character of management, but the more elusive one on the direction of events, and the built-in one on the level of interest rates. The most reckless kind of investment anyone ever makes disregards the element of speculation in it. Bond investment, commonly thought to be the most conservative kind, is nothing but a rank speculation on interest rates. Arthur F. Burns, when he was chairman of the Federal Reserve Board, used to say that interest rates are too speculative and too political for a Fed chairman to discuss in public. His successor, Paul Volcker, made himself the target of attack from every point on the political compass when he disregarded this sage advice and helped to set the markets up for their great fall in 1983.

The Building Blocks of Financial Planning

Traditionally, financial planning has been structured on five premises in the following order of preference: savings, insurance, residential property ownership, investment, and speculation. Of these, saving and investing have become casualties in the last decade. Only residential property ownership, insurance, and speculation (though not necessarily in that order) remain worthwhile. To avoid any misunderstanding, building homes and starting businesses have always offered constructive investment opportunities to Americans. So long as the need for the prescriptions for national prosperity outlined in Part II of this book remain unmet, however, these two basic productive uses for money will not be worth the risk because the high level of interest rates will make them uninsurable. Following are the ones that are worth taking in time of ongoing crisis.

RESIDENTIAL PROPERTY OWNERSHIP FOR PERSONAL USE

Anyone living alone, with a spouse, with a friend, or in an extended household is in financial danger renting living quarters instead of owning them. The only justification for paying rent, aside from being in transit, is while getting started in the work force. At the other end of the demographic spectrum, the elderly inhabitants of nursing homes have no choice. At the worst of the depression of the early 1980s, when the mortgage market and, therefore, the real estate market were both shut, inflation was still fired by a sharp shortage of rental units, while good homes in weak hands went begging. As recovery occurs, it can be expected to turn the rental shortage into a famine and to run the building boom of the second half of the 1980s into bottlenecks of labor, materials, appliances, and machinery, sending costs skyrocketing and delaying completions. Either way Americans will be ahead of the game owning their own residential property during hard times because that is when rents jump from merely expensive to positively extortionate.

Once the argument for owning instead of renting is grasped and accepted, the question of how to go about it falls into place. Get the largest, longest mortgage obtainable—in good times or bad. Notwithstanding the disaster perpetrated by ruinous interest rates in 1981 and 1982, mortgage borrowers subject to amortization payments are always better off trading a higher interest rate in return for a slower pay-down. In fact, the arithmetic built into the tax code calls for mortgage borrowers and lenders to agree that "interest-only" mortgages are best for both parties to the transaction. As we have seen in the national prescription on protecting the real estate market (Prescription #17), everyone in the 50 percent income tax bracket pays interest on mortgage debt at an incentive pre-tax rate of 50¢ on the dollar but pays amortization at a prohibitive after-tax rate of $2 for every dollar in cash paid back. This means that, to anyone in the 50 percent tax bracket on the last $1,000 of taxable income received, the cost of repaying mortgage debt is four times the cost of just paying interest. (The interest-only route would keep everybody happy, including mortgage lenders complaining about their need for more earnings, which interest payments give them but which amortization payments, by virtue of representing a return of capital, deny them.)

The tax subsidy to homeowners and the corresponding penalty against tenants extends beyond mortgage payments to property tax payments. When the backlash from Reaganomics sent property taxes surging at two to four times the official rate of price inflation on goods during the 1982–1983 depression, the advantages of this supplemental form of tax shelter were accentuated. Owners of homes and apartments are entitled to charge property-tax payments against taxable income. Tenants, meanwhile, are obliged to accept "pass-through" rent increases to cover the cost of tax increases to their landlords, who, however, are able to deduct these increases on their state and federal income tax returns. All tax deductions enjoyed by landlords increase their ability to collect rent increases as well as investment income in low income-tax brackets, while all pass-through rent increases absorbed by tenants have the same crippling dollar-for-dollar effect on any hopes they may have had of staying even after cuts in take-home pay. The hardships suffered by local governments during the 1982 depression, reflected in the drastic cuts in basic social services forced on them, guaranteed still sharper ongoing property-tax increases once the pressures of reflation were unleashed.

A special word is in order on the advantages of apartment ownership over leasing for those unable to afford the cost of a down payment for a home or the time needed to commute to a residential neighborhood. Condominium ownership is more conservative in principle than owning shares in a cooperative building for the simple reason that obligations for condominium mortgage debt and taxes are limited to the pro rata share accounted for by each apartment. Liability for the same obligations in a cooperative, determined by the overall expense of operating the building, servicing its debt, and paying its property taxes, extends to the stronger shareholders in the event of a default by the weaker ones. During the worst of the 1929–1933 depression, many luxury cooperative apartment buildings were hit by defaults and vacancies, which left owners who were still able to make their maintenance payments saddled with onerous deficiency assessments. But this traumatic risk remained academic for co-op apartment owners during the 1982–1983 depression, not merely because inflation came to the rescue of the real estate market more quickly and more powerfully than after the 1929 crash but also because hordes of property-buying, cash-rich foreigners showed a keen awareness of how cheap prime American residential property is relative to property around the world. This refugee money took up a great deal of market slack with no need for or interest in mortgage accommodation. The real estate market always benefits from any such noticeable rise in the overall ratio of all-cash to total transactions.

Home or apartment ownership is a continuously paying proposition as an annual tax shelter. Over any period of years, it also works out as an enormously profitable inflation shelter. The reason is rooted in the workings of the political economy. Tax increases and inflation increases spiral on together: Tax increases come as a catch-up for the increased cost of government forced by past inflation, but tax increases are cost increases and therefore also activate an increase in future inflation. This spiral is a Catch-22; tax increases and inflation increases are not alternatives to one another but causes of each other. Consequently, taxes paid out of current income and not recouped cripple current efforts to save, while taxes paid out of capital undo past savings programs. The tax shelter bought with home or apartment ownership subject to an "interest-only" mortgage (or at least a "mainly-interest" mortgage) offers the simplest and surest way to recoup taxes paid out of annual income; and the inflation shelter bought with it is the workhorse vehicle to trust for protecting capital built in the past as well as for building it into the future. People of average means who habitually complain about the burden of making their mortgage payments are startled to discover how much they were saving and how profitably they were investing with each mortgage payment grudgingly made. More savings are embodied in the homes people own than in the passbooks they carry.

Savings in the form of cash reserves meet a basic need for people still able to accumulate and preserve them. Increasingly, however, younger entries into the professional and managerial work force are recognizing their inability to build cash reserves on ordinary income, and older people who regarded themselves as well entrenched with liquid savings until the 1970s are routinely subject to drains of cash for their own needs as well as for those of younger dependents. In any case, the trouble in all age brackets is that savings buy less and less standby insurance, beginning with insurance against geriatric health emergencies and increasingly against educational expenses for younger dependents. The problem of caring for aging parents whose savings have been depleted is also a source of great anxiety. Even during the depression of 1982, when the Reagan administration was congratulating itself because "inflation was down," only the rate of increase in retail-price inflation was actually falling; inflation in the cost of producing goods itself was still on the rise.

More frustrating still for people with savings and hopes of accumulating them, the cost of the services not in the price indexes was still running away—especially taxes but also insurance, repairs, utilities, transportation and transit, education, travel, entertainment, and a host of others. The time-honored right to deduct interest charges from consumer-debt payments was being called into question by the very statesmen who were claiming credit for having beaten inflation back and interest rates down. To car buyers on the installment plan in the 50 percent bracket (and any able to put up down payments and pass credit muster were), a 10 percent nondeductible interest bill on an auto note costs as much as the 20 percent deductible rate that started the squeeze that stopped car sales. Political pressure to cancel the deductibility of consumer-credit interest charges is bound to revive the call to cancel the deductibility of interest on home mortgages as well.

The chilling effect of such extremist talk echoed by self-styled moderates with credentials as reformers furnishes an educational reminder that the inflation of the 1970s was consistently paced by the cost of services more than by the prices of goods, while good news about "disinflation" was making headlines and gunning the markets. Altogether, therefore, savings in reserve were coming to be worth less by the day under the best of circumstances. To prove it, the 50 percent drop in short-term interest rates, which helped borrowers—especially banks, businesses, and governments—hit the saving public with the force of a 50 percent pay cut (or, on the more realistic calculation that income received is the measure of capital owned, as a 50 percent levy on net worth, conservatively appraised). It had a predictably chilling effect on affluent consumers, who had come to count the double-digit interest rates that crippled the productive functions of our political economy as the measure of their financial well-being.

In the main marketplace dominated by consumers—the residential real estate market—the value of savings embodied in homes and apartment houses continued to appreciate in the face of 1982's adverse circumstances as steadily as the value of savings in the form of cash continued to depreciate. Home ownership remained the best hedge against the rising costs of rents. The "can't-lose" bet on home and apartment ownership goes back to the status residential building enjoys as the most volatile basic industry in the country, the first to stop and the first to start. In hard times, its stoppages buoy market prices of existing homes, and in good times, rushes of catch-up buying invite steep markups of existing homes into line with the runaway cost of new construction, which is invariably of inferior quality.

Existing real estate values derive another distinctive advantage from the status of residential property as the only major American industry—not excepting insurance or banking—that obviously enjoys built-in immunity from foreign competition. On the contrary, it benefits from panicked foreign buying of existing property that might otherwise become a drug on the market and which foreign money down through the ages has learned to respect as the prime sanctuary against inflation. Moreover, foreign money makes a hobby of "comparison shopping" for real estate values in metropolitan centers all over the world. It is agreed that American real estate, after its breathtaking inflation, still remains irresistibly cheap alongside values everywhere else, even without allowing for the enormous difference in the valuation basis of Old World and U.S. property. Old World buildings do not come with the land under them; "ground rent" is a separate charge to the landlord, over and above the cost of the building. This traditional practice of leasing land and selling only the structures built and replaced on it is gradually spreading to America. For example, Stanford University in California has adopted the lucrative expedient of leasing tracts to developers in Palo Alto. This trend is further sharpening the appetite of foreign money to gobble up American real estate while it can still be accumulated as "freehold," that is, with the land under it.

Inflationary pressures, then, can be trusted to dominate the real estate market even during depressions, let alone when mere "disinflation" is seen to be the overall trend in the economy and when the interest rates on which real estate activity swings are dropping in apparent proof of the claim. The paradox of an inflationary depression is itself a decisive signal that the inflation is a safe bet to outlast the depression and to outrace any subsequent recovery. The related fact that residential real estate inflation outraces every other form in the marketplace argues that the 1980s will not be a decade in which paying off a mortgage will make sense—or dollars—for either mortgage borrowers or mortgage lenders. Anyway, the American dream, dramatized by the ceremonial burning of the paid-off mortgage prior to settling down to live forever in the family homestead, is a throwback to the golden age when there were no income taxes worth worrying about, when ten years was the top limit of the term of a residential mortgage, and when the purchasing power of the dollar was so stable that the lending institutions wanted their money back instead of just collecting interest on it and relending the interest at the higher rates called for by the faster inflation.

It is well to remember that there are two separate and distinct standards for measuring bargains. The first is the price you pay at the time. The second is the cost you avoid afterwards. The rate of inflation makes the difference. By the Einsteinian standard of relativity, which is worth a trial in the world of money on the record of its practicality in the world of science, the faster the rate of inflation speeds up, the less a long-term investment costs you even when you agree to pay up for it. This goes double if you borrow to buy, that is, to pay slowly for what you bought cheap. Mortgaging, then, is the practical way to approach the financing of a home ownership and to make the cost comfortable to carry in the present as well as profitable to arrange for the future. Admittedly, it is not as simple as plunking down hard cash for the entire deal up front, but neither is the world as simple as it was when cash was king. Here, for example, are two authentic bizarre cases of what has been happening: The first shows the destructive extreme of a self-indulgent life-style; the second, the equally destructive extreme of inflating property for sale.

1. A dentist, sporting a middle-six-figure annual income, wrote me from Hollywood in 1980, just as the California real estate bubble was bursting, complaining about the 24 percent rate of interest he was being charged on his brand-new fourth mortgage. He needed it, he explained, in order to fix up his tennis court. I wrote back that this trip to the bank was not necessary.

2. A cold-sober listing with a real estate broker—again in Hollywood country—told it all. It offered a mansion for sale in an exclusive neighborhood, with all imaginable creature comforts and some museum pieces, at a bargain price of just over $2 million. It invited negotiations on terms guaranteed to be not only generous but flexible. However, it stipulated a firm, rock-bottom cash down payment of $1,100!

These two illustrations from real life are presented as a warning not to abuse the most important personal investment any individual or family can make, and as compelling arguments for the wisdom of the middle course between overspeculation at the extremes just illustrated and overinvestment in the form of all-cash personal ownership. Only nontaxpaying institutional investors, assured of large and steady cash in-flows, can afford to own property outright.

Only one question remains: If you do talk the mortgage lender into a newfangled interest-only mortgage and you do get the benefit of paying all the interest bills, how do you pay off the mortgage? And when? The answer is never pay a mortgage off, or even down, if you can avoid it. If having one pays, why give it up? Instead, why not replace it with a bigger one, or with a second, as market appraisals grow bigger and the eyes of mortgage lenders on the lookout for good loans do too?

A footnote to the residential-property building block, linking it to the insurance building block that follows: It is prompted by the inclination of people to focus on their visible assets and to ignore their creeping liabilities, specifically, property insurance. Homeowners are understandably quick to talk about their steep profits on homes and apartments, but they are just as understandably slow to do anything to pay up for increased property-insurance coverage. America's homeowners are seriously underinsured relative to the present, let alone the prospective, values of their homes. The cost of property insurance would be rising by leaps and bounds even if property tax rates were not catching up with tax appraisals and even if tax appraisals were not catching up with market values. The reason goes back to the staggering losses the casualty companies have been taking on the operating side of their businesses—$11.5 billion in 1982. Until 1982, the industry as a whole was reluctantly willing to continue absorbing higher operating losses because it felt confident in its ability to offset them with higher investment income. As insurance-company managements reconciled themselves to receiving lower dividend income, however, they resolved to raise their premium charges. The bottom line? The prudent homeowner will also be an aggressive insurance buyer.

LIFE INSURANCE AS A SUBSTITUTE FOR SAVING

Life insurance is much maligned because it is widely misunderstood. It was given up as the obvious victim of inflation, yet it has survived as the continuing beneficiary of inflation. The insurance companies can blame themselves for the confusion they have spread, which is rooted in the wrongheaded way insurance has been sold: as an investment. Insurance is always a service offering protection. It is never an investment. Nor is it even a form of compulsory saving. On the contrary, the unique value of insurance, especially during an era of inflation, comes into play as the fallback defense for people who figure out that saving has suffered the fate predicted for insurance. The idea was that insurance would have no value in the future as a death benefit. The reality is that saving is no longer feasible on a meaningful scale in the present. The result is that the insurance dollar is buying the two forms of protection for the cost of one.

While savings programs were still worth the effort and the sacrifice, I advocated the accumulation of six months' income in a reserve fund, not for the interest it would earn but as a source of "appendicitis money." But the rising tide of costs in the 1970s left everyone working for taxable income unable to save enough of it to buy protection against emergencies and unexpected increases in the cost of living. Consequently, it is smart as well as practical to concentrate your defensive priorities on insurance. Stubborn resolves to save will keep you feeling virtuous, but the results will not leave you feeling secure. Thousands of dollars squirreled away each year will not buy you enough protection en route to matter; the same amount plowed methodically into insurance will—especially for policyowners who start young when premium costs per $1,000 face value of protection are dirt cheap.

The advantages of whole life insurance. Specifically, whole life insurance, which is always the first type of insurance to buy, offers the policyholder two advantages, irresistible in an inflationary era. First is the increasing likelihood that everyone is in danger of dying broke. This possibility establishes life insurance as an indispensable substitute for protection against the investment estate that the times prevent most people from accumulating. The unique feature of this first advantage offered by whole life is that the first premium payment starts to endow the policyholder with the equivalent of capital. Therefore, it provides two forms of coverage for the cost of one: the obvious coverage of lump-sum death benefits plus a lifetime capital insurance against pauper status, which is a felt want but not a popularly perceived one. The lifetime fringe benefit offered to whole life policyowners runs the lump-sum death benefit a close second. It guarantees the right to borrow cheap (single-digit) money during a long, drawn-out era of double-digit interest costs. No matter how high interest rates go, policy loans are a bargain, for three reasons. The laws in the various states regulating insurance companies have put single-digit ceilings of 5 to 8 percent on them, depending on the state. Any policy entitling the insured to a fixed-rate option to borrow during his or her lifetime stacks the cards in favor of the policyowner, and against the insurance company, in a period of rising or high interest rates. The losses all the life companies run up meeting calls to divert money from high-yielding investments into low-yielding policy loans explain their increasing inclination to pull back on efforts to sell whole life policies. The morbid fear shown by the life-company managements in their rush for policy loans in response to a bulge in interest rates is prima facie evidence that this fringe benefit to whole life policyholders works as an incentive for them and as a disincentive for the life companies.

No loans come close to matching policy loans; they avoid cash waste, and they achieve capital efficiency. The savings free the borrower from any need to pay interest charges on policy loans in cash from year to year. The dividends earned on the policies cover the cost. They are too low to qualify as investment returns, but they are high enough to meet interest payments subject to statutory ceilings in the event that premium payments cannot be made. A by no means incidental advantage of whole life insurance is the right to remain covered free from the obligation to pay premiums, if a disability waiver of premium is included in the policy. The efficiency comes wrapped in the bargain. The principal need never be repaid because it is covered by the surest collateral in the world: the certainty of death. This explains why insurance companies never ask for amortization payments on policy loans; the risk is always covered by the certainty of the eventual death of the insured.

In 1978, a self-styled investigative reporter published a sketch of me. The unfounded assertions and misleading exaggerations earned him a rebuke from the National News Council, the professional self-policing media tribunal, which in addition refused to entertain his appeal. At one point he accused me of having accepted a fee for an endorsement of whole life insurance when, as he argued, term insurance is clearly cheaper and must therefore be the best form of insurance. It certainly is cheaper, for exactly the same reason that a Volkswagen is cheaper than a Mercedes: It buys less.

The limited uses of term insurance. Whereas whole life insurance covers the several contingencies mentioned above and guarantees the policyholder's alternative rights and privileges, term insurance, which protects the insured for only a limited period of time, is a pure and simple contract with the insurance company. It is a bet on which party to the contract will outsmart the other: Either the insured will die, and in time for the estate to collect the face value of the policy, or the insurance company will collect the premium payments and retain the right to reinvest them free from the obligation to pay benefits after the term of the policy has expired. Since term insurance costs less than whole life, some overzealous consumer protectionists have jumped to the conclusion that term insurance is a better buy. But the all-important benefit offered by the right to borrow is denied the owner of term insurance. So is the right to keep insurance in force without clouding the policy with debt during disability.

Of course term insurance has its uses. Increasingly, couples in their thirties and even forties, let alone their twenties, enjoying incomes once deemed comfortable enough to support savings and investment programs, find themselves in desperate need of interim protection but drained dry of cash. Any couple simultaneously burdened with running expenses for aging parents and healthy children bringing home tuition bills needs to buy the relief term insurance provides. They can take advantage of the bargain offered by the term premium by loading up on term with an eye to converting to whole life when family finances permit. Although this strategy defers access to the privilege offered by whole life, it does conserve cash in early years without sacrificing protection. For those who are not so financially strapped, term insurance is also the way to keep protection in force while taking advantage of the opportunity to use whole life policies to generate low-interest loans. This strategy calls for buying term insurance equal to the amount of loans outstanding on whole life policies.

Warning: Policyholders protected only by term insurance are exposed to the danger of losing their coverage if they are unable to pay their premiums for a couple of years. Policyowners protected by past payments for whole life insurance at least have the right to fall back on the equity accumulated by those premiums to keep their insurance in force if their incomes fall or stop altogether.

While the opportunity to offset borrowings against whole life policies is the most valuable short-term benefit term offers, the right to convert to whole life while a term policy is in force or on its expiration is the most valuable long-term benefit. (In the past, term policyholders could stipulate this privilege, which is obviously valuable as people grow older, but the insurance companies have become so anxious to keep up with the times that they have been waiving the traditional requirement of a medical examination before issuing term policies to younger people.) Older term policy buyers who reserve this right obligate the company issuing the policy to insure them for life even if they contract a disease making them uninsurable between the time they pass the medical examination qualifying them to buy their term policy and the time they exercise their option to convert to whole life. Any company on notice of a term policyholder's shortened life expectancy would be better off letting the term policy expire, but the pressure of competition has forced insurance companies to sweeten term policies with their conversion option free from any requirement to pass a second medical examination or to absorb a higher premium cost on proof of shortened life expectancy.

The value of the medical option available to prudent buyers of term insurance suggests still another course of action—to take out health insurance policies, preferably group policies—made increasingly advantageous by four separate but interrelated social trends: (1) longer life expectancy; (2) increasing probability of living long enough to develop diseases less prevalent in earlier days, most conspicuously cancer; (3)

runaway health costs, especially for diseases like cancer, which call for continuous attention and care; and (4) revolutionary progress in medical technology, particularly in preventive techniques, which, however, puts a high cost on the expertise coming on stream and creates correspondingly strong incentives to finance group insurance.

Using insurance to finance education expenses. A distinctive application of whole life insurance is to use it to ease the increasingly high burden of putting youngsters through college. No doubt some parents will ask what the advantage is of including an insurance policy in their responsibilities to their children instead of simply saving the money and setting it aside. Six separate and distinct advantages are bought for no extra cost by going the more complicated route with an insurance policy.

1. Large life insurance coverage is worth having for an infant with no earning power because of the bargain it brings the prospective student relative to the cost of buying this much insurance later on.

2. It provides reserve borrowing power for college students if their parents run into difficulties. The cost of graduate school training for professional careers is considerably greater than for undergraduate education and runs longer.

3. It provides protection, at no cost, against the risk that parents may run out of money or die prematurely. The annual death benefits go into effect immediately on almost every life insurance policy. After the third year of premium payments, policies begin to build up sufficient loan values to keep them in force if premium payments are missed. In certain cases, the guaranteed cash value of policies in their second year of premium payments, and every year thereafter, increases by more than the annual premium paid.

4. Protection can be increased by increasing the face amount of insurance at any time.

5. Youngsters are entitled to keep their low-cost coverage as long as they live, and, therefore, they will be entitled to rebuild their loan values after their parents have finished their educational borrowings and helped them make their starts in life. If necessary or desirable, they can make further loans as adults once the policy is transferred to their name. In the case of a policy bought at birth, on which $160,000 has been borrowed between the eighteenth and twenty-second year, continuation of premium payments of $6,000 a year will buy the right to borrow another $4 million by the sixty-fifth year.

6. In the event that parents are unable to afford even the minimal cost of whole life on a monthly basis, the grandparents can take over the burden by paying the annual premiums for insurance on the lives of their children in order to earmark death benefits payable to their grandchildren.

Assuming nondeductible tuition charges of $8,000 per year, parents with, say, two children in college at the same time would be obliged to pay $16,000 a year for both—before buying a pair of jeans for either. A couple whose income placed them in a 50 percent tax bracket would require a pretax income of $32,000 a year before family living expenses. If a whole life policy of $1 million is put on each child at birth, with the parents retaining ownership of the policy and paying the premiums, the advantage bought in advance will exceed saving and/or borrowing to meet tuition bills each semester. The coverage bought is impressive in any bracket, but the premium paid is manageable even for parents in middle brackets. Even at the rate at which the cost of education is continuing to inflate, a prefinanced education fund of this amount is likely to prove sufficient to college-educate a child.

The tax code, in addition to the insurance incentive, invites parents or grandparents to finance tuition costs two decades before they fall due on advantageous terms for all concerned, though very few parents and grandparents take advantage of this option. All minors may receive gifts up to $20,000 a year ($10,000 from each parent) free from income tax. (For some years, the ceiling had been $3,000 per year per parent.) A whole life policy taken out on a newborn or a preschool youngster will lock in a deep discount on the annual cost of college tuition in the future. A loan on this policy will set up the child to pay his or her tuition with no pressure for repayment. The dividends paid on the policy cover the low interest rate (5 to 8 percent) charged on the policy loan; the low dividend rate on a whole life policy disqualifies it as an investment but qualifies it to avoid cash outlays for interest to carry the cost of the policy loan. Not even the most alarming inflation projections fifteen to twenty years after the policy has been taken out are likely to anticipate annual tuition costs of $40,000 a year, or $160,000 for a four-year course.

The calculation for infants. Here's how the advantage is secured: The parents (or grandparents) ask their insurance agent how much the annual premium cost will be to buy $1 million of insurance on the baby's life. The arithmetic is a revelation. A yearly outgo of $6,000 for eighteen years will provide $1 million of coverage. By the time the child reaches the age of eighteen, this policy will entitle the parent, as owner of the policy, to borrow $160,000 (for which no interest expense need be paid) to finance education costs. The cash value rises by another $40,000 by the time the child reaches the age of twenty-two. It is understood that the loan value of the policy can be drawn down as needed each year and that annual premiums will continue to be paid during the college years.

For parents unable to afford this amount of premium cost each year, a smaller policy of $100,000 on the life of either parent at age twenty-eight, for example, will cost $1,200 per year (or $100 per month) and accomplish the same purpose, as the table indicates.

Proceeds of a $100,000 Whole Life Policy
Taken Out on an Infant When a Parent Is Twenty-eight

Year	Annual Premium	Guaranteed Cash Value	Cash Value Increase	Net Ledger Change	Death Benefit	Paid-up Insurance
1	$ 1,265	$ 0	$ 0	$ 1,265	$100,000	$ 0
2	1,265	1,300	1,300	−35	100,000	6,800
3	1,265	2,700	1,400	−135	100,000	13,600
4	1,265	4,100	1,400	−135	100,000	19,900
5	1,265	5,500	1,400	−135	100,000	25,700
	6,325		5,500	825		
6	1,265	7,000	1,500	−235	100,000	31,600
7	1,265	8,600	1,600	−335	100,000	37,400
8	1,265	10,300	1,700	−435	100,000	43,200
9	1,265	12,000	1,700	−435	100,000	48,600
10	1,265	13,800	1,800	−535	100,000	53,900
	12,650		13,800	−1,150		
11	1,265	15,500	1,700	−435	100,000	58,400
12	1,265	17,200	1,700	−435	100,000	62,500
13	1,265	19,100	1,900	−635	100,000	67,000
14	1,265	20,900	1,800	−535	100,000	70,800
15	1,265	22,900	2,000	−735	100,000	75,000
	18,975		22,900	−3,925		
16	1,265	24,900	2,000	−735	100,000	78,800
17	1,265	27,000	2,100	−835	100,000	82,500
18	1,265	29,200	2,200	−935	100,000	86,300
19	1,265	31,400	2,200	−935	100,000	89,800
20	1,265	$33,700	2,300	−1,035	$100,000	$93,200
	$25,300		$33,700	$−8,400		

The basic principle to bear in mind is that the annual cost of the policy is determined by the age and, therefore, the life expectancy of the insured. In any case, the death benefit goes into effect the day after the insurance is in force.

After the cost of a college education has been financed by the parent owning such a policy, up to $20,000 a year of accrued and/or accruing cash value in a policy can be borrowed out and transferred to the child free of tax until the entire policy is transferred. Alternatively, the parent can borrow out all the remaining loan value and retain it, transferring only the stripped-down policy to the child. In that case, the college graduate will need to start making premium payments out of his or her own earnings or with a portion of an annual parental gift.

The catch-up calculation for preteens. Here's how the same strategy works if the parents want to make up for lost time and purchase a policy when their child is ten years old. An annual premium payment of approximately $6,000 will buy a whole life policy with a face value of $850,000. Just as in the case of the infant who is insured, the ten year old is named as the insured with the parents retaining the ownership of the policy and the borrowing privileges that accompany it. The cash value that can be borrowed out by the time the child is ready to enter college (age eighteen) comes to $50,000; by graduation (age twenty-two) the cash value increases to $80,000—dependent, of course, on ongoing premium payments by the parents. The cost advantage in taking out such a policy when the insured is still an infant is self-evident.

In order to secure the same $850,000 of coverage and borrowing rights for a child of ten as for a baby, the annual premium payments would need to be increased to $18,000 for a policy with a face value of $2.5 million—or 2.5 times the $1 million policy on the infant. Such a policy, however, would offer the right to borrow approximately $150,000 of cash value by age eighteen and $235,000 by age twenty-two. The other side of this calculation is that the parents do have the option, just as in the policy on the infant, to transfer up to $20,000 of cash value per year to the child free of tax.

The catch-up calculation for teenagers. As a practical matter, many parents who have paid hard, after-tax cash in entire innocence of the uses of whole life insurance to prefinance their youngsters' college educations are waking up to discover the exorbitant costs they face. More frustrating still, they are finding themselves caught in a destructive kind of Catch-22: blight for the future of their children or de facto bankruptcy for themselves. Career opportunities for college graduates increasingly depend upon their qualifying for graduate school training. Moreover, scholarships and grants, just like college and university loan funds, have been evaporating. For middle-aged parents who are discovering that their efforts at capital accumulation are digging them deeper into the hole and who missed the opportunity to buy protection for their families and to prefinance their teenagers' tuition bills looming ahead of them, the second table shows a schedule calculated to provide $100,000 worth of cash value in ten years for an annual premium payment of $8,650. The parent, not the child, is insured in this case. The child or children are the beneficiaries of a $500,000 policy, and the parent has the right to borrow on it beginning in the second year.

In my own case, as a parent and later as a grandparent, I followed the course of action suggested here. I bought a $100,000 whole life policy insuring the lives of each of our two sons, who were born in 1940 and 1943. In that different world, threatened as it was by the ravages of wartime inflation, I estimated this amount of coverage as sufficient to cover the cost of education in the 1960s. It was. Nevertheless, I chose to exercise my option of paying their tuition bills and also of paying the annual premiums on their whole life policies in order to permit future

Ten-Year Proceeds of a $500,000 Policy
Taken Out on the Life of a Thirty-nine Year-Old Parent

Year	Annual Premium	Guaranteed Cash Value	Cash Value Increases	Net Ledger Change	Death Benefit	Paid-up Insurance
1	$ 8,650	$ 0	$ 0	$ 8,650	$500,000	$ 0
2	8,650	10,000	10,000	−1,350	500,000	35,500
3	8,650	20,000	10,000	−1,350	500,000	68,000
4	8,650	30,000	10,000	−1,350	500,000	98,500
5	8,650	40,500	10,500	−1,850	500,000	128,500
	43,250		40,500	2,750		
6	8,650	51,500	11,000	−2,350	500,000	157,500
7	8,650	63,000	11,500	−2,850	500,000	186,500
8	8,650	74,500	11,500	−2,850	500,000	213,000
9	8,650	86,500	12,000	−3,350	500,000	239,500
10	8,650	$99,000	12,500	−3,850	$500,000	$265,500
	$86,500		$99,000	$−12,500		

loan values to build up for them. By the time they were ready to borrow on these policies as adults, the necessary costs of education had been met and they were free to use the proceeds from their loans to make profitable investments for themselves. When our two grandchildren were born at the start of the 1970s, I bought a whole life policy of $250,000 for each of them on the more speculative assumption that by the time the 1990s arrived, the loan values on policies of this size would be sufficient to cover the inflated annual cost of education. As of this writing, they still are.

The federal government's liberalization of the annual gift-tax allowance to minors and to heirs at death points to the eventual elimination of estate and gift-taxes altogether, along with the capital gains tax, on the practical grounds that they yield too little revenue to be bothered with and that the magnitude of the annual deficit and unfunded public debt has deprived the government of the luxury of imposing taxes that fail to harvest annual bumper crops of cash. While estate taxes are still with us, users of insurance for the prefinancing of education will do well to ascertain that their insurance agents are advising them in coordination with the advice of their tax lawyers. Policyowners who contemplate assignments or gifts of their policies (or the death benefits from them) outside the marital relationship will do well to consult their own tax counsel before involving themselves and their beneficiaries in the tax intricacies they will encounter.

Assessing the potential of universal life insurance. The atmosphere of curiosity surrounding the fad known as universal life calls for a perspective on its advantages and disadvantages. Universal life is the response of insurance company marketing managements to the public-relations hype about term insurance as a bargain and money market funds as an investment. It packages a traditional diehard insurance-industry insistence on selling insurance as an investment into this twin appeal of bargains for people who fancy themselves the beneficiaries of usury. The way it works is that customers buy money market funds, presumably yielding higher rates of return, and the companies dedicate the interest to pay premiums on term insurance policies. The amount of term insurance varies with the interest earned. As is invariably the case with the marketing of insurance as an investment product, high up-front charges are levied.

The substantive objection to the universal life concept, however, is that it turns the rationale for insurance bought as protection upside down. The competitive incentive pressing the companies to compete with the money market funds limits the appeal of universal life to prospective policy buyers who already have cash reserves large enough to earn interest income on a meaningful scale. Moreover, it contemplates giving the insurance companies the benefit of the use of those cash reserves over a period of time. By contrast, the strategy I have suggested is meant to help people who need protection buy it at low cost and without confusing money market funds with investment vehicles. As we shall soon see, the purchase of protection frees them to face up to the ugly reality that all of us—those of us who think we are rich and those of us who know we are poor—are under pressure to speculate, subject to the inescapable risk of loss. Last but not least, universal life, by giving the companies the use of their policyholders' lump-sum commitments to money market funds, offers a strategy that is the exact opposite of that which I am recommending, namely, borrowings of cash values at low rates and purchases of term insurance to keep protection in force. The one advantage I can see offered by universal life is that it would enable people inclined to put excess cash into money market funds and to use the interest to pay term insurance premiums to do so without paying taxes on their interest income. The higher short-term interest rates go, the more attractive this incentive will seem.

The insurance business, although—or because—it is dominated by very large companies, is intensely competitive. Moreover, it is axiomatic that where the mass-marketing of financial instruments is concerned, the marketed products that average people end up owning are the ones that are sold to them. By contrast, the course I am recommending calls for people to buy the policies they *need*—especially when financial marketing fads make them seem out of date. The safe way to shop for insurance is to seek guidance from a Chartered Life Underwriter (CLU) whose independence can be verified with a simple question: Can you write life policies with more than one insurance company?

THE DEVALUATION OF INVESTMENT STRATEGIES
INTO SPECULATIVE PLAYS

Times change, and with them traditional axioms of wisdom do. Either savings are still the building blocks to investment, or in changing times they no longer serve this purpose. Either investments for income and reinvestments of income are still the building blocks to capital accumulation, the markets have been telling us, or the markets are no longer investment markets—at least not for the duration of the 1982–1983 crisis.

If tried and tested strategies for saving, investing, and reinvesting income no longer work, the only sensible alternative is to try something else, starting with the recognition that Gresham's law governing devaluation—that bad money drives out good—applies as well to the devaluation suffered by the markets. Any semblance of investment stability has been beaten out of them. They have been transformed into models of speculative instability.

Clinging to the investment approach after the investment markets have been devalued into high-speed gambling casinos is a passport to financial disaster. A speculative strategy suited to the times is needed to cope with the speculative devaluation the investment markets have suffered. None of the traditional speculative devices perfected under the protective cover of our shattered investment markets is likely to work. There is no doubt that random speculating by feel and by gossip can pay in an investment-market environment. Although speculators assume risks when none is forced on them in such an environment, they accept limits on rewards when none is imposed, and they insist on working and worrying to make less than comes the way of patient, passive investors content to get rich sitting still.

But the more speculative the markets get, the greater the odds that people are likely to die broke and to live subject to a high rate of cost inflation paced by a runaway in rents (shelter is the number-one item in the cost of living). The first consideration argues for life insurance as the hedge it is against everyone's final balance-sheet reckoning; the second argues for home ownership as a hedge against out-of-line rent costs en route from the cradle to the grave. Both needs call for cash in larger lump sums—quarterly or annually in the case of life insurance, as a lump sum in the case of home ownership—than "high-earning (and/or -living) paupers" are likely to have on tap or to squirrel away bit by bit. The trick is to find the cash to finance both at the same time. Mastering it depends on being clear about the way the investment markets used to work before they were devalued and the entirely different way the speculative markets work now that this has happened. Here is a summary of functional contrasts.

Analytical Focus—In an investment market, the heavy hitters focus on the direction of events and the thrust of policy moves. In a speculative market, they have eyes only for the leads and lags between the price ticker and the news ticker.

Fallback Position—In an investment market, cash flow from dividends and interest provides insurance. This flow is likely to increase at a significantly faster rate than capital appreciation, from well over 30 percent of portfolio cost by the third year to more than 100 percent by the tenth year. All setbacks in investment markets, by definition, are growing pains soon looked back on with pleasure as buying opportunities and cushioned at the time by cash receipts greater than paper losses. In a speculative market, tax deductions can be a safety net. Up to $3,000 of capital losses may be taken against ordinary income in any year (pending further action by Congress, recommended in Prescription #13). No "high-earning pauper" in need of a lump-sum windfall will want to start speculating with more than $10,000. In the unlikely event that all of it was lost in the first year, all of it would qualify for deductions by the third year. Because capital losses never expire as offsets against capital gains, permitting them to be taken tax-free until all past losses have been recouped, winnings from any subsequent change of luck would be tax-sheltered.

Measuring Profits—In an investment market, the yardstick is capital accumulated in large blocs of securities over a period of years or even decades. The 20 percent capital-gains tax rate in force acts as the criterion for deciding whether to liquidate stock positions held at lower cost. Nontaxpaying portfolios are obviously free to play a more opportunistic hand. In a speculative market, it is by cash, taken out in small amounts weeks, days, or even hours at a time.

Selectivity Standards—In an investment market, selectivity is all-important because leadership is rotated from group to group as the market is subjected to continuous correction by the interplay of buyers and sellers expressing different preferences and responses to profit-taking and bargain-buying opportunities. In a speculative market, timing makes the decisive capital difference because the players have been conditioned to tap out the same selections on the same computers responding to the same signals showing on the same charts at the same time and intent in outsmarting each other while nevertheless following each other. The lead dogs bred in the best kennels heat up a speculative market the way the "thundering herd" broadens an investment market: by stampeding. In a speculative market, the pack is either buying the market blind or selling it blind, with no sensitivity to the investment values behind the ticker action.

Sighting Targets—In an investment market, the hunt is on for future values in securities unrecognized by their present price action, considered a year at a time. In a speculative market, nothing matters but present price action, considered minutes at a time.

Timing Calculation—In an investment market, performance is rated by the annual percentage return on substantial capital investment (reckoned as cash income plus paper profit). In a speculative market, the raising of stakes calls for a monthly multiplier of tiny original input.

Timing Philosophy—In an investment market, prudent investors rely on time as an ally in making more as the result of switching less. In a speculative market, the "action" crowd sees time as an enemy wiping out short-term profits before they can be banked.

So much for the contrasts between a financial atmosphere conducive to investment and one saturated with speculation. "High-earning paupers" cannot be investors. They have nothing to lose but their frustrations, but they have the earnings to sequester for speculation. High incomes invite high life-styles and create the compulsive cash needs that high incomes cannot satisfy. To recall the practical wisdom of Dr. Johnson, they concentrate the mind.

When in doubt about the priorities of life called into question by frustration with its practicalities, consulting writers at random is not enough. The probing of policy quandaries is the business of the philosophers. Providentially, one of the pioneering intellects responsible for fashioning the building blocks of the modern world has a message uniquely helpful and reassuring for the "high-living paupers" in desperate need of learning how to convert income into capital. It is a message relevant and reassuring for the devotees of austerity who have capital in need of conversion to income or supplementation by windfall profits.

Blaise Pascal is our patron philosopher. His career coincided with the seventeenth-century climax of the long, drawn-out war between science and religion. Although he was one of the fathers of modern mathematics, he fought on both sides of the lines. The relevance of his explorations to our travels is established by the mathematical breakthroughs he achieved: analytical geometry, calculus, and, believe it or not, the first computer. Even more prophetically, he switched the focus of mathematical inquiry from trafficking in certainties to calculating probabilities. So Pascal's mathematical philosophy is in sync with the central assumption common to modern nuclear physics and computerized portfolio management.

But it was as an activist on the religious side of the argument that Pascal made the classic case for speculation by doubters living from day to day with nothing to lose and everything to gain. In the history of theology, many arguments have been advanced for the existence of God, but none so terse, so anticlerical, or so downright cynical as Pascal's wager: If you say you believe in God, and you wake up in Heaven, you win. But if you were wrong, you have lost nothing. If, on the contrary, you declare yourself an atheist, you have everything to lose if you are wrong and nothing to gain if you are right. In addition, a profession of faith would placate the authorities in the here and now.

This same logic applies—subject to only one condition—to the plight of today's "high-earning paupers" as well as to income-short capitalists living in dread of pauperization. The condition: no exposure to margin calls or foreclosure claims. In the past, when speculation was winning its bad name, this condition could not be met. As we are about to see, it can be today. More than incidentally, the analogy between Pascal's argument for betting on God and the case for limited-risk speculation in the market extends to placating the authorities. Everyone accruing taxable income and speculating is rewarded for scoring losses by an automatic bank account with the IRS in the form of bankable claims for refunds of taxes paid on past income or deductions against taxes accrued on current income. Pascal proposed his wager on the existence of God as an even-money proposition, an offer that doubters, living from day to day religiously, could not refuse. The two-way street to solvency paved by our much maligned and little understood tax system has stacked the odds in favor of today's doubters who live from day to day financially. If they lose at penny-ante, they get their money back. If they win, they hit the jackpot. The IRS gives losers a better deal than they get at Las Vegas or the racetrack.

Yet we continue to be wary of the IRS bearing gifts. Our thinking is still conditioned to accept the dictum of Chief Justice John Marshall in the early days of the republic—"The power to tax is the power to destroy"—as good for all time. But Marshall reckoned without the Keynesian revolution. Its commitment to welfare economics and its acceptance of deficit financing invited the impression that its thrust was to inflate the power of the government along with the purchasing power of the public. Quite the contrary, it imposed a fiscal Magna Carta on the government in behalf of everyone with earnings subject to income taxes. Marshall defined income taxes as confiscatory levies. The Keynesian revolution redefined them as interest-free advances the government has the right to receive from taxpayers as tokens of its ability to manage the economy, subject to the obligation to refund them with interest as the penalty for mismanaging the money. The fiscal upshot of the Keynesian revolution was to devalue the certainty of taxes into a bet paralleling the one Pascal suggested about belief in God.

Not even the most outspoken critics of the Keynesian system have called for turning the clock back to the discipline of irretrievable taxation. In the spring of 1982, Senator Harry Byrd, Jr. asked me how high I thought the first deficit entirely attributable to Reagan would be. When I guesstimated it at over $100 billion, he gasped, "Great God!" When I asked him if he could imagine Congress repealing the refund privilege, he said, "Certainly not." When the fiscal 1982 deficit came in at $110 billion after $112 billion in refunds had gone out, the illusion that deficits arise on the spending side of the budget was punctured by the reality that it fluctuates with the performance of the economy.

The spectacle of conservatives making a good thing of capturing the heritage of Jefferson has left me wondering why the radicals have not returned the compliment by exploiting the heritage of Hamilton. His operating premise was that the stability of society depends upon a monied class having a stake in the government. His solution was to put the government in debt to them, so that the bonds it owed became the investments they owned. Since the early days, Jefferson's constituents have become Hamilton's customers; everyone has money, but no one has any abiding confidence in how much the government will let or make it be worth. Not until the 1930s did Mr. Justice Owen Roberts hand down the landmark decision recognizing the right of taxpayers to bargain as hard in their own interest against the IRS as against used-car dealers. But Hamilton had recognized 150 years earlier that the government needs solvent taxpayers to draw upon every bit as urgently and as continuously as everybody with income in quest of capital and with capital in quest of income needs a strong government to depend on. So whether anyone planned it that way or not, everybody is better off because the government subsidizes speculation when investment is not safe or smart—not even in its bonds. The more money the speculators make while the government does not know what it is doing, the more they will have for the government to offer to put to work when it finally learns what to do.

THE OPTIONS MARKET

It is a satellite market orbiting around the stock market. At one and the same time, it makes a mockery of the stock market and makes obsolete the use of margin trading for sophisticated speculations. The reason is that it offers a standing opportunity to own options to buy the biggest, the best, and the highest-priced stocks for peanuts, sometimes as low as $1 per option for a $100 stock, with no exposure to the risk of being called on to put up additional margin on pain of being sold out at a loss. Even more attractive to sophisticated speculators, it offers them the opportunity to sell stocks short on the same high leverage—that is, on a low-margin basis without borrowing. Owners of options to sell stocks at prices locked in above quotes in a falling market own them outright, whereas speculators playing the old-fashioned short-selling game have no alternative but to borrow the shares they short. Because options are contracts and not stock certificates, speculators who buy them forgo the right to collect dividends, and speculators who short them are spared the obligation to pass dividends paid on the certificates they have borrowed to the stockholders of record.

Stock options consist of "calls" and "puts." "Calls" are options to buy stocks, and "puts" are options to sell them. Not all stocks sport calls and puts on their future market prices; those that do are listed in the financial press on the options pages. (*Barron's* runs a closely read column on weekly action in the options market.) Call and put contracts entitle their owners to exercise privileges at fixed prices and by fixed dates. Each contract on every stock with a listed option is listed separately, by effective price and month of expiration. The market prices quoted in options from tick to tick vary with their so-called strike prices, that is, the price at which options may be exercised. The further away the price of a stock from the strike price, the less an option on it will cost and, for that matter, be worth; the closer it is to the strike price, the more it will cost and be worth. The closer an option comes to the expiration date with no incentive for it to be exercised, the closer it will come to losing all its market value. Sitting with an option about to expire and not worth exercising is like buying a flight insurance policy, making a safe landing, and complaining about being gypped. The reason for buying it is not to carry it to maturity and then exercise it, but to sell it at a profit before it matures. An option is a speculation, not an investment.

So much for the basics. All market strategies are subject to three interrelated decisions: direction, selection, and timing. Of the three, direction is the most fundamental, selection the most practical, and timing the chanciest. The normal speculative impulse, shared by professionals and amateurs alike, is to target the options on either side of the market that come closest to where the action will be in any given month. It is also where the losses come fastest and easiest. The reason is that any "hot" market move is always subject to a fast and sharp correction, sometimes for as long as a month. But violent corrections in either direction generally start when the market seems topless or bottomless. When an excess of enthusiasm excites the appetite, a price zigzag generally follows. The impending expiration of an options contract generally excites frenetic tugs of war and corresponding volatility in the contract, raising the stakes on hitting a jackpot or being subject to a wipe-out. Being sound as to the direction of the market and shrewd in selecting its price leaders is scant consolation for tearing up an options confirmation killed by the calendar just weeks, or even days, before the stocks controlled make their expected moves.

Because dealing in calls or puts is speculative to begin with, the way to minimize the risk, without forfeiting the reward, is to target contracts not scheduled to mature for the month bought. Sometimes it pays to forgo the fast "hot-money" play and to buy contracts not due to expire for, say, four to six months. This strategy is particularly prudent, and more likely than not to prove profitable, when the speculator is correct about the prospective direction of the market. During frantic periods of volatility, this same strategy minimizes the damage from getting whipsawed when the market could be on the verge of changing direction. Of course, that is when playing calls or puts pays best. It is also when losses are likeliest due to contracts expiring just before the action of the market confirms the judgment on them.

The stakes in options trading are so high that abnormally high profits are not sacrificed—and quick wipe-outs are averted—by adopting a conservative strategy. In a down market, when selections are conservatively in step with the market, small commitments turned over frequently on small moves can substitute for big and continuous returns. With experience and discipline, trading calls and puts in big stocks can make long-term commitments to low- or nonyield stocks pay their way for investors, sacrificing a portion of current income in favor of short-term gains. Also, in a market buffeted by crosscurrents, this technique can be used to provide a cheap form of diversification for speculators who want to generate action without sacrificing marketability in companies thought to be over the hill.

A little knowledge, to paraphrase Alexander Pope, is a dangerous thing. Here is a list of ten rules the prospective options speculator needs to know and/or follow before talking to a broker about taking the plunge:

1. Read Barron's *weekly column on options trading.* Read it even if you can't follow it. Its title, "The Striking Price," pinpoints the speculative problem of buying a call when the underlying stock is "out of the money"—that is, selling below the strike price for the option—on the calculation that it will sell "in the money"—meaning above the strike price—before the expiration date. The same calculation works in reverse when puts are bought in anticipation of stocks selling under strike prices. Options action is lightning fast, but tracking the thoroughly professional yet lucid account of it in this excellent *Barron's* feature after the fact serves the same essential and helpful service as reading a libretto in English before trying to track the action in an Italian or German opera.

2. Learn how to read a computer screen. It's the only way to switch gears in your own thinking, as you will need to do to operate on the fast track of the options market. By comparison, stodgy, old-fashioned trading in stocks moves at the pace of a mule keeping up with a racehorse. Tucking up with the afternoon newspaper to scan the stock quotes or reading the morning comment about them in *The Wall Street Journal* the next morning, as Grandpa used to do, is no substitute for watching the action in options quotes as the computer flashes it up on the screen. The options market is a financial video game; Atari with small stacks of chips for big bucks.

3. Get a broker gaited to this new high-speed game. Devotees of the two-martini, two-hour lunch won't do. (West Coast hot shots might get away with it by making lunch dates at 1:15. The options market runs until then, fifteen minutes later than the stock market in order to give the market makers a chance to take advantage of closing prices and get a head start on likely openings the next morning.) Trainees, bright-eyed, bushy-tailed, and sporting their MBAs, are not likely to have the "street smarts" needed to sense options-market signals and to catch speed-of-sound options-market moves.

4. *Eye the simple, crystal-clear tabulation of daily volume at the top of the options quotes in the newspaper.* It's broken down into call volume and put volume. Anytime call volume outweighs put volume by a significant margin, say three to one, reflecting trader bullishness, figure that the market is in for a tumble and that the green light is flashing for puts against blue chips, like IBM, and glamour stocks, like Texas Instruments. That's the way it was when 1983's spring optimism was inspiring relaxed forecasts of 1,300 to 1,500 on the Dow and the interest-rate reversal brought a predictable tumble. Just as predictably, put volume was way above call volume in early August 1982, reflecting trader bearishness, when the market took off on its record move.

5. *Use options-market action to get a realistic focus on the institutional market action it systematically anticipates.* The options market is where the heavy hitters in the bloc-trading fraternity place their own orders before they start working on institutional orders to execute on the floor of the exchange. This is the way they both abide by the SEC regulation banning broker trading in advance of customer orders and profit from it—after all, an option on a stock is a different security from any stock on which a broker has a buy or a sell order. Elevating hypocrisy to theology, the eerie coincidence of jumps in the options market just ahead of shifts in the wind on the stock market invites smug explanations of the "magic of the market" working its wonderful adjustments and insulates the operators against charges of market manipulation.

6. *Watch new contracts get admitted to trading with each five-point move in the price of a stock on which options are traded.* The normal expectation in trading stocks is that the higher they go, the more money buyers need to put up to buy them or to tie up to ride them. The new era of options trading is a picnic for leverage players. The procedure of admitting new contracts to trading with each five-point price move enables options buyers to continue playing penny-ante poker for high dollar stakes; it offers them new, out-of-the-money, low-priced options on high-priced stocks. It puts blue chips on the auction block priced as chippies. The result recalls the story Judge Jerome Frank used to tell about the hillbilly who, when solicited by an itinerant preacher peddling a novel doctrine of baptism, countered the question whether he believed in baptism by immersion by snorting, "Believe in it? I *seen* it!"

7. *Always target the weakest-performing groups or stocks for the accumulation of puts in contracts with nearby maturities.* Contrariwise, target the strongest performers for the accumulation of calls in nearby months. The opposite calculation applies to the selection of puts

and/or calls for far-out maturities when you expect a reversal of the short-term trend. *The Janeway Letter* is not a registered investment adviser. It therefore avoids making recommendations for the purchase and sale of individual securities and/or options on them, but it does identify ongoing trends and reversals of trends in the economy, domestic and foreign, which determine corresponding behavior in groups of securities.

8. *Discipline yourself to fool with options or play the options game on yellow pads before you try a fling with your checkbook.* Do this for at least three months while you follow your impulses, test your judgments, and accumulate a track record. In feeling your way, discipline yourself, too, to remember that a string of small gains adds up to as much money in your pocket as hitting one big jackpot. Remember, too, that Wall Streeters swear by their old adage that "your first loss is your cheapest one," because they can thank it for having kept so many of them going. Amateurs not content to survive taking small losses again and again go under by saddling themselves with big ones.

9. *Restrain yourself from ever getting fully committed, and feel free to get entirely uncommitted when in doubt.* Always, however, keep a minimum reserve of free and available cash to avoid getting locked into lost positions playing a game that calls for instant and continuous reliquifying, as the model portfolios that follow suggest.

10. *Take your cue in handling profits from the innkeepers in Las Vegas, not from the players.* The house plays the percentages and, therefore, figures that the longer a player crowds his or her luck, the more certainly will it be exhausted. Anyone hitting the jackpot in the options markets will be better off not plunging or pyramiding. Yet, striking it rich on a turn of the market wheel does not argue for retreating into a certificate of deposit (CD) and taking the pledge never to try again. In the case of money made from options, the strategy of retrieving the original investment and reinvesting only profits is a way of buying insurance against the loss of all or even any capital in subsequent speculation. The safest and smartest use of windfall profits is for lump-sum payments to get started on home-buying or insurance programs.

So much for the *how* of the options game. Now let's have a look at the *what* and the *when*.

Portfolio Candidates for Hard Times

GOLD

Gold is the ultimate fallback defense against both depression—as currencies go bad and banks follow—and inflation—as interest rates rise along with government deficits. It benefits from the collapse of currencies, the spread of currency regulations, the fear of banks closing their doors to depositors, the antics of the dictators, and the ravages of war. It has no intrinsic value—contrary to traditional claims—as the ultimate form of money or "store of value." Its value fluctuates with its daily price. The lower the confidence commanded by the government deemed most influential in the world, the higher the price of gold, and vice versa.

SILVER

Like gold, silver bullion is a sterile asset, that is, it yields no unearned income to its holder; only a profit or loss on sales. Unlike gold, however, it attracts no demand from central banks for monetary reserves. Bull markets for silver begin with bull markets for gold, at the outset of inflationary revivals. Because silver is cheaper than gold and usually more oversold than gold before speculative interest in it is rekindled, it generally jumps faster in the first leg of a bull market for precious metals. When gold and silver responded to the renewal of inflationary pressures in the summer of 1982, silver had been broken under $5 an ounce, with gold trading under $300 an ounce as the result of entirely unrealistic fears of "disinflation" resulting from a popular misreading of Federal Reserve Board initiatives and capabilities. Clearly, the odds favored silver doubling from these lows before gold.

Speculators are always in search of "normal" ratios between silver and gold prices. William Jennings Bryan, in his celebrated "Cross of Gold" speech, which won him the Democratic presidential nomination in 1896, called for silver to be pegged at a ratio of sixteen to one against gold. At the worst of the 1982 shake-out in both gold and silver, gold sold at a ratio of more than sixty to one over silver. The subsequent price explosion in both commodities suggested that the market initially "owed" silver a catch-up on gold. When gold jumped to $500 by September 7, 1982, it scored a 67 percent gain in just 10 weeks. Silver, starting out at $5 an ounce, topped out in the first phase of its move at $9—a gain of 80 percent in the same period.

SILVER STOCKS

Silver stocks are priced lower than most gold stocks and, therefore, can be expected to double faster than gold stocks in the first leg of a bull market for both. During the recovery that both gold and silver enjoyed in the summer of 1982, Benguet, the most speculative of the silver stocks, did, in fact, double faster than the speculative stocks in the gold group.

GOLD STOCKS

Gold stocks substantially outperformed the bullion market during its 1982 price recovery. Between June 21, 1982, when gold hit bottom at $297, and February 15, 1983, when the first leg of its recovery topped out at $511.50, a 72 percent rise, Val Reefs, the top-grade investment-rated gold stock, rose 235 percent, and Durban Deep, the most highly leveraged member of the group, jumped 440 percent. Gold stocks and productive stocks generally do not move together for very long, yet they did during the 1982–1983 move in Wall Street. In fact, the gold-stock group outperformed the productive-stock group. The prospect for a long, sharp bear market in productive stocks is the catalyst for gold stocks to move to higher levels. The South African gold-stock group suffered two turns for the worse under cover of this spectacular 1982–1983 move. The first reflected cost pressures in South Africa: Their dividend pay-outs failed to keep pace with their price rises. As interest rates rose, their yields became as uncompetitve as those of productive American stocks. The second reflected the intensification of racial tensions: The risk of violent interruptions to production flows from the mines, and, therefore, to dividend flows to stockholders, surfaced sufficiently to worry the market and, certainly, to prevent any American institutional accumulation of South African gold stocks under the most favorable market conditions. Consequently, a new premium began to attract money to the North American gold stocks, which, despite having never paid dividends worth talking about, are free from political risks or boycotting by institutional investors.

DOMESTIC GAS AND OIL STOCKS

Their collapse in 1981–1982 made them cheap by any standard. The intervention by the antitrust authorities in forcing Gulf Oil to abandon its bid to take over Cities Service, at a price representing a 50 percent premium over the market quote at the time of the bid but a 33 percent discount under its breakup value, made even bigger bargains out of such stocks while discouraging bids for them.

The realistic incentive to own a relatively small portfolio of domestic gas and oil stocks, backed by convertible debentures collateralized to furnish leverage, is to control an option on war in the Caribbean, though the market, after its fashion, is not quick to make the connection between the simultaneous buildup of war dangers and investment values. War in the Caribbean would send domestic gas and oil values back beyond their old highs and send the international oil companies, which are always net buyers of crude, scrambling to take over domestic properties at marked-up prices. Gas and oil stocks offer the dual advantage of rising with gold stocks in response to the spread of war dangers and of continuing to rise after the gold move ends. Gas and oil stocks represent the productive values that will lead the next recovery, for the simple reason that nothing short of a switch to government activism aimed at maximizing America's enormous energy advantages will be needed to start recovery. Then this activism will start a genuine boom.

The oil group offers an asset—namely, Exxon—unique in its claim to lead the next bull market. Exxon is not only the blue chip enjoying the strongest financial condition in the midst of a crisis of corporate illiquidity; it is also the highest-yielding quality money stock on the Big Board and the one most out of favor with the OPM crowd—the hired hands who handle "other people's money" in institutional portfolios. Regard Exxon as you would a Treasury bill with an attractive option on future gain attached to it: money-good, at an acceptable rate of return in a period of high interest rates, readily liquifiable but offering a viable hope for considerable gain when interest rates are brought down and kept down by government policies not dependent on picking daisies in front of a wishing well.

Warning: Exxon made a 1982 high of $31.25 when it was yielding only 9.6 percent. Only sixty days before, it had been selling at a new low of $24.25, yielding 12.4 percent. Clearly, therefore, anyone accumulating it for income was on notice to do so slowly and on a comfortable schedule of dollar averaging, that is, of investing more capital in addition to the original commitment at a scheduled rate during each successive price decline and yield increase in the stock. Exxon, with its high yield, is a prime candidate for switching into from precious metals after any move in them becomes excessive.

DOMESTIC GAS AND OIL DEBENTURES

Domestic oil and gas debentures offer four incentives for gradual accumulation after a major sell-off. Before enumerating them, however, it is relevant to note that any major sell-off in the stock market during the duration of the world economic crisis would most likely be accompanied by an unsettling intensification of political turbulence in Atlantic and Caribbean waters. Any such turn of events would have the predictable effect of putting record new premiums on the assets behind domestic oil and gas convertible debentures, even in a thundering bear market.

- They yield interest income as an offset against interest charges incurred.
- They offer conservative collateral for leveraging.
- The stocks behind these debentures have smaller-share capitalizations and more profit potential than if no leverage had been

created through the issuance of convertible debentures. This leverage offers debenture holders the prospect of getting repaid, not just by getting their money back with interest on the way but also in stock, that is, in ownership of the assets of the company when, presumably, they come to be worth more than when the debentures were issued.

• The renewal of the takeover market in domestic oil and gas values will put the gas-rich stocks behind convertibles at the top of the takeover target list.

Media discussion of convertible debentures is both simplistic and misleading because it calculates the incentive to own them outright. As a practical matter, however, virtually all noninstitutional—that is, tax-paying—owners of convertible debentures use them as vehicles for leveraging. They are motivated by a triple calculation. The first is conservative: The base they provide minimizes the risk of exposure to margin calls during market shake-outs. The second is leverage: The potential for price appreciation they offer during bull markets will send them flying faster than the stocks on which they enjoy conversion privileges, provided they are owned on thin margins. The third is operational: The interest they pay in some cases provides a positive cash flow over the cost of carrying loans against them and, in other cases, provides tax deductions as nominal offsets against gains taken. By contrast, other securities leveraged on thin margins with aggressive gains goals carry high risks of exposure to margin calls at awkward times.

The calculation of plays in convertible debenture is complicated and varies with the price and yield spreads, with the terms of conversion of each debenture, and with the stock on which it offers an option. Although convertible debentures are junior bonds doing double duty as options on stocks, the brokers who are knowledgeable about positioning them are generally not the same ones who are adept at trading stock options. Loans on convertible debentures are best arranged at banks rather than with brokers because banks are permitted to collateralize them on the basis of 70 to 90 percent of market value, depending on the customer's credit rating, without evading the 50 percent margin rule (applicable to stock purchases) to which brokers are subject.

Warning: Companies issuing convertible debentures routinely reserve the right to redeem them at a nominal premium over the issue price. Therefore, speculators who take advantage of the unique features of convertible debentures restrict their accumulations to issues priced under call prices and at discounts under par on the calculation that they will buy their convertibles at nominal or minimal premiums over their bond values, getting free rides on the stock plays in them.

HIGH-TECHNOLOGY DEFENSE STOCKS

Sooner or later, the market will price up the stocks in this group. Even under optimum security conditions for America, projected in the prescriptions for national prosperity formulated in Part II, massive ongoing expenditures for high-cost, innovative weapons systems will remain inescapable for the foreseeable future. The engineering, production, and maintenance requirements of any ongoing joint nuclear policing collaboration, such as the one Senator Sam Nunn has proposed, would be mind-boggling even if NATO and domestic nuclear arms requirements were to be deflated as a result of the proposed collaboration between the hostile superpowers. The production schedules needed to finish the next generation of air-cargo carriers would be mind-boggling as well. Like so much defense technology, the by-product demand for new hot-line command control and communications equipment would by no means be limited to military programs. On the contrary, their commercial application would be limitless.

So long as the stock market is stable, the defense stocks that seem most promising for the future are the minisuppliers of the high-tech specialists (catalogued in Prescription #2, which follows). In a general market collapse, however, the major defense contractors would qualify for inclusion in the portion of any diversified portfolio reserved for patience.

The prudence of patience was underscored as the stock market began to stumble over higher interest-rate hurdles in the not-so-merry month of May 1983. Just when the markets were escalating their familiar discomfort over $40 billion budgets to shock over $40 billion weekly borrowings, the administration won a token vote for its MX intercontinental missile project, purged the State Department of senior Latin American officials deemed hawkish for not being hawkish enough, and, nevertheless, ordered massive cuts in the procurement programs already under way. Even allowing for the likelihood that the next administration will move quickly to cool military "hot spots" and to speed up procurement, the next bull market in defense stocks is not likely to get started until (1) Congress authorizes the Pentagon to allow interest charges in computing recoverable costs of production and (2) the airlines can again finance next-generation fleets of "outsize" cargo carriers. This puts the aeronautical stocks and the "minidefense" specialties in line to come back into their own after the gold stocks and the domestic gas and oil stocks. Reactivation of the V-Loan, with the qualification that interest be an allowable cost of procurement (see Part II, Prescription #12) would ensure major bull markets for the "minidefense" specialty companies when the government finally brings its ongoing defense problem under manageable financial control.

CASH

Don't sell cash short. If you propose to use it, keep your hands on it—preferably on 20 percent of portfolio value in hard times, but at least on 10 percent. A special note is in order here on which instruments you can consider as good as cash: short-term Treasury bills, CDs, and interest-bearing money market funds, all of which invest in nothing but short-term government securities and, therefore, are protected against market and credit risks. None of them qualify as investments, despite the popular impression that they are. All of them are parking lots for cash to which you can get overnight, or at least monthly, access. Bank savings certificates, which tie up reserve cash for longer periods, do not fit this description. They may be safe as parking lots, but they do not allow your investment vehicles to be powered by immediate access to new cash without your paying penalties for early withdrawal or, what comes to the same thing, getting tied up in red tape working for the privilege of unlocking your own cash.

There are two ways to control cash. The first is simpler but not necessarily better: Hold back an uninvested cash residue and put it into Treasury bills. Despite the terms of their maturities, they can be cashed in at any time without penalty. They need not be held to maturity for you to collect your interest any time you want your money back. The second is not all that complicated, but it pays better. Look to the portfolio asset controlled with the most solid value, offering the most stable collateral. Rely on it to create additional buying power as the source of leverage in a large portfolio. Anyone with $1 million worth of invested assets readily convertible to cash can secure from a bank an ultraconservative loan of $100,000 by putting up $300,000 in gold or in gas and oil debentures. The reason: Anyone with $1 million to invest will do well to think in terms of putting more than $1 million to work. Anyone not confident enough to owe on assets is not confident enough to continue owning such a large position in them and has already sold that position in his/her/their mind. The borrow-to-buy test is a pretty good one of the willingness to hold.

The final reason for operating with reserve borrowing power: J. P. Morgan said it all when he gave his unfriendly grunts to a reporter who asked him what he expected the stock market to do. "It will fluctuate," he snapped. And that it will. When securities happen to fluctuate downward, the stubborn investor will want to mobilize standby cash to buy more in order to average down the cost per share of a position with the market. When holdings go up, the alert investor will want to concentrate a position in order to average up the potential profit per share.

Suggested Portfolios for Hard Times

The strategy outlined below for building capital can be put to work by people of modest, moderate, or substantial means willing to accept limited risks of loss. Obviously, investors and speculators of substantial means can afford the luxury of diversification, while people of modest means are obliged to pick one vehicle. People of moderate means can share the wealth by combining both strategies.

In constructing these portfolios, a priority has been given to concentration over diversification. If the purpose of tying money up in a portfolio is to make money, there is no point in being right about selectivity and timing while diluting profits by owning too few shares in too many positions. Again and again, speculators and investors who have been conditioned to give a priority to diversification over concentration end up in the worst of both worlds. Chances are that any profitable moves they make will be eaten up by losses or offset by stagnation, while the meter ticks on the cost of money that is working but not earning its keep. High interest rates are a harbinger of hard times.

The concept of the batting average in baseball is often used in calculating speculative and investment results. Out of ten tries at bat, even champions are not likely to score four hits. In speculation and investment, losing moves are always likely to outnumber winning ones. The analogy goes further: More batters get hits that are wasted than score runs that are counted. The name of the game is not to look good squeezing out a hit here and a hit there but to go for the long ball, as Babe Ruth and Ted Williams and Joe DiMaggio did every time they faced a pitcher, and to make the successful tries pay for the unsuccessful ones.

One practical way for speculators and investors to test their confidence in their impulses is for them to decide whether they are willing to make concentrated commitments in the securities that appeal to them or whether they wish just to dabble. There is no way to make money dabbling. Low-priced positions double more quickly, and more often, than high-priced ones, but the average portfolio is chock-full of small positions in higher-priced securities. The following portfolios embody the exact opposite strategy. They have been constructed on the assumption that concentration pays. Anyone of modest means has no alternative but to concentrate speculation in one kind of effort; anyone of moderate means enjoys the luxury of concentrating in at least five; only substantial market participants are free to concentrate in as many as ten different types of commitments.

Remember: For stockholders, the goal in taking positions is to control at least 1,000 shares per position, or as close to 1,000 shares as money permits. For options players, this means buying no less than ten calls and/or puts at a time; each call or put controls 100 shares of stock.

PORTFOLIO I: START-UP CAPITAL $10,000

40%	$4,000	3- to 6-month puts on worst-acting stocks of previous 3-month period
20%	$2,000	3- to 6-month puts on best-acting stocks of previous 6-month period
20%	$2,000	3- to 6-month calls on gold stocks
20%	$2,000	Reserve or cash equivalents

Strategy of distribution. In a confirmed bear market, that is, one in which the stock of the president is admitted to be dropping and the popular market averages can be seen following, with the breadth of the market bringing up the rear, the probabilities favor recurrent declines in the weakest stocks. This offers an opportunity to cash in moderate profits from a steady deterioration over a period of months while waiting for a major break. The reason for buying a put position against the weakest stocks in a bear market is to minimize the risk inherent in a high-risk strategy. The supplemental strategy for buying a put position against the strongest stocks is to maximize rewards; the stronger stocks, being the highest priced, have the furthest to fall and will fall the most when a break gathers momentum. Ditto the gold calls: They will rise faster than any other group in each stage of a bear market. The recommended "product mix" is likely to build gains without being dependent on an all-or-nothing bet on an instant jackpot. It worked during the euphoric spring and summer of 1983.

Measuring rod: Once a put or call position is taken, time becomes either an ally or an enemy for the speculator (exactly as it does for a country taking a position with a policy). Calculate daily the rate of return on the money in each position. The moment any position shows a profit greater than the yearly rate earned on gilt-edged, fixed-income instruments, take it. If a position shows even a 5 percent profit after commissions, much less a 15 percent profit in a matter of weeks, or even months, it is clearly outperforming the rate at which cash can earn interest by the year. This measures the difference between mere saving and successful speculating, that is, getting nowhere versus getting ahead.

Warning: Don't sit with any loss beyond 10 percent (applicable to puts on best-acting stocks and to calls on gold stocks) unless you are financially prepared to increase the position. Because no start-up portfolio with only $10,000 at work can contemplate the advantages of accumulating more on any price declines in order to average down the cost of the holding, it is safer to take a fast loss and conserve cash for the next try. Treat each position as though your last dollar were in it.

PORTFOLIO II: START-UP CAPITAL $100,000

10%	$10,000	Puts against worst-acting stocks of previous 3 months
10%	$10,000	Puts against best-acting stocks of same period
20%	$20,000	Calls on gold stocks
30%	$30,000	High-grade gold stocks or gold itself
15%	$15,000	Convertible debentures on domestic gas and oil stocks and/or domestic gas and oil stocks on the list of takeover candidates
15%	$15,000	Cash or cash equivalents

Strategy of distribution. **Puts:** The same as in the $10,000 portfolio.

Calls on gold stocks: Same as in the $10,000 portfolio, except that the larger cash availability provides room for maneuvering, specifically in the ability to own more contracts costing more to buy and geared to move faster in response to moves in the underlying gold stocks.

Gold stocks: The gold stocks are the big beneficiaries of bear markets; they are underwritten by realistic anticipations of doing still better during the transition to good times, that is, when the turn from depression to inflation is made. Homestake, the major U.S. gold mine, started from a crash low of $25 in September 1929 and was the only stock of consequence to double in the three bear-market years after that. Between the worst of the Hoover depression and the best of the Roosevelt recovery in 1937, it went to $500, a tenfold gain from its depression high and a twentyfold gain from its prosperity low. In 1937, it paid out $49 a share in dividends, approximately 100 percent of its price on the eve of the bank holiday. It is the only quality American gold mine available for portfolio use by members of the American institutional investing fraternity, none of whom will risk criticism for owning South African stocks. It is unlikely that American institutional investors will regard gold stocks as cheap until gold tops its old high of $800, but at that point Homestake will be their first stop and their last "name" stock with a story. The massive scale of their group buying operation, and its small capitalization, point to a repeat performance of the 1929–1937 price explosion. It can now be bought via the high-leverage call market, which was not around between 1929 and 1937. The fear that prompts investors to dump good stocks, "money-good" bonds, and endangered currencies drives them into the gold markets. When gold stops falling in response to interest-rate rises, and starts rising, its big move is on.

Convertible debentures on domestic gas and oil stocks: They remain the favored quality vehicle of strong and sophisticated investors in a bear market. In the summer of 1982, the explosive potential of oil politics in the Caribbean made the yields on these debentures more attractive than those on money market funds, Treasury bills, or certificates of deposit, and just as safe. They also offered a no-cost option—the best kind—on the rich play to be made when U.S. boiler-fuel use is belatedly switched from imported liquid petroleum to domestic natural gas. (See Prescription #11 in Part II.) Their bear-market attractions were underscored even while the decline in world oil prices was accelerated by the renewed bidding contest for domestic gas and oil properties.

Cash reserve: To be used for the same purposes as in the $10,000 portfolio but on a more comfortable scale. It would buy backup availability to expand the high-grade gold stock position into lower-grade, faster-moving gold stocks taking off in their wake or to increase the stake in oil and gas debentures. In addition, a $15,000 reserve would also leave some room to take advantage of the never-ending takeover opportunities in domestic gas and oil companies. The rule is that once a bidding contest develops for a targeted company, sooner or later a successful bid produces a windfall profit.

PORTFOLIO III: START-UP CAPITAL $1,000,000

10%	$100,000	Gold bullion
2.5%	$25,000	Silver bullion
25%	$250,000	High-grade, high-yielding gold stocks*
2.5%	$25,000	Silver stocks
25%	$250,000	Equity in income-producing real estate (subject to self-financing mortgage)*
10%	$100,000	Convertible debentures on domestic oil and gas stocks*
5%	$50,000	Venture capital "minidefense" specialties (preferably convertible debentures)
20%	$200,000	Puts on productive stocks, calls on gold stocks

*Note: This portfolio seems to be fully invested with no cash reserves. But this is an optical illusion because it can be projected to yield a minimum cash flow of $75,000 from the three sources followed by an asterisk, before collateralization of any securities or bullion. Moreover, anyone with a portfolio of this size and quality is entitled to ready access to cash from bank credit lines.

Strategy of distribution. **Gold:** Gold bullion serves a double purpose in a seven-figure portfolio for hard times: protection against financial crisis to begin with and against the hyperinflationary resolution ahead for it. It also provides instant borrowing power for taking advantage of the upturn when it comes. Therefore, it is an ultraconservative expedient for financing a switch to an aggressive strategy on Day One of the recovery. Note: Bear-market crises climax in recoveries with lightning rapidity and in instant response to the incisive governmental action needed to trigger a comeback and forced when bankruptcies assume epidemic proportions. The onset of crisis lifts bullion with interest rates; the "all clear" explodes it when they collapse.

Silver: Silver adds a more speculative cutting edge to the same strategy. Note: The two smaller model portfolios cannot afford the luxury of either a gold or a silver bullion position. For that matter, not even a $1 million portfolio is big enough to freeze liquidity in a complete coin collection (the only premium-commanding method of accumulating gold or silver coin).

Gold and silver stocks: The rationale for having a position in gold stocks is the same as that in the $100,000 portfolio. The comfortable liquidity provided by a $1 million portfolio permits diversification between the higher-grade gold stocks, preferable for use at the outset of a gold move, and the lower-grade, lower-cost, more highly leveraged stocks that run wild after a major gold move—without sacrificing concentration in either category. The silver stocks add gains potential because, at the outset of a gold move, silver is likely to double at least once before gold will from a $300 takeoff point. No silver stocks offer any dividend-paying incentive; though one of them does swing with a convertible debenture.

Income-producing real estate: The best time to accumulate real estate is during bear markets in securities, coinciding with alarms about a depression spilling over into the real estate market and with strains on the loan portfolios and capital of the banks. A commitment of the size indicated in partnership with proven professional management of reliable character will buy a substantial stake in professionally mortgaged real estate on terms not likely to be matched by an amateur investor. The "product mix" of income-producing, tax-sheltered real estate with bullion and gold and silver stocks is calculated to maximize profits during bear markets and the inflationary recoveries that follow.

Convertible debentures on domestic gas and oil stocks: High-yielding (double-digit) convertibles in this category pay their way while a bear market is running its course and high interest rates are taking their toll. Like gold and silver bullion, they offer extra liquidity with no carrying charges and reasonable income. They also provide cheap war insurance. The moment a bear market responds to the impact of wide-open inflation, gas and oil convertibles are likely to run a respectable third behind (1) calls on gold stocks and puts against productive stocks and (2) gold and silver stocks bought outright. In addition, they are likely to accelerate this move after the turn into a new bull market leads the gold move. Therefore, the domestic gas and oil values offer cheap insurance bought in advance against the risk of missing the top of the gold move.

Venture capital: Companies emerging from the experimental or "idea" stage with new products or processes are covered in this category. By definition, venture-capital companies are long on potential, short on cash. The Bell Telephone Company started out as a venture capital company. So did Ford Motor Company. *Reader's Digest* started in a neighbor's garage, paying no rent. The depression/bankruptcy epidemic of 1982 demonstrated that the worse established companies do, the more money they need too. Strong and sophisticated pools of capital are constantly on the lookout for promising venture capital projects. Bearishness on listed securities sparks interest in growing companies insulated from the public markets.

Every well-balanced seven-figure portfolio makes provision for nominal participation in at least one venture-capital private placement. As with real estate, venture-capital investments are not marketable, at least for a couple of years. As with real estate, too, investments in venture capital projects call for careful scrutiny of the caliber and character of managements and underwriters. Where possible, the prudent way to make initial venture-capital investments is through convertible debentures paying double-digit yields. The most attractive opportunities that turned up during the 1982 bear market were in the defense and health fields. Since both fields are subject to intensive regulation, checking credentials is relatively convenient.

Puts and calls: The comfortable liquidity position of this large a portfolio, including the conservative cushion provided by the ready borrowing power offered by holdings of gold and silver bullion, supports a higher level of put and call participation than a small portfolio does, as well as the greater leverage that comes with it. Of the $150,000 segregated for put and call buying, a "flow"—perhaps $20,000—is best held in reserve to increase options positions already taken or to add new ones.

Implied cash reserve: It serves the same purposes as the cash set aside in the smaller model portfolios, except on a larger scale. A strong cash position comes in handiest when a bear market that has collapsed into a selling panic is about to stage its recovery. Bank lines readily available to the owner of such a portfolio will fortify the cash position and support decisions to take advantage of opportunities offered by distress conditions.

The strategies suggested in these portfolios provide for investment conservatism balanced by high leverage for use during a bear market, as well as during a climactic turn into a proper recovery.

PRESCRIPTION #2
Riding the Wave from Panic to Prosperity

Spotting a Major Market Upturn

The three model portfolios for hard times were meant to protect people knowledgeable enough to take advantage of them from falling into the common error of turning bullish too soon. Bear markets are studded with rallies. By definition, a bear-market rally is bound to be violent and, therefore, to stir up premature, insupportable enthusiasm. While a bear market is running its course, the problem for investors and speculators is to know how to distinguish between a false start and a rally backed by a real recovery.

In the summer of 1982, a false start bearing all the superficial characteristics of a turn into a genuine recovery excited the markets and dominated the headlines. Superficially, the move seemed to pass muster by most of the main tests that matter inside the technical structure of the market itself. The bond market gave the stock market its cue, reflecting the drop in interest rates, on which the brokerage firms had been basing their increasingly desperate hopes for a rally. The stock market traditionally views three successive cuts in the discount rate as indicative of a major upturn. The Federal Reserve Board obliged with no fewer than four initial cuts compressed into the short span of just six weeks; a fifth came during the first week of October. This last action produced an electrifying success with the second test: volume. Overnight, it tripled from just 40 million to 45 million shares a day to well over 130 million shares a day. With interest rates collapsing and trading volume exploding, the market experienced no trouble passing its third interrelated technical test, the breadth test, measured by the number of stocks rising daily versus those declining. Any time more than 1,000 issues a day rise, with the other two tests passed, the market is normally accepted as being on its way up again, with momentum.

Nevertheless, all the technical market tests, which invariably prove reliable as indicators of market fluctuations between crises, proved unreliable during the great market surge from mid-1982 to mid-1983 because the market failed to spread its enthusiasm outside the special world of Wall Street and its amateur followers. True, a significant increase in trading by individuals contributed to the new volume peak, but it was mainly made up of margin buyers, who are weak by definition. The surge of foreign participation in September and early October reflected a frightened flight out of all currencies rather than an exuberant flight into U.S. stocks as investment assets. The solid income-minded investing public refused to participate in it. On the contrary, the plunge in short-term interest rates was greeted by a remarkable $11 billion increase in the amount of money sidelined in the money market funds (up from $222.789 billion to $233.271 billion) in the eight-week period between the Fed's first cut in the discount rate in early August and its fifth cut in early October. The stock market explosion did not stop it.

The only kind of market environment trickier than one dominated by institutional portfolio managers hell-bent on outdoing each other is one in the throes of a volume explosion limited to professional operators intent on outsmarting each other and failing to attract investors for income. In fact, higher volume performance by the stock market is taken as a forecast of higher price performance precisely because it is normally assumed to measure a rising tide of Main Street participation in stock investment. But by the 1980s a record number of elderly people with money, overloaded with responsibilities and petrified of the costs and losses they saw all around them, watched from the sidelines as the market stampeded. The reason was painfully simple: Dividend yields were unacceptably low on stocks trusted not to cut payouts, and the risk of dividend cuts was unacceptably high on stocks whose yields were tempting.

Even brokers benefiting from the explosion were quick to see the danger signal flashed by the lack of participation by the conservative hard-cash public. The word in the better-managed Wall Street firms was that the market would have had to be shut down by noon during each day of the stampede if the computers were being pressed to process 100 million shares a day in 100- and 200-share tickets. True, while the stampede was on, the president of the New York Stock Exchange declared that it could handle 200 million shares a day. The evidence was indisputable that bloc volume was responsible for the trading bulge, but his confidence was clouded with anxiety, and realistically so, when the ticker was becoming clogged with orders for hot new issues in those 100- and 200-share lots, packaged with a flood of 10- and

20-share orders for IBM and other high-priced blue chips bought on margin.

The second suspicion of trouble lurking behind the bullish August explosion revived memories of 1929 among serious market students—not just with margin calls or banking trouble but with a devastating combination of both. In 1982–1983, the evidence of banking trouble was even more unsettling than during the Great Crash because the banking authorities had become so adept at organizing rescue missions. Nevertheless, bank failures continued to spread; so did rumors that bad foreign loans exceeded bank capital.

The margin trouble was more unsettling too, because it was tucked away in a small casino beyond the fringe of the market itself: the stock futures market, increasingly frequented by the institutions, if not directly, certainly through the bloc traders on whom they relied as market makers. The ability of the big hitters to meet margin calls was not the issue, nor had it been in 1929. Prices are broken before margin players are. The trouble arises when the small fry's failure to meet margin calls forces huge blocs to be thrown on the market and when the shock effect of dumping produces a failure of nerve in the players with money. Institutional portfolio managers built up huge hedge positions on margin in the futures markets. These positions were not large by institutional standards, but they were large for the new top-heavy markets in which fast switching is the rule. Trading in stock futures produced a margin vulnerability that was at once more concentrated and more destructive than that which built up when the amateur public was attracted to 10 percent margin speculation in small lots and by large numbers of players in 1929. In 1982, the margin exposure was allowed to build up in large lots at 4 percent by small numbers of players.

Coming into 1983, a decided downgrading in the quality of market leadership accentuated the technical deterioration that the market was suffering, even as stock prices continued to be marked up. The hallmark of any market is in the quality of that leadership. During its 1982 phase, the market recovery was paced by high-priced stocks; Pan American and International Harvester painted the tape with their tarnished images. The downgrading of institutional portfolios was dominated by a massive switch from stocks selling above $75 a share into stocks selling at under $40 a share. This move into lower-priced stocks was led by the international oils and was a can't-win play. The empty hope of higher oil prices posed a threat to their costs, and the inescapable pressure for lower oil prices guaranteed a threat to their asset values and their incomes.

But the danger signs that surfaced outside the stock market in 1982–1983—four of them, to be exact, all fundamental—were even more ominous than the technical troubles enumerated above. The most obvi-

ous and the most disconcerting was the failure of the economy to develop comparably vigorous momentum when the stock market did.
Such a follow-through is a condition of a genuine recovery from a
depression-time bear market, as the revival in 1933 demonstrated. The
early 1983 try at recovery was weak, suspect, and brief. It failed to
support price increases, to spur inventorying, or to breathe life into
capital investment. The second disturbing rumble from the world beyond Wall Street showed up in the political polls. Not even Ronald
Reagan's gift for communication could reassure the representative
cross section of voters that was becoming increasingly alarmed about
the shrinkage in their pocketbooks. No market revival in history had
ever before gotten under way with an incumbent president starting to
get into trouble, with no charismatic challenger coming into view carrying a Christmas tree, with incomes unrelated to the stock market showing no surge, and with both the stock market and improving industries
developing visible vulnerability to the threat of higher interest rates.
Before it materialized, Reagan ran into his first veto, with disaffected
Republicans leading the charge. Predictably, the veto was overridden
on a confrontation over cash for the elderly. Just as predictably, the
amount involved was petty cash; it merely acted out the studied concern on the congressional side of the argument for weighing the balance between frugality and compassion.

America's foreign relations were the source of another major disturbance to the fundamental structure of stock market confidence. Upturns from bear markets that win trust as they score points depend
upon one of two separate but equivalent developments in America's
foreign relations for their momentum: either a lead that is followed
abroad or a solo move that does not wait for a foreign lead. The summer
of 1982 found Reagan wrangling with his most important allies, America's NATO partners, over the Soviet gas pipeline. He had rushed into
a maze of his own making and, more inexcusable still in Europe's eyes,
without having taken advantage of the ceremonial visits at the Versailles economic summit to warn his opposite numbers that he intended
to do so. At one and the same time, he was warning the Europeans not
to go ahead with the pipeline yet urging them to improvise a formula
they were expecting him to suggest. Worse still, the political wrangle
was punctuated by salvos of financial distress from all around the banking world, which Europe's "pipeline powers" took as urgent notice to
disregard sermons from the White House and to do what was good for
them. The market began to buckle under interest-rate pressure just as
the Williamsburg summit convened for its fiasco in May 1983.

On top of this, the fourth and most frightening hurdle looming in
the way of the market's effort to attract long-term investment buying
was put in its way by the gold market. Under cover of the major explosion that sent the stock market rocketing, the gold market took a mini-

rocket ride of its own. It jumped from a precarious perch at $330 an ounce to $525 an ounce within the short span of a few weeks, and then reverted to the $440 level. The gold markets and the stock market often start together, but they never stay together. The stock market does not like banking or currency defaults. The gold markets feed on both, and they take off when government borrowing pressures burst all budgetary restraints, as America's did in mid-1983.

These four fundamental pressures gnawing away at the foundation of the market under cover of its late-1982 surge surfaced with its mid-1983 break. A real bull market, by contrast with a false takeoff, is powered by two engines: the fundamental one as well as the technical one. No market rebound from the twin trauma of economic depression and financial panic can take hold without a domestic economic recovery, a show of political confidence in American leadership, a foreign policy lead from America, and a cooling of the gold fever. Add to these fundamental factors the technical ingredient mentioned earlier, which was missing from the 1982 takeoff: the participation in force of the conservative, hard-cash, income-minded public. The stubborn departure of these conservative people from the market, as it boiled over with bullishness, was the decisive missing link between the bullish technical pressures that sparked the climactic bear-market rally and the bearish fundamental pressures that splintered it. Neither engine of a bona fide bull market will power it unless the other is running at full throttle. No "insider's rally" unleashing mind-boggling volume to a computer can sustain itself with only a narrow base of fast-buck players buying small lots of the blocs being distributed—that is, so long as the financial institutions doing the selling lend the fast-buck players what they need to do their buying.

Profiting from the Start of a New Round of Inflation

Shrewd, realistic speculation during the climactic phase of the previous bear market will provide not only a sound but a swift head start on personal prosperity. Every commitment that does well at the worst of a bear market will do better still in the first transition wave of a new bull market. Real estate will outperform the pack, and for a much longer run, with gold and silver running neck and neck with it at the outset. The striking resilience of real estate was dramatized by the 1981–1982 depression. When the pace of transactions slowed down, market values held their own at worst and continued to rise at best. The striking new feature of the real estate market coming into the 1980s is that demand for residential units continued to rise after new supply was cut off; it did not fall with the amount of disposable income available to pay for the higher cost of shelter.

A return of realism to government, measured by its ability to manage a durable recovery, would bring mortgage rates down into line with short-term interest rates, which the plunge in short-term rates failed to do in 1982. Long-term mortgage rates remained well into double-digit territory, although short-term rates and long-term bond rates broke 10 percent. Moreover, though the depression made the unions susceptible to pressure from employers on concessions, it made no discernible impression on local environmental authorities. The resultant prospect of a steady hardening of environmental restrictions on new construction signaled a further lengthening of lead times for builders and developers when, finally, they got back into business. This, in turn, meant that owners of real estate ready for occupancy could look forward to a dramatic easing of credit terms when the upturn came as well as to a parallel scramble for space on the part of buyers and renters. The practical market upshot of a seller's market for real estate, even in hard times, and a buyer's scramble for it during a transition to good times, is always to send developers and builders to neighborhoods previously regarded as rural, that is, where land is cheap but safely outside the reach of entrenched environmental authorities. The need to break ground for new roads, sewers, etc. lengthens the time lag involved in new construction and spurs price increases on existing property values.

A rising real estate market at the outset of a revival in the economy recreates the inflationary climate in which gold and silver flourish. Looking back on the first gold-and-silver move of the twentieth century, the New Deal led the inflationary trend of the 1930s; and the bullion markets followed. In fact, it was not until the spring of 1934, after the New Deal had been going full blast for a full year, that silver flared up into a hot headline issue. By that time, Roosevelt's demonetization and revaluation of gold had been a fait accompli for several months. It established gold as the only basic commodity able to engineer a striking price rise (from $20.65 to $35) and, more impressive still, able to trust it to hold (thanks to the government peg).

The arms ingredient of inflation is as necessary in firing up a gold-and-silver move as inflation itself. The emphasis given to the politics and economics of the Roosevelt administration has obscured the priority Roosevelt gave to naval rearmament during the start-up New Deal phase of his presidency. At the time, the Japanese military had been riding roughshod across Asia for four years, and Hitler was getting ready to do the same across Europe.

Two historical asides will explain the theories and recall the personalities involved in the two interrelated episodes. The first pair of characters, George Warren and Frank Pierson, were commodity price chartists who enjoyed the status of professors at the Cornell College of Agriculture. Roosevelt had picked them up while he was still governor of New York at the initiative of Henry Morgenthau, subsequently FDR's secretary of the Treasury but at that time chairman of his agricultural advisory committee in New York. The Warren-Pierson Theory, as it came to be called, was tailored perfectly to the times. Roosevelt was running for the Democratic nomination against Al Smith, his former sponsor, whose trademarks were a New York accent and the label "Roman Catholic," not an asset in those days. To counter Smith's Eastern power base, Roosevelt needed to build one in the West and South, which were then (and are now) Protestant country. Therefore, he embraced the first economic theory to come along that was guaranteed to explain in one word and one number how he could promise to put farm and mining prices up.

Warren and Pierson had the answer. The magic word was *gold;* the magic number was $35. In 1932, gold was still selling for about $20 an ounce. The two cow-college professors assured the new President that all he had to do to get credit for ending the Depression was to sign a law putting the price of gold up. Inflation then, far from being the taboo it was until the Reagan depression rehabilitated it, would have been as welcome as water in the desert. Accordingly, Roosevelt, relying in good part on the strength of this quackish professorial promise, broke up the World Economic Conference in June 1933 with a blistering telegram denouncing its ditherings in London and reminding the world that he had been elected president of the United States "to raise the level of prices, wages and incomes inside the United States." Suffice it that the gold nostrum did not produce the promised effect of promoting prosperity, though the gold move held because the price was pegged at $35. The Warren-Pierson Theory was filed away in the archives, and Roosevelt moved on to the pursuit of other panaceas until Pearl Harbor solved the problem for him.

The failure of this simplistic mechanical theory was responsible for catapulting the silver bubble of 1934 into the headlines. The bubble was burst by a controversial political schemer who happened to be a Roman Catholic priest with a parish at Royal Oak, Michigan, a suburb of Detroit, where the bank panic of 1932–1933 originated. His name was Father Charles Coughlin and he had a silver tongue to match the silver panacea he peddled. He picked up the Warren-Pierson Theory that a higher pegged price for gold would work magic for commodity prices, and he applied it to silver after Roosevelt had moved the price of gold to $35 without, however, galvanizing the economy into motion.

Coughlin, who was then in the process of building a huge nationwide radio audience, charged that Roosevelt had sold out the common people to the international bankers by pegging the price of gold. Coughlin demanded that silver be monetized at the ratio of three to one for gold. Roosevelt would have none of it, on the sober political calculation that going all out for gold in pursuit of inflation would leave him looking good with conservatives even if it failed to work, but that silver was poison bearing the brand name of William Jennings Bryan. Enough voters and opinion makers to matter in 1932 recalled how Bryan, as the boy orator from the Plains, had intoxicated the Democratic Convention of 1896 with his impassioned plea not to crucify mankind on a cross of gold. As I noted earlier, Bryan's call for the monetization of silver at a ratio of sixteen to one for gold had won him the presidential nomination but saddled the Democratic party with him or his record for the next five presidential elections and made Democratic candidates targets for charges of fiscal irresponsibility. In two elections, Bryan was the defeated candidate; in the other three, he played the part of Uncle Fud, relegated to the attic but refusing to stay out of sight. Woodrow Wilson was forced to carry the burden of supporting Bryan during his first presidential campaign and to take him on as his first secretary of state. No wonder Roosevelt was afraid to touch silver.

When Roosevelt repudiated Coughlin, the party got rough. Coughlin teamed up with the Fisher brothers, who were the major inside stockholders of General Motors and who had become notorious for their market miscalculations all the way up to and down from the crash of 1929. They let Coughlin in on their private pool, and he took the silver panacea public on his radio program. To spice it up, he began to blame the "international Jewish bankers" for steering Roosevelt onto gold and away from silver.

Roosevelt, meanwhile, had put Tommy Corcoran on Coughlin's trail; FDR had made a lifelong hobby of the arcane art of clerical politics, and Corcoran, a Catholic himself, was his scout on this sensitive front. Corcoran, comparing notes with Bernie Baruch and Joe Kennedy over Coughlin's unholy alliance with "the Fisher boys," as they were known in Wall Street's pool-hall circles, quickly discovered that they were mixed up with a pair of New York commodity speculators who were being hit by margin calls on their cotton position. (This crew comprised the small-time Hunts of their day. The plot never changes; only the characters do.) Corcoran also unearthed the juicy item that Coughlin's secretary was sitting on a tremendous silver position in the name of the Shrine of the Little Flower, which Coughlin had built with the cash received by mail in response to his radio show. The idea behind the scheme to prod the government into propping silver was that where gold had failed to help cotton and the rest of the list, silver would succeed.

This sordid episode in the silver saga ended when Roosevelt's principal ally in the Catholic hierarchy, George Cardinal Mundelein of Chicago, resolved to silence Coughlin. (Mundelein was more than an ally and a fatherly counselor to FDR; he was the major influence outside his administration who encouraged Roosevelt to take up the cudgels against Hitler from the first day of his presidency.) While the Detroit archdiocese and the Vatican were passing the buck to one another, the cardinal prepared a blistering statement against Coughlin, which he proposed to deliver in the Chicago cathedral on Easter Sunday, 1939. Mundelein died before he could read the statement, but it was read by his auxiliary, Bishop Bernard J. Sheil, who told me that he picked up the private phone connecting the cardinal to the president's bedroom and woke him up to say, "The cardinal is dead." A massive heart attack had killed Mundelein at the pinnacle of his remarkable career, when he was still in his early fifties.

The bishop told me that FDR's immediate reaction was to say, "Benny, you must not read the cardinal's statement, or you will never be cardinal." (Benny was the bishop's nickname, used by friend and foe alike, in recognition of his fiery militancy against Nazism.)

Sheil replied, "Mr. President, it's the way the cardinal would have wanted it."

He went ahead and read the statement, and he was not named to succeed Mundelein. The Detroit archdiocese, however, took Coughlin off the air. Silver never had a chance to do more for commodities than gold had done. All its price did was rise with all the other speculative commodities when the Roosevelt recovery simultaneously pumped inflation back into the system and benefited from it. From a Hoover-depression low in 1933 of 24.5¢, silver took a high, hard bounce up to a 1935 peak of 81¢. Its average price in 1933 was 34.7¢; in 1934, it was 47.97¢. It failed to stay there, however, despite all the speculative excitement stirred up by the high-pressure touting of its supposedly miraculous properties by the silver lobby and the silver pool. By 1940, the year after Coughlin was banished, silver was back in the doldrums of 1933: Its average price was 34.77¢. Inflation remained an issue, and stagnation remained a problem.

This case history dramatizing the background in which gold and silver flourish repeated itself three times during the 1970s: first in 1972, as the first repercussions of Watergate; then again in 1974, in uneasy response to the oil embargo; and yet again in 1977, in shocked recognition that the oil war was going military. The first two shocks made their impact in an inflationary atmosphere saturated with armament pressures, which intensified as the oil war drove up the cost of munitions and as the evolution in military technology lengthened their production cycles. The third and largest gold move of the 1970s was driven upward by the same force as the second move: the visible failure of the American presidency, this time under Jimmy Carter, from whom more had been expected than from Gerald Ford. Two reversals tell the story of Carter's political bankruptcy: his retreat to massive deficits and his advance to massive armaments. They also tell the story of the gold explosion that sent bullion rocketing to $875 in January 1980.

The transition between the false alarm over disinflation in 1982 and the revival of concern over inflation in 1983 set up the fourth—and biggest—gold move. Just as in 1933 and 1934, when the stirrings of an aggressive inflationary drive and the rumblings of an arms race in the making had planted the roots in which gold and silver came into their own as crisis-time commodities, they did so again at the outset of the 1980s, but in a more fear-ridden atmosphere, at a much higher rate of inflation than had touched off the three earlier moves, and at a time when arms expenditures were enormously higher and guaranteed to go higher still. Moreover, the great gold inflation of the 1980s started from a level three times higher ($300) than the previous one in 1977 ($100), and, therefore, it traveled toward correspondingly higher goals. Gold and silver never do well when international confidence rides high, but they are havens for "funk" money during troubled times. Though gold and silver positions do well while bear markets in stocks and bonds are deepening, the precious metals do not pay off in a major way until a deflationary crisis has been resolved by an inflationary takeoff. Then, silver is the tail that wags; gold is the dog that runs.

With the Caribbean in the 1980s an armed camp and the arms business the only one in the world doing well or helping to pay for the government deficits mushrooming everywhere, the incentive to take bear-market crisis-time positions in domestic gas and oil values revived in the wake of high gold and silver prices. With wars breaking out in two or three trouble spots at once, the attraction offered by domestic gas and oil values was new and different from that which had attracted money to them in the 1970s. Then, the incentive was to cash in on the presumed oil shortage. In the 1980s, it was to buy insurance against blockage of the world's oil-carrying sea channels. Defensive positions taken during depressions and amid cries of disinflation offer a double attraction: They protect the investor as defensive strategies during hard times, they are the first to pay off, and they are the most profitable of ongoing aggressive strategies, when inflation sends money rampaging out of cash and into assets again.

Gold and/or silver bullion positions taken before depressions explode into inflation are best owned outright. The same goes for gas and oil debentures bought before a depression starts "bottom fishing." Depressions—especially depressions on the verge of panic—are no time to invite exposure to margin calls. But both groups of defensive values offer instant access to cash (because they are the easiest to borrow on) without any need to sell them the moment panic becomes, as always, the catalyst for the transition from depression to inflation.

The time to borrow on a mixed portfolio of gold bullion and convertibles is after the inflationary turn comes and the economic engines start up again. The market values of both groups will go up first and fastest when the securities markets revive. The way to get the edge on any start-up recovery, therefore, is to regard securities bought for hard cash during the previous bear market as a store of credit from which to raise more cash to buy more securities. Hyperinflation subsidizes discretionary borrowing.

A word about interest rates during a depression. The source? Joe Kennedy: "Sticking up banks at the point of a gun is old-fashioned. It's smarter, as well as cheaper, to use the point of a fountain pen by signing a note." Money was a giveaway in the world of the 1930s; there was no government debt worth worrying about. The funny thing that has happened on the way to the world of the 1980s is that Kennedy's judgment about the smart money strategy, when money cost 1 percent, has become operative again with money costing more than 10 percent. When inflation is about to blow the lid off asset values, the dollar debt taken on beforehand becomes easier to carry thanks to the appreciation of the assets controlled by the borrowed dollars. The time to play with other people's money is at the start of a new cycle of devaluation. The place to put those borrowings first is in calls on gold and silver, the stocks those calls control, convertible debentures on gas and oil stocks, and, where cash and credit permit, into income-producing real estate. As a matter of fact, the gas and oil companies play the game Joe Kennedy's way when they issue convertible debentures. They borrow on the reserves they have and give their debenture holders an opportunity to get paid by converting the bonds they own into shares of stock promising to be worth more over a period of time than the money originally put up to buy the debenture.

The strategy of borrowing on both bullion and convertibles—known among professionals as leveraging—will pay at the start of a run of inflationary recovery, whether it comes with the inflation more pronounced than the recovery or with the recovery absorbing the inflation as it gathers momentum. In the first, and more likely, case, interest rates will rise as the economy speeds up; but any time inflation is out of control, borrowing pays, no matter how high interest rates go. The assets carried by the borrowings are marked up enough to cover the cost of the money and more.

A pragmatic version of Albert Einstein's theory of relativity, translated into financial terms, tells us that, given hyperinflation, the cost of money falls as the price of borrowing it rises. The experiences of Argentina, Brazil, and Mexico among the weak countries during the late 1970s and early 1980s prove it; so does the experience of Israel among the strong countries. Inflation rates have been running over 100 percent a year in all four countries, yet the interest rates that accompany them have not restrained borrowing. In Argentina, the habit of automatic borrowing seems to have broken banks, not their customers —a decided departure from the experience of 1929–1933 in the United States when, in the absence of inflation, the banks broke their customers, who then returned the compliment.

The second case—that is, recovery absorbing inflation—will not develop until America finds a government able to trigger a solid economic recovery instead of waiting for one to start by spontaneous combustion or apologizing for a resurgence of inflation amid a deflation of investment values. As the prescriptions for prosperity outlined in Part II of this book explain, there is only one way recovery can outpace inflation —and that is for Washington to devise methods for dealing with the rest of the world from economic strength backed up by usable military strength brought to bear with realistic political restraint. Once America snaps out of her self-indulgent trance, she will effect still another reversal of familiar business-cycle expectations: She will bring interest rates down as she speeds up economic productivity. If anything is surer than death and taxes, it is that this economic miracle will not unfold as an answer to a political evangelist's prayer. Only a political operator can kill both birds with one stone and keep control of the stone.

The following model portfolios have been structured into investment vehicles for riding a transition from depression into hyperinflation. The need for such a vehicle became urgent in my calculations when I perceived a return of hyperinflation beginning in the early 1980s; it had not been in use since the great European inflations of the 1920s. As with the three portfolios presented for hard times, these are offered for use by people with either no capital, moderate capital, or a backlog of capital. As anyone with common sense and a will to play the do-it-yourself game can see, they are ready to do double duty: defensively, when the economy and the markets are depressed, and aggressively, when Washington gets its act together and America's next economic takeoff is triggered. These money-using vehicles are reliable whether the "product mix" fueling the upward climb generates more inflation or more recovery.

The defense stocks, technically referred to as the aeronautical stocks, are the first candidates for inclusion in any portfolio designed to do well during the inflationary transitional stage from hard times to good times. The distinctive advantage of the three alternative portfolios is that no asset in them need be sold to improve performance once the government takes the steps needed to get the transition to good times started. Only one minor adjustment would be indicated on that happy day: to switch out of puts against big-name stocks and into calls on the big aeronautical/defense stocks. Moreover, no new money is needed to add the extra dimension of aeronautical stocks to the classifications in the start-up portfolios for hard times. If no transition starts, the original investments will do well; in that case, any changes made would increase risks run without increasing rewards in prospect.

The moment the government were to take the timely steps indicated in Part II to make sense of the budget by bringing the defense budget under control, interest rates would collapse contracyclically and the economy would be catapulted forward into a borrower's picnic. The two bigger hard-times portfolios could be drawn upon for borrowings to pay for defense stocks, as well as to add to the gold- and silver-stock positions and the gas and oil debentures; all three hard-times portfolios allowed for at least a 10 percent cash reserve for maneuvering room. The cash income earned by the securities borrowed would be adequate to pay for carrying charges on any borrowings during the transition, when presumably interest rates would be falling.

The way to hedge bets when borrowing at high rates is to reserve the right to prepay the debt, without penalty, at any time. If rates really do drop during a recovery, any borrower remains free to make a cheaper and bigger loan at the bank across the street and to use part of the money to pay off the high-cost loan. Loans made to carry securities can always be paid off in this way, without penalty.

Another Joe Kennedy coup, his "steal" of the Chicago Merchandise Mart, which had been a family heirloom property, explains how. Marshall Field, the prototype of the "guilty-rich" liberal philanthropist (or, as *Time* magazine would have said in its saucy days, no bank robber, he), owned it—outright, of course. I remember Field with warmth as the gentlest of souls, not knowing how to use the wealth he had inherited to help the needy and haunted by the shame of his buccaneering merchant-prince father, who was shot to death in the high-toned sporting house operated by Chicago's famous Everleigh sisters—familiarly known by their patrons as the 'Everlays.

Despite Field's readiness to support every New Deal cause in the late 1930s, FDR's Treasury was permitting the IRS to give the Chicago philanthropist a hard time over a tax matter. Though he was all for anything Roosevelt said or did—even when he said one thing and did the opposite, and Kennedy was bitterly opposed—Field turned to Kennedy to fix his case. Kennedy said he would, but only if Field would sell him the Merchandise Mart for something less than $20 million—all cash. How Kennedy arranged for the IRS to roll over is part of another story.

For this exploit, Kennedy had arranged a mortgage of over $20 million on the property with an insurance company, so that he walked away from the closing with the title to the Merchandise Mart in one pocket and something like $5 million in cash in the other—just before rents and property values riding on them ran wild, while interest rates stood still. Not everyone can fix a federal tax case for a "guilty-rich" liberal philanthropist, or would be willing to try, but anyone can see that Joe Kennedy's formula for getting a free ride on the tranquil money of insurance policyowners beats working.

Suggested Portfolios for Transition Times

PORTFOLIO I: START-UP CAPITAL $10,000

40%	$4,000	Calls on gold stocks
20%	$2,000	Calls on gas and oil stocks (including oil-gas-gold combinations)
20%	$2,000	Calls on aeronautical stocks
20%	$2,000	Cash or cash equivalents

Strategy of distribution. The strategy involves a switch out of the put positions on productive stocks, a doubling of the call positions on gold stocks, and the accumulation of moderate call positions on gas and oil stocks, as well as on the big aeronautical stocks.

Calls on gold stocks: The reason for doubling the position in calls on gold stocks—from 20 percent in hard times to 40 percent during the transition—is that the start of the transition period from depression to recovery will unleash a tremendous blast of inflation, and the gold stocks will set the pace in the market response to it. The gold stocks will outpace the other gold markets, and calls on them will be priced up much faster than the gold stocks themselves.

Calls on gas and oil stocks: Gas and oil stocks will follow gold stocks at a slower start-up rate, which, however, will reenact Aesop's fable of the hare and the tortoise. The move in the gas and oil stocks will last longer. Note: At least two domestic gas and oil producers also produce gold on a significant scale.

Calls on aeronautical stocks: Thanks to the failure of the Reagan administration to prevent the depression of 1982, the two branches of the aeronautical group—the manufacturing companies and the airlines—are likely to make their start-up moves together. The manufacturing stocks will move in response to the step-up in Pentagon cash outlays; the belated launching of the intercontinental cargo-carrier program that is needed will be very bullish for the industry. As for the air carriers, their stocks lost enormous leverage with the shrinkage of volume in the economy, and they will regain it when volume recovers.

Cash reserve: The same rationale as for hard times, subject to the added consideration that the transition from depression to inflationary recovery will speed up the pace of all market action. This argues for the prudence of keeping cash on hand to ensure flexibility of action.

Note: A special comment is in order on the use of cash during the takeoff into a transitional bull market. This is the time for testing whether inflation will swamp recovery or whether recovery will soak up inflation. It will be a time of high uncertainty and correspondingly high risks and rewards. It will be a time to have cash even though, if inflation does end by swamping recovery, cash will then become less attractive than hard assets.

PORTFOLIO II: START-UP CAPITAL $100,000

30%	$30,000	Domestic gas and oil debentures (70–90% of market value borrowed)
20%	$20,000	Low-grade, high-leverage gold stocks
10%	$10,000	High-technology defense stocks
20%	$20,000	Calls on gold stocks
10%	$10,000	Calls on aeronautical stocks
5%	$5,000	Calls on domestic gas and oil stocks
5%	$5,000	Cash or cash equivalents (supported by investment-income cash flow, plus bank loans)

Strategy of distribution. **Domestic gas and oil debentures:** Four reasons dictate assigning the largest percentage of cash in this portfolio to domestic gas and oil debentures.

- They are the easiest to borrow the most on at the banks and the safest for protecting against margin calls, so less cash will stay in them after the upturn than goes into them beforehand.
- Borrowing is the intent in this portfolio and, therefore, income is needed to meet interest charges.
- They are inflation/war hedges.
- They will be money makers whether the transition culminates in hyperinflation or prosperity.

Gold stocks: The three-phase chain reaction from depression into panic into an inflationary explosion will thrust the low-grade, high-leverage gold stocks into market leadership. When a major move in an industry group takes off, the stocks likely to benefit the most are invariably those with smaller capitalization and higher break-even points, commanding the greatest leverage.

Defense-aeronautical stocks: Gain, not income, will be the reason for owning them. Like the domestic-gas-and-oil-stock group, they will outrun the pack, whether the transition is headed into an inflationary war crisis or a happy landing into peace and prosperity. Once a transitional inflationary bull market explodes, it will be safe to borrow against defense stocks, but their low yields will need enriching by the high yields from the other stock groups to carry interest charges. Consequently, aeronautical and gold stocks will make good fellow travelers in a transitional portfolio.

Calls on gold stocks: The same rationale as for the $10,000 portfolio. This will be the biggest profit play of all once the transition starts. But yellow lights will flash behind the green. If a transition is made into peace and prosperity, the trick will be to put on the hit-and-run play and get out of gold—in that case, before the next transition starts the productive stocks flying again. No mixed motives about buying calls on the gold stocks amid a return to reflation, just a sharp eye on whether, and/or when, good news dictates selling them. Once the time comes to do so, forget them for a generation if my prescriptions for prosperity are adopted.

Calls on aeronautical stocks: A switch from owning puts on productive stocks in either the blue-chip or the growth category to owning calls on the aeronautical stocks will pay in a well-hedged way with the first inflationary turn into recovery.

Calls on domestic gas and oil stocks: The income from the gas and oil debentures will help pay for the cost of carrying them; so will the dividend windfalls from the low-grade gold stocks. Calls are an aggressive speculation and, therefore, go with owning convertible debentures in this group and borrowing on them. In an inflationary recovery, they will begin by running right behind the golds and end, in a genuine bull market, by outrunning them. If war does come, no one owning an option to buy gas and oil stocks will suffer.

Cash reserve: Refer to the strategies described above to keep options open and to the strategy described below to broaden them.

Strategy for borrowing. Borrowing strategies come into play after the double bounce from depression into panic and from panic into reflation. That is the time for the prudent speculator to ask whether he/she trusts any asset enough to own it without also trusting it enough to owe on it. The strategy of owning calls, mentioned above, is highly aggressive to begin with. If, in addition to owning calls, a portfolio also owns equities borrowed against them, it is a very aggressive stance indeed, and it is positioned to cash in handsomely on the historic market takeoff that the transition to prosperity will trigger.

The trick is to make earning assets, like debentures and dividend-paying stocks, cover the cost of sitting with assets paying no income, or under-market income, while watching the clock and giving assets a chance to score gains. Almost everybody will eventually have a desk or home computer tailored to help play the do-it-yourself game. The fast way to get back an investment in a home computer is to use it to calculate how much income the overall portfolio needs to generate to pay for the cost of borrowing against a portion of it. The computer can also be asked to determine how fast gains need to be made on the nonyielding assets owned in order to pay for the cost of sitting with them instead of switching to income-yielding assets.

PORTFOLIO III: START-UP CAPITAL $1,000,000

25%	$250,000	Income-producing real estate (leveraged with mortgaging)*
20%	$200,000	High-grade, high-yielding gold stocks*
10%	$100,000	Lower-grade, high-leveraged gold stocks*
12.5%	$125,000	Gold and silver positions
2.5%	$25,000	Silver stocks
20%	$200,000	Calls on gold, gas, oil, and aeronautical stocks
10%	$100,000	Aeronautical stocks
10%	$100,000	Domestic gas and oil debentures*
5%	$50,000	Venture capital
10%	$100,000	Cash or cash equivalents

*Note: The mix of this portfolio adds up to more than $1 million because it assumes reinvestment of dividend and interest income from the four asterisked items.

Strategy of distribution. **Income-producing real estate:** There is no need to reduce the size of the commitment made in the portfolio for hard times, but there is good reason to increase the allocation for income-producing real estate once the inflationary turn comes. There are two ways to do so: either to tell the real estate partner chosen in hard times to look for additional property, or to ask a bank to turn over a foreclosed property. It is safe to assume that properties foreclosed on by lenders during hard times will practically be given away to new owners after the worst is over. Remember: A 25 percent commitment to real estate made during hard times invites borrowing to generate cash or, what comes to the same thing, to collect more property, by "financing out," Joe Kennedy fashion, during the first bounce-back, when borrowing puts more money to work on top of the original investment and when real estate prices and supporting appraisals are marked up. It is axiomatic that $250,000 of equity put into income-producing property in a depression year will generate more cash in comfortable borrowings once the turn comes.

High-grade gold stocks: The same rationale as for the $100,000 portfolio. Keep a sharp eye on whether inflation is outracing recovery in order to determine whether to reinvest profits taken from the gold stocks, when gold is over $1,000 an ounce, in more of the same or in other assets worth holding during the transition.

Low-grade gold stocks: The purpose of taking such positions is to maximize price action during the transition. Income from these gold stocks is best diverted to more conservative uses, like down payments, real estate, or additions to domestic gas and oil debentures or to domestic gas and oil stocks.

Gold and silver bullion: The reason for maintaining these positions accumulated during hard times is for insurance during the transition. If inflation swamps recovery and wars become the prognosis, the way to sit with gold bullion is to begin borrowing on it. In that case, it is best to switch silver into real estate and/or lower-grade gold stocks.

Silver stocks: After the third double from the 1982 lows, switch silver stocks into lower-grade, high-yielding gold stocks or more real estate. Limit commitments to domestic U.S. silver stocks.

Mixed-call positions: gold, gas, and aeronautics: Invest in these positions on the assumption that all three will continue to outpace the stock market, whether it fizzles or sizzles.

Aeronautical stocks: The same rationale as for the $100,000 portfolio. Note: Increasing the total sum employed by borrowing will call for increasing this allocation in order to keep the ratio of participation for this group constant.

Domestic gas and oil debentures: Keep them as income-earning assets. Borrow on them aggressively. Note: Keeping the ratio of participation constant calls for putting more money into them.

Venture capital: Several top-grade established investment firms with proven records specialize in private placements with sophisticated and substantial investors to finance venture capital starts. High-technology health and defense-related technology lead the list. Where possible, buy income-bearing convertible debentures, limiting the risk and cost of waiting for these companies to realize their start-up potential. Remember: Venture capital placements lock money up for a minimum of two years. During uncertain times, some money is prudently employed when insulated from market risk.

Cash reserve: Use it to do double duty to protect borrowed positions as well as to scout for the new opportunities that turn up in a transitional market. Anyone with a large investment position will always do well to hold a reasonable margin of cash in reserve, relying on bank lines to do so.

PRESCRIPTION #3
Calling the Turn to Good Times

Ever since it peaked, floundered, and fell in the aftermath of the Vietnam crisis, the stock market has been impaled on the twin horns of the inflation-versus-recovery dilemma. On scrutiny, however, this has not been the basic cause of what has gone wrong with the market. Its troubles have been rooted in the budget, as the market itself has gradually come to realize. What has gone wrong with the budget, in turn, is rooted in the defense budget. Both are in chaos.

Defense is the shifting unknown in the tug of war between inflation and recovery. America will not resolve it until she resolves her ambivalence and her inhibitions about defense. As we have seen, the destructive waste built into America's defense is not in her housekeeping but in her planning. America is not likely to manage by trying to finance token defense programs, which will not pull her out of the number-two position vis-à-vis Russia, and by failing to "stay the course," as Reagan referred to his commitment to balance the budget when America still had one, to finance functional defense programs. The pragmatic test for grading any recovery once it has started is to determine whether the prudent investor will want to buy the defense/aeronautical stocks. If so, it would be yet another case of history repeating itself.

The aeronautical stocks emerged as the real leaders of the great bull market launched under the clouds of World War II. They were the lineal successors of the automotive stocks and the electrical stocks, including American Telephone and Telegraph. The Boeing Corporation is the leader of this group of which Telephone, in its manufacturing capacity, is a member. Boeing is a double-duty stock, the industrial leader in time of emergency and the leader when times are normal. Eugene Zuckert, when he was secretary of the Air Force during the Kennedy administration, told me in mixed tones of resentment and respect that Boeing will always charge the Air Force more than it is prepared to pay, and that its surcharges will always be worth paying. When I was most controversially bullish, after the Sputnik crisis of 1957 and at the onset of the market recovery of 1958, Boeing was my test pilot of the stock market's ability to fly. It did, and so did the market.

To design a third set of portfolios for good times in the decade of the 1980s would be quixotic so long as the precious metals offer the most profitable form of insurance against disaster in the economy and its markets. The completion of the transition from bad times to good times will flash the signal to sell gold and silver in all their forms—by then at dizzying, all-time highs. The resumption of capital flows into America's splintered workshop industries—not just from corporate earnings internally generated but also from external injections of new investment— will pull money back into the stocks offering ownership of steel and other basic metals, chemicals, machinery, transportation, utilities, building, and communications stocks. The next bull market is theirs.

In any case, however, the signal transmitter is located in Washington, not in Wall Street. By the same token, the dead charts of market sequences relied on to confirm economic theories of proven impracticality are not the omens to read. The prudence of skepticism about charts applies with particular force to charts about gold. The reason is rooted in the on-again, off-again rhythm of gold moves, depending on the level of financial confidence in political arrangements in Washington. The gold market either fizzles or sizzles in response to it. When gold is not moving, no charts are needed to see that it is sinking. By the time it does move, however, charts are invariably useless as early warning signals. That's why gold moves always take the markets by surprise.

Joe Kennedy's realism about borrowing at the trough of an economic cycle assumed that it would pay even, and especially, as interest rates rose, and it certainly did for him when this happened. As I explained in the case of inflation outrunning recovery, borrowing would pay over the span of a healthy recovery even on Kennedy's assumption that recovery would push interest rates up, as it always has. But a recovery, coinciding with a drop in interest rates, would hand an endowment, richer than any professional bank robber could hope for, to everyone with a fountain pen on the borrower's side of a bank desk. Don't bet on it, but don't rule it out either.

No chartist can be a forecaster. As Karl Marx, student and disciple of Hegel that he was, warned his own disciples as well as his enemies, the cunning of history always discloses when and how history is about to repeat itself, short of revealing, however, with what treacherous twist. Marx himself, though never in doubt, wavered between thundering that history would confirm his prophecies and exhorting his disciples to take matters into their own hands and storm the barricades.

So the proposition is as long as it is broad. Just as no chartists can be prophets in a world flung into chaos by the clash of hostile forces buffeted by unfamiliar pressures, so some practitioners of the ancient art of politics with a sense of the drift of events can sometimes make a difference for the better. More than an incidental purpose of this book is to help the voting leaders of our political leaders make this same difference.

INDEX